AP 7 '11

Frommer's®

W9-CEI-990

Maine Coast

4th Edition

by Paul Karr

Wauconda Area Library
801 N. Main Street
Wauconda, IL 60084

WILEY

Wiley Publishing, Inc

ABOUT THE AUTHOR

Paul Karr has been visiting the Maine coast since he could walk and has lived on the coast part- or full-time for more than 20 years. Today he divides his time between Maine and New York. Paul is the author or co-author of more than 25 guidebooks, including *Frommer's Vermont, New Hampshire & Maine*, while writing articles for *Sierra* and *Sports Illustrated*, among other publications.

Published by

WILEY PUBLISHING, INC.

111 River St.
Hoboken, NJ 07030-5774

Copyright © 2011 Wiley Publishing, Inc., Hoboken, New Jersey. All rights reserved. No part of this publication may be reproduced, stored in a retrieval system or transmitted in any form or by any means, electronic, mechanical, photocopying, recording, scanning or otherwise, except as permitted under Sections 107 or 108 of the 1976 United States Copyright Act, without either the prior written permission of the Publisher, or authorization through payment of the appropriate per-copy fee to the Copyright Clearance Center, 222 Rosewood Drive, Danvers, MA 01923, 978/750-8400, fax 978/646-8600. Requests to the Publisher for permission should be addressed to the Permissions Department, John Wiley & Sons, Inc., 111 River Street, Hoboken, NJ 07030, 201/748-6011, fax 201/748-6008, or online at http://www.wiley.com/go/permissions.

Wiley and the Wiley Publishing logo are trademarks or registered trademarks of John Wiley & Sons, Inc. and/or its affiliates. Frommer's is a trademark or registered trademark of Arthur Frommer. Used under license. All other trademarks are the property of their respective owners. Wiley Publishing, Inc. is not associated with any product or vendor mentioned in this book.

ISBN 978-0-470-88154-5 (print); ISBN 978-1-118-05669-1 (ebk);
ISBN 978-1-118-05670-7 (ebk); ISBN 978-1-118-05671-4 (ebk)

Editor: Linda Barth
Production Editor: Lindsay Conner
Cartographer: Andrew Dolan
Photo Editor: Richard Fox
Production by Wiley Indianapolis Composition Services

Front Cover Photo: Sunrise, Otter Cliff, Acadia National Park © Pat & Chuck Blackley / Alamy Images
Back Cover Photo: Moose in Maine Kappy / Frommers.com Community

For information on our other products and services or to obtain technical support, please contact our Customer Care Department within the U.S. at 877/762-2974, outside the U.S. at 317/572-3993 or fax 317/572-4002.

Wiley also publishes its books in a variety of electronic formats. Some content that appears in print may not be available in electronic formats.

Manufactured in the United States of America

5 4 3 2 1

CONTENTS

Wauconda Area Library
801 N. Main Street
Wauconda, IL 60084

4 SUGGESTED MAINE COAST ITINERARIES 63

5 SOUTHERN MAINE 74

6 PORTLAND 106

7 FREEPORT TO MONHEGAN ISLAND 132

8 MIDCOAST MAINE 160

9 MOUNT DESERT ISLAND 196

10 THE DOWNEAST COAST 241

11 SIDE TRIPS FROM THE MAINE COAST 262

12 FAST FACTS & WEBSITES 288

Index 294

LIST OF MAPS

ACKNOWLEDGMENTS

Gracious thanks to all who cooperated with this and previous editions, especially Wayne Curtis, who authored the original title; a boatload of editors and higher-ups at Frommer's and Wiley, including Linda Barth, Anuja Madar, Naomi Kraus, and Mike Spring (and dozens before them); and countless unsung copy editors, designers, printers, web jockeys, sales folk, and bean-counters who ensure that books are actually assigned, edited, printed, and sold. Thanks to the many tourism officials, PR liaisons, and hotel and restaurant staff who tirelessly answered questions, arranged itineraries, checked facts, provided tours, cooked meals, made beds—and then let me do my job without trying to tell me how to do it. Thanks to the staticky web of AM radio stations crisscrossing northern New England, who kept me in the Red Sox loop throughout the short summer. If only your signals reached to Gotham . . . Thanks to Gibson, Epiphone, and Harmony for making fine guitars that travel well. And finally, this goes out to my lovely girl.

—Paul Karr

HOW TO CONTACT US

In researching this book, we discovered many wonderful places—hotels, restaurants, shops, and more. We're sure you'll find others. Please tell us about them, so we can share the information with your fellow travelers in upcoming editions. If you were disappointed with a recommendation, we'd love to know that, too. Please write to:

Frommer's Maine Coast, 4th Edition
Wiley Publishing, Inc. • 111 River St. • Hoboken, NJ 07030-5774
frommersfeedback@wiley.com

AN ADDITIONAL NOTE

Please be advised that travel information is subject to change at any time—and this is especially true of prices. We therefore suggest that you write or call ahead for confirmation when making your travel plans. The authors, editors, and publisher cannot be held responsible for the experiences of readers while traveling. Your safety is important to us, however, so we encourage you to stay alert and be aware of your surroundings. Keep a close eye on cameras, purses, and wallets, all favorite targets of thieves and pickpockets.

FROMMER'S STAR RATINGS, ICONS & ABBREVIATIONS

Every hotel, restaurant, and attraction listing in this guide has been ranked for quality, value, service, amenities, and special features using a star-rating system. In country, state, and regional guides, we also rate towns and regions to help you narrow down your choices and budget your time accordingly. Hotels and restaurants are rated on a scale of zero (recommended) to three stars (exceptional). Attractions, shopping, nightlife, towns, and regions are rated according to the following scale: zero stars (recommended), one star (highly recommended), two stars (very highly recommended), and three stars (must-see).

In addition to the star-rating system, we also use seven feature icons that point you to the great deals, in-the-know advice, and unique experiences that separate travelers from tourists. Throughout the book, look for:

special finds—those places only insiders know about

fun facts—details that make travelers more informed and their trips more fun

kids—best bets for kids and advice for the whole family

special moments—those experiences that memories are made of

overrated—places or experiences not worth your time or money

insider tips—great ways to save time and money

great values—where to get the best deals

The following abbreviations are used for credit cards:

AE	American Express	DISC	Discover	V	Visa
DC	Diners Club	MC	MasterCard		

TRAVEL RESOURCES AT FROMMERS.COM

Frommer's travel resources don't end with this guide. Frommer's website, **www.frommers.com,** has travel information on more than 4,000 destinations. We update features regularly, giving you access to the most current trip-planning information and the best airfare, lodging, and car-rental bargains. You can also listen to podcasts, connect with other Frommers.com members through our active-reader forums, share your travel photos, read blogs from guidebook editors and fellow travelers, and much more.

THE BEST OF THE MAINE COAST

Humor columnist Dave Barry once suggested that Maine's state motto should be changed to "Cold, but damp," thereby emphasizing its two primary qualities. That's cute, but it's also sort of true. Spring here tends to last just a few days or weeks; November features bitter winds alternating with gray sheets of rain; and the long winters often bring a mix of blizzards and ice storms.

Ah, but summer. Summer on the coast of Maine brings osprey diving for fish off wooded points, fogs rolling in poetically from the Atlantic, and long, timeless days when the sun rises well before visitors do. (By 8am, it can already feel like noon.) Maine summers offer a serious dose of tranquillity; a few days in the right spot can rejuvenate even the most jangled city nerves.

The trick is *finding* that right spot. Rte. 1 along the Maine coast is mostly an amalgam of convenience stores, tourist boutiques, and restaurants catering to bus tours. The main loop road, single beach, and most popular mountain peaks in Acadia National Park tend to get congested in summer. And arriving without a room reservation in high season? Simply a bad idea.

On the other hand, Maine's remote position and size often work to your advantage. The state has an amazing 5,500 miles of coastline, plus 3,000 or so coastal islands (admittedly, some of these are nothing more than rocks). With a little homework, you can find that little cove, island, or fishing village that isn't too discovered yet, book your room well in advance, and enjoy coastal Maine's incredibly lovely scenery without sweating any of the last-minute details.

Getting to know the locals is fun, too. They're mostly fishermen (as opposed to the farmers who colonized the rest of New England) and other seafaring folk, or the descendants of such, and today's coastal Mainers—even the transplanted ones—exhibit both a wry, dry sense of humor and a surprising gregariousness. (There's a Bait's Motel in Searsport, complete with worm-hanging-off-its-hook motif, for instance, and a tiny street called Fitz Hugh Lane in Somesville.) And fishermen's stories, of course, are the stuff of legend. Take the time to get to know some folks, and you'll smile a lot more.

Basically, your main challenge when preplanning a vacation in coastal Maine boils down to simply this: Where to start? Here's an entirely biased list of destinations—some places I enjoy returning to time and again. During my years of traveling through the region, I've discovered that places like these merit more than just a quick stop; instead, they're worth a detour or an extended stay of a few days to a week.

THE NATURAL WONDERS OF COASTAL MAINE

o **The Beaches of Southern Maine** (southern Maine): The flat, white-sand beaches of southernmost Maine are gorgeous and perfect for playing Frisbee, walking, tanning, kite flying, and photography. Just watch your tootsies: That water's cold. See chapter 5.

o **Casco Bay's Islands** (southern Maine): Locals call 'em the Calendar Islands for a reason: They claim there are 365 of these rocky islands dotting Casco Bay, in every shape and size. (I'd wager there are more than that, though.) Catch a mail boat from Portland harbor and see how many *you* can count. See chapter 6.

o **Rocky Peninsulas** (southern, Midcoast, and Downeast Maine): Everywhere you go—from the Cape Neddick area to just south of Portland, from Harpswell to Georgetown, from Blue Hill to Boothbay to Schoodic Point—you'll find long fingerlings and headlands carved of sheer bedrock. Once these were mountaintops high above an ancient sea; now they comprise some of the East Coast's most beautiful scenery. Try some back-road wandering to find the best ones. Just remember that these take time to traverse. See chapters 5, 8, and 10.

o **The Camden Hills** (Midcoast Maine): They're not huge, yet this run of hills comes with a bonus you'll only understand when you get to the top: eye-popping coastal vistas of boats, villages, and islands. In the winter, you can even toboggan-run from crest to valley. See chapter 8.

o **Acadia National Park** (Downeast Maine): New England's only national park is also one of the most beautiful (and popular) in the entire U.S. The fractured, rocky, surf-pounded coastline here is the main attraction, but don't overlook the quiet, boreal forests and open summits of low mountains that afford spectacular coastal views, either. And don't forget to rent a mountain bike or horse-drawn carriage for further exploration. See chapter 9.

o **The Appalachian Trail and Mount Katahdin** (side trip from Downeast Maine): All right, they're not on the coast. But Maine's highest peak is well worth a short detour inland. Rising abruptly from a thick blanket of North Woods forest, the nearly mile-high Mount Katahdin has an ineffable spiritual quality to it. It's the centerpiece of equally inspiring Baxter State Park, one of the last, best wildernesses remaining in the eastern U.S. While here, don't forget to check out the trail itself, which stretches 2,100 rugged miles from Georgia before winding uphill to the finish line here on Katahdin. These stretches in Maine include some of the most magnificent scenery in New England. See chapter 11.

THE best SMALL TOWNS

o **York Village** (southern Maine): What else can you say? It's Maine's oldest settlement, so it's got history and fine architecture. It's also got a set of beaches and a coastal trail nearby. And people just seem friendly here. See chapter 5.

- **Camden** (Midcoast Maine): This seaside town has everything—a beautiful harbor; great Federal, Queen Anne, and Greek Revival architecture; and even its own tiny mountain range affording great hikes with sweeping ocean views. With lots of elegant bed-and-breakfasts, it's a perfect base for explorations farther afield. See chapter 8.

- **Castine** (Midcoast Maine): Soaring elm trees, a peaceful harborside setting, grand historic homes, and a selection of good inns make this a great spot to soak up some of Maine's coastal ambience off the beaten path. See chapter 8.

- **Blue Hill** (Midcoast Maine): A tiny town with fine harbor views; a general store; central green; museum; a lazy, summery feeling; and no—absolutely no—pretense nor tourist tack (so far). See chapter 8.

- **Northeast Harbor** (Mount Desert Island, Downeast Maine): Northeast has a waterside setting, sure, but also a gentle mixture of seafaring locals and art-loving summer folks, giving it an aura of a place that's still living life from a century ago. The single, sleepy main street anchors one of Mount Desert Island's best little villages. See chapter 9.

- **Eastport** (Downeast Maine): Sure, it's basically a fish-processing town, yet Eastport is making a slow transition from working-class town to (gasp) tourist destination. Don't be surprised if it gets more popular as time goes on; or see it now, and be ahead of the curve. See chapter 10.

THE best PLACES TO SEE FALL FOLIAGE

- **The Camden Hills** (Midcoast Maine): The surrounding countryside is full of blazing color, with whitewashed homes and sailboats to offset it. See chapter 8.

- **Acadia National Park** (Downeast Maine): This national park possesses some of the finest foliage in northern New England, all the more so because it's set right beside the dramatic, rocky coastline. See chapter 9.

- **Blueberry Barrens** (Downeast Maine): Downeast Maine's vast wild blueberry fields suddenly turn a brilliant cranberry-red color each fall, practically setting the landscape ablaze with color. This is one of Maine's unappreciated scenic treasures. Wander the dirt roads northeast of Cherryfield through the upland barrens, or just drive Rte. 1 between Harrington and Machias past an experimental farm atop (of course) Blueberry Hill. See chapter 10.

THE best COASTAL VIEWS

- **From Hiking Trails on Monhegan:** The village of Monhegan is clustered around the harbor of the same-named island, quite a way off the coast. The rest of the 700-acre rock is comprised of picturesque wild lands, with miles of trails crossing open meadows and tracing rocky bluffs. See chapter 7.

- **From the Deck of a Windjammer:** See Maine as many saw it for centuries—from the ocean, looking inland. Sailing ships depart from various harbors along the coast, particularly from Rockland and Camden. Spend between a night and a week exploring the dramatic shoreline. See chapter 8.

- **From Merchant's Row via Kayak:** The islands between Stonington and Isle au Haut, rimmed with pink granite and capped with the stark spires of spruce trees,

The Maine Coast

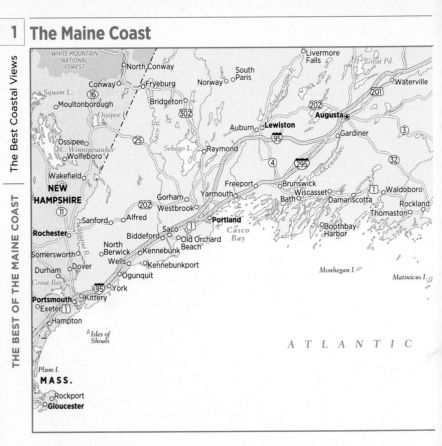

are among the most spectacular on the entire East Coast. They're inaccessible by motorboat, but wonderful to explore by sea kayak if you've got the skill (or the will). Some outfitters even offer overnight camping trips on the islands. See chapter 8.

o **From Acadia's Park Loop Road:** Forming the heart of Acadia National Park, this is New England's premier oceanside drive. Start along a ridge with views of Frenchman Bay and the Porcupine Islands, then dip down along the rocky shores to watch the surf crash against the dark rocks. Plan to do this 20-mile loop at least twice to get the most out of it. See chapter 9.

o **From a Well-Located Rocking Chair:** Views are never better than when you're caught unaware—such as glancing up from an engrossing book on the front porch of an ocean-side inn and catching a great sunset or angle of light on the water. This book includes many hotels and inns on the water. A list of the best porch views in Maine could run for pages, but it would certainly include those gleaned from the Beachmere Inn (in Ogunquit), the Black Point Inn (in Scarborough), Grey Havens (on Georgetown Island), East Wind Inn (in Tenant's Harbor), the Samoset Resort (outside Rockport), the Inn on the Harbor (in Stonington), the Tides Inn (in Bar Harbor), and the Claremont (in Southwest Harbor). But feel free to find your own best front porch, too.

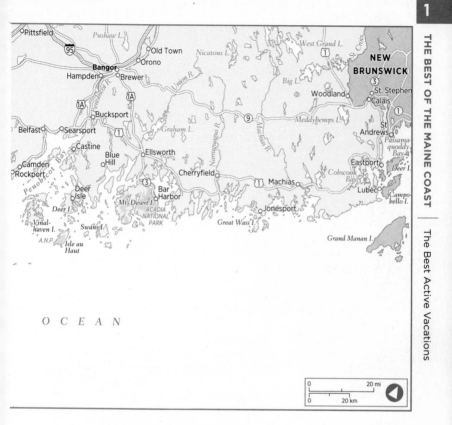

- **New Hampshire Route 1A by Bike:** This beautiful little ride packs a sampling of all sorts of coastal scenery into a tiny slice of New Hampshire coastline running approximately from Hampton Beach. You begin among sandy beaches, then pass rocky headlands and handsome mansions before coasting into the scenic, appealing little city of Portsmouth. See chapter 11.

THE best ACTIVE VACATIONS

- **Mountain Biking at Acadia:** Oil magnate John D. Rockefeller, Jr., built the carriage roads of Mount Desert Island so that the gentry could enjoy rambles in the woods on horseback—far away from those pesky cars that were just then filling his bank accounts with huge profits. His extensive network today offers some of the most scenic and enjoyable mountain biking in the U.S. Thanks, John! See chapter 9.
- **Kayaking the Coast:** With its massive and serpentine coastline and thousands of islands, most of them uninhabited, Maine is a world-class destination for those who know their way around a sea kayak. The Stonington area is considered the best spot for kayaking in Maine, but it's hard to go wrong anywhere northeast of

Portland. Just beware the dangers that lurk in the form of tricky tides or weather—kayak with a guide if you're at all a novice.

o **Canoeing the North Woods:** Maine has thousands of miles of flowing rivers and streams, and hundreds of miles of shoreline along remote ponds and lakes. Happily, these are not all that far inland from the coast. Bring along a tent, sleeping bag, and cooking gear, and you're good to go: It will be just you, the stars, and the sounds of the loons. See chapter 11.

THE best DESTINATIONS FOR FAMILIES

o **York Beach** (southern Maine): This beach town is actually a set of three towns; head for Short Sands with the kids, where they can watch a taffy-pulling machine, play video games in an arcade, ogle seashells in a trinket shop, or scarf cotton candy at a small amusement park. The Long Sands section is ideal for tanning, Frisbee tossing, or kite flying, and nearby Nubble Light (a scenic lighthouse) is close to a kid-friendly ice-cream shop. See chapter 5.

o **Freeport** (southern Maine). It's almost impossible to knock Freeport as a family vacation spot. We're talking about a town with tons of shopping, outdoor music in summer, about a half-dozen L.L.Bean stores (including one focused exclusively on kids' outdoor wear), and tons of quick eats and chain hotels. Plus lobsters. Plus a souvenir shop with a moose theme. Heck, there's even a McDonald's—tastefully designed, of course. About the only thing this place *lacks* is a go-kart track and an Elmo theme park. And that's a good thing. See chapter 7.

o **Old Orchard Beach** (southern Maine): This place has sort of a carnival atmosphere—there are french fries, hot dogs, and fried dough galore. Though it might be a bit much for adults, the kids will probably love it. See chapter 6.

o **Monhegan Island** (southern Maine): The mail boat from Port Clyde out to Monhegan is rustic and intriguing, the inns are a rustic overnight adventure, and the smallish island's scale is perfect for kids to explore, especially kids in the, say, 8-to-12-year-old range. See chapter 7.

THE most INTRIGUING HISTORIC HOMES

o **Victoria Mansion** (Portland): The Victorians went all out for grandiose material excess in a Trumpian-before-the-Donald sort of style. You'll find Victorian decorative arts at their zenith in this elaborate Italianate mansion, which was built during the Civil War. It's open to the public for tours throughout the summer, and then again during the Christmas season. See chapter 6.

o **Castle Tucker** (Wiscasset): It may not be a "castle" per se, but it certainly does have the look of one—and that's by design, of course. The fellow who built it made his fortunate trading something you just don't hear much about in Maine: cotton. It's fun to note how successive layers were built onto the house over time. Today this oddball find is safely preserved under the watch of the region's preeminent historic-homes organization. See chapter 7.

- **Musical Wonder House** (Wiscasset): Two odd houses in one little town? Yes, indeed. I'll wager you'll never find another house in the 50 states with as many music boxes as this one, whose amazingly curated collections of the mechanical wonders (sorry) are compromised a bit by the strange admissions policy: you pay per floor. Really. See chapter 7.
- **Parson Fisher House** (Blue Hill): Parson Jonathan Fisher, who served as minister to the quiet town of Blue Hill in the late 18th century, was a man of extraordinary talents, from designing his own house to building his own clocks and preaching sermons in five languages (including Aramaic). As if that wasn't enough, his primitive landscape paintings of the region are surprisingly good. See chapter 8.

THE best PLACES TO REDISCOVER THE PAST

- **Sabbathday Lake Shaker Community** (New Gloucester): This is the last of the active Shaker communities in the nation and the only one that voted to accept new converts rather than die out. The 1,900-acre farm about 45 minutes outside of Portland has a number of exceptional buildings, including some dating from the 18th century. Visitors can view examples of Shaker craftsmanship and buy herbs to bring home. See chapter 6.
- **Mount Desert Island & Bar Harbor:** In the mid-1800s, America launched a love affair with nature and never looked back. See where it started, here amid surf-wracked rocks, and where some of the nation's most affluent families ventured to erect vacation "cottages," with bedrooms by the dozen. The area still offers lessons on how to design with nature as accomplice rather than adversary. See chapter 9.
- **Portsmouth** (New Hampshire): Portsmouth is a salty coastal city that also happens to possess some of the most impressive historic homes in all New England. Start at Strawbery Banke, a 10-acre compound of 42 historic buildings. Then visit some of the many other grand homes in the surrounding neighborhoods. See chapter 11.

THE best RESORTS

- **Black Point Inn Resort** (Scarborough; © **207/883-2500**). Just outside Portland, this resort offers expansive views of the sea and walking-distance proximity to famed landscape painter Winslow Homer's former studio, which will open to the public in just a few years. It remains a Maine classic resort experience. See p. 109.
- **Inn at Ocean's Edge** (Lincolnville Beach; © **207/236-0945**). This resort delivers exactly what the name promises: a resort, perched right on the edge of the ocean (or, in this case, Penobscot Bay). The place has its own vanishing-edge pool, a very good seaside restaurant, a real sense of hospitality, and rooms that range from comfortable to luxe. See p. 175.
- **The Samoset Resort** (Rockport; © **800/341-1650** or 207/594-2511). The new heated pool and hot tub possess an incredible view of the bay, and so do many of the rooms and suites. Plus there's an outstanding golf course right at your feet—the best in Maine—and even a little lighthouse you can walk to from your room. The dining room is outstanding. See p. 166.

o **Wentworth by the Sea** (Portsmouth, New Hampshire; ✆ **866/240-6313** or 603/422-7322). Actually just across the state line in New Hampshire, the Wentworth is an old grand hotel that faded out, then was brought back to life. It works: the red-roofed, turreted main inn holds a swimming pool, spa, and wonderful dome-ceilinged dining room, while the suites by the water are among the most luxurious in the state. See p. 269.

o **White Barn Inn** (Kennebunkport; ✆ **207/967-2321**): Much of the White Barn staff hails from Europe, and they treat guests graciously. The rooms and suites here are a delight, and the meals (served in a gloriously restored barn) are among the best in northern New England. See p. 98.

THE best BED & BREAKFASTS

o **The Captain Lord Mansion** (Kennebunkport; ✆ **800/522-3141** or 207/967-3141): You'll transcend all those "wannabe&Bs" at this genuine article, chock-full of grandfather clocks, Chippendale highboys, and other antiques. This mansion is just off the village center in Kennebunkport, perfectly situated for relaxing strolls to the beach or into town. See p. 100.

o **The Hartstone Inn** (Camden; ✆ **800/788-4823** or 207/236-4259). Among the zillions of inns and B&Bs in Camden, the Hartstone probably tops them all. The combination of food, fun, and comfort here can't be beat—absolutely sign on for at least one dinner in the dining room. Later, relax in your suite. And you couldn't be more centrally located in this lovely town—the town drugstore, opera house, and greengrocer are literally on the same block as the inn. See p. 175.

o **Lindenwood Inn** (Southwest Harbor; ✆ **800/307-5335** or 207/244-5335): This place features a jovial owner, good rooms, a refreshingly laid-back and summery feel, a fine pool and deck, and proximity to one of Mount Desert Island's key lobster piers. It's a uniquely relaxing retreat, just a short drive from the main street of one of MDI's best small towns. See p. 236.

THE best AFFORDABLE ACCOMMODATIONS

o **Driftwood Inn & Cottages** (Bailey Island; ✆ **207/833-5461**): Where else can you find a double room at the edge of the rocky Maine coast starting at around $80? This classic shingled compound dates from 1910 and offers mostly rooms with shared bathrooms, but the views might be worth that inconvenience. See p. 146.

o **Maine Idyll Motor Court** (Freeport; ✆ **207/865-4201**): The 1932 Maine Idyll Motor Court is a classic—a cluster of 20 cottages scattered about a grove of beech and oak trees. Each cottage has a tiny porch, wood-burning fireplace (birch logs provided), TV, fridge, modest kitchen facilities (no ovens), and timeworn furniture. The downside? A little highway noise. Cottages start at $63 for two. See p. 138.

o **Seawall Motel** (Southwest Harbor; ✆ **800/248-9250**): The rooms here are modest, but the location, next to wetlands and across the street from the rocky shore of Mount Desert Island, is hard to beat. Plus, owners David and Vickie Lloyd are excellent hosts, providing insider information on the area's best trails (hint: not all of them are in Acadia National Park), restaurants, and bird-watching sites. The fact that rooms are offered as low as $80 a night is just an added bonus. See p. 237.

THE best ALTERNATIVE ACCOMMODATIONS

○ **Maine Island Trail:** About 70 remote islands along the Maine coast are open to camping, and from these remote, salty wildernesses, you'll see some of the best sunsets imaginable. See "Outdoor Activities," in chapter 3, for an introduction.

○ **Windjammers** (Midcoast and Downeast Maine): Maine has the East Coast's largest fleet of windjammers, offering adventures on the high seas throughout the summer. You can explore offshore islands and inland estuaries and learn how sailors once made the best of the wind. Accommodations in private cabins are typically spartan, but you'll spend most of your time on the deck luxuriating in the stunning views. See chapter 8.

THE best RESTAURANTS

○ **Hurricane** (Kennebunkport; ✆ 207/967-1111): Talented chef Brooks MacDonald's restaurant emphasizes local seafood and lobster with a creative flair right in Kennebunkport's Dock Square. See p. 104.

○ **White Barn Inn** (Kennebunkport; ✆ 207/967-2321): The setting, in an ancient, rustic barn, is magical. The tables are draped with floor-length tablecloths, and the chairs feature Italian upholstery. The menu—and the decor—changes seasonally, but is always top-notch. See p. 104.

○ **Fore Street** (Portland; ✆ 207/775-2717): Fore Street is one of New England's most celebrated restaurants, and has been previously selected as one of *Gourmet* magazine's 100 best restaurants in the U.S. Chef Sam Hayward has been getting lots of press. His secret? Simplicity: Some of the most memorable meals are prepared over an applewood grill. See p. 114.

○ **Primo** (Rockland; ✆ 207/596-0770): Melissa Kelly and Price Kushner create culinary magic on two floors of a century-old home at this winning Rockland bistro. Expect fancy treatments of foie gras, scallops, duck, steak, and more; outstanding desserts; and a long, impressive wine list. See p. 168.

THE best LOCAL DINING EXPERIENCES

○ **Becky's** (Portland; ✆ 207/773-7070): Five different kinds of home fries on the menu? It's breakfast nirvana at this local institution right on Portland's working waterfront. This is *the* favored hangout of Portland's fishermen, not to mention high school kids, businessmen, and lots of other folks. See p. 118.

○ **Silly's** (Portland; ✆ 207/772-0360): Hectic and fun, this tiny, kitschy restaurant serves up delicious finger food in a no-frills setting. Expect pita wraps, thick burgers, kabobs, hamburgers, and pizzas, among many other things. The milkshakes alone are worth the detour. See p. 120.

- **Dolphin Chowder House** (South Harpswell; ℂ 207/833-6000): The fish chowder and lobster stew are so reasonably priced and delicious at this hidden spot—which is part of a marina at the very end of a dead-end road—that you'll want to find it. Blueberry muffins come with most meals. See p. 147.

- **Thurston's Lobster Pound** (Bernard; ℂ 207/244-7600): It doesn't get much more local than this eatery, perched on stilts right above the lobster boats with atmospheric views on the so-called "quiet side" of Mount Desert Island. Choose your lobster from the tank at the counter, plus sides of corn on the cob, steamed clams, blueberry cake, and beer, then join the happy crowds either upstairs or down. See p. 240.

- **Helen's Restaurant** (Machias and Ellsworth; ℂ 207/255-8423). Everyone in Midcoast and Downeast Maine knows about Helen's, last of a dying breed of local-food diners that used to dot this coast from top to bottom. Order pork chops, fried fish, burgers, or meatloaf, but whatever you do, save room for the widely famous pies: blueberry is the signature selection. And the chocolate cream and meringue pies put up good fights, too. The original Helen's is in Machias, and I recommend you get there if you possibly can, but there's also a second location between Ellsworth and Mount Desert Island—very convenient if you're headed to Acadia.

THE best DESTINATIONS FOR SHOPPERS

- **Kittery:** There are tons of outlets on Rte. 1 of this otherwise sleepy hamlet; you're bound to find something good at a low price at Crate & Barrel, Coach, Seiko, Gap, or wherever. See chapter 5.

- **Portland:** A city this size really ought to have more shops than it does—the Old Port, the chief shopping district, is in serious danger of becoming a bit too precious, and is pretty small—but you can still find great little boutiques and shops if you look hard enough. See chapter 6.

- **Freeport:** L.L.Bean is the anchor store for this thriving town of outlets, but you'll also find places such as Patagonia, J. Crew, Dansk, Brooks Brothers, and about 100 others. This is somehow among the most aesthetically pleasing of the outlet centers scattered around northern New England. See chapter 7.

- **Portsmouth, New Hampshire:** Downtown Portsmouth offers a grab bag of small, eclectic shops ranging from funky shoe, vintage, and toy shops to classy art galleries. The downtown is small enough to browse on foot, and you'll find a broad assortment of stuff for sale appealing to almost any taste. See chapter 11.

THE best SMALL TOWNS

- **Ogunquit** (southern Maine): Take a couple of beaches, mix 'em in with more than a smidgeon of art and culinary art, swirl in a ton of good-to-excellent mid-priced and luxurious inns and resorts, and sprinkle a top-flight museum on top. What do you get? Ogunquit. This longtime summer resort town is extremely agreeable, and it's got one of the best little coastal walking trails in Maine. See chapter 5.

- **Wiscasset** (southern Maine): Why not? It already dubs itself the "prettiest little village in Maine," and I've got to admit, there is quite a bit of cuteness to go around, not to mention history and a pair of the more unusual museums you're going to come across. See chapter 7.

o **Stonington** (downeast Maine): Maine's heritage as a fishing town is never more on display than it is here on Stonington, the biggest "town" (if you want to call it that) on little Deer Isle. You get a fair number of blow-ins here, too, who came for the views and stayed to paint pictures, paddle kayaks, do yoga, or whatever. See chapter 8.

o **Eastport** (downeast Maine): Now this is truth in advertising: You can't get any farther east in the U.S. than Eastport. You'd think this place would be a lonely outpost, but it's actually a thriving little hub of artistic culture, historic architecture, brawny fishing exploits, and briny eats. See chapter 10.

THE MAINE COAST IN DEPTH

Boiled down to its simplest facts, the Maine coast basically consists of two regions: southern Maine—"down there," also sometimes referred to as "Vacationland" or "not Maine"—and Downeast—"up there" or "the real Maine." The two regions are as different as night and day; broadly speaking, the gourmet cuisine, fine cars, and luxury inns of the south coast gradually (and then quickly) give way to cottages, used cars tacked together with duct tape, and fried fish.

Maine's legendary aloofness is important to keep in mind when visiting the area, because getting to know the region requires equal amounts of patience and persistence. New England doesn't wear its attractions on its sleeve. It keeps its best destinations hidden in valleys and on the side streets of small villages. Your most memorable experience might be cracking open a boiled lobster at a roadside lobster pound marked by a scrawled paper sign, or exploring a cobblestoned alley that's not even on Google Maps. There's no Disneyland or Eiffel Tower here. This coast is, instead, the sum of dozens of smaller attractions and resists being defined by a few big ones.

Of course, the natural elements here—the wind, the soft hazy light, the shining or roiling seas—always seem to have the greatest draw on the traveler, and these elements are as rejuvenating as they are capricious. You're as likely to get a blue-sky day when the islands sparkle like coins in the harbor as you are 3 days of fog and spitting rain or snow. Maybe both in the same week. Attempting to understand this weather—just like trying to explore the coast as a regular tourist, hitting attraction after attraction—is pointless. It's better to just let the mood of each day catch you, cycling or driving a back road in search of something (a byway, an old house, a handmade sign advertising PIES) you've never seen before. Or, if the weather's really nasty, stay inside and do crossword puzzles; paint a watercolor; listen to the Red Sox on the local radio station. *Now* you're getting the real Maine.

Some writers believe Maine's character is still heavily influenced by Calvinism, by such ideas as *nothing can change my fate* and *hard work is the only virtue*. It's hard not to agree, but Mainers aren't completely stone-faced—there are wonderful characters, smiles, and stories to be had in abundance here. And you don't need to expect rock-hard mattresses and tasteless meals, either; as these pages demonstrate, spas, luxurious country inns, and restaurants serving London-class meals have swiftly arrived on the coastal Maine scene (displacing some of the boardinghouses and chowder houses of old). Be sure to visit these places, but also set aside time to spend an afternoon rocking in a chair on a simple inn porch, or wandering a rocky beach path unhurriedly. You'll be glad you did.

THE MAINE COAST TODAY

You might be on Monhegan Island, or traveling downeast along Rte. 1. You'll see a few houses and a few people. A store. A pickup truck. And you'll wonder, "What do these people do to earn a living, anyway?"

Only a few decades ago, the answer was almost always this: living off the land. They might have fished the ocean, harvested their own woodlots, or managed gravel pits, but *work* here usually fell into a category that was awfully close to that of *survival*. Of course, many still do three jobs, but hardscrabble work is no longer the only game in town. Today a coastal Mainer just as likely might have once been a former editor for the *New Yorker*, a farmer who grows organic produce for gourmet restaurants, or a financial consultant who handles his clients by fax and e-mail. And you'll find *lots* of folks whose livelihood is dependent on tourism, whether it's the lone tour guide, the high school kid working the local T-shirt shop, or the tow-truck driver hauling fancy cars around Mount Desert Island after they break down.

This slow change in the economy is but one of the big shifts facing Maine and New England. The most visible and wracking change involves development and growth; for a region long familiar with poverty, a spell of recent prosperity and escalating property values has threatened to bring to Maine that curious homogenization already marking suburbs in the rest of the nation. Once a region of distinctive villages, green commons, and courthouse squares, coastal Maine is just starting to resemble suburbs everywhere else in a few places—a pastiche of strip malls dotted with fast-food chains, big-box discount and home-improvement stores, and the like.

While undeniably convenient, this is nothing short of shocking to longtime residents. Coastal towns have long maintained their identities in the face of considerable pressure. The region has always taken pride in its low-key, practical approach to life. In smaller communities, town meetings are still the preferred form of government. Residents gather in a public space to speak out about—sometimes forcefully—and vote on the issues of the day, such as funding for their schools, road improvements, fire trucks, or even symbolic gestures such as declaring their towns nuclear-free. "Use it up, wear it out, make do, or do without" is a well-worn phrase that aptly sums up the attitude of many longtime Mainers—and it's the polar opposite of the designer-outlet ethos filtering in.

It's not clear how town meetings and that sense of knowing where your town ends and the next one begins will survive the slow but inexorable encroachment of chain stores like Walmart and Banana Republic in places like a mall-heavy area outside Portland, the shopping outlets of Kittery and Freeport, and the conglomeration of U.S. Rte. 1 near Bucksport and Ellsworth. In these spots, little regional identity can be found.

Meanwhile, the rest of coastal Maine is figuring out how best to balance the principles of growth and conservation—how to allow the economy to edge into the modern age without sacrificing those qualities that make Maine such a distinctive place. Development is a hot issue, but it isn't white-hot—yet. Few locals feel that development should be allowed at all costs. And few locals tend to think that the land should be preserved at all costs, either. They're not all that happy about rising property taxes and land prices—unless they happen to own a chunk of the coast, in which case they're probably putting up the for sale signs as we speak.

Pinching off all development would mean that the offspring of longtime Maine families will have no jobs, and that Maine would be fated to spend its days as a sort of quaint theme park. But if development continued unabated, many of the characteristics that make this place unique—and attract tourist dollars—would vanish. Will the Maine coast be able to sustain its tourism industry if it's blanketed with strip malls and fast-food joints, making it look like every other town in America? Unlikely. The question is how to respect the conservation ethic while leaving room for growth, but that question won't be answered anytime soon.

Complicating things, Maine's economy has been quixotic, with tourism on the uptick but in no way growing steadily. The mid-1990s saw a slump, and things have been flat of late; even when the economy nosed back downward, however, resourceful locals somehow found a way to buy and fix up farmhouses and keep their pickup trucks and dogs happy. Turn over a few stones, and it's remarkable how many self-owned enterprises you'll find along this coast.

One change is all but inevitable: Property values will continue to rise as city folks increasingly seek a piece of whatever it is that makes rural Maine special. Commentators believe this change, while welcome after decades of slow growth, will bring new conflicts. The continuing rise of an information culture will make it increasingly likely that telecommuters and info-entrepreneurs will move in and settle the coast's most pristine villages, running their businesses via modem or satellite. How will these affluent newcomers feel about increased coastal development or increasing numbers of tour buses cruising their quaint harborside streets? How will locals respond to all the new money—with envy, or with open arms? And how much will the state's priceless natural resources become stressed by increased tourism or development?

Local Wisdom

Welcome to Vacationland
    —former Maine state motto
Maine: The Way Life Should Be
    —former Maine state motto

Change doesn't come rapidly to the Maine coast. But there's a lot to sort out, and friction will certainly continue to build, one waterfront condo at a time. One thing is for sure: It will be interesting to see how it plays out.

LOOKING BACK AT MAINE

Viewed from a distance, Maine's history mirrors that of its progenitor, England. This coastline rose from a sparsely populated, inhospitable place to a place of tremendous historical importance in a relatively short time, thanks to its tremendous natural resources (such as white pine trees for ship's masts, and endless schools of fish that could be caught offshore). For a time, Maine captured a good deal of America's overseas trade and became a legitimate world industrial and marine powerhouse—not to mention a center of literary and creative thought and even fine art.

Don't believe me? That's because the party ended almost as suddenly as it began, when commerce and culture sought more fertile grounds to the west and south.

To this day, Maine refuses to separate itself from the past. When you walk through downtown Portland, layers of history pile up at every turn: modern buses and punk-rock wannabes crouching before fine church steeples dating from colonial times; oceanview parks; elaborate mansions by world-class architects that speak to the refined sensibilities of the late Victorian era.

This history is even more inescapable as you proceed up the coast and off the beaten track. Travelers in Downeast Maine—an overlooked, economically depressed area today—can still find clues to what Henry Wadsworth Longfellow called "the irrevocable past" in everything from the stone walls running through the woods to the handsome Federal-style homes once built by wealthy merchants.

Here's a brief overview of some historical episodes and trends that have shaped coastal Maine:

INDIGENOUS CULTURE   Native Americans have inhabited Maine since about 7000 B.C. The state was inhabited chiefly by Algonquins and Abenakis, who lived a nomadic life of fishing, trapping, and hunting; they changed camp locations several times each year to take advantage of seasonal fish runs, wildlife movements, and the like.

After the arrival of the Europeans, French Catholic missionaries succeeded in converting many Native Americans, and most tribes sided with the French in the French and Indian War in the 18th century. Afterward, the Indians fared poorly at the hands of the British and were quickly pushed to the margins. Today they are found in greatest concentration at several reservations in Downeast Maine. Other than that, the few remnants left behind by Indian cultures have been more or less obliterated by later settlers.

THE COLONIES   In 1604, some 80 French colonists spent winter on a small island on what today is the Maine–New Brunswick border. They did not care for the harsh weather of their new home and left in spring to resettle in present-day Nova Scotia. In 1607, 3 months after the celebrated Jamestown, Virginia, colony was founded, a group of 100 English settlers established a community at Popham Beach, Maine. The Maine winter demoralized these would-be colonists, as well, and they returned to England the following year.

The colonization of the region began in earnest with the arrival of the Pilgrims at Plymouth Rock in 1620. The Pilgrims—a religious group that had split from the Church of England—established the first permanent colony, although it came at a hefty price: Half the group perished during the first winter. But the colony began to thrive over the years, in part thanks to helpful Native Americans. The success of the Pilgrims lured other settlers from England, who established a constellation of small towns outside Boston that became the Massachusetts Bay Colony. Throughout the 17th century, colonists from Massachusetts pushed northward into what is now Maine (but was once actually part of Massachusetts). The first areas to be settled were lands near protected harbors along the coast and on navigable waterways.

The more remote settlements came under attack in the 17th and early 18th centuries in a series of raids by Native Americans conducted both independently and in concert with the French. These proved temporary setbacks; colonization continued throughout New England into the 18th century.

THE AMERICAN REVOLUTION   Starting around 1765, Great Britain launched a series of ham-handed economic policies to reign in the increasingly feisty colonies. These included a direct tax—the Stamp Act—to pay for a standing army.

The crackdown provoked strong resistance. Under the banner of "No taxation without representation," disgruntled colonists engaged in a series of riots, resulting in the Boston Massacre of 1770, when five protesting colonists were fired upon and killed by British soldiers.

In 1773 the most infamous protest took place in Boston (and, at the time, Maine was still part of Massachusetts). The British had imposed the Tea Act, which prompted a group of colonists dressed as American Indians to board three British ships and dump 342 chests of tea into the harbor. This well-known incident was dubbed the Boston Tea Party. Hostilities reached a peak in 1775 when the British sought to quell unrest in Massachusetts. A contingent of British soldiers was sent to seize military supplies and arrest high-profile rebels John Hancock and Samuel Adams. The militia formed by the colonists exchanged gunfire with the British, thereby igniting the revolution ("the shot heard round the world"). Hostilities formally ended in February 1783, and in September Britain recognized the United States as a sovereign nation.

While no notable battles were fought in Maine, a number of forts were established along the coast of Maine—first for the purpose of defending the British from the French, and then for the purpose of defending the new America from, well, the British. Many of these forts remain well preserved today, as state parks.

FARMING & TRADE As the new republic matured, economic growth in New England followed two tracks. Residents of inland communities survived by farming and trading in furs.

On the Maine coast, however, boatyards sprang up anywhere there was a good anchorage, and ship captains made tidy fortunes trading lumber for sugar and rum in the Caribbean. Trade was dealt a severe blow following the Embargo Act of 1807, but commerce eventually recovered, and Maine-ported ships could be encountered everywhere around the globe. Entire towns such as Searsport developed almost solely as exclusive (at the time) hometowns for the sea captains who stayed at sea for long months on these difficult journeys; many of their homes contained distinctive "widow's walks," from which their wives could watch for their returns.

The growth of the railroad in the mid–19th century was another boon. The train opened up much of the coast to trade by connecting Maine with Boston. The rail lines allowed local resources—such as timber from the Maine woods, floated downriver to the coast via log drives—to be much more easily shipped to markets to the south.

INDUSTRY Maine's Industrial Revolution found seed around the time of the embargo of 1807. Barred from importing English fabrics, New Englanders simply pulled up their bootstraps and built their own textile mills. Other common household products were also manufactured domestically, especially shoes. Coastal towns such as Biddeford, Saco, and Topsham became centers of textile and shoe production. Today, however, industry no longer plays the prominent role it once did—manufacturing first moved to the South, then overseas.

TOURISM In the mid- and late 19th century, Mainers discovered a new cash crop: the tourist. All along the eastern seaboard, it became fashionable for the gentry and eventually the working class to set out for excursions to the mountains and the shore. Aided by the dramatic paintings of the Hudson River School painters, Acadia and the downeast coast were suddenly lifted by a tide of summer visitors; this tourism wave crested in the 1890s in Bar Harbor. Several grand resort hotels from tourism's golden era still host summer travelers in the area.

ECONOMIC DOWNTURN   While the railways helped Maine to thrive in the mid–19th century, the train played an equally central role in undermining its prosperity. The driving of the Golden Spike in 1869 in Utah, linking America's Atlantic and Pacific coasts by rail, was heard loud and clear in Maine, and it had a discordant ring. Transcontinental rail meant manufacturers could ship goods from the fertile Great Plains and California to faraway markets; the coastal shipping trade was dealt a fatal blow. And the tourists, too, began to set their sights on the suddenly accessible Rockies and other stirring sites in the West.

Beginning in the late 19th century, Maine lapsed into an extended economic slumber. Families commonly walked away from their farmhouses (there was no market for resale) and set off for regions with more promising opportunities. The abandoned, decaying farmhouse became almost an icon for the Maine coast, and vast tracts of farmland were reclaimed by forest. With the rise of the automobile, the grand resorts further succumbed, and many closed their doors as inexpensive motels siphoned off their business.

BOOM TIMES   During the last 2 decades of the 20th century, much of Maine rode an unexpected wave of prosperity. A massive real-estate boom shook the region in the 1980s, driving land prices sky-high as prosperous buyers from New York and Boston acquired vacation homes or retired to the most alluring areas. In the 1990s, the rise of the high-tech industry also sent ripples from Boston north into Maine. Tourism rebounded as harried urbanites of the eastern seaboard opted for shorter, more frequent vacations closer to home.

Travelers to more remote regions, however, will discover that some communities never benefited from this boom; they're still waiting to rebound from the economic downturn earlier in the 20th century. Especially hard hit have been places such as Downeast Maine, where many residents still depend on local resources—lobsters, fish, farmland, maybe a bed-and-breakfast or crafts business on the side—to eke out a living. And, remarkably, it still works.

COASTAL MAINE ART & ARCHITECTURE

ARCHITECTURE   You can often trace the evolution of a place by its architecture, as styles evolve from basic structures to elaborate mansions. The primer below should help you with basic identification.

- **Colonial** (1600–1700): The New England house of the 17th century was a simple, boxy affair, often covered in shingles or rough clapboards. Don't look for ornamentation; these homes were designed for basic shelter from the elements, and are often marked by prominent stone chimneys.

- **Georgian** (1700–1800): Ornamentation comes into play in the Georgian style, which draws heavily on classical symmetry. Georgian buildings were in vogue in England at the time, and were embraced by affluent colonists. Look for Palladian windows, formal pilasters, and elaborate projecting pediments. Portsmouth, New Hampshire, has abundant examples of later Georgian styles.

- **Federal** (1780–1820): Federal homes (sometimes called Adams homes) may best represent the New England ideal. Spacious yet austere, they are often rectangular or square, with low-pitched roofs and little ornament on the front, although carved swags or other embellishments are frequently seen near the roofline. Look for fan windows and chimneys bracketing the building. In Maine, excellent Federal-style homes are found throughout the region in towns such as Kennebunkport, Bath, and Brunswick.

o **Greek Revival** (1820–60): The most easy-to-identify Greek Revival homes feature a projecting portico with massive columns, like a part of the Parthenon grafted onto an existing home. The less dramatic homes may simply be oriented such that the gable faces the street, accenting the triangular pediment. Greek Revival didn't catch on in New England the way it did in the South, however.

o **Carpenter Gothic and Gothic Revival** (1840–80): The second half of the 19th century brought a wave of Gothic Revival homes, which borrowed their aesthetic from the English country home.

o **Victorian** (1860–1900): This is a catchall term for the jumble of mid- to late-19th-century styles that emphasized complexity and opulence. Perhaps the best-known Victorian style—almost a caricature—is the tall and narrow Addams Family–style house, with mansard roof and prickly roof cresting. You'll find these scattered throughout the region. The Victorian style also includes squarish **Italianate** homes with wide eaves and unusual flourishes, such as the outstanding Victoria Mansion in Portland.

o Stretching the definition a bit, Victorian can also include the **Richardsonian Romanesque** style, which was popular for railroad stations and public buildings.

o **Shingle** (1880–1900): This uniquely New England style quickly became preferred for vacation homes on the Maine coast. They're marked by a profusion of gables, roofs, and porches, and are typically covered with shingles from roofline to foundation.

o **Modern** (1900–present): Maine has produced little in the way of notable modern architecture; you won't find a Fallingwater (one of Frank Lloyd Wright's best-known works, near Pittsburgh), though you might spy a surprising modernist building somewhere on an enclave of wealth such as Mount Desert Island or Cape Elizabeth—if you can get past the security.

ART   New England is also justly famous for the **art** it has produced, particularly the seascapes painted on Cape Cod, along the coast of Maine, and by **Hudson River School** artists such as Thomas Cole and his student Frederic Church. Some of the other artists who have memorably painted New England landscapes and seascapes include **Winslow Homer** (1836–1910), **Fairfield Porter** (1907–75), **John Marin** (1870–1953), **Neil Welliver** (1929–2005), and **Andrew Wyeth** (1917–2009), he of the iconic *Christina's World,* painted in a coastal Maine field.

To showcase these works, and the works of other local and traveling artists, there are a surprising number of excellent art museums and galleries in Maine. Consult the individual chapters for more details on local art offerings.

COASTAL MAINE IN POPULAR CULTURE

BOOKS   Mainers have generated whole libraries, from the earliest days of hellfire-and-brimstone Puritan sermons to Stephen King's horror novels set in fictional Maine villages.

The tales of Bowdoin graduate **Nathaniel Hawthorne** (1804–64) captivated a public eager for native literature. His most famous story, *The Scarlet Letter,* is a narrative about morality set in 17th-century Boston, but he wrote numerous other books that wrestled with themes of sin and guilt, often set in the emerging republic.

Henry Wadsworth Longfellow (1807–82), the Portland poet who settled in Cambridge (another Bowdoin man), caught the attention of the public with evocative narrative poems focusing on distinctly American subjects. His popular works included "The Courtship of Miles Standish," "Paul Revere's Ride," and "Hiawatha." Poetry in the mid–19th century was the equivalent of Hollywood movies today—Longfellow could be considered his generation's Steven Spielberg (apologies to literary scholars).

Thoreau's *The Maine Woods* explored Maine (although not the coast) in detail, at a time when few white men had yet penetrated the interior of the state—and there were still significant dangers involved in doing that. His canoe trip to Katahdin was a genuine adventure.

Other regional writers who left a lasting mark on American literature include **Edna St. Vincent Millay** (1892–1950), a poet from Camden, and **Sarah Orne Jewett** (1849–1909), who wrote the indelible *The Country of the Pointed Firs.* The best-selling *Uncle Tom's Cabin,* the book Abraham Lincoln half-jokingly accused of starting the Civil War, was written by **Harriet Beecher Stowe** (1811–86) while in Brunswick.

And the former *New Yorker* scribe **E. B. White** (1899–1985) wrote many fine, wide-ranging essays and books (including children's books such as the classic *Charlotte's Web*) about rural Maine from his perch in North Brooklin, near Blue Hill, where he moved in 1939.

Finally, Maine is still the home of **Stephen King,** who is considered not so much a novelist as Maine's leading industry.

FILM & TV   Maine is frequently captured through the lens of Hollywood, thanks in equal parts to its natural beauty and, probably, the unusually high numbers of actors and actresses (John Travolta, for example) who maintain vacation homes here.

Lillian Gish's 1920 silent film ***Way Down East*** was perhaps the first movie to bring cinematic attention to the region. A host of horror films written by Maine's **Stephen King**—from *Carrie, Cujo,* and *The Dead Zone* down to a welter of TV miniseries—make it sometimes seem like the only inhabitants of small New England towns are ghosts, creeps, and other supernatural forces. However, King also penned the short story upon which the wonderful flick starring Morgan Freeman and Tim Robbins, ***The Shawshank Redemption*** (one of my all-time favorites), was later based. The story and film are both based in Maine, though the prison and events are completely fictional.

EATING & DRINKING ON THE MAINE COAST

All along the coast you'll be tempted by seafood in its various forms. You can get fried clams by the bucket at divey shacks along remote coves and busy highways. The more upscale restaurants offer fresh fish, grilled or gently sautéed.

Live lobster can be bought literally off the boat at lobster pounds, especially along the Maine coast. The setting is usually rustic—maybe a couple of picnic tables and a shed where huge vats of water are kept at a low boil.

In summer small farmers set up stands at the end of their driveways offering fresh produce straight from the garden. You can usually find berries, fruits, and sometimes home-baked breads. These stands are rarely tended; just leave your money in the coffee can.

Restaurateurs haven't overlooked New England's bounty. Many chefs serve delicious meals consisting of local ingredients—some places even tend their own gardens. Some of the fine dishes I've enjoyed while researching this guide include curried pumpkin soup, venison medallions with shiitake mushrooms, and wild boar with juniper berries.

But you don't have to have a hefty budget to enjoy the local foods. A number of regional classics fall into the "road food" category. Here's an abbreviated field guide:

○ **Baked beans:** Boston is forever linked with baked beans (hence the nickname "Beantown"), but they remain amazingly popular in Maine. A local Saturday-night church supper on the coast often consists of just baked beans and brown bread at "bean hole" suppers featuring the food. There's also a famous B&M baked-bean plant in Portland.

○ **Lobster rolls:** Lobster rolls consist of some pretty basic fixings: fresh lobster meat plucked from the shell, mixed with just enough mayonnaise to hold it together, and served on a hot-dog roll (preferably buttered and grilled). There are fancier permutations in touristy areas, with stuff such as celery and onions mixed in, but you want this basic version: It's meatier and more succulent. You'll find the rolls almost everywhere along the Maine coast; expect to pay between $9 and $15 per roll (more in lean lobster-harvest years). One of the meatiest in Maine is served at Red's Eats, a hot-dog stand by the side of the road in downtown Wiscasset. For info on where to find some of the best *boiled* lobsters off the pier, see the box "Pier, Beer & Lobster," on p. 21).

○ **Moxie:** It's hard to imagine it now, but early in the 20th century, the Maine-made soft drink Moxie outsold Coca-Cola. Part of its allure was the fanciful story behind its 1885 creation: A traveler named Moxie was said to have observed South American Indians consuming the sap of a native plant, which gave them extraordinary strength. The drink was then helpfully "re-created" by Maine native Dr. Augustin Thompson. It's still very, very popular among old-timers in Maine, although some others say it tastes worse than cough medicine. Think Coke plus quinine, minus any sweetener.

○ **Wild blueberries:** You sometimes get the feeling, traveling in Downeast Maine, that the entire state's economy would implode if anything ever happened to the blueberry crop; it's grown and harvested (and added to recipes) everywhere in these parts. Look for roadside stands and diners advertising pies made with fresh berries in mid- to late summer. Also note that the tiny wild blueberries (which grow on low shrubs, often on wind-swept rocks or hilltops) are tastier than the bigger, commercially grown high-bush variety you're probably familiar with.

Finally, no survey of Maine foods would be complete without a mention of the local beer. Maine *alone* probably has more microbreweries than any other *region* in the U.S. except for the Pacific Northwest. Popular brewpubs to hit include Federal Jack's Brewpub (Kennebunkport); the Sea Dog Brewing Co. (now located in

PIER, BEER & lobster

The best lobster restaurants are those right on the water, where there's no pretension or frills. The ingredients for a proper feed at a local lobster pound are a pot of boiling water, a tank of lobsters, some well-worn picnic tables, a good view, and a six-pack of Maine beer. Among the best on Mount Desert Island is famous **Beal's Lobster Pier** (✆ 207/244-3202) in Southwest Harbor, one of the oldest pounds in the area. **Thurston's Lobster Pound** (✆ 207/244-7600) in tiny Bernard (across the water from Bass Harbor) is atmospheric enough to have been used as a backdrop for the Stephen King miniseries *Storm of the Century;* it's a fine place to linger toward dusk, with great water views from the upstairs level. **Abel's Lobster Pound**

(✆ 207/276-5827) on Rte. 198, 5 miles north of Northeast Harbor, overlooks the deep blue waters of Somes Sound; eat at picnic tables under the pines or indoors at the restaurant. It's quite a bit pricier than other lobster restaurants at first glance, but they don't charge for the extras that many other lobster joints do—and some visitors claim that lobsters here are more succulent. Then there's **Trenton Bridge Lobster Pound ★** (✆ 207/667-2977) on Rte. 3 in Trenton (on the mainland) just before the bridge across to the Island, a personal favorite of mine where the lobsters are boiled in seawater. It's salty and unpretentious as all get-out. A container of their smoky lobster stew and a slice of homemade blueberry pie make for ideal takeout.

Topsham, originally in Camden); and Portland's clutch of terrific mini-breweries—at least a half-dozen, at last count, all making mighty good beer.

LIGHTHOUSES: A TOUR UP THE COAST

Unlike its neighbor Nova Scotia, Canada, Maine doesn't maintain, advertise, or market a "Lighthouse Trail"—but it might be a good idea to cobble one together, because this state has quietly assembled some of the best lighthouses in the U.S. Most were built of stone in the early to mid–19th century, and nearly all were automated in the 1960s or 1970s with very few exceptions. (Today no keepers live full time in any Maine lighthouses.) To see them all, you'd need to drive the coast bottom to top—in other words, follow the chapters of this book in geographical order—and also be in possession of a boat.

Let's forget about the boat for a minute and concentrate on those most easily seen by car; I've sprinkled references to Maine's most visible lighthouses throughout this guidebook, but henceforth, a quick primer on connecting the dots and seeing them one by one, beginning with the southern coast. (**Note:** If you're tacking on a side trip to Portsmouth, New Hampshire—described in greater detail in chapter 11—you've got a shot at even adding a few *more* lighthouses to your "seen-in-lifetime" list. See below for more on those.)

THE SOUTHERN COAST Almost from the moment you cross the state line in Kittery, you're on the scent of our imagined Lighthouse Trail. Make a beeline for Fort McClary, on the back road from Portsmouth to York (Rte. 103); from Portsmouth, simply follow State Street across the bridge to Maine, then turn right at the sign for Rte. 103. Follow the winding road a few miles to a sharp right-hand bend, and the park's there on the right before you round the bend. From here, you can view squat, gray-granite **Whaleback Light.** It's not much to look at, though a private boat would help you get closer; public access to the lighthouse grounds is not permitted, however.

A few miles north of Kittery, detour off Rte. 1 to York Beach and head for Long Sands. Here, from the comfort of nothing more than a blanket or beach chair, you can—with good eyes—spy *two* lighthouses at once.

The first one, **Nubble Light** (p. 80), is obvious at the northern end of the beach. It sticks far out on a promontory and is the archetypal Maine light. For a closer look at it, drive to the northern end of the beach and hang a right, then drive the winding cape road to the turnoff for Sohier Park (parking is free). Here, from a rock or bench, you can get almost close enough to the fabled light to touch it—don't try however; a dangerous narrow passage of water separates the viewing area from the rock-bound lighthouse. Snap a photo, then head up the hill for an ice-cream cone at Brown's, again keeping your gaze fixed on the lighthouse as you eat.

The other lighthouse visible from Long Sands, the tall, slim, ghostly **Boon Island light,** demands a perfectly clear day and binoculars or exceptional vision. Gaze out to sea, roughly in the middle of the stretch between both ends of crescent-shaped Long Sands, and its hazy outline may appear to you. Though nearly 10 miles offshore, the granite tower stands more than 13 stories tall—New England's tallest—and that's why it can be seen.

Tiny, wind-swept Boon Island itself has an appropriately murky history: When a British ship ran aground here in 1710, survivors resorted to cannibalism for nearly 3 weeks to survive until a member of the party somehow sailed ashore and fetched help. Author Kenneth Roberts wrote a popular novel, *Boon Island,* fictionalizing parts of this incident. Incredibly, the barren rock and its lighthouse was still inhabited as recently as 1978, when one of the worst winter storms in New England history destroyed all the outbuildings and part of the tower, where the keeper's family cowered for several days awaiting rescue. Soon afterward, it was automated.

It's a bit farther north to the next light. The small **Goat Island Light** lies just off the lovely little hamlet of Cape Porpoise, north of Kennebunkport. (From Dock Sq. in the center of Kennebunkport, follow coastal Rte. 9 about 2½ miles north and east to find the village.) The light has a storied history, including its use as a command post for U.S. Secret Service agents defending the family compound of President George H. W. Bush; a keeper who did a 34-year stint of duty on the rock; a caretaker who died in a boating accident in 2002; and Maine's last lighthouse-keeping family, the Culps, who departed the light in 1990 and turned it over to automation and the care of the Kennebunkport Conservation Trust, which maintains the 25-foot tower and keeper's house and plans to restore the property further in the future. Boat visits are welcome.

At the mouth of the Saco River, where the big river enters the Atlantic at the Biddeford-Saco line, the cute little **Wood Island Lighthouse** and its keeper's house still guard this passage—though you'd never know it, as the light's almost impossible to view, except by boat. The light has a rich history, however, including tales of ghosts, murder most foul, and a keeper's dog smart enough to ring bells by himself. The Friends of Wood Island Lighthouse (www.woodislandlighthouse.org) offer summertime boat tours to the island; otherwise, its premises can't be visited by the public.

GREATER PORTLAND   Greater Portland contains perhaps the finest—and most visited and photographed—lights on the whole of the Maine coast.

To view **Cape Elizabeth Light,** the southernmost light in the Portland area, head straight for Two Lights State Park (there were previously two working lights here; one was phased out). The light-keeper's home is now privately owned, but this lighthouse has a rich lore, including daring rescues of shipwrecked sailors in the boiling, stormy sea and the work of painter Edward Hopper, who featured the light in several early-20th-century paintings. It is still an important signal on this rocky part of the coast. If you're hungry after viewing it, be sure to drop by the outstanding Two Lights Lobster Shack (see the sidebar "Lucky 77: Hitting the Beaches," in chapter 6) for a bite, and also visit the small souvenir shack on the rocks.

Just to the north, **Portland Head Light** (p. 122) possesses lovely proportions, an 80-foot beveled tower, a handsome keeper's home (now a small museum), and a scenic position on a cliff before the horizon and the Atlantic. This is one of the very best lighthouses in Maine to view with the family—and one of the most popular and often photographed, as well. (Don't come here for solitude.) Hundreds of thousands of visitors come each year to the free park from which it can be viewed, just off Shore Road in Cape Elizabeth. There's also a gift shop.

From Portland Head Light, you can get a very good view of another lighthouse just offshore: the often-overlooked (probably due to its crude looks) **Ram Island Light,** built of Maine granite in 1905.

Next up, reachable by following South Portland's Broadway to its end, is the **Spring Point Light,** an amusingly shaped light that somewhat resembles a fire hydrant. But take it seriously: It guards the heavily trafficked passage between Portland Harbor and the so-called Calendar Islands, a passage critical to oil and freight transport into and out of Maine. The light is set out at the end of the narrow stone breakwater, and can be walked up to and viewed but not entered except during special open houses held periodically, when you may view the keeper's room, which is slowly being outfitted with period furnishings. There's a museum, the Portland Harbor Museum (© 207/799-6337), on the land side of the breakwater with plenty more information about the area. The light is also adjacent to both the pretty campus of Southern Maine Community College and the ruins of Fort Preble, good places for a picnic and a walk.

Nearby around the point, the Portland Breakwater Light—locally known as **"Bug Light"**—is a smaller, squatter version of the Spring Point light sitting on land that was once an important shipbuilding complex. A small, free city park surrounds the light.

FREEPORT TO MIDCOAST   From either Bath or South Freeport, you can take a boat tour to view the attractive high rock housing **Seguin Island Light** a few miles off Popham Beach. Contact Atlantic Seal Cruises (© 207/865-6112), which runs twice-weekly tours in summertime, or the Maine Maritime Museum (© 207/443-1316), which offers periodic cruises past the light. Due to the heavy fogs that frequently move into this area, the house sports Maine's strongest (and most valuable) lens; it's 12 feet high, and has been operating since 1857, the same year the keeper's home and stone light tower were also constructed.

Smaller, weaker **Pond Island Light, Cuckolds Light,** the **Perkins Island Light, Ram Island Light,** and the mainland-based **Squirrel Point Light** are all located in the same general vicinity as Seguin, and they can also be viewed during the

Maine Maritime Museum's cruises or during other charter runs from the Boothbay Harbor waterfront. Squirrel Point's light can also be hiked to via a rough trail that begins off Bald Head Road in Arrowsic.

Also in Arrowsic, some of **Doubling Point Light**'s grounds are free to roam—reach it by crossing the huge bridge from Bath, making an immediate right onto Rte. 127 south, and following signs to the Doubling Point Road turnoff on the right. The light is connected to the keeper's quarters by a long causeway, which is closed to the public. Two small related lights, known as the **Range Lights,** are housed in octagonal wooden towers near the Doubling Point grounds; these lighthouse grounds are also free to visit, and the towers are architecturally singular on the coast, though unsigned and a bit difficult to find. Once again, the Maine Maritime Museum's special lighthouse cruises often pass by this set of lights.

From the Boothbay Harbor pier, it's easy to visit the handsome **Burnt Island Light** and its attractive complex of outbuildings: Catch an excursion from the pier, then settle in for one of the twice-daily summertime tours. Plan ahead, however; the tours take 2 to 3 hours apiece. Now owned by the state of Maine, the complex, still active as a navigational aid, is also home to a program of nature, arts, and even music courses—a real success story.

Before leaving Boothbay Harbor, you may wish to detour down the long peninsula to West Southport (take Rte. 27 to the turnoff for the village) to get a view of offshore **Hendricks Head Light,** now privately owned and beautifully restored.

Finally, there's the **Pemaquid Point** (in Bristol) and its museum and the **Marshall Point Lighthouse** (in Port Clyde) and its museum, both of which I describe in greater detail in chapter 7; and, offshore, there's the **Monhegan Island Light** and *its* museum (open July–Sept; ✆ **207/596-7003**), which I haven't mentioned. But it's well worth a look if you're out on the island, and makes a fine, fitting end to this section of our ad hoc lighthouse trail.

PENOBSCOT BAY   The Midcoast region harbors plenty of lights, though many are small and posted on offshore rocks, thus inaccessible (and unviewable) by car. However, the squat **Owls Head Light,** now owned by the Coast Guard and still active, sits on a promontory in Knox County Lighthouse Park (✆ **207/941-4014**); it can be viewed by anyone who can wrangle a parking spot in the lot. (The light itself, though, is off-limits.) Interestingly, there's a long walkway and set of stairs connecting the keeper's house to the actual light, making this one of the most visually pleasing of all Maine's lighthouses.

The southernmost light of the two in the city of Rockland is known as **Rockland Harbor Southwest Light,** and this light is fascinating: It's the only one in Maine that was built by a private citizen. A local dentist constructed the light as both an aid to ships and a kind of homage to the other Rockland light (see below), and it began blinking on and off in 1987; today it's an official navigational light and still privately held. From downtown Rockland, head south about 2 miles on Rte. 73 and hang a left onto North Shore Road.

The **Rockland Breakwater Light** is at the northern edge of the harbor, sitting atop a handsome brick home about a mile out on a rugged stone breakwater; it's easily viewed from the Samoset resort complex (see "Where to Stay," in chapter 8), but the grounds are only open to the public during summer weekends.

Rockport's Marine Park is a good spot to look out at the attractive keeper's house and its **Indian Island Light;** however, the light itself no longer functions. Just north in Camden, the **Curtis Island Light** is quite attractive—it sits on a private island, now owned by the city—but can only really be seen well from the deck of a sightseeing charter or windjammer cruise leaving from the harbor.

Again just north, in Lincolnville, stand on the ferry dock for a look at the **Grindle Point Light,** with its unusual squarish light tower—or, better yet, hop the ferry for an up-close look; it docks on Isleboro nearly beside the lighthouse. The light is part of a public park that includes a small museum built as a memorial to sailors.

Continuing north, pull off Rte. 1 at signs for Stockton Springs if you want a look at the tiny **Fort Point Light,** still active and now a state historic site. It's not the most impressive of the state's lights, however.

Castine is already attractive enough, but the presence of the **Dice Head Light** makes it even more so; the light, privately owned and resided in, features an unusual rough, conical stone tower (though the actual light is no longer atop this interesting structure). Simply follow Rte. 166 to its very end at the water for a look. Do not approach the tower, however; it's private property.

There are three lighthouses on or just offshore Deer Isle, but one is no longer active and the other two can only be seen from a boat cruising off the island's back shore.

Finally, the **Robison Point Light** on Isle au Haut is accessible to the public—in fact, this is the only lighthouse in Maine where you can sleep in the keeper's house (May–Oct). Contact the Keeper's House (✆ **207/460-0257;** www.keepershouse.com) for current rates and availability; there's no phone and no electricity, but the owners will prepare a gourmet meal for you if you wish.

MOUNT DESERT ISLAND & DOWNEAST   Mount Desert Island and its surrounding islands are home to very few lights that can be visited or viewed by the public. One that can is the **Bass Harbor Head Light,** on Mount Desert's western lobe, down Rte. 102A past Southwest Harbor. The complex includes a cylindrical light tower, simple keeper's house, triangular fog signal, and even a barn.

From Bass Harbor, head for another light that can be visited by the public: the **Burnt Coat Harbor Light** (also known as Hockamock Head Light). To get here, however, you'll need to catch a ferry from Bass Harbor to Swan's Island. The squared brick tower and keeper's home were built in 1872.

The downeast section of the Maine coast is rife with little ledges and lighthouses, often steeped in fog and usually off-limits to the public (and too far offshore or too indistinct to be seen anyway). The inactive **Winter Harbor Light** can be glimpsed from the Schoodic Peninsula loop road, although distantly.

The slim stone tower of the **Petit Manan Light** near Milbridge pokes an impressive 120 feet above the surrounding sea. However, it's off-limits and difficult to see anyway. You can get a better look at it while taking a tour of the Maine Coastal Islands National Wildlife Refuge (see "What to See & Do" in chapter 10).

Finally, the **West Quoddy Head Light** in Lubec is part of the state park of the same name I've described in chapter 10. This is America's easternmost point, and there's a museum on the lighthouse grounds, open daily from spring through Columbus Day. Check it out, then sit awhile to reflect on all you've seen on your lighthouse tour.

A LITTLE SOMETHING EXTRA   If you decide to begin your Maine coasting in Portsmouth, New Hampshire, you can take a side trip to the coast and glimpse a few more lighthouses. The cast-iron **Fort Point Light,** part of the state's Fort Constitution Historic Site (✆ **603/436-1552**), is located on Rte. 1B near the Wentworth by the Sea resort described in "Where to Stay" in chapter 11. It can be viewed from the historic site—which is free to enter—from May through October, but can only be entered on one special open-house day each month during that season; check with the park for the open-house dates.

There's also the brick **White Island Light,** offshore in the Isles of Shoals and too far to be seen except when taking a cruise of the islands. Contact the Isle of Shoals Steamship Co. (© **603/431-5500;** www.islesofshoals.com) about periodic lighthouse cruises of the area.

For more on Maine's (and New Hampshire's) lighthouses and preservation efforts, contact the **American Lighthouse Foundation,** P.O. Box 565, Rockland, ME 04841 (© **207/594-4174;** www.lighthousefoundation.org).

PLANNING YOUR TRIP TO THE MAINE COAST

This chapter provides the nuts-and-bolts travel information you'll need before setting off for coastal Maine. Browse through this section before hitting the road to ensure you've touched all the bases.

WHEN TO GO

The Seasons

The well-worn joke about the climate in coastal Maine is that it has just two seasons: winter and August. There's a kernel of truth in this, but it's also probably a ploy to keep outsiders from moving here. In fact, the ever-shifting seasons make Maine distinctive, and with one exception, the seasons are well defined.

SUMMER   The peak summer season runs from July 4th to Labor Day. Vast crowds surge up the Maine coast during and between the two holiday weekends, swelling traffic on the turnpike and Rte. 1, and causing countless motels and inns to hang NO VACANCY signs. Expect to pay premium prices at hotels and restaurants along the coast in midseason. This should be no surprise: Summers are exquisite, in spite of the occasional stretches of fog or rain. (In Portland it tops 90°F/32°C only 4 or 5 days a year, on average.)

Maine's coastal weather is largely determined by whatever breezes are prevailing. Southerly winds bring haze, heat, humidity, fog (thick fogs occasionally linger for days), and even thunderstorms. Northwesterly winds bring cool weather and knife-sharp vistas. (Northeasters bring wind and storms, though these are rare in summer.) These systems tend to alternate during summer, with the heat arriving stealthily and slowly, then getting exiled by stiff, cool winds a few days later. (The change from hot to cool sometimes occurs in a matter of *minutes.*) Along the immediate coast it's often warmest in the late morning, because sea breezes typically kick up daily around lunchtime, pushing temperatures back down for the rest of the afternoons. Rain is rarely far away—some days it's an afternoon thunderstorm, sometimes it's a steady drizzle that brings a 4-day soaking. On average, about 1 day in 3 will bring at least a little rain. Travelers should come prepared for some.

Also be aware that early summer brings out black flies and mosquitoes in multitudes, a state of affairs that has ruined many a camping and hiking trip. While this is especially true inland, it applies along the coastline and on islands as well. Outdoors enthusiasts are best advised to wait until July 4 or later for long camping-out adventures unless they want to end up resembling human pincushions.

AUTUMN   Don't be surprised to sense fall approaching even as early as mid-August, when you'll first notice a few leaves turning orange on the maples at the edges of wetlands. Fall comes early to Maine, puts its feet up on the couch, and hangs around for some time. The foliage season truly begins in earnest in the northern part of the region by the third week in September; in the south, it reaches its peak around mid-October.

Fall is to Maine what the Grand Canyon is to the Southwest. It's one of the great natural spectacles of the place, and when the rolling hills become saturated in brilliant reds and stunning oranges (every year's foliage is different; some years are amazing, others downright dreary), the season is almost garish. Even hardened locals still get dewy-eyed at the sight of the annual colors year after year.

Happily, thanks to Maine's low elevation and the moderating influences of ocean temperatures along the coast, foliage season tends to run even longer along the coast than it does just inland. Maine's mountains can become brown and brittle by mid-October, when coastal foliage is just hitting its stride; sometimes the tart colors even linger into the first few days of November.

Keep in mind that this is also the most popular time of year for *other* travelers, however—bus tours flock like migrating geese to all parts of New England in early October. As a result, hotels are invariably booked solid, and advance reservations are essential. Don't be surprised if you're assessed a foliage surcharge of $10 to $50 per night at some inns. Pay it and be glad you're here.

Maine also maintains a recorded **foliage hot line** and **website** to let you know where and when the leaves are at their brightest peaks. Call ⓒ **888/624-6345** for the latest updates, or log onto the state's foliage website at www.mainefoliage.com.

WINTER   Maine winters are like wine; some years are good, some are lousy. During a good season, mounds of light, fluffy snow blanket the deep woods and fill the ski slopes. A good winter offers a profound peace and tranquillity. The muffling qualities of fresh snow bring a great silence to the region, and the hiss and pop of a wood fire at a country inn can sound like a heavenly symphony. During these winters, exploring the powdery forest floors on snowshoes or cross-country skis is an experience bordering on the magical.

During those *other* winters, though (the lousy ones), the weather gods bring a nasty mélange of rain, freezing rain, and sleet. The woods become filled with dirty crusty snow; the cold is damp and numbing, and the sky seems perpetually cottony and bleak. In 1998, a destructive ice storm wreaked so much havoc on the woods that you can still see evidence (fallen trees) today; more than half of all Maine's homes lost power, for periods up to 2 weeks. During times like this, even the stoutest residents wish they'd been born in the Caribbean.

Things are particularly tricky along the coast during winter; a winter vacation can be spectacular (not much beats cross-country skiing at the edge of the pounding surf), but it's a venture that could as likely yield rain as snow.

Where to go during winter? Beach towns such as York Beach and Ogunquit and tourist destinations such as Boothbay Harbor shut down almost entirely and become almost depressing in winter. Skip those. Winter visitors are better off heading for places with more substantial year-round communities and a good selection of year-round lodging and cultural attractions, such as Kennebunkport, Portland, and Camden. (A foray inland to Baxter State Park is also a fine idea in a cold clear winter; see chapter 11.)

SPRING   Maine's spring seemingly lasts only a weekend or so, often appearing around mid-May but sometimes as late as June. One day the ground is muddy, the trees barren, and gritty snow is still collected in shady hollows. The next day it's in the 70s or 80s, trees are blooming, and kids are jumping off docks into the ocean. Travelers need to be crafty and alert if they want to experience spring in Maine; it's also known as "mud season" in these parts, and many innkeepers and restaurateurs actually close up shop for a few weeks for repairs or to venture someplace a lot more cheery.

That said, April and May can offer superb days when a blue sky arches overhead and it's warm in the sun. This might be the most peaceful time of year—a good season for taking solitary walks on the beach or sitting on rocky promontories with only seagulls for company. And here's another secret: Maine hotel rooms are never cheaper than they are in springtime. Just be aware that as soon as that sun slips behind a cloud or over the horizon, it'll feel like winter again; don't leave the parka or gloves far behind.

Portland's Average Monthly Temperatures

		JAN	FEB	MAR	APR	MAY	JUNE	JULY	AUG	SEPT	OCT	NOV	DEC
Avg. High	(°F)	31	32	40	50	61	72	76	74	68	58	45	34
	(°C)	-1	0	4	10	16	22	24	23	20	14	7	1
Avg. Low	(°F)	16	16	27	36	47	54	61	59	52	43	32	22
	(°C)	-9	-9	-3	2	8	12	16	15	11	60	-6	

CALENDAR OF EVENTS

JANUARY

New Year's Portland. Ring in the New Year with a smorgasbord of events and entertainment throughout downtown Portland. Events for families are scheduled in the afternoon; adult entertainment, including loads of live music, kicks off later in the evening at numerous auditoriums, shops, and churches. One admission price buys entrance to all events. December 31 and January 1.

FEBRUARY

U.S. National Toboggan Championships, Camden. A raucous and lively athletic event where being overweight is an advantage. Held at the Camden Snow Bowl's toboggan chute. Call ✆ **207/236-3438.** Early February.

MARCH

Maine Boatbuilders' Show, Portland. More than 200 exhibitors and 9,000 boat aficionados gather as winter fades to make plans for the coming summer. A great place to meet boat builders and get ideas for your dream craft. Call ✆ **207/774-1067.** Mid-March.

Maine Maple Sunday. Maple sugarhouses throughout the state open their doors to visitors. Call ✆ **207/287-3491.** Fourth Sunday in March.

APRIL

Boothbay Harbor Fisherman's Festival. Local fishermen display their talents in fish filleting, clam shucking, and even lobster eating. Enjoy seafood feasts, exhibits, games, and a Blessing of the Fleet on Sunday afternoon. Call ✆ 207/633-2353. End of April.

MAY

Annual Fiddlers Contest, Ogunquit. Rosin up your bow and whip out your best version of Sally Goodin. Or just come and listen to others. Call ☎ **207/646-6170.** Early May.

JUNE

Old Port Festival, Portland. A block party in the heart of Portland's historic district with live music, food vendors, and activities for kids. Call ☎ **207/772-6828.** Early June.

Market Square Weekend, Portsmouth, New Hampshire. This lively street fair attracts 300 vendors and revelers from throughout southern New Hampshire and Maine into downtown Portsmouth to dance, listen to music, sample food, and enjoy summer's arrival. Call ☎ **603/436-3988.** Early June.

Annual Windjammer Days, Boothbay Harbor. For nearly 4 decades, windjammers have gathered in Boothbay Harbor to kick off the summer sailing season. Expect music, food, and a parade of magnificent sailboats. Call ☎ **207/633-2353.** Late June.

JULY

Independence Day, regionwide. Communities all along the coast celebrate with parades, greased-pole climbs, cakewalks, cookouts, road races, and fireworks. The bigger the town, the bigger the fireworks. But many small coastal towns feature seafood and/or lobster-boat racing, an unusual and fun way to celebrate the occasion; Eastport's celebration is particularly impressive (it's 4 days long); see chapter 10. Check local newspapers or contact chambers of commerce for details. July 4.

Summer Performance Series, Portland. Relax and enjoy one of the 50 free noontime performances in Portland's downtown parks. Music includes classical, folk, jazz, rock, country, and children's shows. Call ☎ **207/874-8793** for a complete listing. July and August.

York Days, York Village. Enjoy a quintessential coastal Maine celebration complete with crafts, road races, parades, dances, concerts, fireworks, and much more. Call ☎ **207/363-1040.** Late July to early August.

AUGUST

Maine Lobster Festival, Rockland. Fill up on the local harvest at this event marking the importance and delectability of Maine's favorite crustacean. Enjoy a boiled lobster or two, and take in the ample entertainment during this informal waterfront gala. Call ☎ **800/LOB-CLAW** (562-2529) or 207/596-0376. Usually held first week of August.

Wild Blueberry Festival, Machias. A festival marking the harvest of the region's wild blueberries. Eat to your heart's content. Call ☎ **207/794-3543** or 255-6665. Mid-August.

Blue Hill Fair, Blue Hill. A classic country fair just outside one of Maine's most elegant villages. Call ☎ **207/374-3701.** Late August.

SEPTEMBER

Windjammer Weekend, Camden. Come visit Maine's impressive fleet of old-time sailing ships, which host open houses throughout the weekend at this scenic harbor. Call ☎ **207/236-4404.** Labor Day weekend.

Common Ground Country Fair, Unity. A sprawling, old-time state fair with a twist: The emphasis is on organic foods, recycling, and wholesome living. Call ☎ **207/568-4142.** Late September.

October

Fall Foliage Fair, Boothbay. More than 100 exhibitors display their arts and crafts at the Railroad Village; plenty of festive foodstuffs and live music, too. Call ☎ **207/633-4727.** Early October.

Mount Desert Island Marathon, Bar Harbor. Scenic 26.2-mile race through gorgeous island scenery. Call ☎ **207/276-4226** for more information. Mid-October.

Festival of Scarecrows and Harvest Day, Rockland. A local scarecrow-making contest, plus a farmers market and other activities, spread over a 2-week period. Call ☎ **207/596-6256** for details. Mid-October.

OgunquitFest, Ogunquit. A 3-day pre-Halloween bash, featuring arts, crafts, costumes, and a parade. Call ✆ **207/646-2939.** Late October.

Festival of Lights, Rockland. Horse-drawn carriages, singing, shopping, and open houses of local inns. Call ✆ **207/596-0376** for details. Late November.

Victorian Holiday, Portland. From late November until Christmas, Portland decorates its Old Port in a Victorian Christmas theme. Enjoy the window displays, take a free hayride, and listen to costumed carolers sing. Call ✆ **207/772-6828** or 207/780-5555. Late November to Christmas.

DECEMBER

Christmas Prelude, Kennebunkport. This scenic coastal village greets Santa's arrival in a lobster boat, and marks the coming of Christmas with street shows, pancake breakfasts, and tours of the town's splendid inns. Call ✆ **207/967-0857.** Early December.

Candlelight Stroll, Portsmouth, New Hampshire. Historic Strawbery Banke gets in a Christmas way with old-time decorations and more than 1,000 candles lighting the 10-acre grounds. Call ✆ **603/433-1100.** First 2 weekends in December.

York Village Festival of Lights. This beautiful festival displays an entire York Village and York Beach lit with Christmas lights, carolers, a parade, and much more. Call ✆ **207/363-4974.** Early December.

ENTRY REQUIREMENTS
Passports

Virtually every air traveler entering the U.S. is required to show a passport. U.S. and Canadian citizens entering the U. S. at land and sea ports of entry from within the western hemisphere must now also present a passport or other documents compliant with the Western Hemisphere Travel Initiative, or WHTI; see **www.getyouhome.gov** for details.

It is advised to always have at least one or two consecutive blank pages in your passport to allow space for visas and stamps that need to appear together. It is also important to note when your passport expires. Many countries require your passport to have at least 6 months left before its expiration in order to allow you into the destination.

For an up-to-date, country-by-country listing of passport requirements around the world, go to the "International Travel" tab of the U.S. State Department at **http://travel.state.gov**.

International visitors to the U.S. can obtain a visa application at the same website. *Note:* Children are required to present a passport when entering the United States at airports. More information on obtaining a passport for a minor can be found at http://travel.state.gov. Allow plenty of time before your trip to apply for a passport; processing normally takes 4 to 6 weeks (3 weeks for expedited service) but can take longer during busy periods (especially spring). And keep in mind that if you need a passport in a hurry, you'll pay a higher processing fee.

For Residents of Australia: You can pick up an application from your local post office or any branch of Passports Australia, but you must schedule an interview at the passport office to present your application materials. Call the **Australian Passport Information Service** at ✆ **131-232,** or visit the government website at www.passports.gov.au.

DESTINATION: COASTAL MAINE—RED ALERT checklist

- Did you make sure to book advance reservations for popular tours and restaurants you don't want to miss?

- Did you make sure your favorite attractions are open? Especially if you're traveling early or late in the season, you should call ahead for opening and closing hours if you have your heart set on seeing certain places.

- Do you have a safe, accessible place to store money?

- Did you bring identification that could entitle you to discounts, such as AAA and AARP cards, student IDs, and so on?

- Did you bring emergency drug prescriptions and extra glasses and/or contact lenses?

- Do you have your credit card PINs?

- If you have an e-ticket, do you have documentation?

- Did you leave a copy of your itinerary with someone at home?

- If renting a car, have you checked your insurance and credit card policies to see what's covered? You may be able to save money by declining the extra insurance (collision-damage waiver) offered by the rental agency.

For Residents of Canada: Passport applications are available at travel agencies throughout Canada or from the central **Passport Office,** Department of Foreign Affairs and International Trade, Ottawa, ON K1A 0G3 (✆ **800/567-6868;** www. ppt.gc.ca). **Note:** Canadian children who travel must have their own passport. However, if you hold a valid Canadian passport issued before December 11, 2001, that bears the name of your child, the passport remains valid for you and your child until it expires.

For Residents of Ireland: You can apply for a 10-year passport at the **Passport Office,** Setanta Centre, Molesworth Street, Dublin 2 (✆ **01/671-1633;** www. irlgov.ie/iveagh). Those under age 18 and over 65 must apply for a 3-year passport. You can also apply at 1A South Mall, Cork (✆ **21/494-4700**) or at most main post offices.

For Residents of New Zealand: You can pick up a passport application at any New Zealand Passports Office or download it from their website. Contact the **Passports Office** at ✆ **0800/225-050** in New Zealand or 04/474-8100, or log on to www.passports.govt.nz.

For Residents of the United Kingdom: To pick up an application for a standard 10-year passport (5-year passport for children under 16), visit your nearest passport office, major post office, or travel agency. Or contact the **United Kingdom Passport Service** at ✆ **0870/521-0410,** or search its website at www.ukpa.gov.uk.

Visas

For information on obtaining a Visa, please visit "Fast Facts," on p. 292.

The U.S. State Department has a **Visa Waiver Program (VWP)** allowing citizens of the following countries to enter the United States without a visa for stays of up to 90 days: Andorra, Australia, Austria, Belgium, Brunei, Czech Republic, Denmark,

Estonia, Finland, France, Germany, Hungary, Iceland, Ireland, Italy, Japan, Latvia, Liechtenstein, Lithuania, Luxembourg, Malta, Monaco, the Netherlands, New Zealand, Norway, Portugal, San Marino, Singapore, Slovakia, Slovenia, South Korea, Spain, Sweden, Switzerland, and the United Kingdom. (**Note:** This list was accurate at press time; for the most up-to-date list of countries in the VWP, consult http://travel.state.gov/visa.) Even though a visa isn't necessary, in an effort to help U.S. officials check travelers against terror watch lists before they arrive at U.S. borders, visitors from VWP countries must register online through the Electronic System for Travel Authorization (ESTA) before boarding a plane or a boat to the U.S. Travelers must complete an electronic application providing basic personal and travel eligibility information. The Department of Homeland Security recommends filling out the form at least 3 days before traveling. Authorizations will be valid for up to 2 years or until the traveler's passport expires, whichever comes first. Currently, there is no fee for the online application. **Note:** Any passport issued on or after October 26, 2006, by a VWP country must be an **e-Passport** for VWP travelers to be eligible to enter the U.S. without a visa. Citizens of these nations also need to present a round-trip air or cruise ticket upon arrival. E-Passports contain computer chips capable of storing biometric information, such as the required digital photograph of the holder. If your passport doesn't have this feature, you can still travel without a visa if the valid passport was issued before October 26, 2005, and includes a machine-readable zone; or if the valid passport was issued between October 26, 2005, and October 25, 2006, and includes a digital photograph. For more information, go to **http://travel.state. gov/visa**. Canadian citizens may enter the United States without visas, but will need to show passports and proof of residence.

Citizens of all other countries must have (1) a valid passport that expires at least 6 months later than the scheduled end of their visit to the U.S.; and (2) a tourist visa.

Customs

WHAT YOU CAN BRING INTO THE U.S.

Every visitor 21 years of age or older may bring in, free of duty, the following: (1) 1 U.S. quart of alcohol; (2) 200 cigarettes, 50 cigars (but not from Cuba), or 3 pounds of smoking tobacco; and (3) $100 worth of gifts. These exemptions are offered to travelers who spend at least 72 hours in the United States and who have not claimed them within the preceding 6 months. It is forbidden to bring into the country almost any meat products (including canned, fresh, and dried meat products such as bouillon or soup mixes). Generally, condiments including vinegars, oils, pickled goods, spices, coffee, tea, and some cheeses and baked goods are permitted. Avoid rice products, as rice can often harbor insects. Bringing fruits and vegetables is prohibited since they may harbor pests or disease. International visitors may carry in or out up to $10,000 in U.S. or foreign currency with no formalities; larger sums must be declared to U.S. Customs on entering or leaving, which includes filing form CM 4790. For details regarding U.S. Customs and Border Protection, consult your nearest U.S. embassy or consulate, or **U.S. Customs** (www.customs.gov).

WHAT YOU CAN TAKE HOME FROM MAINE

For information on what you're allowed to bring home, contact one of the following agencies:

Canadian Citizens: Canada Border Services Agency, Ottawa, Ontario, K1A 0L8 (© **800/461-9999** in Canada, or 204/983-3500; www.cbsa-asfc.gc.ca).

U.K. Citizens: **HM Customs & Excise,** Crownhill Court, Tailyour Road, Plymouth, PL6 5BZ (📞 **0845/010-9000;** from outside the U.K., 020/8929-0152; www.hmce.gov.uk).

Australian Citizens: Australian Customs Service, Customs House, 5 Constitution Avenue, Canberra City, ACT 2601 (📞 **1300/363-263;** from outside Australia, 612/6275-6666; www.customs.gov.au).

New Zealand Citizens: New Zealand Customs, The Customhouse, 17–21 Whitmore St., Box 2218, Wellington, 6140 (📞 **04/473-6099** or 0800/428-786; www.customs.govt.nz).

Medical Requirements

Unless you're arriving from an area known to be suffering from an epidemic (particularly cholera or yellow fever), inoculations or vaccinations are not required for entry into the United States.

GETTING THERE & AROUND

Getting to Maine

BY PLANE

Several commercial carriers serve the coast of Maine, though airlines more commonly connect to Maine's airports after stopping first in New York or Boston; direct connections from other cities, such as Chicago and Philadelphia, are also available. Remember that some of the scheduled flights to Maine from Boston are aboard small propeller-driven ("prop") planes; ask the airline or your travel agent if this is an issue for you.

Portland International Jetport (abbreviation: PWM) is Maine's largest airport. The airport is served by airlines including **JetBlue** (📞 800/538-2583; www.jetblue.com); **Continental** (📞 800/525-0280; www.continental.com), **Northwest** (800/225-2525; www.nwa.com), **United Express** (📞 800/241-6522; www.ual.com), and **US Airways** (📞 800/428-4322; www.usair.com). For general airport information, see the airport's website, www.portlandjetport.org, or call 📞 207/874-8877.

Some savvy visitors to northern New England find cheaper fares and a wider choice of flight times by flying into **Boston's Logan Airport** (code: BOS), then rent a car and drive north (or take a connecting bus or train). Boston is about 2 hours by car from Portland, 5 hours from Bar Harbor. Almost every major airline in the U.S. (and many others worldwide) flies into Boston daily, so the fare competition can result in a better ticket price. Boston's airport can become congested, especially at check-in and security; delayed flights are common; and traffic can snarl. But the fare savings can be large.

When researching fares, also check flights going into **Manchester Airport** (airport code: MHT) in New Hampshire, a regional hub for **Southwest Airlines** (📞 800/435-9792; www.southwest.com). The airport is less than 2 hours from Portland by car (1 hr. to York or Kittery), and you can sometimes find deep discounts on routes from Southwest hub cities such as Chicago, Dallas, Orlando, Los Angeles, Houston, and Baltimore-Washington.

Travelers to Downeast Maine might check on rates to the **Saint John, New Brunswick** (airport code: YSJ) airport, about 2 hours from Eastport by car—just remember to budget additional time for the border crossing.

LONG-HAUL FLIGHTS: HOW TO STAY comfortable

- Your choice of airline and airplane will definitely affect your legroom. Find more details about U.S. airlines at **www.seatguru.com**. For international airlines, the research firm Skytrax has posted a list of average seat pitches at **www.air linequality.com**.

- Emergency exit seats and bulkhead seats typically have the most legroom. Emergency exit seats are usually left unassigned until the day of a flight (to ensure that someone able-bodied fills the seats); it's worth checking in online at home (if the airline offers that option) or getting to the ticket counter early to snag one of these spots for a long flight. Many passengers find that bulkhead seating offers more legroom, but keep in mind that bulkhead seats have no storage space on the floor in front of you.

- To have two seats for yourself in a three-seat row, try for an aisle seat in a center section toward the back of coach. If you're traveling with a companion, book an aisle and a window seat. Middle seats are usually booked last, so chances are good you'll end up with three seats to yourselves. And in the event that a third passenger is assigned the middle seat, he or she will probably be more than happy to trade for a window or an aisle.

- To sleep, avoid the last row of any section or the row in front of an emergency exit, as these seats are the least likely to recline. Avoid seats near highly trafficked toilet areas. Avoid seats in the back of many jets—these can be narrower than those in the rest of coach. Or reserve a window seat so you can rest your head and avoid being bumped in the aisle.

- Get up, walk around, and stretch every 60 to 90 minutes to keep your blood flowing. This helps avoid **deep vein thrombosis,** or "economy-class syndrome."

- Drink water before, during, and after your flight to combat the lack of humidity in airplane cabins. Avoid caffeine and alcohol, which will dehydrate you.

Finally, if you need a quick connection directly to Midcoast Maine, check with **Cape Air** (✆ **800/352-0714** or 866/227-3247; www.capeair.com). This regional airline operates two to seven *daily* flights from Boston to the **Knox County Regional Airport** (airport code: RKD) in the lovely Camden-Rockland region, using small nine-seat twin-engine business jets. If you book well ahead and choose off-peak dates and hours, a round-trip fare from Boston can cost as little as $120 per person. There's even a **Budget** (✆ **888/594-0822** or 207/594-0822; www.budget.com) auto rental kiosk at the little airport, open daily until 5pm.

For a fuller listing of who flies where, check the "Getting There" information at the beginning of each chapter in this book.

Foreign visitors arriving by air, no matter what the port of entry, should cultivate patience and resignation before setting foot on U.S. soil. Clearing immigration control can take as long as 2 hours.

From Memorial Day through Labor Day, sometimes longer, I-95 from Boston to Maine becomes sluggish (even stopped-to-a-standstill) on Friday afternoons and evenings as weekend traffic backs up at the toll gates for miles. Sunday nights bring a reverse-repeat of this scene. It might sound comical that you could be stuck immobile in a Dubai-esque gridlock here in the middle of a tidal flat in the middle of nowhere; trust me, it's not nearly so funny once you're ensnared in it. U.S. Rte. 1 along the coast *seems* like an escape route—but it's not. Instead, it bottlenecks at the same times of day and week, especially in spots where two-lane bridges span the local tidal rivers. There's really no cure for this condition; you can, however, do a few things to prevent the affliction from striking. To avoid the very worst of the summer tourist traffic, try to stay put on weekends and during the big summer holidays. Travel midweek or midday if at all possible. Or simply take an extra day off work and head back after the holiday crush. It'll pay handsome dividends in lowered blood pressure—and you'll save a few hours you would have wasted idling your engine going nowhere.

BY CAR

From Boston, New York, and points farther beyond, **I-95** is by far the quickest way to get to the coast of Maine. Note that I-95 is a toll road for stretches through New Hampshire, New Jersey, Delaware, and Maryland—you'll need to pay cash at tollgate, or go through an "E-ZPass" lane with an electric transponder subscribed to the network. The **Maine Turnpike** is also a toll road for long stretches, and it also accepts the E-ZPass. To reach Portland, exit the Turnpike at Exit 44 and follow I-295 (a free highway) into the city, then exit for the waterfront (exit 4) and follow Commercial St. to reach the Old Port and waterfront. To get to the Midcoast or Downeast Maine, follow the same directions but continue north about half an hour past Portland, then exit onto **U.S. Rte. 1 North.**

Note: From New York City, I-95 can sometimes be congested for much of its length, particularly on summer weekends. It's often quicker to take **I-91** north from New Haven, Connecticut, then cutting north on **I-84** toward Boston and then circumventing Beantown via **I-495** north, which then joins **I-95** again near Portsmouth, New Hampshire. Either way, note that some stretches of I-95 are toll roads.

Road maps can sometimes be deceptive, so keep in mind that Maine is much **bigger than it looks** on a one-page road map. Budget time for driving accordingly. I have noted driving distances or driving times in this book wherever possible, but a good rule of thumb to follow is that 50 miles of rural driving takes about 1 hour if there's little traffic. (In summer, passing through a string of busy towns, it might take up to twice that long.)

BY TRAIN

Train service to coastal Maine is very limited, but it does exist. **Amtrak** (© **800/872-7245;** www.amtrak.com) relaunched rail service to Maine in late 2001, restoring a line that had been idle since the 1960s.

Amtrak's **Downeaster** service operates four to five times daily between North Station in Boston and Portland, Maine. If you're coming from elsewhere on the East

Coast, however, you will need to change train stations in Boston—a slightly frustrating exercise requiring either a taxi ride through congested streets or a ride and transfer on Boston's aging subway system. The train stops in **Wells** (7 miles from **Ogunquit**), **Saco**, and **Old Orchard Beach** before arriving in Portland.

Total travel time is about 2½ hours from Boston to Portland. Bikes are allowed to be loaded or off-loaded at Boston, Wells, and Portland. The one-way fare from Boston to Portland is $24 (with a discount for same-day round-trips). The line even has its own website, located at **www.thedowneaster.com**, with fares, schedules, and other useful information.

International visitors can buy a **USA Rail Pass,** good for 15, 30, or 45 days of unlimited travel on **Amtrak** (*©* **800/USA-RAIL** [872-7245]; www.amtrak.com). The pass is available online or through many overseas travel agents. See Amtrak's website for the cost of travel within the western, eastern, or northwestern United States. Reservations are generally required and should be made as early as possible. Regional passes are also available.

BY BUS

Express bus service is well run, but spotty, in coastal Maine. You'll be able to reach the major cities and tourist destinations by bus but only a few of the smaller towns or villages. Tickets from Boston to Portland usually cost between $15 and $30 per person, one-way, depending on such factors as day of week, time of day, and how far in advance you purchase the tickets. Taking the bus requires no advance planning or reservations, but in summer it's still a good idea to buy as early as possible; often you can also save money this way.

Two major bus lines serve coastal Maine from Boston and New York City. **Greyhound** (*©* **800/231-2222;** www.greyound.com) serves Portsmouth, New Hampshire; Portland; Bangor; and points in between with frequent departures from Boston's South Station.

Concord Coach Lines (*©* **800/639-3317** or 603/228-3300; www.concord coachlines.com) serves Portsmouth, New Hampshire; Portland; and Bangor from Boston, and it also connects a few of the key smaller towns like **Belfast, Camden, Rockport, Brunswick,** and **Damariscotta.**

Neither line any longer travels to Bar Harbor, however.

Getting Around

Maine is like much of the rest of America: A set of small cities and suburbs, strung together by transportation corridors, with a whole bunch of small towns and rural areas filling in the rest of the map. Bus, train, and regional plane services are sporadic at best. This all means you will almost certainly need to travel by car (yours, or one you have rented) if you really want to see the coast of Maine in any detail.

BY CAR

Mark my words: You'll need a car. Portland's airport (see above) has plenty of rental options. Among the outfits at the terminal are **Alamo** (tel) 877/222-9075 or 207/775-0855; www.alamo.com), **AVIS** (*©* 800/331-1212 or 207/874-7500; www.avis.com), **Budget** (*©* 800/527-0700 or 207/772-6789; www.budget.com); **Enterprise** (*©* 800/261-7331 or 207/615-0030; www.enterprise.com), **Hertz** (*©* 800/654-3131 or 207/774-4544; www.hertz.com), and **National** (*©* 877/222-9058 or 207/773-0036; www.nationalcar.com).

YOUR car: DO LEAVE HOME WITHOUT IT

If you're *really* green-friendly, options exist for a vacation in New England *without* a car. Here are four suggestions:

○ From New York City or Boston, take an **Amtrak** (www.amtrak. com) train to Brattleboro, Vermont, and explore this small town of brick architecture, good restaurants, and quirky shops. Cross the river to hike Wantastiquet Mountain one afternoon. Another day, rent a canoe and explore the Connecticut River, or get a bike and head off into the hilly countryside. There's a canoe touring center just north of town, and a bike rental outfit or two on the main street.

○ From Boston, take a Concord Coach bus directly to the **Appalachian Mountain Club's Pinkham Notch Visitor Center** (© 603 /466-2721), high in the White Mountains. Spend a night or two, then backpack for 2 days across demanding, rugged mountains, staying at AMC's backcountry huts (all meals provided). At the end of your sojourn, catch the AMC shuttle back to North Conway or Pinkham Notch, and then hail the return bus back to Boston.

○ Bus, fly, or train it to Portland, Maine, where you can sign up for a guided sea-kayak excursion. The **Maine Island Kayak Co.** (© 207/ 766-2373; www.mita.org) on Peaks Island is reached by a quick and pleasant 20-minute ferry ride (the terminal is at the corner of Commercial and Franklin sts.) and offers trips throughout the state all summer long. You can even camp within city limits on remote Jewell Island at the edge of Casco Bay, or head out for a few days along more remote parts of the coast. Portland's museums, restaurants, and bars don't require wheels to reach, either.

○ Fly to tiny airports in Bar Harbor or Rockland, Maine, and then settle into one of the numerous inns or B&Bs downtown. There's even a free shuttle bus from the Bar Harbor airport running downtown and around the island from spring through late fall. Rent a mountain bike and explore the elaborate network of carriage roads at Acadia National Park, then cruise along picturesque Park Loop Road. Another day, sign up for a sea-kayak tour or whale-watching excursion. By night, enjoy lobster or other fine meals at Bar Harbor's fine restaurants. Mountain bikes can be easily rented along Cottage Street in Bar Harbor and in the Camden/Rockland area.

An automobile-association membership is recommended. **AAA, the American Automobile Association** (© 800/222-4357; http://travel.aaa.com), is the country's largest auto club and supplies its members with maps, insurance, and, most important, emergency road service. (Helpfully, it honors cross-memberships with Great Britain's **AA** and Canada's **CAA**.)

I've tried to lay out driving directions to every spot mentioned in this book, but there are dozens of peninsulas, points, and villages I couldn't include in these tours due to space limitations. To find more of those special places, I highly recommend you get your hands on a copy of the wonderful *Maine Atlas and Gazetteer*

(© **800/642-0970** or 800/561-5105; www.delorme), an oversized book of detailed grid maps of the state. With its close-ups of everything from hill contours and historic attractions to hiking trails and even individual boat launches, it's a handy companion. Pick it up at local bookstores, convenience stores, gas station, or company headquarters in **Yarmouth.**

Traffic in Maine is generally light compared with that in urban and suburban areas of the East Coast, but the Maine Turnpike and U.S. Rte. 1 are a couple of notable exceptions during summer weekends. Expect **heavy delays** during peak times, and try to travel off-peak if possible; mid-week traffic is vastly different from that entering Maine on a Friday evening or departing it on a Sunday night. North-south travel is fairly straightforward in Maine, thanks to **I-95 and Rte. 1.** Don't underestimate the length of the Maine coast, though—from Kittery to Eastport (the easternmost city in the United States) is 293 miles, much of it winding slowly through coastal villages or sitting at stoplights. Driving times can be longer than you'd expect due to narrow roads and zigzagging peninsulas, not to mention high-season traffic.

For what are promised to be live, real-time updates of weather, accidents, and traffic conditions on the state's roads and highways, also check out the useful web site **Maine 511** online at **www.511maine.gov.** It's maintained by the Maine Department of Transportation.

If you're still in doubt about a route, use a Web service such as **Google Maps** (maps.google.com), **MapQuest** (www.mapquest.com), or **Yahoo! Maps** (maps.yahoo.com). These handy websites calculate distances and driving directions from any point in the country to any other point. Type in where you want to start and where you want to go, and the online software calculates the total distance and provides detailed driving instructions, along with maps if you want them. Before departing, you can plot your route and print out a daily driving itinerary.

Also, if you're visiting from abroad and plan to rent a car in the United States, keep in mind that **foreign driver's licenses** are usually recognized in the U.S., but you should get an international one if your home license is not in English.

Here are some representative distances between points:

NEW YORK CITY TO	
Bar Harbor, Maine	493 miles
Portland, Maine	319 miles
PORTLAND, MAINE, TO	
Eastport, Maine	250 miles
Bar Harbor, Maine	174 miles
Manchester, New Hampshire	95 miles
North Conway, New Hampshire	65 miles
Camden, Maine	85 miles
York, Maine	45 miles
Kennebunk, Maine	27 miles
Burlington, Vermont	232 miles

BY BUS

As I have already mentioned in the "Getting to Maine" section earlier in this chapter, express bus service *into* the region is pretty good, but beware of trying to travel *within*

BEWARE: MOOSE X-ing

Driving across the northern tier of Maine, you'll often see MOOSE CROSSING signs, complete with silhouettes of the gangly herbivores. These are not placed here to amuse the tourists. In Maine, the state with the most moose (an estimated 30,000, at last count), crashes between moose and cars are increasingly common.

These encounters are usually more dramatic than deer-car collisions. For starters, the large eyes of moose don't reflect in headlights like those of deer, so you often come upon them with less warning when driving late at night. Moose can weigh up to 1,000 pounds, with almost all of that weight placed high atop spindly legs. When a car strikes a moose broadside in the road, it usually knocks the legs out and sends a half-ton of hapless beast right through the windshield. Need we dwell on the results of such an encounter? I thought not. In 1998 alone, the state of Maine recorded 859 crashes involving moose, with 247 injuries and five fatalities. When in moose country, drive slowly and carefully.

Maine by bus. Quirky schedules and routes may send you well out of your way, and what may seem like a simple trip could take hours. Traveling north-south between towns along a single bus route (for example, Portland to Bangor) is feasible, but east-west travel across Maine is, by and large, impractical.

For information on bus travel within Maine, contact either **Greyhound** or **Concord Coach Lines** (see earlier in this chapter, in "Getting to Maine") for service in New Hampshire and Maine.

BY PLANE

Service between airports in Maine is sketchy at best. You can find limited direct flights between some cities (such as Portland to Bangor), but for the most part, you'll have to backtrack to Boston and fly out again to your final destination. Convenient, it's not. See the "Getting There & Getting Around" section, earlier in this chapter, for details.

US Airways (🕾 800/428-4322; www.usair.com) and its commuter subsidiaries handle many of the scheduled flights to Rockland and Bar Harbor.

BY TRAIN

As I have noted above, **Amtrak** (🕾 800/872-7245; www.amtrak.com) provides limited rail travel on the southernmost coast of Maine. See the "Getting to Maine" section, earlier in this chapter, for details. There is also talk of expanding passenger rail lines *north* of Portland to Brunswick, Camden, and even Bar Harbor—basically, back to where they once went in days of yore. But this hasn't happened quite yet.

MONEY & COSTS

THE VALUE OF A DOLLAR VS. OTHER POPULAR CURRENCIES

US$	Can$	UK£	Euro (€)	Aus$	NZ$
1	C$1	£.63	€,74	A$1	NZ$1.29

Frommer's lists exact prices in the local currency. The currency conversions quoted above were correct at press time. However, rates fluctuate, so before departing, consult a currency exchange website, such as **www.oanda.com/convert/classic**, to check up-to-the-minute rates.

Costs

Here's a scene I've seen repeated dozens of times in Maine. It's late Saturday afternoon, maybe early in July. A young (or not-so-young) couple has driven up from the city by car or motorcycle, "just for the day," in sparkling clear weather. But something magical has happened. They've fallen in love with each other all over again, and with the quaint lovely Maine-ness of (insert town here). They've decided to stay for the night in a feather bed, eat a nice meal, and maybe watch the sun set over the (ocean/mountains/lake) and have a beer, and head home tomorrow morning fully assured that all is right with the world.

Except that here they stand, before a tourist information center staff member, looking despondent (or even desperate) as the staffer holds a phone in one hand, waiting for an answer.

"Isn't there *anything* cheaper?" pleads one of the lovebirds. "No, and that's a good price," responds the person behind the desk as kindly as possible. "You won't find anything better. Now, do you want me to book it, or not?"

Yes, travelers are in for a little sticker shock on the coast of Maine, at least during peak travel seasons. In midsummer, there's simply no such thing as a cheap motel room in places such as Portland, Camden, or Bar Harbor. Even no-frills mom-and-pop motels can and do sometimes happily charge $100 a night or more for a bed that could fairly be described as a notch above car-camping. Blander-than-bland chain hotels demand even more.

To be fair, innkeepers in some of these tourist areas must reap nearly all their annual profits in what amounts to just a 2- or 3-month season each year, so that's one reason for the approaching-bank-stickup rates. It's not like they enjoy your misery (I don't think).

Anyhow, take heart. Except during peak foliage season and holidays, the cost of rooms, meals, and day-to-day expenses is generally a lot less here than you'd pay in a major non–New England city. You can find excellent entrees at upscale, creative restaurants for around $20, comparing favorably with similar dishes at big-city restaurants that would top $30.

Still, lodging here is more expensive than in almost any other rural part of the United States (see above about the paucity of cheap motels), and planning can prove tricky for budget travelers.

So you'll need money to enjoy yourself here. It's always advisable to bring money in a variety of forms on a vacation: a mix of cash, credit cards, and traveler's checks. You should also exchange enough petty cash to cover airport incidentals, tipping, and transportation to your hotel before you leave home, or withdraw money upon arrival at an airport ATM.

Money

The most common bills in the U.S. are the $1 (a "buck"), $5, $10, and $20 denominations. There are also $2 bills (seldom encountered), $50 bills, and $100 bills (the last two are usually not welcome as payment for small purchases).

Coins come in six denominations: 1¢ (1 cent, or a penny); 5¢ (5 cents, or a nickel); 10¢ (10 cents, or a dime); 25¢ (25 cents, or a quarter); 50¢ (50 cents, or a half dollar); and $1 coins, which come in several iterations, including the gold-colored Sacagawea coin and the relatively rare silver dollar.

ATMs

Nationwide, the easiest and best way to get cash away from home is from an ATM (automated teller machine), sometimes referred to as a "cash machine" or "cash-point." The Cirrus (© 800/424-7787; www.mastercard.com) and PLUS (© 800/843-7587; www.visa.com) networks span the country; you can even find them in remote regions. Look at the back of your bank card to see which network you're on, then call or check online for ATM locations at your destination. Be sure you know your personal identification number (PIN) and daily withdrawal limit before you depart. Note: Many banks impose a fee every time you use a card at another bank's ATM, and that fee can be higher for international transactions (up to $5 or more) than for domestic ones (where they're rarely more than $2). In addition, the bank from which you withdraw cash may charge its own fee. To compare banks' ATM fees within the U.S., use www.bankrate.com. For international withdrawal fees, ask your bank.

Credit Cards & Debit Cards

Credit cards are the most widely used form of payment in the United States: Visa (Barclaycard in Britain), MasterCard (Eurocard in Europe, Access in Britain, Chargex in Canada), American Express, Diners Club, and Discover. They also provide a convenient record of all your expenses, and they generally offer relatively good exchange rates. You can withdraw cash advances from your credit cards at banks or ATMs, provided you know your PIN.

Visitors from outside the U.S. should inquire whether their bank assesses a fee on charges incurred abroad, usually 1% to 3%.

It's highly recommended that you travel with at least one major credit card. You must have one to rent a car, and hotels and airlines usually require a credit card imprint as a deposit against expenses.

ATM cards with major credit card backing, known as debit cards, are now a commonly acceptable form of payment in most stores and restaurants. Debit cards draw money directly from your checking account. Some stores enable you to receive "cash back" on your debit-card purchases as well. The same is true at most U.S. post offices.

Traveler's Checks

Traveler's checks are still accepted in the U.S., although not as widely as they once were. They're denominated in U.S. dollars; foreign-currency checks are often difficult to exchange. At smaller destinations, such as backwoods camps in Maine, you might find they are not accepted at all—if in doubt, check in advance.

You can buy traveler's checks at most banks. Most are offered in denominations of $20, $50, $100, $500, and sometimes $1,000. Generally, you'll pay a service charge ranging from 1% to 4%.

The most popular traveler's checks are offered by American Express (© 800/807-6233, or 800/221-7282 for cardholders—this number accepts collect calls, offers service in several foreign languages, and exempts Amex gold and platinum cardholders

WHAT THINGS COST ON THE MAINE COAST	US$
Taxi from Portland airport to downtown Portland	18.50 + tip
Double room, moderate	120.00
Double room, inexpensive	75.00
Three-course dinner for one, moderate, no wine	25.00–35.00
Bottle of Imperial beer	1.00–1.50
Bottle of Coca-Cola	1.29
Cup of coffee	1.50–2.50
1 gallon of gas	2.80
Admission to Ogunquit Museum of American Art	7.00–8.00 per person
Admission to Acadia National Park, May to Oct	10.00–20.00 per vehicle
Admission to Acadia National Park, Nov to Apr	Free

from the 1% fee) and **Visa** (© **800/732-1322**). AAA members can obtain Visa checks for a $9.95 fee (for checks up to $1,500) at most AAA offices or by calling © **866/339-3378.** Call © **800/223-9920** for information on MasterCard traveler's checks.

If you do choose to carry traveler's checks, keep a record of their serial numbers separate from your checks in the event that they are stolen or lost. You'll get a refund faster if you know the numbers.

STAYING HEALTHY
Local Health Concerns

Mainers by and large are a healthy bunch, something locals ascribe to clean living, brisk northern air, vigorous exercise (leaf raking, snow shoveling, and so on), and a sensible diet. Other than picking up a germ that may lead to a cold or flu, you shouldn't face any serious health risks when traveling in the region.

Exceptions? Well, yes—you may find yourself at higher risk when exploring the outdoors, particularly in the backcountry. A few things to watch for when venturing off the beaten track:

○ **Poison ivy:** The shiny, three-leafed plant is common throughout the region. If touched, you may develop a nasty, itchy rash that will seriously erode the enjoyment of your vacation. The reaction tends to be worse in some people than others. It's safest to simply avoid it. If you're unfamiliar with what poison ivy looks like, ask at a ranger station or visitor information booth for more information. Many have posters or books to help with identification.

○ **Giardia:** That crystal-clear stream coursing down a backcountry peak may seem pure, but it may be contaminated with animal feces. Gross, yes, and also dangerous. Giardia cysts may be present in some streams and rivers. When ingested by humans, the cysts can result in copious diarrhea and weight loss. Symptoms may not surface until well after you've left the backcountry and returned home. Carry your own water for day trips, or bring a small filter (available at most camping and sporting-goods shops) to treat backcountry water. Failing that, at least boil water or treat it with iodine before using it for cooking, drinking, or washing. If you detect symptoms, see a doctor immediately.

○ **Lyme disease:** Lyme disease has been a growing problem in New England since 1975 when the disease was identified in the town of Lyme, Connecticut, and some 14,000 cases are reported nationwide annually. The disease is transmitted by tiny deer ticks—smaller than the more common, relatively harmless wood ticks. Look for a bull's-eye-shaped rash (3–8 in. in diameter); it may feel warm but usually doesn't itch. Symptoms include muscle and joint pain, fever, and fatigue. If left untreated, heart damage may occur. It's more easily treated in early phases than later, so seek medical attention as soon as any symptoms are noted.

○ **Rabies:** Since 1989, rabies has been spreading northward from New Jersey into New England. The disease is spread by animal saliva and is especially prevalent in skunks, raccoons, bats, and foxes. It is always fatal if left untreated in humans. Infected animals tend to display erratic and aggressive behavior. The best advice is to keep a safe distance between yourself and any wild animal you may encounter. If bitten, wash the wound as soon as you can and immediately seek medical attention. Treatment is no longer as painful as it once was, but still involves a series of shots.

Those planning longer excursions into the outdoors may find a compact first-aid kit with basic salves and medicines very handy to have along. Those traveling mostly in the towns and villages should have little trouble finding a local pharmacy, Rite Aid, or Walmart to stock up on common medicines (such as calamine lotion or aspirin) to aid with any minor ailments picked up along the way.

If You Get Sick

If you suffer from a chronic illness, consult your doctor before your departure. Pack **prescription medications** in your carry-on luggage, and carry them in their original containers, with pharmacy labels—otherwise they won't make it through airport security. Visitors from outside the U.S. should carry generic names of prescription drugs. For U.S. travelers, most reliable healthcare plans provide coverage if you get sick away from home. Foreign visitors may have to pay all medical costs upfront and be reimbursed later. See "Insurance" on p. 289.

If you get sick while in Maine, consider asking your local hotel concierge to recommend a local doctor—even his or her own. You can also try the emergency room at a local hospital. Some hospitals in Maine have walk-in clinics for emergency cases that are not life-threatening. There are large, good hospitals and clinics in the cities of Maine, as well as many small towns. Check with your hotel or the local tourism office if you're concerned about proximity to hospitals.

If you suffer from a chronic illness, consult your doctor before your departure. For conditions like epilepsy, diabetes, or heart problems, wear a **MedicAlert identification tag** (© **888/633-4298;** www.medicalert.org), which will immediately alert doctors to your condition and give them access to your records through MedicAlert's 24-hour hot line.

Pack **prescription medications** in your carry-on luggage, and carry prescription medications in their original containers, with pharmacy labels—otherwise they won't make it through airport security. Also carry copies of your prescriptions in case you lose your pills or run out. Don't forget an extra pair of contact lenses or prescription glasses.

For domestic trips, most reliable healthcare plans provide coverage if you get sick away from home.

CRIME & SAFETY

Maine boasts some of the lowest crime rates in the country. The odds of anything bad happening during your visit here are very slight. But all travelers are advised to take the usual precautions against theft, robbery, and assault.

Travelers should avoid any unnecessary public displays of wealth. Don't bring out fat wads of cash from your pocket, and save your best jewelry for private occasions. If you are approached by someone who demands money, jewelry, or anything else from you, do what most Americans do: Hand it over. Don't argue. Don't negotiate. Just comply. Afterward, immediately contact the police by dialing ✆ 911 from almost any phone.

The crime you're statistically most likely to encounter is theft of items from your car. Don't leave anything of value in plain view, and lock valuables in your trunk. Better still, keep them with you at all times.

Late at night you should look for a well-lighted area if you need gas or you need to step out of your car for any reason. Also, it's not advisable to sleep in your car late at night at highway rest areas, which can leave you vulnerable to robbers.

Take the usual precautions against leaving cash or valuables in your hotel room when you're not present. Many hotels have safe-deposit boxes. Smaller inns and hotels often do not, although it can't hurt to ask to leave small items in the house safe.

SPECIALIZED TRAVEL RESOURCES

Travelers with Disabilities

Most disabilities shouldn't stop anyone from traveling to the coast of Maine. Thanks to provisions in the Americans with Disabilities Act, most public places are required to comply with disability-friendly regulations. Almost all public establishments (including hotels, restaurants, museums, and so on, but not including certain National Historic Landmarks) and at least some modes of public transportation provide accessible entrances and other facilities for those with disabilities.

The **America the Beautiful—National Park and Federal Recreational Lands Pass—Access Pass** (formerly the **Golden Access Passport**) gives visually impaired or permanently disabled persons (regardless of age) **free lifetime entrance** to federal recreation sites administered by the National Park Service, including the Fish and Wildlife Service, the Forest Service, the Bureau of Land Management, and the Bureau of Reclamation. This may include national parks, monuments, historic sites, recreation areas, and national wildlife refuges.

The America the Beautiful Access Pass can only be obtained in person at any NPS facility that charges an entrance fee. You need to show proof of a medically determined disability. Besides free entry, the pass also offers a 50% discount on some federal-use fees charged for such facilities as camping, swimming, parking, boat launching, and tours. For more information, go to **www.nps.gov/fees_passes.htm**, or call the United States Geological Survey (USGS), which issues the passes, at ✆ **888/275-8747**.

For more on organizations that offer resources to travelers with disabilities, go to frommers.com.

LGBT Travelers

Though coastal Maine isn't exactly a hotbed of gay culture, it has been rapidly growing as a gay travel destination, and many gays and lesbians now live and travel here. Larger cities tend to be more accommodating to gay travelers than smaller towns, but many small coastal towns now also show gay and lesbian presence. In general, gay and lesbian travelers should feel very comfortable in all vacation areas of coastal Maine.

Portland is now home to a substantial gay population. The city hosts a sizable pride festival early each summer that includes a riotous parade and a dance on the city pier, among other events. In early 1998, Maine narrowly repealed a statewide gay-rights law that had been passed earlier by the state legislature. In Portland, however, the vote was nearly four to one against the repeal and in support of equal rights. Portland also has a municipal ordinance that prohibits discrimination in jobs and housing based on sexual orientation.

Ogunquit is hugely popular among gay travelers, a longtime (even historic) gay resort area that features a lively beach-and-bar scene in the summer. In the winter it's still active but decidedly more mellow. Several Ogunquit B&Bs are owned by gay entrepreneurs. A website, **www.gayogunquit.com**, is a good place to find information on locally gay-owned inns, restaurants, and nightclubs.

Senior Travel

Mention the fact that you're a senior when you make your travel reservations. Although all the major U.S. airlines except America West have canceled their senior discount and coupon book programs, many hotels still offer lower rates for seniors. In most cities people over the age of 60 qualify for reduced admission to theaters, museums, and other attractions and discounted fares on public transportation.

Maine is well suited to older travelers, with a wide array of activities for seniors and discounts commonly available. Members of **AARP** (formerly known as the American Association of Retired Persons), 601 E St. NW, Washington, DC 20049 (© **888/687-2277;** www.aarp.org), get discounts on hotels, airfares, and car rentals. AARP offers members a wide range of benefits, including *AARP The Magazine* and a monthly newsletter. Anyone 50 and over can join.

The U.S. National Park Service offers an **America the Beautiful—National Park and Federal Recreational Lands Pass—Senior Pass** (formerly the **Golden Age Passport**), which gives seniors 62 years or older lifetime entrance to all properties administered by the National Park Service—national parks, monuments, historic sites, recreation areas, and national wildlife refuges—for a one-time processing fee of $10. The pass must be purchased in person at any NPS facility that charges an entrance fee. Besides free entry, the America the Beautiful Senior Pass also offers a 50% discount on some federal-use fees charged for such facilities as camping, swimming, parking, boat launching, and tours.

For more information, go to **www.nps.gov/fees_passes.htm**, or call the United States Geological Survey (USGS), which issues the passes, at © **888/275-8747.**

Family Travel

The family vacation is a rite of passage for many households, one that in a split second can evolve into a *National Lampoon* farce. However, it can be among the most pleasurable and rewarding times of your life.

Families will have little trouble finding fun, low-key things to do with kids in Maine. The natural world seems to hold tremendous wonder for the younger set—an afternoon exploring mossy banks and rocky streambeds can be a huge adventure. Older kids may like the challenge of climbing a mountain peak or learning to paddle a canoe in a straight line, and the beach is always good for hours of afternoon diversion.

Some recommended destinations for families in Maine include **York Beach** and **Acadia National Park.** Be sure to ask about family discounts when visiting attractions. Many places offer a flat family rate that costs less than paying for each ticket individually. Some parks and beaches charge by the carload rather than the head count.

To locate accommodations, restaurants, and attractions that are particularly kid friendly, see the "Kids" icon throughout this guide.

Frommer's Family Vacations in the National Parks, by Charles Wohlforth, includes useful material on traveling with kids to Acadia National Park in Maine.

Traveling with Pets

No surprise: Some places allow pets, some don't. I've noted inns that allow pets, but even here I don't recommend showing up with a pet in tow unless you've cleared it over the phone with the innkeeper. Note that many establishments have only one or two rooms (often a cottage or room with exterior entrance) set aside for guests traveling with pets, and they won't be happy to meet Fido if the pet rooms are already occupied. Also, it's increasingly common for a surcharge of $10 or $20 to be charged to pet owners to pay for the extra cleaning. On the positive side, all **Motel 6** hotels accept pets as a matter of policy, and so (surprisingly) do some upscale inns.

Keep in mind that dogs are prohibited on hiking trails and must be leashed at all times on federal lands administered by the National Park Service (this includes Acadia National Park in Maine). But **no pets of any sort are allowed at any time** (leashed or unleashed) into Baxter State Park in Maine, a short side trip from the coast. Most other Maine state parks *do* allow pets on a leash, however.

Student Travel

Check out the **International Student Travel Confederation (ISTC)** (www.istc.org) website for comprehensive travel services information and details on how to get an **International Student Identity Card (ISIC),** which qualifies students for substantial savings on rail passes, plane tickets, entrance fees, and more. It also provides students with basic health and life insurance and a 24-hour help line. The card is valid for a maximum of 18 months. You can apply for the card online or in person at **STA Travel** (© **800/781-4040** in North America; 132 782 in Australia; 0871 2 300 040 in the U.K.; www.statravel.com), the biggest student travel agency in the world; check out the website to locate STA Travel offices worldwide. If you're no longer a student but are still under 26, you can get an **International Youth Travel Card (IYTC)** from the same people, which entitles you to some discounts. **Travel CUTS** (© **800/592-2887;** www.travelcuts.com) offers similar services for both Canadians and U.S. residents. Irish students may prefer to turn to **USIT** (© **01/602-1904;** www.usit.ie), an Ireland-based specialist in student, youth, and independent travel.

SUSTAINABLE TOURISM

Sustainable tourism is conscientious travel. It means being careful with the environments you explore and respecting the communities you visit. Two overlapping components of sustainable travel are **eco-tourism** and **ethical tourism.** The

International Ecotourism Society (TIES) defines eco-tourism as responsible travel to natural areas that conserves the environment and improves the well-being of local people. TIES suggests that eco-tourists follow these principles:

- Minimize environmental impact.
- Build environmental and cultural awareness and respect.
- Provide positive experiences for both visitors and hosts.
- Provide direct financial benefits for conservation and for local people.
- Raise sensitivity to host countries' political, environmental, and social climates.
- Support international human rights and labor agreements.

You can find some ecofriendly travel tips and statistics, as well as touring companies and associations—listed by destination under "Travel Choice"—at the **TIES** website, www.ecotourism.org. Also check out **Ecotravel.com,** which lets you search for sustainable touring companies in several categories (water-based, land-based, spiritually oriented, and so on).

While much of the focus of eco-tourism is about reducing impacts on the natural environment, ethical tourism concentrates on ways to preserve and enhance local economies and communities, regardless of location. You can embrace ethical tourism by staying at a locally owned hotel or shopping at a store that employs local workers and sells locally produced goods.

Responsible Travel (www.responsibletravel.com) is a great source of sustainable travel ideas; the site is run by a spokesperson for ethical tourism in the travel industry. **Sustainable Travel International** (www.sustainabletravelinternational.org) promotes ethical tourism practices, and manages an extensive directory of sustainable properties and tour operators around the world.

In the U.K., **Tourism Concern** (www.tourismconcern.org.uk) works to reduce social and environmental problems connected to tourism. The **Association of Independent Tour Operators (AITO)** (www.aito.co.uk) is a group of specialist operators leading the field in making holidays sustainable.

Volunteer travel has become increasingly popular among those who want to venture beyond the standard group-tour experience to learn languages, interact with locals, and make a positive difference while on vacation. Volunteer travel usually doesn't require special skills—just a willingness to work hard—and programs vary in length from a few days to a number of weeks. Some programs provide free housing and food, but many require volunteers to pay for travel expenses, which can add up quickly.

Before you commit to a volunteer program, it's important to make sure any money you're giving is truly going back to the local community, and that the work you'll be doing will be a good fit for you. **Volunteer International** (www.volunteerinternational.org) has a helpful list of questions to ask to determine the intentions and the nature of a volunteer program.

Animal-Rights Issues

Whale-watching is increasingly popular in New England, particularly in downeast parts of Maine. For those who may be concerned about the sensitivity of the animals to these visits, there are a number of animal-rights organizations that provide good information. The organization **Tread Lightly** (www.treadlightly.org) is one. For more specific information about the current status of various species of whales, visit the **Whale and Dolphin Conservation Society** (www.wdcs.org).

IT'S EASIER BEING green

Here are a few simple ways you can help conserve fuel and energy when you travel:

○ Each time you take a flight or drive a car greenhouse gases release into the atmosphere. You can help neutralize this danger to the planet through "carbon offsetting"—paying someone to invest your money in programs that reduce your greenhouse gas emissions by the same amount you've added. Before buying carbon offset credits, just make sure that you're using a reputable company, one with a proven program that invests in renewable energy. Reliable carbon offset companies include **Carbonfund** (www.carbonfund.org), **TerraPass** (www.terrapass.org), and **Carbon Neutral** (www.carbonneutral.org).

○ Whenever possible, choose nonstop flights; they generally require less fuel than indirect flights that stop and take off again. Try to fly during the day—some scientists estimate that nighttime flights are twice as harmful to the environment. And pack light—each 15 pounds of luggage on a 5,000-mile flight adds up to 50 pounds of carbon dioxide emitted.

○ Where you stay during your travels can have a major environmental impact. To determine the green credentials of a property, ask about trash disposal and recycling, water conservation, and energy use; also question if sustainable materials were used in the construction of the property. The website **www.greenhotels.com** recommends green-rated member hotels around the world that fulfill the company's stringent environmental requirements. Also consult **www.environmentallyfriendlyhotels.com** for more green accommodations ratings.

○ At hotels, request that your sheets and towels not be changed daily. (Many hotels already have programs like this in place.) Turn off the lights and air conditioner (or heater) when you leave your room.

○ Use public transport where possible—trains, buses, and even taxis are more energy-efficient forms of transport than driving. Even better is to walk or cycle; you'll produce zero emissions and stay fit and healthy on your travels.

○ If renting a car is necessary, ask the rental agent for a hybrid, or rent the most fuel-efficient car available. You'll use less gas and save money at the tank.

○ Eat at locally owned and operated restaurants that use produce grown in the area. This contributes to the local economy and cuts down on greenhouse gas emissions by supporting restaurants where the food is not flown or trucked in across long distances. Visit **Sustain Lane** (www.sustainlane.org) to find sustainable eating and drinking choices around the U.S.; also check out **www.eatwellguide.org** for tips on eating sustainably in the U.S. and Canada.

FROMMERS.COM: THE COMPLETE TRAVEL RESOURCE

Planning a trip or just returned? Head to **Frommers.com,** voted Best Travel Site by *PC Magazine.* We think you'll find our site indispensable before, during, and after your travels—with expert advice and tips; independent reviews of hotels, restaurants, attractions, and preferred shopping and nightlife venues; vacation giveaways; and an online booking tool. We publish the complete contents of over 135 travel guides in our **Destinations** section, covering more than 4,000 places worldwide. Each weekday, we publish original articles that report on **Deals and News** via our free **Frommers. com Newsletters.** What's more, **Arthur**

Frommer himself blogs 5 days a week, with cutting opinions about the state of travel in the modern world. We're betting you'll find our **Events** listings an invaluable resource; it's an up-to-the-minute roster of what's happening in cities everywhere—including concerts, festivals, lectures, and more. We've also added weekly **podcasts, interactive maps,** and hundreds of new images across the site. Finally, don't forget to visit our **Message Boards,** where you can join in conversations with thousands of fellow Frommer's travelers and post your trip report once you return.

SPECIAL INTEREST & ESCORTED TRIPS

Special Interest Trips

One rewarding way to spend a vacation is to learn a new outdoor skill or add to your knowledge while on holiday. You can find plenty of options in Maine, ranging from formal weeklong classes to 1-day workshops.

There are lots of options; here are a couple of the most popular:

o **Fly-fishing in Maine.** What says Maine more than L.L.Bean? The world-famous outdoors-store's educational offerings are growing by leaps and bounds, and are highly recommended by travelers of all ages. Among the many options, the intriguing fly-fishing outings (© **800/343-4552**) are worth a look. There's a good catalog available by mail or at the flagship store (open 24 hr.) on Main Street in Freeport. L.L.Bean also offers a number of shorter workshops on various outdoor skills through its **Outdoor Discovery Program** (www.llbean.com/adventures; call © **888/552-3261**).

o **All About Birds.** Budding and experienced naturalists can expand their understanding of marine wildlife while residing on 333-acre Hog Island in Maine's wild and scenic Muscongus Bay through the **Maine Audubon Society.** You're brought by boat, then stay on the island for 5 nights; see the web site **www.projectpuffin. org** for more details. (Famed birder Roger Tory Peterson once taught birding classes here.) I can personally vouch for Maine Audubon's *other* outdoors and educational programs, too. Call or visit their lovely headquarters at 20 Gilsland Farm Rd. in Falmouth (© **207/781-2330;** www.maineaudubon.org), 10 minutes north of Portland.

Indeed, Maine especially lends itself to outdoorsy adventures that combine fresh air and exercise with Mother Nature as your instructor in Maine's vast, beautiful classroom.

Adventure & Wellness Trips

Outdoors travel in Maine is such a huge and fascinating endeavor that I have treated this category separately. See the next section of this chapter, "The Active Traveler," for a complete discussion of these types of tours.

Escorted General Interest Tours

Escorted tours are structured group tours, with a group leader. The price usually includes everything from airfare to hotels, meals, tours, admission costs, and local transportation.

Despite the fact that escorted tours require big deposits and predetermined hotels, restaurants, and itineraries, many people derive security and peace of mind from the structure they offer. Escorted tours—whether they're navigated by bus, motorcoach, train, or boat—let travelers sit back and enjoy the trip without having to drive or worry about details. They take you to the maximum number of sights in the minimum amount of time with the least amount of hassle. They're particularly convenient for people with limited mobility, and they can be a great way to make new friends.

On the downside, you'll have little opportunity for serendipitous interactions with locals. The tours can be jampacked with activities, leaving little room for individual sightseeing, whim, or adventure—plus they often focus on the heavily touristed sites, so you miss out on many a lesser-known gem.

One good source of package deals is the airlines themselves. Most major airlines offer air/land packages, including **American Airlines Vacations** (© 800/321-2121; www.aavacations.com), **Delta Vacations** (© 800/800-1504; www.deltavacations.com), **Continental Airlines Vacations** (© 800/829-7777; www.covacations.com), and **United Vacations** (© 888/854-3899; www.unitedvacations.com). Several big **online travel agencies**—Expedia, Travelocity, Orbitz, LastMinute.com—also do a brisk business in packages.

Travel packages are also listed in the travel section of your local Sunday newspaper and in national travel magazines such as *Arthur Frommer's Budget Travel Magazine*, *Travel + Leisure*, *National Geographic Traveler*, and *Condé Nast Traveler*.

For Those Who Love Historic Homes

Historic New England is a nonprofit foundation that owns and operates 36 historic properties around New England, ranging from places built in the 17th century to the present, including a number of properties profiled in this book. Members get into all of the organization's properties for free, and receive a number of other benefits including a subscription to *Historic New England* magazine; a guide to the group's properties; and invitations to members-only events and other perks. Memberships cost $45 per year for individuals, $55 for households. For more information on Historic New England and its properties, visit the group's website at www.historicnewengland. org, or call the organization's Boston headquarters at © **617/994-5410.**

📎

ASK before YOU GO

Before you invest in a package deal or an escorted tour:

- Always ask about the **cancellation policy.** Can you get your money back? Is a deposit required?

- Ask about the **accommodations choices and prices** for each. Then look up the hotels' reviews in a Frommer's guide and check their rates online for your specific dates of travel. Also find out what types of rooms are offered.

- Request a complete **schedule.** (Escorted tours only)

- Ask about the **size** and demographics of the group. (Escorted tours only)

- Discuss what is included in the **price** (transportation, meals, tips, airport transfers, and so on). (Escorted tours only)

- Finally, look for **hidden expenses.** Ask whether airport departure fees and taxes, for example, are included in the total cost—they rarely are.

THE ACTIVE TRAVELER

Coastal Maine is a superb destination for those who don't consider it a vacation unless they spend some time far away from their cars. Hiking, canoeing, and skiing are among the most popular outdoor activities, but you can also try rock climbing, sea kayaking, mountain biking, road biking, sailing, winter mountaineering, and snowmobiling. In general, the farther north you go in the region, the more remote and wild the terrain becomes. For pointers on where to head, see "Outdoor Activities," below. More detailed information on local services is included in each regional section.

General Advice

The best way to enjoy the outdoors is to head to public lands where the natural landscape is preserved. Wild areas in coastal Maine include **Acadia National Park**'s various sections, **Cobscook Bay State Park,** and (a bit inland) **Baxter State Park.** You can often find adventure-travel outfitters and suppliers in towns around the perimeter of these areas.

To find real adventure, plan to stay put. I'd advise prospective adventurers to pick just one area, then settle in for a few days or a week, spending the long summer days exploring locally by foot, canoe, or kayak. This will give you the time to enjoy an extra hour lounging at a rocky beach, or to spend an extra day camped by a cove. You'll also learn a lot more about the area. Few travelers ever regret planning to do too little on their vacations. A lot of travelers regret attempting to do too much.

Outdoor Activities

BEACHGOING Swimming at Maine's ocean beaches is for the hardy. The Gulf Stream, which prods warm waters south toward the Cape Cod shores, veers toward Iceland south of Maine and leaves the state's 5,500-mile coastline washed by a brisk Nova Scotia current, an offshoot of the arctic Labrador current. During summer, water temperatures along the south coast may top 60°F (16°C) during an especially warm spell where water is shallow, but it's usually cooler than that.

Maine's best beaches are found mostly between the New Hampshire border and Portland. Northeast of Portland a handful of fine beaches await—including popular **Reid State Park** (p. 146) and **Popham Beach State Park** (p. 146)—but rocky coast defines this territory for the most part. The southern beaches are beautiful but rarely isolated. Summer homes occupy the low dunes in most areas; mid-rise condos give **Old Orchard Beach** a "mini-Miami" air.

Some of the best swimming beaches in the region can be found at **Ogunquit,** which boasts a 3-mile-long sandy strand (some of which has a mildly remote character), and **Long Sands Beach** (p. 80) and **Short Sands Beach** (p. 80) at York. Long Sands possesses great views of the sea and a nearby lighthouse plus great walking at low tide (at high tide, the sand disappears completely), while Short Sands has a festive, carnival atmosphere. Both lie right on Rte. 1A. There are also a number of fine beaches in the greater **Portland** area; for a primer on the very best, see chapter 6.

If you love swimming but aren't especially keen on shivering, head inland to the sandy beaches at Maine's wonderful lakes, where the water is tepid by comparison. A number of state and municipal parks offer access. Among the most accessible to the coast is **Sebago Lake State Park** (© **207/693-6613**), about 20 miles northwest of Portland; a small admission fee is charged.

BIKING   In southern Maine, **Rte. 103** and **Rte. 1A** offer pleasant scenery for bikers as well. Offshore, bring your bike to the bigger islands for car-free cruising. In Casco Bay I recommend two islands for cycling. Rustic **Chebeague Island** offers a pleasantly wooded excursion (the path cuts through forests to the sea), while more populous **Peaks Island** (p. 124) has a few cafes, more culture, and the advantage of a bicycle-rental shop near the ferry dock. Both are flat, and both are conveniently connected to Portland by Casco Bay Lines ferries. (Peaks is a much shorter ferry ride, if time matters.)

Serious mountain biking is also available in parts of coastal Maine, for those who like to get technical on two wheels. Your best bet is to consult area bike shops for the best trails, which are typically a matter of local knowledge.

The Maine Department of Transportation (DOT) publishes a booklet, *Explore Maine by Bike,* describing 25 popular bike trips around the state; log on to **www. exploremaine.org/bike** to get it. The Maine DOT also publishes a map marked up with state biking information, including traffic volumes and road shoulder conditions along popular routes.

BIRDING   Birders from southern and inland states should lengthen their life lists along the Maine coast, which attracts migrating birds cruising the Atlantic flyway (there are warblers galore in spring) and boasts populations of numerous native shorebirds, such as plovers (including the threatened piping plover), terns, whimbrels, sandpipers, and dunlins. Gulls and terns are frequently seen; you'll see a surfeit of herring and great black-backed gull, along with the common tern. Less frequently seen are Bonaparte's gull, the laughing gull, the jaeger, and the arctic tern.

For a recording of recent sightings of rare birds, call © **207/781-2332.**

CAMPING   For information about state parks, many of which offer camping, contact the **Department of Conservation,** State House Station #22, Augusta, ME 04333 (© **207/287-2211**). To make camping reservations at most state park campgrounds, call during business hours on a weekday between February and early September (© **800/332-1501** in Maine, or 207/287-3824).

Maine also has more than 200 private campgrounds spread throughout the state, many offering full hookups for RVs. For a guide to the private campgrounds, contact the **Maine Campground Owners Association** (© 207/782-5874; www.camp maine.com), 10 Falcon Rd., Ste. #1, Lewiston, ME 04240. Campsites get booked quickly for summer weekends, so call ahead for reservations.

FISHING   Anglers from all over the Northeast indulge their grand obsession on Maine's 6,000 lakes and ponds and its countless miles of rivers and streams. And deep-sea-fishing charters are available at many of the harbors along the Maine coast, with options ranging from inshore fishing expeditions for stripers and bluefish to offshore voyages in search of shark, cod, and pollock. Prices might typically range from $25 per person for day trips to $395 to charter an offshore boat for the day. Visitor information centers and chambers of commerce listed in this guide will be able to match you up with the right boat to meet your needs.

Saltwater fishing in Maine requires no license. For freshwater fishing, nonresident **licenses** are $64 for the season or $23 for 3 days. One-, 7-, and 15-day licenses are also available. Fees are reduced for children (ages 12–15), and no license is required for those 11 and under. These licenses are available at many outdoor shops and general stores throughout the state or by mail from the address below. For a booklet of fishing regulations, contact the **Department of Inland Fisheries and Wildlife,** State House Station #41, Augusta, ME 04333 (© 207/287-8000; www.state.me.us/ifw).

GOLFING   Many of the Maine coast's best courses are private, but a few of these gems are open to the public. Kennebunkport's **Cape Arundel Golf Club** (© 207/967-3494) is favored by a certain ex-president when he's in town (© 207/967-3494; www.capearundelgolfclub.com). Other courses I like along the coast—nearly all of them wafted by sea breezes—include **Cape Neddick Country Club** in Ogunquit (© 207/361-2011; www.capeneddickgolf.com), the **Kebo Valley Golf Club** in Bar Harbor (© 207/288-3000; www.kebovalleyclub.com), the **Web-hannet Golf Club** in Kennebunk Beach (© 207/967-2061; www.webhannetgolf club.com), the **Riverside Golf Course** in Portland (© 207/797-3524; www. portlandmaine.gov/riverside), and South Portland's **Sable Oaks Golf Club** (© 207/775-6257; www.sableoaks.com). But the *best* public course on the whole coast of Maine might be the **Samoset Resort Golf Club** in Rockport (© 207/594-1431; www.samoset.com): several holes run right alongside the Atlantic and past a mini-lighthouse. It's as scenic as golf gets.

HIKING   Southern Maine's walks are not hikes but rather less-demanding strolls; many of these are a matter of local knowledge. Two fine pathways skirt the water in **York** (see chapter 5), and even in **Portland** (see chapter 6) you can saunter on well-maintained (and heavily used) recreational pathways along about 5 miles of tidal waters.

SEA KAYAKING   Sea kayakers nationwide migrate to Maine for world-class sea kayaking. Thousands of miles of deeply indented coastline and thousands of offshore islands have created a wondrous kayaker's playground. Paddlers can explore protected estuaries far from the surf or test their skills and determination with excursions across choppy, open seas to islands far offshore. It's a sport that can be extremely dangerous (when weather shifts, the seas can turn on you in a matter of minutes), but can yield plenty of returns with the proper equipment and skills.

The nation's first long-distance water trail, the **Maine Island Trail,** was created here in 1987. This 325-mile waterway winds along the coast from Portland to Machias, incorporating some 70 state and privately owned islands on its route. Members of the Maine Island Trail Association, a private nonprofit group, help maintain and monitor the islands and in turn are granted permission to visit and camp on them as long as they follow certain restrictions (for example, no visiting designated islands during seabird nesting season). The association seeks to encourage low-impact, responsible use of these natural treasures, and joining is a good idea if you'll be doing some kayaking. The MITA guidebook, published annually, provides descriptions of all the islands in the network and is free with association membership (note that the guide is available only to members).

For membership details, contact the **Maine Island Trail Association,** 58 Fore St., Ste. 30-3, Portland, ME 04101 (© **207/761-8225;** www.mita.org).

The islands and protected bays around **Portland** make for great kayaking, as do the cliffs, parks, and beaches just south of the city—though surf can be rough at times. Make sure you're experienced enough to handle it.

For novices, a number of kayak outfitters take guided excursions ranging from an afternoon to a week. Outfitters include the **Maine Island Kayak Co.** on Peaks Island (© **207/766-2373;** www.maineislandkayak.com) in the Portland area and **Maine Sport Outfitters,** located on Rte. 1 in Rockport (© **800/722-0826** or 207/236-8797; www.mainesport.com).

Finding Your Way

Travelers used to hire guides to ensure they could find their way out of the woods. With development encroaching on many once-pristine areas, it's now helpful to have guides to find your way *into* the woods and away from civilization and its long reach. Clear-cuts, second-home developments, and trails teeming with weekend hikers are all obstacles to be avoided. Local knowledge is the best way to find the most alluring, least congested spots.

Travelers have three options: Hire a guide, sign up for a guided trip, or dig up the essential information yourself.

HIRING A GUIDE Guides of all kinds may be hired throughout the region, from grizzled fishing hands who know local rivers like their own homes to young canoe guides attracted to the field because of their interest in the environment. Alexandra and Garrett Conover of Maine's **North Woods Ways,** 2293 Elliotsville Rd., Willimantic, ME 04443 (© **207/997-3723;** www.northwoodsways), are among the most experienced in the region. The couple offers canoe trips on northern Maine rivers (including a Thoreau's Maine Woods trip), and are well versed in North Woods lore.

Maine has a centuries-old tradition of guides leading "sports" into the backwoods for hunting and fishing, although many now have branched out to include recreational canoeing and more specialized interests, such as bird-watching. Professional guides are certified by the state; you can learn more about hiring Maine guides by contacting the **Maine Professional Guides Association,** P.O. Box 336, Augusta, ME 04332. The association's website (www.maineguides.org) features links to some of its members.

Elsewhere, contact the appropriate chambers of commerce for suggestions on local guides.

GUIDED TOURS   Guided tours have boomed in recent years, both in number and variety. These range from 2-night guided inn-to-inn hiking trips to weeklong canoe and kayak expeditions, camping each night along the way. A few reputable outfitters to start with include the following:

- **Country Walkers,** P.O. Box 180, Waterbury, VT 05676 (✆ **800/464-9255** or 802/244-1387; www.countrywalkers.com), has a glorious color catalog (more like a wish book) outlining supported walking trips around the world. Among the offerings: walking tours in coastal Maine. Trips run 4 or 5 nights and include all meals and lodging at appealing inns.
- **Maine Island Kayak Co.,** 70 Luther St., Peaks Island, ME 04108 (✆ **800/796-2373** or 207/766-2373; www.sea-kayak.com), has a fleet of seaworthy kayaks for camping trips up and down the Maine coast. The firm has a number of 2- and 3-night expeditions each summer and has plenty of experience training novices.
- **New England Hiking Holidays,** P.O. Box 1648, North Conway, NH 03860 (✆ **800/869-0949** or 603/356-9696; www.nehikingholidays.com), has an extensive inventory of trips, including extended excursions on the Maine coast. Trips typically involve moderate day hiking coupled with nights at comfortable lodges.
- **Vermont Bicycle Touring,** P.O. Box 711, Bristol, VT 05442 (✆ **800/245-3868;** www.vbt.com), is one of the more established and well-organized touring operations, with an extensive bike tour schedule in North America, Europe, and New Zealand. VBT offers several trips in Maine, including a 6-day Acadia trip.

GETTING MORE INFORMATION   Guidebooks to the region's backcountry are plentiful and diverse. L.L.Bean in Freeport, Maine, has an excellent selection of guidebooks for sale, as do many local bookshops throughout the region. An exhaustive collection of New England outdoor guidebooks for sale may be found online at **www.mountainwanderer.com**. The **Appalachian Mountain Club,** 5 Joy St., Boston, MA 02108 (✆ **617/523-0636;** www.outdoors.org), publishes a number of definitive guides to hiking and boating in the region.

Map Adventures, P.O. Box 15214, Portland, ME 04112 (✆ **207/879-4777**), is a small firm that publishes a growing line of good recreational maps covering popular local areas including the Camden Hills and Acadia National Park. See what they offer online at **www.mapadventures.com**.

Local outdoors clubs are also a good source of information, and most offer trips to nonmembers. The largest of the bunch is the Appalachian Mountain Club (see address above), whose chapters run group trips almost every weekend throughout the region, with northern New Hampshire especially well represented.

STAYING CONNECTED

Mobile Phones

Just because your cellphone works at home doesn't mean it'll work on the back roads of Maine—or even at that rustic country B&B, thanks to our nation's (and the region's) fragmented and competing cellphone coverage systems and the mostly rural nature of the state. You may or may not be within your roaming area, even if you have a national calling plan. It's a good bet that your phone will work in the region's major cities, so look over your wireless company's coverage map on its website before heading out to be sure; T-Mobile, Sprint, and Nextel are particularly weak at covering rural areas.

The **AT&T** and **Verizon** networks covers most (though not all) of coastal Maine, usually without incurring roaming charges. T-Mobile, Sprint, and Nextel are notably weaker in coverage. Foreign cellphones may or may not work here due to the poorly developed GSM network; they will probably work on the southern Maine coast, but probably not on the rest of the coast. Foreign phones may or may not be able to use SMS to send text messages.

Need to rent a cellphone? Check at the airport in Boston or Portland when you arrive. Or head for a shopping mall or the central business district/main street of the town or city you're visiting.

Internet & E-mail

Most hotels, resorts, airports, and coffee shops in Maine offer **Wi-Fi** (wireless fidelity "hotspots" that offer high-speed Wi-Fi access—usually for free, sometimes for a small fee. Wi-Fi can also be found in Maine's campgrounds, RV parks, and even towns. If you're traveling from outside the U.S., bring along a **connection kit** of electrical and phone adapters, a spare phone cable, and an extra Ethernet network cable—and, if you've forgotten, ask at the reception desk whether your hotel can loan these items to guests.

Avoid **hotel business centers,** which often charge exorbitant rates, unless you're desperate and have no other choice. Portland has a couple of **cybercafes**, which are a good value for quick e-mail checking (figure a $3 minimum charge); in small towns, though, it's hit-or-miss (usually miss). Fortunately, coastal Maine's **public libraries** are superb at offering Internet access, nearly always for free (you may need to submit a driver's license, library card, or other piece of identification as a deposit). The local library in a large coastal town such as York, Kennebunk, or Belfast could prove vital in a pinch—but be courteous, and do not overstay your welcome.

For help locating cybercafes and other establishments where you can go for Internet access, please see "Internet Access" on p. 290.

Newspapers & Magazines

The *Portland Press Herald* is Portland's daily newspaper, with decent listings; the free *Portland Phoenix* is also very handy for listings of southern Maine concerts, shows at local clubs, art shows. The biggest paper in the Downeast and Midcoast regions is the daily *Bangor Daily News*. Regional newspapers—in print, remember that?—still abound in the rest of coastal Maine, too, from the *York Weekly* to the *Biddeford Journal Tribune, Bar Harbor Times, Brunswick Times-Record,* and the *Camden Herald Gazette*.

Starved for news of the "outside" world? Most grocery stores in Maine stock a few copies of the *Boston Globe* and the *New York Times*.

There are also a surprising number of quality glossy magazines based in Maine, from longtime star *Down East* to *Portland Monthly* to *WoodenBoat*.

Telephones

You can still find public pay phones and phone booths in Maine, but they're getting scarcer. Count on using a cellphone (see above) or your in-room phone at the hotel to make calls.

AN ONLINE TRAVELER'S toolbox

Savvy travelers know that it's a great idea to use online resources when planning a trip to the coast of Maine. Here are a few websites I keep bookmarked:

- **www.pressherald.com**
  Portland Press Herald, Maine's largest newspaper
- **www.maine.gov** Maine state government website

- **www.nps.gov/acad**
  Acadia National Park
- **www.visitmaine.com**
  Maine Office of Tourism
- **www.campmaine.com**
  Maine Campground Owners Association
- **www.downeast.com**
  Down East magazine

Many convenience groceries and packaging services sell **prepaid calling cards** in denominations up to $50. Many public pay phones at airports now accept American Express, MasterCard, and Visa. **Local calls** made from most pay phones cost either 25¢ or 35¢. Most long-distance and international calls can be dialed directly from any phone. **To make calls within the United States and to Canada,** dial 1 followed by the area code and the seven-digit number. **For other international calls,** dial 011 followed by the country code, city code, and the number you are calling.

Calls to area codes **800, 888, 877,** and **866** are toll-free. However, calls to area codes **700** and **900** (chat lines, bulletin boards, "dating" services, and so on) can be expensive—charges of 95¢ to $3 or more per minute. Some numbers have minimum charges that can run $15 or more.

For **reversed-charge or collect calls,** and for person-to-person calls, dial the number 0 then the area code and number; an operator will come on the line, and you should specify whether you are calling collect, person-to-person, or both. If your operator-assisted call is international, ask for the overseas operator.

For **directory assistance** ("Information"), dial 411 for local numbers and national numbers in the U.S. and Canada. For dedicated long-distance information, dial 1, then the appropriate area code plus 555-1212.

TIPS ON ACCOMMODATIONS

"The more we travel," said an unhappy couple one morning at a nameless New England inn, "the more we realize why we go back to our old favorites time and again." The reason for their chagrin? They had been forced to switch rooms at 2am when rain had begun dripping right onto them through the ceiling. I hasten to add that this story is not an isolated incident. Small, quaint inns here often come with their own drips, creaks, and quirks.

Maine is famous for its plethora of country inns and bed-and-breakfasts, which offer a wonderful alternative to the sort of cookie-cutter, chain-hotel rooms that line U.S. highways from coast to coast. But (as the unhappy couple learned) there are reasons why some people *prefer* the cookie-cutter hotels. In a chain hotel, you can be reasonably sure that water won't drip through your ceiling in the middle of the night. Likewise, the beds will be firm, the sink will be relatively new, and you'll have a TV, telephone, and counter space next to the bathroom sink.

Every **inn** and **B&B** listed in this guide yields a decent, and often a high-quality, experience. Just keep in mind that each place is different, and you need to match the personality of the place with your *own* personality. Some inns are more polished and fussier than others; this is a rural area, so a lot of them (even some calling themselves "resorts") lack basic amenities to which business travelers have grown accustomed in chain hotels. (In-room phones and air-conditioning lead the list.)

Surfing for Hotels

I regularly use online travel booking sites to compare prices and book hotels in Maine. The best include **Travelocity, Expedia, Orbitz, Priceline, Hotwire, Hotels. com,** and **Quikbook.**

I use **TripAdvisor.com** for helpful independent consumer reviews of hotels and resort properties.

It's always a good idea to **get a confirmation number** and **make a printout** of every online booking transaction.

Saving on Your Hotel Room

The **rack rate** is the maximum rate that a hotel charges for a room. Hardly anybody pays this price, however, except in high season or on holidays. To lower the cost of your room:

o **Ask about special rates or other discounts.** You may qualify for corporate, student, military, senior, frequent-flier, trade union, or other discounts.

Inn vs. B&B: Everybody Wins

The difference between an inn and a B&B may be confusing for some travelers, since the gap between the two narrows by the day. A couple of decades ago, inns were full-service affairs, whereas B&Bs consisted of private homes with an extra bedroom or two and a homeowner looking for a little extra income. These old-style B&Bs still exist around the region. I've occupied a few evenings sitting in a well-used living room watching Tom Brokaw with the owner, as if visiting with a forgotten aunt.

Today, B&Bs are more commonly professionally run affairs, where guests have private bathrooms, a separate common area, and attentive service. The owners have apartments tucked away in the back, prepare sumptuous breakfasts in the morning (some B&Bs offer "candlelight breakfasts"), and offer a high level of service. All of the

B&Bs in this guide are of the more professionally run variety (although several or more still have shared bathrooms). Other guidebooks are available for those searching for home-stay lodging.

The sole difference between inns and B&Bs—at least as defined by this guide—is that inns serve dinner (and sometimes lunch). B&Bs provide breakfast only. Readers shouldn't infer that B&Bs are necessarily more informal or in any way inferior to a full-service inn. Indeed, all of the places listed in "The Best Bed & Breakfasts" in chapter 1 have the air of gracious inns that just happened to have overlooked serving dinner. That's true for many of the other B&Bs listed in this guide; and with a little luck, you'll stumble into Ralph Waldo Emerson's idea of simple contentment: "Hospitality consists in a little fire, a little food, and an immense quiet," he wrote in his journal.

Even in Maine, when making reservations, it's essential that you get down (in writing, via printed-out website promise, by e-mail) some confirmation of your hotel's or inn's exact **cancellation policy.** Since they're going to take your credit card as a deposit in almost every case, you'll need this information in case your trip is waylaid for any reason at all.

There's an amazing variety of policies out there. Some places give you all your money back if you cancel early enough; a cutoff of **24 hours before arrival is standard** as a deadline, but some lodging establishments require 1 week's advance notice of a cancellation, and some will let you cancel at 6pm on the *day of arrival.* Some properties refund all your deposit back even if you missed the deadline (mostly very small places do this, when they know they can sell the room again). Most properties **keep 1 night's fee** if you missed the deadline. And a few give you nothing back, no matter what.

As you can see, **policies range from generous to outrageous.** One Frommer's reader wrote me that she canceled a reservation at a New England motel 2 days before arriving because a hurricane had just veered into her home state. "Sorry," she was told, "cancellations must be made 1 week in advance." To which I would have swiftly replied: "Fine. I'm canceling this motel from my life, forever."

○ **Dial direct.** When booking a room in a chain hotel, you'll often get a better deal by calling the individual hotel's reservation desk rather than the chain's main number.

○ **Book online.** Many hotels offer Internet-only discounts, or supply rooms to Priceline, Hotwire, or Expedia at rates much lower than the ones you can get through the hotel itself.

○ **Remember the law of supply and demand.** Resort hotels are most crowded and therefore most expensive on weekends, so discounts are usually available for midweek stays. Business hotels in downtown locations are busiest during the week, so you can expect big discounts over the weekend.

○ **Look into group or long-stay discounts.** If you come as part of a large group, you should be able to negotiate a bargain rate. Likewise, if you're planning a long stay (of at least 5 days), you might qualify for a discount of 1 free night for a 7-night stay; buy 6 nights, get 1 free.

○ **Sidestep excess surcharges and hidden costs.** Many hotels have the unpleasant practice of nickel-and-diming their guests with opaque surcharges. When you book a room, ask what is included in the room rate, and what is extra. Avoid dialing direct from hotel phones, which can have exorbitant rates. And don't be tempted by the room's minibar offerings: Most hotels charge through the nose for water, soda, and snacks. Finally, ask about local taxes and service charges, which can increase the cost of a room by 15% or more.

○ There are a small handful of **all-inclusive** resorts in Maine. The term "all-inclusive" means different things at different hotels; here, it means three meals daily and use of the resort's sports equipment (such as canoes and kayaks).

○ Carefully consider your hotel's meal plan. If you enjoy eating out and sampling the local cuisine, it makes sense to choose a Continental plan (also known as B&B),

or a European plan, which doesn't include any meals and allows you maximum flexibility. If you're more interested in saving money, opt for a **Modified American plan (MAP),** which includes breakfast and dinner, or the American plan, which includes all three meals (pretty rare in this region). If you must choose a MAP, see if you can get a free lunch at your hotel if you decide to do dinner out.

o **Book an efficiency.** A room with a kitchenette allows you to shop for groceries and cook your own meals. This is a big money saver, especially for families on long stays.

o **Consider enrolling in hotel "frequent-stay" programs,** which are upping the ante lately to win the loyalty of repeat customers. Frequent guests can accumulate points or credits to earn free hotel nights, airline miles, in-room amenities, merchandise, tickets to concerts and events, or discounts on sporting facilities. Perks are awarded not only by many chain hotels and motels (Hilton HHonors, Marriott Rewards, Wyndham ByRequest, to name a few), but some individual inns and B&Bs. Many chain hotels partner with other hotel chains, car-rental firms, airlines, and credit card companies to give consumers additional incentives to return.

o **Ask if the hotel charges extra for additional guests** (beyond two). The room rates published in this guide are all for two people sharing one room. Most places charge $10 and up per extra guest sharing the room. Don't assume that children traveling with you can stay for free—usually they can, but ask first about extra charges—and don't assume that every room can hold more than two.

o **Ask about a minimum stay requirement and discounts for multiday stays.** Many inns now require guests to book a minimum of 2 nights or more during the busiest times (holiday weekends, peak ski season, peak fall foliage season). These policies are mentioned in the following pages if known, but check anyway. And they might not apply if you walk in off the street; innkeepers develop sudden amnesia when faced with a chance to sell an empty room on a Saturday night despite a policy against such a stay.

Service Charges

Rather than increase room rates in the face of rising competition, hotels, inns, and B&Bs are increasingly tacking on nickel-and-dime fees to their guests' bills. Most

 Renting a House or Cottage in Maine

Renting a house or cottage in Maine for a week is another good option, particularly outside the summer high season, though there really isn't a centralized resource for doing so. You get the comforts of having your own kitchen or kitchenette and not worrying about parking, checkout times, or untimely "room service" knocks on your door. For a nice house with an ample supply of bedrooms and an unobstructed ocean view, expect to pay anywhere from $2,000 to $10,000 per week; a simpler cottage will run you less but might still cost more than you expected. Do a Web search for Maine house or cottage rentals, or go to a nationwide rent-by-owner website such as www.vrbo.com. While these certainly aren't the only choices along the Maine coast, they'll give you a good head start.

innkeepers will tell you about these fees when you reserve or check in; a few will surprise you at checkout.

The most common surcharge is an involuntary "service charge" of 10% to 15%. Coupled with state lodging taxes (even "sales-tax-free" New Hampshire hits tourists with an 8% levy), that bumps the cost of a bed up by nearly 25%. (The rates listed in this guide don't include service charges or sales tax.)

Other charges may include a pet fee ($10 or more per day extra), a foliage-season surcharge ($10–$50 per room), and a "resort fee" (of 15%–20% tax at certain resorts). Some hotels even tack on a $1 per day fee for the presence of an in-room safe, whether it is used or not.

SUGGESTED MAINE COAST ITINERARIES

M any travelers look at a coast-of-Maine trip as their only chance in a lifetime to see this part of the world. They try to race around the region seeing everything from Kittery to Portland to Acadia, plus even (maybe) a moose in the Maine Woods along the way . . . all in less than a week.

Trust me: That's nothing but a formula for disappointment, and has all the makings of a trip on which you'll probably end up seeing the inside of your windshield more than anything else. The coast of Maine has very few attractions that lend themselves to snap-a-photo tourism. Instead, it's best seen by moving slowly—on foot, in a canoe, on a bike, driving the back roads. The happiest visitors to this region tend to be those who stay more or less in one place or region, getting to know that place especially well through a series of carefully crafted day trips.

With that in mind, here are a few itineraries to use as a starting point; feel free to mix and match, improvise, or even devise your own. The first tour shows you the best of the entire Maine coast, but it takes from 1 to 2 weeks to do right; don't try to compress it into a couple of days. A second set of tours focuses on the city of Portland, Maine's cultural capital, geared toward the perspective of those traveling with families. I have devised three separate itineraries, according to how much time you have available. Finally, a third tour takes visitors through the often-neglected Bath-Brunswick area, focusing on the museums, art, and historic homes that reside there.

If you have somehow gotten to Maine without a car, and won't have time to rent or borrow one during your visit, see my suggestions for touring the coast without a vehicle in "Your Car: *Do* Leave Home Without It," in chapter 3.

The Regions in Brief

Southern Maine From the state line at Kittery to the Freeport-Bath-Brunswick area, Maine's southern coast features most of the state's best beaches and beach resorts. It's also home to the region's largest and most vibrant city, Portland. In addition, I recommend dipping a few miles south of the Piscataqua River to experience the adjacent New

Hampshire coast and its anchor city of Portsmouth (which I will cover separately in chapter 11). For the purposes of this guidebook, I have divided southern Maine into three chapters: Kittery to the Kennebunks; Portland; and Freeport to Monhegan Island.

Midcoast Maine   Midcoast Maine begins, depending on whom you ask, somewhere around the big bridge in downtown Bath and ends somewhere around Bucksport or Ellsworth. In between, you'll discover more rocky headlands, bays, and coves than you ever dreamed existed, as well as quaint villages with names such as Blue Hill, Camden, and Rockport and even some small hills and mountains. For the purposes of this book, I have shoehorned this entire, wonderfully scenic region into one action-packed chapter.

Downeast Maine   Maine's rocky coast is the stuff of legend, art, and poetry, and in Downeast Maine—which goes from the Ellsworth area all the way up the coast to the Canadian border—you'll find plenty of empty back roads and room to roam, not to mention rocky islands, foggy mornings, lobster boats aplenty, and a breathtakingly beautiful national park. In this book, I have dedicated one entire chapter to MDI (as Mount Desert Island is known by locals)— and that chapter is necessarily dominated by Acadia National Park. A second chapter treating the rest of Downeast Maine details the quieter pleasures of exploring north and east from the MDI area up to the Canadian border.

Side Trips from the Maine Coast   Once you've reached the Maine coast, it's worth exploring some dandy nearby areas and attractions, as well. In my final chapter, I describe three such side trips: first, heading a few miles south to experience small-town Portsmouth, New Hampshire, and its lovely surrounding coastline; second, pushing inland from Belfast or Bangor to sample the Great North Woods of Maine, which could legitimately be called the Northeast's last bit of untrammeled wilderness; and third, pressing north across the Canadian border an hour by car or boat to experience a lovely slice of coastal New Brunswick.

THE BEST OF THE MAINE COAST IN 2 WEEKS

Maine's coast tends to confound hurry-up tourists—there are simply too many dead-end peninsulas to backtrack along, and too many inlets that cleave the coast too far inland. You must sometimes drive great distances just to get from one rocky, wave-beaten point to the next, so finding a single home base and fanning out from there is the best strategy. Most of this Rte. heads north along U.S. Rte. 1, which can be a bit slowpokey in high summer season, but take heart: You'll have more time to soak up the views, which are pretty good for stretches, particularly once you get north of Bath.

Day 1: York ★★

Drive into Maine from the south on I-95, and head immediately for **York Village** ★ (the first exit; p. 74). Spend some time snooping around the historic homes of the **Old York Historical Society,** and stretch your legs on a walk through town or the woods.

Drive northward through **York Beach** ★★ (stocking up on saltwater taffy at the Goldenrod); stay near the beach.

From York, drive 20 miles north on the Maine Turnpike (I-95) or U.S. Rte. 1 to find:

Day 2: The Kennebunks ★★ & Ogunquit ★★

The Kennebunks are definitely worth a day if you enjoy the old blue-blood New England quaintness and luxury accommodations. There are some pretty fancy inns and bed-and-breakfast establishments in these parts.

Kennebunk, the lesser-known of the twin towns (they're separated by a slim tidal river), is a mixed bag of attractions, with the so-called **Wedding Cake House ★**, a very good public beach, a monastery (yes, really), and a natural-products factory store, among other things to see and do. See p. 96.

Across the river in **Kennebunkport,** you can stroll the leafy town, gawk at George Bush the elder's summer home (from a short distance away; those Secret Service guys mean business), and have a relaxed dinner at a fine restaurant. There is also a small shopping district and plenty of pleasure boats and yachts moored in the area. See p. 96.

While staying in the area, be sure to visit **Ogunquit,** a small town justly famous for its beaches, ocean views, and summery atmosphere. While there, be sure to stop in at the small but truly excellent **Ogunquit Museum of American Art ★★★**. Also hit the antiques shops lined up along Rte. 1 as you trend northward if you're so inclined. See p. 87.

From the Kennebunks, drive 27 miles north either on the Maine Turnpike (I-95, exiting onto Rte. 295 and following signs) or U.S. Rte. 1 to the Greater Portland area.

Days 3, 4 & 5: Portland ★★★

Plan to stay in **Portland** or on a nearby beach for up to 3 days, shopping for jewelry, souvenirs, or even kites or toys; taste-testing chowder recipes and micro-brewed beers; and just generally soaking up the salty air and atmosphere.

And don't forget to take a walk along the **Eastern Promenade ★★** or a day cruise on a local ferry, either. See p. 120.

From Portland, drive north 17 miles on I-295 or U.S. Rte. 1 to the Freeport area. There's a Maine state tourist information facility on Rte. 1 just north of Yarmouth, stocked with brochures and staff (daytime hours).

Day 6: Freeport & Surrounding Areas

Head north early to beat the shopping crowds in the outlet haven of **Freeport.** (You can't leave too early for **L.L.Bean**—it never closes!) See p. 132.

From Freeport, continue northward to **Brunswick,** home to **Bowdoin College ★** (p. 140) and its two small but excellent museums. Then press a few miles farther north to atmospheric **Bath ★**, with plenty of ancient sea captains' homes, a shipyard, and the **Maine Maritime Museum & Shipyard ★** (p. 143). Stay in a B&B in any of the three towns.

From Freeport, drive about 70 miles north along U.S. Rte. 1 to the Camden-Rockland-Rockport area; summer traffic congestion can slow this to a 2-hour-plus stretch. Wiscasset (about halfway to Camden) and Waldoboro (home of Moody's Diner) make two nice stopping points along the way.

Days 7 & 8: Camden ★★ & Penobscot Bay ★★

Heading north from the Bath-Brunswick area, detour down to **Pemaquid Point ★★** for a late picnic and to watch the surf roll in. Then head back to Rte. 1 and set your sights on the Camden-Rockland area, the commercial heart of the **Penobscot Bay** region. See p. 154.

Rockland ★, which comes first, is the workaday half of the equation. You'll find funky cafes, an excellent museum, and good restaurants. See p. 162.

Nearby **Rockport** ★ is a tiny harbor town with superb views and a tiny, artsy main street. See p. 170.

Finally, head a few miles north to wander around **Camden's** ★★ downtown, poke into shops and galleries, hike up one of the impressive hills at **Camden Hills State Park** ★★, hop a ferry to an island (North Haven and Isleboro are both great for biking), sign up for a daylong sail on a windjammer, or just spend a long afternoon unwinding on the deck of a local restaurant. It's also fun to grab an ice cream or hot dog down by the harbor.

From Camden, drive U.S. Rte. 1 40 miles north to state Rte. 15, turn south, and drive 12 more miles to:

Day 9: Blue Hill ★★ & Deer Isle ★★

Have dinner and find accommodations in scenic **Blue Hill** (p. 190). There are good views here, and the mixture of a Maine fishing town with bookshops and restaurants is quite appealing. Also take a spin around the peninsula to even smaller towns such as **Blue Hill Falls** and **Brooklin,** where you'll see boat-yards, old-fashioned general stores (post offices included), and Maine ingenuity holding it all together. *This* is the real Maine.

Continue an additional 18 miles south on Rte. 15 to **Deer Isle.** The roads here are great for aimless drives, but aim anyway for **Stonington** ★ at the far end of the peninsula. If distant **Isle au Haut** ★★, visible from the town docks, makes you pine for an offshore adventure, plan a boat trip for early the next morning; secure lodging in Deer Isle; and adjust your schedule accordingly. Otherwise, explore the area by car or sign up for a kayak tour with **Old Quarry Charters** (p. 189).

From Stonington, backtrack 18 miles on Rte. 15 to Blue Hill, then follow Rte. 172 north 14 miles to U.S. Rte. 1. Follow Rte. 1 just a short distance before bearing right onto Rte. 3 (following signs to Acadia National Park), and continue 6 miles to the bridge to Mount Desert Island. Cross the bridge and follow Rte. 3 about 10 more miles to Bar Harbor.

Days 10, 11, 12 & 13: Bar Harbor ★ & Acadia National Park ★★★

Bar Harbor is the most convenient, if not the prettiest, base for exploring **Mount Desert Island** ★★, which is well worth at least 4 days on any Maine itinerary. You might want to plan at least 2 nights in Bar Harbor, especially if you're here with your family: This town provides access to comforts and services such as a movie theater, souvenir shops, bike and kayak rentals, free shuttle buses fanning out all over the island, and numerous kinds of restaurants that other island towns don't have. Yes, it's a lot more developed (perhaps too much so) than the rest of the island, but think of it as a supply depot.

Hike, bike, boat, or do whatever you have to do to explore the island and this national park—in my humble opinion, one of America's finest. What it lacks in "bigness," it more than makes up for with intimate contact with nature. Explore at your own pace, via a beginner's kayak trip down the eastern shore, a hike out to Bar Island, or a mountain bike trip along one of the many carriage roads built by the Rockefeller family: Only bicycles and horses are allowed on these roads, making them a good respite from the island's highways, which—almost unbelievably—*do* get crowded in summer.

The scenic **Park Loop Road** ★★★ offers a good introduction to what's in store for you later (crashing waves, big mountains, drop-dead-gorgeous views). Make sure to buy a park pass that lasts more than 1 day.

While exploring the rest of the island, hit some of the towns off the beaten track, too. **Northeast Harbor** ★ and **Southwest Harbor** ★ are both fishing villages that have been transformed by tourism into small centers of art, music, and shopping, but they still have local grocery stores where fishermen slush in to shop for slickers and Wonder Bread, too.

The things you wanted to do, but didn't have time for? Do them on your last day in Acadia. Cap off your visit with a cold-water dip at Sand Beach and tea and popovers at **Jordan Pond House** ★★ (p. 210). Maybe watch a sunrise from the top of Cadillac Mountain, take a quick last hike up The Bubbles, or paddle a canoe on Long Pond. Or just enjoy one last lobster from atop a wooden pier before setting off back south.

From Bar Harbor, follow Rte. 3 10 miles back to the island bridge, cross it, and continue 6 miles to Rte. 1. Follow Rte. 1 a mile south to junction with Rte. 1A, then turn onto Rte. 1A and continue about 25 miles to Bangor.

Day 14: Bangor ★ & Home

Heading home, you don't need to head south on Rte. 1 again. In fact, it's far quicker to bypass the coast and use I-95—part of which comprises the Maine Turnpike (a toll road)—to get home. On the way, you might want to stop in **Bangor,** especially if you're a big fan of horror writer Stephen King. His house is pretty obvious once you get downtown. There are several museums in and around the city, as well; it's the only place that passes for a cultural center in the vastly empty spaces of inland northern Maine, so stock up (and fuel up) while you've got the chance.

From Bangor, take the Maine Turnpike (I-95) south 180 miles to the state line at Kittery. With no stops, it takes less than 3 hours.

PORTLAND FOR FAMILIES IN 1 DAY

A family can easily spend a pleasant 3 days exploring the cobblestones, shops, museums, and attractions of Portland. Day 1 of this tour begins in the city's emerging Arts District, which is home to a number of museums, and then makes its way to Portland's historic Old Port.

1 Portland Museum of Art ★★★

Located on Congress Square, Portland's outstanding museum of art is almost directly in the center of the city proper, making it a good jumping-off point for a tour of the rest of Portland. Make a deal with your kids: If they behave during a trip to the art museum, they'll be rewarded with a couple of hours in their own museum (just next door). Or simply split your party up, sending teens and college-age family members to the art museum while younger kids and a lucky adult muck about in the Children's Museum. See p. 122.

2 Children's Museum of Maine ★

Kids will love the opportunity to run from exhibit to exhibit in their own museum. In addition to its legendary camera obscura, the museum also sports permanent and rotating exhibits of interactive stuff such as a firehouse pole and mock space shuttle. Be sure to check out the Explore Floor, which offers a series of interactive science exhibits focusing on Maine's natural resources. See p. 121.

As you exit the Children's Museum, turn right on Free Street. At Oak Street, cross the street and continue half a block down Free Street to the back entrance of the:

3 L.L.Bean Outlet Store

Fans of L.L.Bean shouldn't miss its Portland outlet, located in the Arts District a few blocks away from the museums. The outlet sells both kids' and adults' clothes; the best deals are usually the (very) slightly damaged or imperfect goods, which can often be had for a steal. See p. 128.

Either backtrack to your car or, if it's a nice day, consider hoofing it down to the Old Port. Continue left (as you leave the outlet's back door) down Free Street 4 short blocks to Temple Street. Turn right, continue a short half block to the traffic light and intersection, then make a left on Middle Street (also called Spring St.). Continue straight 1 block to Exchange Street and find yourself in the heart of:

4 The Old Port ★★★

Spend the rest of the day exploring the historic Old Port. If you haven't stopped for lunch yet, you'll find plenty of options in the Old Port, particularly along Commercial Street. **Exchange Street** is the key shopping address, though the other cobblestone side streets and the harbor area are also nice.

In summer, free concerts are sometimes held in a small park, and the city's tourist office—stocked with free info—is down at the bottom on Commercial Street. Kids will enjoy the ice-cream shops, boats, and knickknacks.

Don't miss a seafood feed of lobster, fish, or clam chowder at a place such as **Gilbert's Chowder House,** 92 Commercial St. (p. 119). There are plenty of choices for all of these in town.

Coffee Break

Portland is chock-full of great coffee shops, and more of them seem to open all the time. My two current favorites are both on the fringes of the Old Port: Arabica (2 Free St.; ✆ 207/879-0792), with great wall art and a hospitable Portland vibe, and newcomer Bard Coffee (185 Middle St.; ✆ 207/899-4788), with a younger feel and good espresso drinks. They're both open 7 days a week.

PORTLAND FOR FAMILIES IN 2 DAYS

On day 2 of your Portland stay, you'll focus on tiny trains and the islands dotting Casco Bay. Kids will love riding a tiny choo-choo back and forth along the waterfront, while adults enjoy the island vistas, sea breezes, and dreams of second homes.

If you're driving, think about parking in the ferry terminal garage for this tour—it's expensive, but unavoidable if you're out on the islands. To begin the tour, walk downhill to the base of the Old Port: the waterfront boulevard known as Commercial Street. Turn left and continue past the ferry docks to the:

1 Maine Narrow Gauge Railroad Co. & Museum ★

This combo of a mini–choo-choo and museum is inexpensive and fun for the kiddies. Admission to the museum is free and educational, while the (*very* slow) train ride traces the foot of the cliffs framing Portland's east end. Parents will be popping the NoDoz, but, hey, at least it's short. See p. 122.

From the railroad, backtrack along Commercial Street 1 block to the ferry terminal, where you can:

2 Take a Ferry to an Island

One of the don't-miss experiences of a Portland visit is a cruise around Casco Bay on a **Casco Bay Lines** (p. 124) ferry that departs from a terminal at the foot of Franklin Arterial (across from the blockish Hilton Garden Inn). You can take anywhere from a 20-minute run to a half-day mail-boat cruise. Two of my recommended destinations are **Peaks Island**—a favorite among mothers pushing baby strollers, for its easy-to-cruise streets with Portland views—and **Long Island,** with an excellent beach.

From the ferry terminal, it's an uphill hike to the next stop; those with small children will want to drive. Exit the ferry terminal and turn right on Commercial Street. Loop around left to India Street, then take the first right onto Fore Street. The street will change its name to Eastern Promenade and open up some good views. At the top, you have two choices: Take the high road, and park for free on the street in front of the long grassy slope leading down to the water, or angle downhill to the right, where boats await. Either way, you've reached:

3 The Eastern Promenade ★★

Young and old alike enjoy the sunrises, sunsets, picnics, sailboat views, swing sets, and ball fields of the Eastern Promenade, a 68-acre hillside park with broad, grassy slopes extending down to the water and superb views of Casco Bay and its islands. It's one of Portland's true gems. See p. 120.

From the Eastern Promenade, with the water on your right, continue by car or foot a few more blocks to Congress Street. You'll find this corner easily: There's a statue marking it. Turn left on Congress. You'll go up a slight rise, and after about 7 blocks, at the crest of the hill at 138 Congress St., find the:

4 Portland Observatory ★

Kids like checking out the stupendous views from the top of this distinctive, shingled observatory, built in 1807 to signal ship arrivals into the city's port. (It's also locally called the Munjoy Hill Observatory, if you're asking directions.) It's said to be the last working maritime signal tower in the nation and was designated as a National Historic Landmark in 2006. It's open from spring through fall to tours. See p. 121.

PORTLAND FOR FAMILIES IN 3 DAYS

You'll spend day 3 of your stay in Portland having a ball on the beach and taking in some action at a Portland Sea Dogs baseball game. Remember that some of these activities depend on good weather. Portland's summer temperatures are normally lovely—but in case Mother Nature doesn't cooperate, I've also added some backup plans. (Also, be sure to consult a daily paper, television, or the website www.seadogs.com to make certain the Sea Dogs are actually playing a home game.)

From downtown Portland, begin at Monument Square downtown (that's the square surrounded by the Portland Public Library, office buildings, and an open square, which sometimes holds a farmers market). Here you'll find the:

1 Public Market House

This newish market house at 28 Monument Sq. replaced the bigger Portland Public Market nearby, and is now your best bet for one-stop picnic shopping while in downtown Portland. The complex includes a cheese shop, a beer-and-wine vendor, a florist, a coffee shop, a pizza shop, and a bakery: Portland, distilled into a single building. It's open daily year-round.

With picnic packed, head up to Congress Street. Turn left and continue ½ mile to State Street. Turn left on State and continue downhill, following signs for Rte. 77. Bear right and cross a big bridge into South Portland; stay the course for several traffic lights until you reach a right turn at Ocean Street (Rte. 77). Turn right and continue about 6 more miles to reach:

2 Cape Elizabeth

On a sunny summer day, you can't go wrong with any of a number of beaches and lighthouses out Rte. 77 in the quiet suburb of Cape Elizabeth and its associated areas. Be sure to bring a swimsuit, sunscreen, and a camera.

Kids especially enjoy the **Two Lights** and **Portland Head Light** lighthouses, and everyone likes the eats at Two Lights Lobster Shack (a separate outbuilding dispenses ice-cream treats for lobster-phobes). There's also romping around in the sand and surf on Scarborough and Willard beaches nearby.

Backtrack the way you came: From Cape Elizabeth, drive 6 miles along Rte. 77 to South Portland, then cross the big bridge. After a few blocks, turn left (from the two left lanes) onto High Street and continue uphill 4 blocks to Congress Street. Turn left at the light and continue about 1 mile downhill along Congress until you reach the Maine Medical Center parking garage (on the left). Park here, cross busy Congress Street, walk 2 blocks downhill, and turn right to find Hadlock Field, home of the:

3 Portland Sea Dogs ★★★

If your kids tend more toward the teens and they're crazy about baseball, an outing at Hadlock Field can't be beat; it's one of the better minor league parks at which I've ever attended a ballgame. And there's a bonus for New Englanders: The Sea Dogs are the minor-league club for the Boston Red Sox, with a chance to catch up-and-coming talent. Yankee fans, deal with it. See p. 124.

Fill 'Er Up

You'll likely fill up on peanuts, popcorn, and hot dogs at the game. If you're looking for a healthy bite before or after the contest, the surrounding industrial district doesn't seem promising at first. However, one of my favorite Thai restaurants in Maine just happens to sit a few blocks away from the park. Seng Thai (📞 207/879-2577) is at 921 Congress St. Too experimental for you? The bar/red-sauce restaurant Sportsman's Grill, 911 Congress St. (📞 207/772-9324), is half a block away. Both places are also handy in case the game's rained out.

BATH & BRUNSWICK FOR CULTURE LOVERS

This tour takes in the often-neglected Bath-Brunswick sliver of the Maine coast, which is usually passed by but is in fact packed with colonial history, brick buildings, great residential architecture, and a fistful of good little museums.

Our tour starts at the Brunswick town green, in the center of town. From here, walk 1 block to the:

1 Federal Street District, Brunswick ★

Just a block off the main street, Federal Street is several eras removed from the present. This is where the town's wealthy first set up shop, and a stroll down the long, straight thoroughfare produces plenty of **Greek Revival, Victorian,** and **Federal-style homes** to please the eye. Many of these architectural gems were designed by Samuel Melcher III, a local architect and master builder of the 19th century who also worked on Bowdoin College nearby (see below).

The Parker Cleaveland house at **no. 75 Federal** is a good example of Melcher's work; a pathbreaking Bowdoin mineralogy professor, Cleaveland lived here for nearly half a century.

2 Time for a Cuppa

When in downtown Brunswick and needing a quick snack and some java, look no farther than the Bohemian Coffee House (☎ 207/725-9095) at 4 Railroad Ave., close to the large Hannaford's grocery store (itself set back in a plaza from the town green on Maine St.). Yes, they have free wireless Internet access. And a patio. And their own homemade gelato. Gelato? 'Nuff said.

3 Bowdoin College Campus ★

Just up the street from no. 75 Federal, you come upon the campus of **Bowdoin College,** which is built around a lovely and expansive central green in classic Ivy style. (In fact, Bowdoin is considered a "little Ivy.") Among the famous folks to have taught or studied here: Nathaniel Hawthorne, Olympic marathon gold medalist Joan Benoit Samuelson, Henry Longfellow, and Civil War Gen. Joshua Chamberlain.

The campus buildings, mostly constructed in the 19th century—the oldest dates from 1802—are remarkable. Sturdy little **Massachusetts Hall ★**, still my favorite building, originally contained the entire Bowdoin campus within its walls. **Winthrop Hall,** close by, was the first of the line of brick dormitories that march in a prim line away from **Hubbard Hall** (1934), a drippingly Gothic library.

Memorial Hall, also close to Massachusetts Hall, was constructed of stone in the late 19th century but is now overshadowed by the Pickard and Wish theaters, whose performances are open to the public.

The steepled granite **chapel** is worth peeking inside if it's open. Designed by Richard Upjohn, it's unmistakably the visual focal point of the campus.

4 Bowdoin College Museum of Art ★★

On the Bowdoin College campus, within a McKim, Mead, and White–designed structure, this jewel of a museum holds work from big-shot Maine artists such as the **Wyeths, Marsden Hartley, Winslow Homer,** and **John Singer Sargent.** And admission is free.

The **exterior** was designed to echo Brunelleschi's Renaissance Piazzi Chapel in Florence. The interior isn't too shabby, either: Look up at the **central dome** as you enter, where four murals were painted by LaFarge and others to symbolize the great European cultural centers of Rome, Florence, Venice, and Athens.

The **Winslow Homer Collection** ★ consists not only of Homer paintings but also memorabilia and even some of his painting tools—a must-see for true art buffs. In addition to all the New England landscape artists mentioned above, the museum's collections also hold European treasures such as the **cassone panel *Nymphs of Fiesole,*** recently attributed to the important 15th-century Renaissance artist Fra Angelico (who apparently painted it when he was a teenager). Look for other permanent or visiting work by such artists as Corot, Magritte, Picasso, and Braque. See p. 142.

5 Peary-MacMillan Arctic Museum ★★

Bowdoin's "other" museum is equally splendid, yet in a different way. Beyond the fascinating historical items pertaining to Peary and MacMillan's historic journeying to the North Pole (Peary alone donated some 5,000 photographs and a glass lantern from his travels), there's also a growing collection of Inuit artifacts, arts, and crafts here. See p. 143.

From Brunswick, head northeast 8 miles on U.S. Rte. 1 or slower Bath Road to reach Bath and its historic district.

6 Bath Historic District ★★

Bath was once sea-captain-central for these parts, and many built their lovely Greek Revival, Federal, and Georgian homes on the brow of a hill overlooking the harbor. **Washington, Hill,** and **Middle streets** are the best lanes to explore; many of the homes now house excellent bed-and-breakfast inns.

There's a striking Gothic Revival **church** (1843) at 880 Washington St., now home to the local historic preservation organization; noted Maine architect John Calvin Stevens did some interior work here about a half century later.

And just try to miss the oversize, Gothic Revival **Chocolate Church,** now home to a local arts organization. It's dipped in paint the color of . . . well, you can guess, I think.

You'll find a few antiques shops and a bookshop on nearby **Front Street,** the heart of the commercial district that has somehow managed to retain a still-part-of-yesteryear look.

7 Dining in Style

While hotfooting it among Bath's and Brunswick's museums and historic homes, you're sure to wilt from hunger at some point. Thank goodness, then, for Mae's Café, 160 Centre St. (✆ 207/442-8577), in a wonderful old house in downtown Bath. In addition to serving two to three meals a day, they offer great baked goods such as pecan-studded sticky buns, pies, and cookies.

8 Maine Maritime Museum & Shipyard ★

One of Maine's two primary maritime museums (there's another north along Rte. 1 in Searsport), this one offers plenty for the kids, but also adults who appreciate seafaring history. It's housed in a former shipyard and is chock-full of art, artifacts, and exhibits on marine-related topics such as boat building and lobstering. There's a nice gift shop here, too, and the museum sometimes operates boat trips along the Kennebec River. See p. 143.

Drive 10 miles northeast on Rte. 1 to reach Wiscasset.

9 Wiscasset ★★

Many call this the cutest village in Maine. There's certainly no arguing that there are plenty of fine buildings to poke through (though no museums) in a relatively small area here. More than two dozen structures in this tiny town are listed on, or have been nominated to, the National Register of Historic Places, including **Castle Tucker** ★ (p. 149), which isn't really a castle, and the elegant 1807 **Nickels-Sortwell House,** 121 Main St. (© **207/882-6218**), a hard-luck shipbuilder's home and former hotel, which you can tour for a small admission fee; it contains great period furnishings. Afterward, stroll the lanes and waterfront and see whether you can find the former U.S. Customs house, old jail, so-called "Octagon House," and brick schoolhouse, too. See p. 148.

SOUTHERN MAINE

Maine's southern coast runs roughly from the state line at Kittery to Portland, and is the primary destination of most travelers to the state. (These statistics include many day-trippers from the Boston area.) While it takes some doing to find privacy or remoteness here, there are at least two excellent reasons to come: the long, sandy beaches and a sense of history in the coastal villages . . . some of them, anyway.

Thanks to quirks of geography, nearly all of Maine's sandy shores occur along this stretch of coastline. It's not hard to find a relaxing spot whether you prefer dunes, the lulling sound of breaking waves, or a carnival-like atmosphere in a beach town. Waves depend on the weather; during a good Northeast blow, they pound the shores, rise above the roads, and threaten beach houses built decades ago. During balmy midsummer days, though, the ocean can be gentle as a farm pond, its barely audible waves lapping timidly at the shore as the tide creeps in, inch by inch, covering tidal pools full of crabs, snails, and starfish.

One thing all the beaches here share in common: They're washed by the chilled waters of the Gulf of Maine, which makes for, er, invigorating swimming. Though the beach season is generally brief and intense, running only from July 4th to Labor Day, some towns are making an effort to stretch the tourist season out into fall.

KITTERY & THE YORKS ★★

Kittery is 60 miles N of Boston and 266 miles NE of New York City

Driving into Maine from the south, as most travelers do, **Kittery ★** is the first town to appear after crossing the big bridge spanning the Piscataqua River from New Hampshire. Once famous for its (still operating) naval yard, Kittery is now better known for its dozens of factory outlets.

"The Yorks," just to the north, are three towns that share a name, but little else. In fact, it's rare to find three such well-defined and diverse New England archetypes within such a compact area. **York Village ★** is full of 17th-century American history and architecture in a compact area, and has a good library. **York Harbor ★★** reached its zenith during America's late Victorian era, when wealthy urbanites constructed cottages at the ocean's edge; it's the most relaxing and scenic of the three. Finally, **York Beach ★★** is a fun beach town with amusements, taffy shops, a small zoo, gabled summer homes set in crowded enclaves, a great lighthouse,

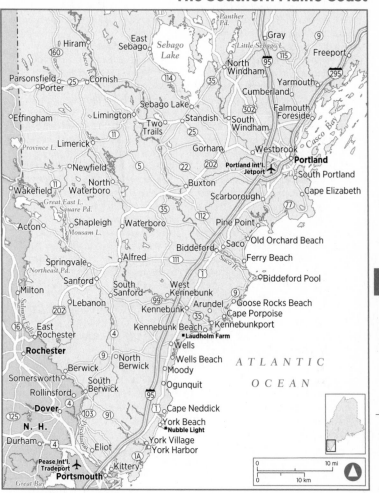

and two excellent beaches with sun, sand, rocks, surf, surfers, fried-fish stands, and lighthouse views.

Just outside York Village, the protrusion of land known as **Cape Neddick ★★** is an excellent back-road route to Ogunquit, *if* you can find it (go past the police station in Short Sands, then bear right at the sign for the Cape Neddick Lobster Pound).

Essentials

GETTING THERE

Kittery is accessible from either **I-95** or **Rte. 1,** with well-marked exits. Coming from the south, the Yorks are reached most easily by heading for (but not taking) the Maine Turnpike; follow I-95 to a point just south of the turnpike exit, then exit to the right

Think Maine is your little secret get-away? Think again: This coast has seen wave after successive wave of visitation, beginning at least 3 centuries ago when European newcomers tried to settle it, only to be driven off by Native Americans. (It's also locally believed that Vikings may have touristed—er, pillaged?—the region even longer before that.) By the early 19th century, the Maine coast had become well colonized and blossomed into one of the most prosperous places in all the U.S. Shipbuilders constructed brigantines and sloops, using stout pines and other trees floated downriver from Maine's North Woods; ship captains built huge, handsome homes in towns such as Searsport, Kittery, Bath, and Belfast; and merchants and traders built vast warehouses to store the booty from the

excursions, as well as their own grandiose homes.

Then things quieted down for a while, until landscape artists "rediscovered" Maine. They brought a fresh influx of city dwellers in their wake in the mid-to-late 19th century from Boston, New York, and Philadelphia, seeking relief from the heat and congestion of the city. They built huge, shingled estates facing the sea in places such as Bar Harbor and Camden. Then, at the beginning of the 20th century, a newly moneyed emerging middle class (a third wave?) showed up to discover Maine yet again, building smaller, less expensive bungalows by the shore in places such as York Beach, Kennebunk Beach, and Old Orchard Beach. The next arrival? That's you, dear reader.

("last exit before tolls"). Coming from the north, pay your toll exiting the turnpike and then take the first exit, an immediate right.

Amtrak (📞 800/872-7245; www.amtrak.com) operates four to five Downeaster trains daily from Boston's North Station (which does not connect to Amtrak's national network; you must take a subway or taxi from Boston's South Station first) into southern Maine, stopping outside Wells, about 10 miles away from the Yorks; a one-way ticket costs $19, and the trip takes 1¾ hours. From Wells, though, you'll need to phone for a taxi or arrange for a pickup to get to your final destination.

No bus lines serve the stretch of Maine between Portland and Kittery. However, several competing bus lines run regular buses daily from Boston's South Station to downtown Portsmouth, New Hampshire, which is very close to Kittery (you can actually walk over a bridge into Maine from Portsmouth). The two chief carriers are **Greyhound** (📞 800/231-2222; www.greyhound.com)—which has absorbed former competitor Vermont Transit—and **C&J Trailways** (📞 800/258-7111; www.ridecj.com). For more details, see "Getting There" in the Portsmouth, New Hampshire, section of chapter 11. Taking a bus from New York City's Port Authority to Portsmouth costs from $45 to $60 one-way and takes 6 to 7 hours; from Boston, figure on paying a fare of $17 to $22 one-way and a ride of slightly more than 1 hour to Portsmouth.

From mid-June through Labor Day, a trackless **"trolley"** (a bus painted to look like a trolley) runs back and forth between Short Sands and Long Sands, providing a convenient way to explore without having to be hassled with parking. Hop on the trolley (📞 207/363-9600; www.yorktrolley.com) at one of the well-marked stops; it's $1.50 each way, $3 to sit on board for the entire loop without debarking. The trolley makes a circle through the Short Sands business district before heading out to Long Sands and proceeding all the way to the Libby's and Camp Eaton campgrounds at the far southern end of that beach, before turning around again. (It does not travel to Nubble Light, but if you want to see the famous lighthouse, debark the bus at Nubble Light Rd. and hoof it a little more than a mile out to the point.) The trolley operates from late June through Labor Day daily on the half-hour, from about 9:30am until around 10:15pm.

VISITOR INFORMATION

The **Maine State Visitor Information Center** (✆ **207/439-1319**) is at a well-marked rest area on I-95. It's full of info and helpful staff; has a pet exercise area and copious vending machines; and is open daily from 8am to 6pm in summer, from 9am to 5:30pm the rest of the year. (The vending machines and restrooms are open 24 hrs.)

The **Greater York Region Chamber of Commerce** (✆ **207/363-4422;** www.gatewaytomaine.org) also operates another helpful **visitor center,** one that mirrors the shape of a stone cottage. It's across Rte. 1 from the Maine Turnpike access road (right beside the Stonewall Kitchen headquarters and cafe) on Stonewall Lane. In peak season, it's open Monday to Saturday from 9am to 5pm and Sunday from 10am to 4pm; from Labor Day through June, it's open Monday to Friday 9am to 4pm and Saturday from 10am to 2pm.

Exploring Kittery & the Yorks

Kittery has become a shopping mecca thanks to the establishment of colonies of little factory outlet shopping malls clustered along both sides of U.S. Rte. 1, about 4 miles south of York. More than 100 of these outlets flank the highway, in more than a dozen strip malls. It's aesthetically ugly, but if you're looking to score a deal, you just might find it beautiful.

Name-brand retailers with factory shops here purveying cut-rate designer stuff include Coach, Crate & Barrel, Orvis, Samsonite, Gap, Eddie Bauer, Banana Republic, Calvin Klein, Brookstone, and Polo Ralph Lauren, among many others. On rainy summer days, hordes of disappointed beachgoers head here and swarm the aisles; thus, parking can become tight on bad-weather days.

Father of Our Country; Flop As a Wharf Owner

John Hancock is justly famous for his oversize signature on the Declaration of Independence, his tenure as governor of Massachusetts, and the insurance company and tall Boston building that were named for him. What's not so well known is his involvement as a proprietor of **Hancock Wharf,** a failed wharf-and-warehouse enterprise that went bust. Hancock never actually set foot on the wharf, but for years locals believed he used it to stash arms, contraband, and/or goods he didn't want taxed by those tax-happy British. It now appears that wasn't the case, but it still makes for one of the many intriguing sites and stories in the **York Village** section of downtown York. (See p. 78 for more details on this neighborhood.)

Surprisingly, the wharf has a happy ending: It's more famous today than it was then, the only 18th-century warehouse still standing on the York River. It has been designated a National Historic Site, and the York Historical Society sometimes uses it to launch or receive the occasional historic boat passing through town.

Information on current outlets is available from the **Kittery Outlet Association.** Call ℂ **888/548-8379** (which spells KITTERY, by the way), or visit the website at www.thekitteryoutlets.com.

Only have time for one set of outlets? For a comparison between the outlets here and the ones about an hour north in Freeport, see "Tale of the Tags: Freeport vs. Kittery," in chapter 7.

Kittery has no true town center, but is instead made of several disconnected villages (all of them quite old) and a long, skinny shopping strip. On the waterfront, the historic **Portsmouth Naval Shipyard** faces Portsmouth, New Hampshire. This active shipyard isn't open to the public for security reasons, but you can visit the engaging displays at the nearby **Kittery Historical & Naval Museum** (ℂ **207/439-3080;** www.kitterymuseum.com) to get a quick overview of maritime history. You'll find ship and sub models, lighthouse lenses, scrimshaw work, diving suits, and the like—plus muskets, utensils, and tools from another era. It's not a bad effort at all. The museum is open from June through October daily, from 10am to 4pm. Admission is $3 for adults, $1.50 for children, and $6 for a family. Find it by taking U.S. Rte. 1 to the Kittery traffic circle, then exiting for Rte. 236 south; that's Rogers Road. Continue to the end and Rogers Road Extension.

From Kittery, an attractive alternative route north to York follows winding Rte. 103—perfect for driving, though a bit busy and narrow for biking. This road passes through the historic, lost-in-time village of Kittery Point, where homes seem to be just inches from the roadway and there are not one but *two* historic forts; both are parks open to the public.

York is split into several village centers, described above; the best for walking around in is **York Village ★★**, a fine destination for those curious about early American history. First settled in 1624, the village opens several homes to the public.

For a duck's-eye view of the local terrain, visit **Excursions Coastal Maine Outfitting Co.** in Cape Neddick (ℂ **207/363-0181;** www.excursionsinmaine.com). This outfitter offers half- day, daily, and weekly sea-kayak rentals and tours—it costs $60 per adult for a guided half-day excursion, $50 for a child, for example—along the lovely local coastline. For more dramatic paddling, ask about sunrise, sunset, full-moon, and overnight kayaking trips. The shop is located on Rte. 1, between Ogunquit and York; go north 5 or 6 miles from York's information hut near the turnpike exit.

Finally, while visiting Kittery and the Yorks, don't forget that Portsmouth, New Hampshire makes a worthwhile side trip—in fact, if you're seeking culture, arts, coffee shops, and top-flight restaurants, it's a much *better* base than either of those towns. Best of all, it's just a half-mile from Kittery, or a few minutes' drive from the Yorks. I've described this city as a side trip in greater detail in chapter 11 of this book.

Old York Historical Society ★★★ York's local historical society oversees the bulk of the town's collection of historic buildings, some of which date to the early 18th century, and most of which are astonishingly well preserved or restored. Tickets are available to eight Old York–operated properties in all; one good place to start is at the **Jefferds Tavern ★**, across from the handsome **old burying ground ★**. Changing exhibits document various facets of early life. Next door is the School House, furnished as it might have been in the 19th century. A 10-minute walk along lightly traveled Lindsay Road brings you to **Hancock Wharf,** next door to the **George Marshall Store.** Also nearby is the Elizabeth Perkins House, with its well-preserved Colonial Revival interiors. A 10-minute walk along Lindsay Road brings you to **Hancock Wharf,** next door to the **George Marshall Store.** (Also nearby is the

Wheeling It to the Sayward-Wheeler House

If you'd like to get a taste of York's long history, but lack the stamina for the full-court Old York visit, here's your best option: stop by the **Sayward-Wheeler House** ★ at 9 Barrell Lane Extension in York Harbor, run by the group **Historic New England.** In this well-preserved merchant's home dating from 1760, you'll find booty (such as fine china) plundered during the 1745 Siege of Louisbourg, which routed the French out of Nova Scotia. But you'll have to do some planning: The home is open alternate Saturdays only, from June through mid-October; tours are given hourly from 11am to 4pm. Admission is $5 for adult, $4 for seniors, and $2.50 for students—but free if you join Historic New England. For more information, call the home (✆ **207/384-2454**) or the organization's home office in Boston (✆ **617/227-3956**; www.historicnewengland.org).

Elizabeth Perkins House, with its well-preserved Colonial Revival interiors.) Finally, there are two "don't-miss" buildings in the society's collection: the barn-red, hill-topping **Old Gaol ★★** was built in 1719 as a jail to hold criminals, debtors, and other miscreants. It's said to be the oldest surviving public building in the United States, and you can still see the dungeons. Then, just down the knoll from the jail, is the bright yellow **Emerson-Wilcox House ★**, built in the mid-1700s and periodically added onto through the years. It's a virtual catalog of architectural styles and early decorative arts.

207 York St., York. ✆ **207/363-4974.** www.oldyork.org. Admission per building $5 adults, $4 seniors, $3 children 6–15; pass to all buildings $10 adults, $9 seniors, $5 children 6–15, $20 family. Museum Mon–Sat 10am–5pm; some properties shorter hours. Closed mid-Oct to mid-June.

Sohier Park ☺ ★★★   The small peninsula known as Cape Neddick shoots off from York's beach areas, circles through beach views, and winds up here, at Sohier Park—a great place to look out onto Nubble Light, probably one of the ten most photographed lighthouses in the world. The light is especially lovely because it's set on a tiny island. The park is free; gaze at the lighthouse and snap pictures from the safety of a parking lot across the swift little inlet that separates it from the mainland. There are coin-operated looking-glasses to get a better view, and small gift shop and information kiosk in the park. In high summer season, expect a parking lot jam-packed with RVs and motorcycles—watching the crowd is half the fun. There's also a lobster hut adjacent to the park, and an outstanding ice cream stand about 100 yards uphill from it. If you're coming to take photos, remember that the lighthouse is trimmed in additional white lighting twice a year, for a week during July's York Days festival and again from Thanksgiving through New Year's.

Nubble Rd. (off Long Sands Dr.), Cape Neddick. www.nubblelight.org. Free admission. Park open year-round, 24 hr.; welcome center and restrooms open daily May to mid-Oct, 7am–7pm.

Two Wonderful Walks

Two local strolls will allow visitors to stretch their legs and get the cobwebs out of their heads.

York Harbor and York Village are connected by a quiet pathway that follows a river and passes through gently rustling woodlands. **Fisherman's Walk ★** departs from below Edward's Harborside Inn, near the Stage Neck Inn. (There's limited parking at tiny York Harbor Beach.) Follow the pathway along the river, past lobster shacks and along lawns leading up to grand shingled homes. Cross Rte. 103 and walk over the **Wiggly Bridge** (said to be, not implausibly, the smallest suspension bridge in the world), then head into the woods. You'll soon connect with a dirt lane; follow this and you'll emerge at Lindsay Road near Hancock Wharf (see above). The entire walk is about a mile long and, depending on your pace, will take a half-hour to 45 minutes.

Also departing from near York Harbor Beach is the **Cliff Walk ★★**, a scenic little trail that follows rugged terrain along rocky bluffs and offers sweeping views of the open ocean as well as glimpses of life in some of the town's grandest cottages. The far end of this trail has been destroyed by ocean waves and has not been rebuilt; you'll have to retrace your steps back to the beach. The pathway remains the subject of recent disputes between the town and landowners seeking to limit access. Check signs for any new restrictions on trespassing before you set off.

Finally, there's the small peninsula ending at an island capped by the scenic **Nubble Light ★★★** lighthouse. This lighthouse, probably one of the most photographed in the world, is undeniably attractive—and absolutely free to view from the safety of a parking lot set across the swift little inlet that separates it from the mainland. There's little walking to be done, but this is a terrific spot for a picnic; walk a minute uphill to **Brown's Ice Cream ★★** for some of Maine's best homemade ice cream for dessert. (The lighthouse is lit up for the holiday season around Thanksgiving each year. If you happen to be here in late November inquire about the shuttle from Short Sands Beach out to the vantage point.) For information on additional lighthouses, see "Lighthouses: A Tour Up the Coast," in chapter 2.

Beaches

York Beach actually consists of *two* beaches, **Long Sands Beach ★★** and **Short Sands Beach ★**, separated by a rocky headland. Both have plenty of room for sunning and Frisbees when the tide is out. When the tide is in, though, both become narrow and cramped. Short Sands fronts the honky-tonk town of York Beach, with its candlepin bowling, taffy-pulling machine, and video arcades. It's a better pick for families traveling with kids who have short attention spans. Long Sands runs along Rte. 1A, directly across from a line of motels, summer homes, and convenience stores. Parking at *both* beaches is metered in summer; pay heed, as enforcement is strict and you must feed the meters until 9pm, all 7 days of the week. (At the end of summer, though, they decapitate the meters—literally—and parking is subsequently free and plentiful until the next Memorial Day.)

Public restrooms are available at both beaches; other services, including snacks, are provided by local restaurants and vendors.

Where to Stay

York Beach has a large supply of no-frills motels facing Long Sands Beach, with rooms ranging from very basic to suites with private seaside decks and kitchenettes. Reserve ahead during high season. Among those with simple accommodations are the **Anchorage Inn** (© **207/363-5112;** www.anchorageinn.com), the **Grand View Inn Motel** (© **207/363-3838** or 207/363-9815; www.grandview-york.com), and the **Sunrise Motel** (© **800/242-0750;** www.sunrisemotel.net), all directly across the highway from the ocean.

HISTORY TAKES A detour TO SOUTH BERWICK

It's tiny, it's not on the tourist map, and it's not on the coast, yet little South Berwick, Maine, provides a worthwhile detour back into Maine's colonial—and literary—history. Think about taking a few hours to explore it if raindrops happen to be pelting York Beach and ruining your beach outing.

The two most important structures in town are the late-18th-century **Hamilton House,** 40 Vaughan's Lane (✆ **207/384-2454**)—a solid riverside home, with fine gardens and grounds—and its contemporary, the **Sarah Orne Jewett House,** 5 Portland St. (✆ **207/384-2454**), a 1774 Georgian where the famous Maine author lived. Her desk overlooks the village's main crossroads. Both homes are open to the public from June through mid-October, on slightly different schedules. Hamilton House is open Wednesday to Sunday from 11am to 4pm, while the Jewett House is open Friday through Sunday (same hours); tours are offered on the hour at each property. It costs $8 per adult ($7 seniors, $4 students) to visit Hamilton House, and $5 per person ($4 seniors, $2.50 students) to tour the Jewett House.

If you're looking for some nature, drop by one of the area farms or orchards, or take the kids to **Vaughan Woods State Park** (✆ **207/490-4079**), down Oldsfields Road just off Rte. 236 (a bit south of the town center). Set along the quiet Salmon Falls River, the park features picnic areas and a hiking trail through groves of old-growth pine and hemlock. It's open Memorial Day to Labor Day; the admission fee is $3 per non-Maine resident adult, $1 for seniors and children age 5 to 11.

For golfers, the outstanding **The Links at Outlook** golf course (✆ **207/384-4653**; www.outlookgolf.com) on Rte. 4 is a fine, links-style track of bent grass fairways and greens. The greens fees for 18 holes will run you around $45 per person in high summer season; it's cheaper on weekdays, afternoons, and in spring and fall. Carts cost extra.

From York, South Berwick is quickly reached via Rte. 91 (which shoots west off Rte. 1 just south of the Maine Tpk. interchange for York). It's a ride of about 20 minutes.

Campers lack good options around here, but might head for **Dixon's Campground** (✆ **207/363-3626**), which has a mix of wooded tenting and RV sites set back from busy Rte. 1 (just north of York proper) for $30 to $44 per night. Monthly (yes, monthly) rates are cheaper. There's a 3-night minimum on holiday weekends; it's open from mid-May through Columbus Day.

IN THE YORKS

Dockside Guest Quarters ★ David and Harriette Lusty established this quiet retreat in 1954, but more recent additions and new management (son David and his wife) haven't changed the friendly, maritime flavor of the place. Situated on an island connected to the mainland by a small bridge, the inn occupies nicely landscaped grounds shady with maples and white pines. A few of the rooms are in the cozy main house, built in 1885, but the bulk of the accommodations are in small, shared, townhouse-style cottages added between 1968 and 1998 down by the water. These are simply furnished, but bright and airy; most have private decks overlooking the entrance to York Harbor. Several also have woodstoves, fireplace, and/or kitchenettes (though you do pay quite a bit extra for the kitchenette units and suites). The inn also maintains a simple restaurant (run by yet another son), and offers personalized boat tours of the harbor from its own private dock.

22 Harris Island Rd., York, ME 03909. ✆ **888/860-7428** or 207/363-2868. www.docksidegq.com. 25 units. $117–$265 double; $236–$312 suite. Rates include breakfast. Closed Jan–Apr and closed Mon-Fri in May, Nov, and Dec. 2-night minimum stay in summer. Packages available. DISC, MC, V. From Rte. 1A in York Harbor, turn onto Rte. 103 and cross bridge over York River; make an immediate left and follow signs to end of road. **Amenities:** Restaurant; badminton; bike rentals; boat tours; croquet' rowboats. *In room:* A/C, TV, fireplace (some units), kitchenette (some units).

Edwards' Harborside Inn ★ 🎁 Work your way downhill off Rte. 1A toward the sprawling Stage Neck Inn and the public beach, and before you get there you'll come across a beautifully kept home on the water, with a private dock and a lawn whose Adirondack chairs possess wonderfully quaint views of fishing boats. Ten units vary from simple to elegant (the York Suite is also known as the "Spoil Me Suite," with its tiled Jacuzzi and water views on all sides); all are lovely and homey, with touches such as chocolates. Add in a fireplace in winter, hearty hospitality, board games for relaxing, and splendiferous views from the front rooms, and you've discovered a cozy sort of place you might never want to leave.

Stage Neck Rd. (P.O. Box 866), York Harbor, ME 03911. ✆ **800/273-2686** or 207/363-3037. www.edwardsharborside.com. 13 units (3 with shared bathroom). July–Aug and holidays $200–$240 double; $270–$350 suite; May–June and Sept–Oct $170–$200 double, $240–$270 suite; Nov–Apr $130–$160 double, $220–$250 suite. Rates include breakfast. Rates do not include 8% hotel service charge or 7% Maine state tax. Minimum stay some times of year. MC, V. *In room:* A/C.

Union Bluff Hotel ★★ With its turrets, dormers, and porches, the Union Bluff looks like a 19th-century beach hotel—but it was actually built in 1989, replacing the previous (circa 1870) version of the hotel, which had burned down. Inside, the hotel is modern if bland; but rooms have oak furniture, wall-to-wall carpeting, and small refrigerators, and the place is slowly morphing into a sort of boutique hotel. There are about 20 rooms in an annex next door, but the main inn's rooms and views are better—the best ones are the suites on the top floor, with beach vistas (and some Jacuzzis, fireplaces, and decks). It's amazing how low rates can plummet here midweek and off-season; but weekends, even before and after the summer, are quite expensive. The hotel's restaurant recently underwent a face-lift, and is excellent (see "Where to Dine," below). What to do? Step outside and you're a half-block from Short

---

📷 Jam Sessions in York

Need a souvenir but too weak with hunger to shop another minute? At **Stonewall Kitchen's** flagship store, on Stonewall Lane (✆ **207/351-2712**)—just behind the huge tourist information complex at the corner of Rte. 1 and the access road leading to and from I-95 and the Maine Turnpike—you can sample from among the company's delicious jams and spreads before tucking into a soup-and-sandwich special from the on-site deli (see "Where to Dine," below). Then, hunger and birthday lists both satisfied in one fell swoop, keep browsing through a good selection of handy kitchen accessories: knives, lobster bibs, graters, and the like. Staff is friendly and helpful. It's open daily until 8pm; the cafe, though, closes at 3pm.

Sands beach, T-shirt and shell shops, and a bowling alley and arcade. The hotel assigns one parking spot for each room, which is great because parking is supertight in summer in Short Sands; but if you've brought an RV or second car, you'll need to use the big town parking lot adjacent to the hotel—bring quarters. Lots of quarters.

8 Beach St. (P.O. Box 1860), York Beach, ME 03910. © **800/833-0721** or 207/363-1333. www.union bluff.com. 61 units. Mid-June to Aug $179–$379 double and suite; rest of the year $59–$289 double and suite. Packages available. AE, DISC, MC, V. **Amenities:** Restaurant; pub. *In room:* A/C, fireplace (some units), fridge (some units), Jacuzzi (some units).

York Harbor Inn ★★ Once known as the Hillcroft, the rambling York Harbor lords over the best views of York Harbor and the sea. It's also got some history of its own: the "Cabin Room" in the main building is made of original 1637 beams (once a sail loft) shipped over from the Isles of Shoals, and lanterns came from a trolley line that once ran along what is now the highway here. The basement pub has original hitching posts where travelers tied up horses as they drank. The handsome blue Harbor Crest building uphill is from the early 18th century, and contains wonderful tilework; another outbuilding dates from 1783. The main inn's 22 rooms are simplest, and are closest to the convivial basement pub. The adjacent Harbor Hill Inn contains the best units: all have Jacuzzis, gas fireplaces, heated bathrooms, CD players, and sea views, plus a hot tub out back. Nearby Harbor Cliffs is also a good choice, with breakfast included and a variety of room styles. The latest addition to this collection is actually the oldest building: the 1730 Harbor Crest Inn, a half-mile up the road, with wonderful common areas, porches, a variety of color schemes, king-size beds, big Jacuzzi tubs, and black-and-white tiled bathrooms.

Rte. 1A (P.O. Box 573), York Harbor, ME 03911. © **800/343-3869** or 207/363-5119. Fax 207/363-7151. www.yorkharborinn.com. 54 units. May–Oct $149–$349 double and suite (weekend rates may be higher); Nov–Apr $99–$349 double and suite (weekend rates may be higher). Packages available. Some rates include breakfast. AE, DISC, MC, V. **Amenities:** Restaurant; bar. *In room:* A/C, TV.

Where to Dine

In addition to the choices below, there are plenty of fried-fish joints but also several options that go beyond the usual takeout fare. On Rte. 1 in Kittery, not far north of the island bridge to Portsmouth, the **Beach Pea Baking Co.** (© **207/439-3555**) turns out outstanding sandwiches, breads, and pastries. Eat at one of the tables outside or on the front porch. Open Monday through Saturday until 6pm, it's closed Sunday.

York Village harbors **Fazio's,** 38 Woodbridge Rd. (turn just before the town library; © **207/363-7019**), a good Italian family restaurant with atmosphere. Directly on Long Sands in York Beach, **Sun & Surf** (© **207/363-2961**) has a takeout window proffering fried seafood and ice cream—but also a dining room with standout ocean views and an increasingly sophisticated menu that now incorporates steaks, salads, pastas, tuna, and lamb.

If you're hankering for nothing more complicated than simple Chinese takeout, have no fear. **Chun Ping Lau** (© **207/439-6055**) is a friendly place just north of the Kittery outlets on Rte. 1 serving amazingly inexpensive Cantonese and Szechuan combo plates of tofu, cashew chicken, egg rolls, and the like.

IN KITTERY

Bob's Clam Hut FRIED SEAFOOD Operating since 1956, Bob's manages to retain an old-fashioned flavor—despite now being surrounded on all sides by factory outlet malls, and with prices that have steadily escalated out of the "budget eats"

In York the best place for a picnic is on the beach—any of them. **Long Sands** (p. 80) and **Short Sands** (p. 80) are best: The former has views of a lighthouse and boats far out to sea; the latter is more compact and surrounded by quaintly appealing arcades, hotels, and grand summer homes. Parking can be tight at both—and tickets are written with regularity. Bring lots of quarters.

Speaking of that lighthouse, **Nubble Light** (p. 80) is hard to beat for the quintessential Maine postcard-view picnic. Reach it from Long Sands. If you need sweets, stock up at the **Goldenrod** (p. 85), a real live working candy shop just a block off Short Sands beach. For a bite, I like the **Long Sands General Store** (*✆* **206/363-5383**), near the northern end of Long Sands beach, with pizzas, sandwiches, and other essential picnicking supplies.

category. It still does one thing very well: fries up plump heaps of clams and other seafood for miles, sides them with french fries and coleslaw in baskets, and puts them out with tremendous efficiency. Order at the window, get a soda from the machine, and stake out a table inside or on the deck (with its lovely view of, er, Rte. 1) while waiting for your number to be called. The food is surprisingly light, cooked in cholesterol-free vegetable oil; the onion rings are especially good. Fish-and-chips are also on the menu. To ensure that your diet is irrevocably busted, Bob's also serves good New England–made ice cream at an adjacent scoop shop: now, that's just overkill. But count us in.

Rte. 1 (west side), Kittery. *✆* **207/439-4233.** www.bobsclamhut.com. Reservations not accepted. Sandwiches $4–$13; dinners $8–$29. AE, MC, V. Mon–Thurs, Sun 11am–7pm; Fri–Sat 11am–8pm.

IN THE YORKS

Brown's Old Fashioned Ice Cream ☺ ★ ICE CREAM A minute's walk uphill from Nubble Light and Sohier Park (see "Exploring Kittery & the Yorks, above), Brown's literally cranks out some of Maine's best homemade ice cream every summer from its lovely seaside perch. Kids pile into line to enjoy cones and sundaes made with the shack's churned ice cream, which comes in such interesting flavors as Indian pudding, Maine moose tracks, pumpkin, blueberry, Danish cream, and checkerberry. This isn't a gourmet ice cream scoop shop, just a fun and scenic place to lick a cone— the views from the weathered picnic tables are better than those from almost any hotel or resort in the state of Maine. Warning: the cones here are *huge*. And they melt fast. Plan to order a size smaller than you thought you wanted, and to eat faster than you planned.

Nubble Rd., Cape Neddick. No phone. Memorial Day to Labor Day, daily 11am–8pm. Cones $3–$6.

Fox's Lobster House ☺ SEAFOOD Fox's is unabashedly commercial, and charges more than it could, but so what? You're sitting outside, eating precracked lobsters and breathing salt air, on a headland that would be worth zillions in real estate terms. Looking straight at Nubble Light. Fox's has been here since 1966, and I can see why: It delivers a pretty intensively "Maine" experience just a few miles across the state line. You can also dine inside, in a wood-and-nautical-themed dining room, where you can get platters including side dishes: a better deal for families, just without that great lighthouse view. There's an ice-cream window for kids, as well.

8 Sohier Park Rd., Cape Neddick. *C* **207/363-2643.** Lobsters $25 and up. May–Oct, daily 11:30am–9pm.

Goldenrod Restaurant ☺ TRADITIONAL AMERICAN   Follow the neon to this beach-town classic—a York summer institution ever since it opened in 1896. It's easy to find: Look for visitors gawking through plate-glass windows at ancient machines hypnotically churning out taffy (millions of pieces a year). The restaurant, across from the candy-making operation, is low on frills but big on atmosphere: Diners sit on stout oak furniture around a stone fireplace or elbow-to-elbow at an antique soda fountain. Breakfast offerings are New England standards, and for lunch you can eat soups, burgers, and overpriced sandwiches. But what saves the place is the candy counter, where throngs line up to buy boxes of wax-wrapped taffy "kisses" (check the striping on each candy for its flavor; I like molasses and peppermint), almond-pocked birch bark, and other penny-candy treats. The shakes, malts, and sundaes are on the sweet side.

Railroad Rd. and Ocean Ave., York Beach. *C* **207/363-2621.** www.thegoldenrod.com. Lunch and dinner entrees $2–$8. MC, V. Memorial Day to Labor Day daily 8am–10pm (until 9pm in June); Labor Day to Columbus Day Wed–Sun 8am–3pm. Closed Columbus Day to Memorial Day.

Lobster Cove ☺ ★ SEAFOOD/FAMILY FARE   Right across the street from the pounding surf of Long Sands Beach, dependable Lobster Cove is a good choice when the family is too tired to drive far in search of a feed. And a "feed" is what you'll get here. Breakfast consists of standard, inexpensive choices such as omelets, pancakes, and eggs Benedict. Lunch runs to burgers and sandwiches, but dinner is prime time, when a standard shore dinner of lobster, corn on the cob, clam chowder, and steamed clams is hefty and good. Lobster pie is an old-fashioned New England favorite. They also do lobster rolls, clam rolls, steaks, broiled seafoods, and traditional Maine desserts such as wild blueberry pie and warm bread pudding with whiskey sauce.

756 York St., York (south end of Long Sands Beach). *C* **207/351-1100.** Main courses $7–$21. AE, MC, V. Daily 7:30am–9pm.

Stonewall Kitchen Café ★★ CAFE   Stonewall Kitchen's York-based gourmet foods operation has taken a step forward with this quality, inexpensive cafe, smartly located in its York headquarters/store right beside the local tourist information office. The cafe serves simple, hearty items such as fish chowder, changing soups, lobster rolls (and lobster BLTs), muffulettas (a New Orleans–style, olive-salami sandwich), turkey wraps with cranberry spread, and much more. Check the board to find out what's on daily. Finish with a dessert such as a lemon square, brownies, or fresh-baked cookies. The cafe kitchen also prepares gourmet meals to go.

Stonewall Lane (set back from U.S. Rte. 1), York. *C* **207/351-2719.** www.stonewallkitchen.com. Sandwiches and salads $7–$11. AE, DC, DISC, MC, V. Cafe seating Mon–Sat 8am–3pm, Sun 9am–3pm; takeout available until 4pm. See box p. 82 for store.

OGUNQUIT

15 miles NE of Kittery

Ogunquit (Oh-*gun*-quit) is a busy little beachside town that has attracted vacationers and artists for more than a century. Although it's certainly notable for the abundant and elegant summer-resort architecture, Ogunquit is probably most famous for the

3½-mile white-sand beach, backed by grassy dunes, that dominates the town. This beach serves as the town's front porch, and most everyone drifts over there at least once a day when the sun is shining. As a bonus, a wonderful walking trail known as the Marginal Way begins at the beach, then climbs the cliffs above tide pools to great views back onto the sand and ocean.

Ogunquit's fame as an art colony dates from around 1890, when Charles H. Woodbury arrived and declared the place an "artist's paradise." He was soon followed by artists such as Walt Kuhn, Elihu Vedder, and Yasuo Kuniyoshi, not to mention Rudolph Dirks, author of the "Katzenjammer Kids" comic. (During the latter part of the 19th century, the town later found another sort of fame as a quiet destination for gay regional travelers; today, many local enterprises here are still owned by gay proprietors.)

Despite its architectural grace and civility, the town is narrow—there's only one main street—and can become seriously overrun with tourists (and their cars) during peak summer season, especially on weekends. If you don't like crowds, try to visit in the shoulder seasons or simply visit another destination along the coast. Other advice: If you arrive early in the morning, stake out a spot on the long beach.

A pre-Halloween festival in late October, the **Ogunquit Fest,** offers 3 days of arts, crafts, costumes, and a parade; it's best for families with kids. Call ℂ **207/646-2939** for more information.

Essentials

GETTING THERE

Ogunquit is right on U.S. Rte. 1, exactly midway between York and Wells—which means it's a long way to either of the nearest convenient turnpike exits. Take either exit 7 (York) or exit 19 (Wells) off the Maine Turnpike, a toll road. Proceed to U.S. Rte. 1 and follow it north from York or south from Wells, turning seaward (left if you're traveling south, right if you're coming from the south) at the confusing intersection at the center of town (see below) and follow Shore Road to reach Perkins Cove and the bulk of the shops, accommodations, and eateries. Or, for the best beach access, take the other prong of the intersection to Beach Street.

VISITOR INFORMATION

The **Ogunquit Welcome Center,** P.O. Box 2289, Ogunquit, ME 03907 (ℂ **207/646-2939;** www.ogunquit.org), is on U.S. Rte. 1, just south of the village center. It's open daily from Memorial Day to Columbus Day (until 8pm weekends during the peak summer season), and Monday to Saturday during the off season. Helpfully, it has restrooms.

Take the Trolley

A number of trackless "trolleys" (ℂ **207/646-1411**)—actually buses—with names like *Dolly* and *Ollie* (you get the idea) run all day from mid-May to Columbus Day between Perkins Cove and the Wells town line to the north, with detours to the sea down Beach and Ocean streets. These trolleys are very handy, and they stop everywhere. (There's a map of stops posted online at **www.ogunquit.com/trolley.cfm.**) Rides cost $1.50 one-way (children free); it's worth the expense to avoid driving and parking hassles and limits.

GETTING AROUND

Ogunquit's entrance is a horrid three-way intersection that seems intentionally designed to cause massive traffic tie-ups. Parking in and around the village is tight and relatively expensive for small-town Maine ($6–$15 per day in various lots). As a result, the town is best navigated on foot or by bike.

Exploring Ogunquit

The village center is good for an hour or two of browsing among the boutiques, or sipping a cappuccino at one of the several coffee emporia. From the village, you can walk to scenic Perkins Cove along **Marginal Way ★★★**, a gorgeous mile-long ocean-side pathway that departs across from the Seacastles Resort on Shore Road. En route, it passes tide pools, pocket beaches, and rocky, fissured bluffs, all worth exploring. This is one of Maine's best public trails. The seascapes can be spectacular, but the Way can also get extremely crowded during fair-weather weekends or toward sunset. Early morning is a good time to avoid crowds.

Perkins Cove ★, accessible either from Marginal Way or by driving south on Shore Road and veering left at the Y-shaped intersection, is a small, well-protected harbor that attracts many visitors and is often heavily congested. A handful of galleries, restaurants, and T-shirt shops cater to the tourist trade from a cluster of quaint buildings between harbor and sea. (If teeming crowds and tourist enterprises are *not* the reason you came to Maine, steer clear of Perkins Cove.) An intriguing pedestrian drawbridge is operated by whoever happens to be handy.

Not far from the cove is the lovely, newly relocated **Ogunquit Museum of American Art ★★★**, 543 Shore Rd. (© **207/646-4909;** www.ogunquitmuseum. org), one of the best—and most beautiful—small art museums in the nation (that's not just me talking; the director of New York's Metropolitan Museum of Art said so, too). It's only open in summer and early fall, however. Set back from the road in a grassy glen overlooking the rocky shore, the museum's spectacular view initially overwhelms the artwork as visitors walk through the door. But stick around for a few minutes—the changing exhibits in this architecturally engaging modern building of cement block, slate, and glass will get your attention soon enough; its curators have a track record of staging superb shows and attracting national attention, and the permanent collection holds work by seascape master Marsden Hartley and many members of the Ogunquit Colony, including Woodbury, Hamilton Easter Field, and Robert Laurent. The museum is open from July to October, Monday to Saturday from 10am to 5pm and Sundays from 1pm to 5pm. Admission costs $7 for adults, $5 for seniors, and $4 for students; it's free for all children 11 and under.

For evening entertainment, head for the **Ogunquit Playhouse ★** (© **207/646-2402**), a 750-seat summer-stock theater right on U.S. Rte. 1 (just south of the main town intersection) with an old-style look that has garnered a solid reputation for its careful, serious attention to stagecraft. The theater has entertained Ogunquit since 1933, attracting noted actors such as Bette Davis, Tallulah Bankhead, and Sally Struthers performing in shows like *A Chorus Line* and *Guys and Dolls*. Performance tickets generally cost in the range of $30 to $45 per person, and the season runs from mid-May through mid-October.

Another evening alternative is the tiny summer-stock **Booth Theatre,** at the Betty Doon Motor Hotel, Village Square (© **207/646-8142;** www.boothproductions. com). Summer season runs for about 11 weeks. Recent shows have included favorites such as *Snoopy!*, *Nunsense,* and *Kiss Me Kate*. Tickets are inexpensive, about $20 for adults and less for seniors and students.

Beaches

Ogunquit's **main beach ★★** is more than 3 miles long, though its width varies with the tides. This beach appeals to everyone: the livelier scene at the south end near the town itself; the more remote and unpopulated stretches to the north, with their sand dunes; and the clusters of summer homes that lie beyond. The most popular access point is the foot of Beach Street, which runs into Ogunquit Village. This beach ends at a sandy spit, where the Ogunquit River flows into the sea; here you'll find a handful of informal restaurants. It's also the most crowded part of the beach. Less congested options are **Footbridge Beach** (turn on Ocean Ave. off Rte. 1 north of the village center) and **Moody Beach** (turn on Eldridge Ave. in Wells). Restrooms and changing rooms are maintained at all three beaches.

A Side Trip to Laudholm Farm

About 8 miles north of Ogunquit (bear right from Rte. 1 onto Rte. 9 just north of the beach town of Wells) is **Laudholm Farm ★** (② 207/646-4521), a historic saltwater farm owned by the nonprofit Laudholm Trust since 1986. The 1,600-acre property was originally the summer home of 19th-century railroad baron George Lord, but is now used for estuarine research. The farm has 7 miles of trails through diverse ecosystems, which range from salt marsh to forest to dunes. A visitor center in the regal Victorian farmhouse will get you oriented. Tours are available, or you can explore the grounds on your own. Parking costs $2 per adult (or $10 per car, whichever is less) daily from Memorial Day through Labor Day, $1 per guest 6 to 16. You pay by donation the rest of the year. There's never an admission charge to the grounds or visitor center, and the 7 miles of trails here are open daily from 7am to dusk. The visitor center is open 10am to 4pm Monday to Saturday and noon to 4pm on Sunday (closed weekends in the off season, also closed mid-Dec to mid-Jan).

The farm is reached by turning east from Rte. 1 on Laudholm Farm Road at the blinking light just north of Harding Books. Bear left at the fork, then turn right into the farm's entrance.

Where to Stay

In addition to the selections below, there are many family-owned budget to moderately priced motel operations around town. Simply cruising Rte. 1 can yield dividends (don't forget your AAA card if you're a member). In July and August you'll be hard-pressed to find a bargain, but try the following three economical choices first for a combination of affordability and amenities.

The family-friendly **Colonial Village Resort** (② 800/422-3341; www.colonial villageresort.com) on Rte. 1 is not a resort—but with two pools, a Jacuzzi, tennis court, free doughnuts, coin-op laundries, a few weekly rental cottages and apartments, and free rowboats to get you across the tidal river to the beach, it's almost a steal for families on the go most of the year. Most rooms contain kitchenettes consisting of stovetops, microwaves, and full-size refrigerators. It's usually open from April until December, with double rooms starting as low as $54; summer rates, however, begin at around $160 per night.

Just a few steps from Ogunquit's main downtown intersection is the meticulously maintained **Studio East Motel**, 267 Main St. (② 207/646-7297; www.studioeast motel.com). It's open April to mid-November, with peak-season rates running from $99 to $169 double. The rooms are basic, but all have refrigerators, telephones, and

Ogunquit

ATTRACTIONS ●
Laudholm Farm **1**
Ogunquit Museum of
American Art **25**

ACCOMMODATIONS ■
Above Tide Inn **9**
Beachmere Inn **16**
Cliff House Resort &
Spa **26**
Colonial Village Resort **2**
Dunes on the Waterfront **3**
Grand Hotel **19**
Marginal Way
House & Motel **10**
Nellie Littlefield House **13**
Riverside Motel **24**
Studio East Motel **6**
Terrace by the Sea **11**

DINING ◆
Amore Breakfast **17**
Arrows **15**
Barnacle Billy's **21**
Bread & Roses Bakery **7**
Cove Cafe **20**
Egg & I **5**
Fancy That **8**
Five-O Shore Road **12**
La Pizzeria's **14**
MC Perkins Cove **23**
98 Provence **18**
Oarweed **22**
Ogunquit Lobster
Pound **4**
Village Food Market **8**

5

SOUTHERN MAINE | Ogunquit

---

televisions, and there are a few two-bedroom suites. Microwaves are available for free to those staying 3 nights or more. And the quiet **Riverside Motel,** 50 Riverside Lane (© **207/646-2741;** www.riversidemotel.com), has great marina views and Wi-Fi, as well as a convenient footbridge leading directly over the tidal inlet to Perkins Cove, which saves you the parking hassles and fees. Rooms here run $99 to $209 double, depending on the season.

Another upscale choice in addition to those listed below is **Terrace by the Sea,** 23 Wharf Lane (© **207/646-3232;** www.terracebythesea.com), with great sea views, a nice heated outdoor pool, and excellent customer service. Eight of the motel-style rooms have kitchenettes. From late May through October, rates range from $69 to $242 double; in the shoulder seasons (late Mar to late May and Nov to mid-Dec), they range from $52 to $182 double. Children 5 and under are welcome in the off season. The inn is closed from early December through late March.

Beachmere Inn ★★ ☺ In a town of motels, simple B&B's, and condos, the Beachmere excels. Operated by the same family since 1937, this quiet, well-run cliff-top inn sprawls across a scenic lawn where repeat visitors have reclined for decades. Nearly every unit gives you an amazing look up or down the beach, and all have

Cruising the Wells-Ogunquit axis, foodies will want to check out venerable **Congdon's Doughnuts Family Restaurant & Bakery ★★** (© 207/646-4219) on Rte. 1 between the two towns. Clint and Dot "Nana" Congdon moved to Maine and opened a family style restaurant in 1945; Nana's sinkers proved so popular that she relocated the whole operation to Wells 10 years later and went into the doughnut business full-time. Chocolate-chocolate is ever-popular, but you can't go wrong with almost anything else among the dozens of choices—pillowy raised doughnuts; filled blueberry doughnuts; butter crunch, honey-dipped, sugar twist, and chocolate honey doughnuts . . . or one of the seasonal specials such as maple, apple, or pumpkin doughnuts. You can also eat diner meals here, most of which involve fried food and/or breakfast fare. Despite a newish drive-through window, this place retains its original character (and that includes the local characters dining inside). The secret? They use lard. Yes, lard. Schedule the EKG now. Congdon's is open daily, except Wednesdays, year-round from 6am to 2pm.

kitchenettes. The original Victorian section dates from the 1890s and is the most fun; it's all turrets, big porches, angles, and bright beachy interiors. Next door is the modern Beachmere South, with spacious rooms and plenty of private balconies or patios—those on the end have absolutely knockout views. A new wing (Beachmere West) was added in 2008, with a small but nice little hot tub, exercise room, and children's play area; units in this wing have sitting rooms and bigger bathrooms. The adjacent Marginal Way footpath (see above) is terrific for walks and beach access, and groups can inquire about several off-property cottages a short walk away. The inn's now open year-round: you can rent snowshoes in winter to (carefully) stroll the path.

62 Beachmere Place, Ogunquit, ME 03907. © **800/336-3983** or 207/646-2021. Fax 207/646-2231. www.beachmereinn.com. 53 units. June–Aug $175–$250 double, $275–$380 suite, $460 cottage; May and Sept to mid-Oct $105–$220 double, $195–$265 suite, $270–$305 cottage; Apr and mid-Oct $95–$160 double, $155–$195 suite, $235 cottage. Rates include continental breakfast. 3-night minimum in summer. AE, DC, DISC, MC, V. **Amenities:** Lounge; beach access; children's play room; Jacuzzi. *In room:* A/C, fireplaces (in some), kitchenettes (in some), patios and balconies (in some).

Cliff House Resort and Spa ★★ This complex of modern buildings replaced a former grand hotel, and now offers some of the best hotel-room ocean views in Maine: nearly a 360-degree panorama, in some cases. There are a number of different styles of rooms, most with comforts such as digital televisions and recliners; other updates include new beds and furniture in the Cliffscape wing and a covered corridor linking all terraces and guest rooms with the dining areas. A vanishing-edge pool fronting the sea does indeed seem to disappear into the blue yonder, and there's an upscale restaurant with knockout vistas. The state-of-the-art spa and fitness facility dispenses a wide range of soothing treatments and exercise programs.

Shore Rd. (P.O. Box 2274), Ogunquit, ME 03907. © **207/361-1000.** Fax 207/361-2122. www.cliffhouse maine.com. 200 units. July–Aug $265–$385 double and suite, mid-Apr to June and Sept-Nov $160–$335 double and suite. Meal plans available. 3-night minimum stay July–Aug and holiday weekends; 2-night minimum other weekends. Packages available. No children in "spa room" units. AE, DISC, MC, V. Closed Dec to mid-Apr. **Amenities:** Restaurant; bar; fitness center; Jacuzzi; indoor pool; 2 outdoor pools; room service; spa. *In room:* A/C, TV, hair dryer.

The Dunes on the Waterfront ★★   This classic motor court (built ca. 1936) has made the transition into the modern luxury age more gracefully than any other vintage motel I've seen. It has one six-unit motel-like building, but most of the rooms are in gabled cottages of white clapboard and green shutters; these have full kitchens and bathrooms. Plenty of old-fashioned charm remains in many of the units, with vintage maple furnishings, oval braided rugs, maple floors, knotty pine paneling, and louvered doors. Most of the cottages also have wood-burning fireplaces. The complex is set on 12 acres, wedged between busy Rte. 1 and the ocean, but somehow stays quiet and peaceful; Adirondack chairs overlook a lagoon, and guests can borrow a rowboat to get across to the beach.

518 U.S. Rte. 1 (P.O. Box 917), Ogunquit, ME 03907. © **888/295-3863.** www.dunesmotel.com. 36 units. $95–$345 double; $160–$435 cottage. July–Aug 1-week minimum stay in cottages; 3-night minimum stay in motel. All other weekends, 2-night minimum stay in motel. MC, V. Closed Nov to late Apr. **Amenities:** Outdoor pool; watersports equipment rental. *In room:* A/C, TV, fridge.

Marginal Way House and Motel ★   This simple, old-fashioned compound centers on a four-story, mid-19th-century guesthouse with summery, basic rooms and white-painted furniture; the whole complex is plunked down on a large, grassy lot on a quiet cul-de-sac, and it's hard to believe you're smack in the middle of busy Ogunquit. But you are: the beach and village are each just a few minutes' walk away. Room no. 7, despite its skinny twin beds, has a private porch and canopy and ocean views. The main building is surrounded by four more contemporary buildings that lack charm, but rooms here are mostly comfortable and bright; the "motel" building only has rooms with double beds, but the Wharf House has a cool quietude about it, enhanced by white linens and shady trees. Some units have little decks with views; all rooms have refrigerators and televisions, but none have phones. The property also maintains some one- and two-bedroom efficiency apartments (some have minimum stays); inquire when booking.

22-24 Wharf Lane (P.O. Box 697), Ogunquit, ME 03907. © **207/646-8801.** www.marginalwayhouse. com. 30 units (1 with private bathroom down hall). Early June to Labor Day $86–$208 double; mid-Apr to early June and early Sept to Oct $49–$146 double. $15 extra charge for more than 2 people (except kids under 3). Minimum stay requirements some weekends. MC, V. Closed Nov to mid-Apr. Pets allowed in off season only; advance notice required. *In room:* A/C (most units), TV, fridge, no phone.

Nellie Littlefield House ★★ 🎁   Of the many B&Bs and boardinghouses filling downtown Ogunquit, this might be the friendliest. The handsome 1889 home stands at the edge of the town's compact commercial district, and features elegant Queen Anne–style detailing. All rooms are carpeted and feature a mix of modern and antique reproduction furnishings; several have refrigerators. Rooms to the rear have private decks, although views are limited—mostly looking out on a motel next door. The most spacious room is the third-floor J. H. Littlefield suite, with two televisions and a Jacuzzi tub, and the most unique unit is probably the circular Grace Littlefield room in the upper turret, overlooking the street. The basement features a compact fitness room. Hospitality remains a strong selling point here.

27 Shore Rd. (P.O. Box 1341), Ogunquit, ME 03907. © **207/646-1692.** www.visit-maine.com/nellielittle fieldhouse. 8 units. June–Sept $108–$230 double; Mar–May and Oct–Dec $85–$170 double. Holiday rates higher. Rates include full breakfast. 3-night minimum on high-season weekends and holidays. DISC, MC, V. Closed Jan–Feb. Children 13 and older are welcome. **Amenities:** Fitness center. *In room:* A/C, TV, fridge (some units), Jacuzzi (few units).

Where to Dine

The main strip, where Rte. 1 converges with Perkins Cove Road, is packed with a tremendous variety of bakeries, coffee shops, markets, and restaurants, and this has got to be the latest-open-hours town in Maine: Amazingly, many places stay open until 10 or 11pm in summer. Among them is **Bread & Roses Bakery,** 246 Main St. (℗ **207/646-4227**), whose kitchen skillfully turns out cupcakes, peanut-butter-and-chocolate cake, raspberry mousse, cookies, and the like; there's outdoor seating as well. **Fancy That** (℗ **207/646-4118**) is a cafe nearby with sandwiches, hot panini, slices of Boston cream and other pies, and a Wi-Fi–equipped patio great for people-watching. The **Village Food Market,** 230 Main St. (℗ **877/646-2122** or 207/646-2122), stocks good wines, ready-to-go meals, and staples, and it also has a small deli; try the house red-eye coffee.

There are also myriad breakfast-only places scattered about the town. In addition to the excellent Amore (below), check out the reliable **Egg & I,** 501 Main St. (Rte. 1; ℗ **207/646-8777**), and the little **Cove Café,** 4 Oarweed Rd. (℗ **207/646-2422**), near Perkins Cove. Or, if you're not in the mood for a fancy dinner, **La Pizzeria's,** 239 Main St. (℗ **207/646-1143**), sandwiches, meatballs, and pizza pies are as dependable as the name—plus it's friendly and stays open later than just about anyplace else in Maine (usually until 11pm in summer). Like most places in town, though, it's closed in winter.

There are also several lobster pounds packed into and around the little downtown, most of them seasonal (sometime in Apr through Labor Day or Columbus Day). Try the **Ogunquit Lobster Pound** (504 Main St.; ℗ **207/646-2516**), **Oarweed** (65 Perkins Cove Rd.; ℗ **207/646-4022**), or **Barnacle Billy's** (Perkins Cove Rd.; ℗ **800/866-5575** or 207/646-5575).

Amore Breakfast ★ 🍴 BREAKFAST   Now relocated to Ogunquit's Perkins Cove neighborhood, Amore is a breakfast-only place—but what a breakfast it is. Look for numerous variations on the eggs Benedict theme (including a popular one with a big hunk of lobster on top), plus Belgian waffles, wonderful bananas Foster–style French toast with pecans outside and cream cheese inside, and more than a dozen types of yummy omelets. Coffee is from a small-batch San Diego coffee roaster. And they've got heart, too: Annual benefit meals are held, with the proceeds going to CARE packages for a Dominican orphanage. Italian owner Leanne Cusimano deserves (and gets local) kudos. This is *not* a place for waist-watchers. But, hey, you're on vacation, right?

309 Shore Rd. ℗ **866/641-6661** or 207/646-6661. www.amorebreakfast.com. Breakfast items $5–$14. MC, V. Summer daily 7am–1pm; off season closed Wed–Thurs. Closed Dec to mid Apr.

Arrows ★★★ NEW AMERICAN   When owner/chefs Mark Gaier and Clark Frasier opened Arrows in a gray farmhouse outside town in 1988, they quickly put Ogunquit on the national culinary map (and it's still ranked among the nation's top 15 by *Gourmet* magazine). They've done so not only by creating an elegant and intimate atmosphere, but by serving some of the freshest, most innovative cooking in New England. The emphasis is on local products—often very local. The salad greens are grown in gardens on the grounds, and much of the rest is produced or raised locally. The food transcends traditional New England fare and is deftly prepared with exotic twists and turns. The menu changes nightly, but among the more popular recurring appetizers is the house-cured prosciutto—hams are hung in the restaurant to cure in the off season. Entrees might include some interpretation of lobster; wild salmon in four preparations (including a portion steamed with pine needles); roasted

WHAT COULD BE FINER THAN A MAINE diner?

One thing you'll notice as you traverse the Maine coast is a preponderance of diners.

What gives? This isn't New Jersey, after all, yet the humble diner remains as much a culinary staple of coastal Maine as the lobster shack—probably more so, in fact. Locals congregate daily in their kaffeeklatsches on the diner stools; expect a steady stream of hunting caps, thick accents, doughnuts and eggs, and Red Sox or Patriots talk (depending on the season). You'd do well to sample one or two of them while on the road. Here are a few that are easily reached if you're taking Rte. 1.

From the New Hampshire state line heading north, your first opportunity on Rte. 1 comes rather quickly, almost on top of the town line that separates York from Kittery a few miles north of the Kittery outlets. **York's Best Seafood** (✆ **207/439-3401**) has been serving heralded fried clams and other local diner favorites in this location (though under several names) since 1945, and remains a steady favorite among locals.

Heading north from York to Ogunquit along Rte. 1, you could easily blow right by the reddish-hut icon that is **Flo's Steamed Hot Dogs** (no phone) in Cape Neddick—a couple of miles north of York, in the middle of nowhere, at a bend in the road—without noticing. But if you crave a winner of a wiener, screech to a halt in the dirt parking lot and give it a whirl. You'll wait in the line, which resembles an assembly line: The steamed dogs here with "special sauce" are cheap ($2) and good, but they can only do them 50 at a time. If your dog's number 51, bring a paperback. There are only six seats, so you'll probably have to eat in the car, too. Come anyway. The hut is closed Wednesdays, and they don't take credit cards—what did you expect?

A little farther north, also on Rte. 1 but in Wells, the **Maine Diner** (✆ **207/646-4441**) is a classic, though perhaps getting a little too famous for its own good. (They'll page you when a table is ready.) But worry not, there's a reason why they've just passed the "four million served" mark. The lobster pie and hot lobster roll are famous and delicious, as is a plate of baked scallops. Red flannel hash? Pot roast? They've got it—as well as the "Clam-o-rama," a sampler of clam items. They serve wine and beer here, too—very unusual.

An entire book could be written about **Moody's Diner** (✆ **207/832-7785**) in Waldoboro—in fact, it has. This is *the* place to stop on Rte. 1 when traversing north toward Acadia and points beyond. From the sublime cream pies to the only-in-Maine specials (boiled dinner on Thurs, haddock with egg sauce on Fri, and of course, baked beans on Sat), the place simply serves food you can find almost nowhere else in the state. The old food ways are disappearing that fast. Finish with Indian pudding or one of those mile-high pies—walnut cream and rhubarb are two good choices, though any of them will satisfy. The prices, too, seem nearly locked in 1948, when Moody's opened.

Finally, way farther downeast, I'd be remiss if I didn't mention the two **Helen's** restaurants, one on Rte. 1 in Ellsworth just north of the Rte. 3 split (✆ **207/667-2433**), and another, truly timeless one (expect sweet ladies waiting on you) on Main Street in downtown Machias (✆ **207/255-8423**). Though neither eatery is, strictly speaking, a diner, they serve some of the very best home-cooked meals and pies in all of the great state o' Maine, in fine old diner tradition. Look for seasonal specials such as turkey with the fixings, pork with fiddleheads, or just order a piece of the marvelous seasonal blueberry, strawberry, chocolate cream, or other widely renowned pies.

Bread & Breakfast

A good spot for bread and snacks in southern Maine is **Borealis Breads** (ℂ 207/641-8800), between Ogunquit and Kennebunkport on the east side of U.S. Rte. 1 in a strip mall just north of the turnoff to Wells Beach. (Look for the Aubuchon hardware store.) You'll find a good selection of hearty, warm-from-the-oven breads, plus sandwiches, local specialties, and macaroons. Open daily, it's a good pit stop before an afternoon on the beach.

squab in a "crystal lantern" with tangerine and fermented black beans; or halibut cooked three ways. The wine list is top-rate. Note that there is a moderate dress code: jackets preferred for men, and no shorts allowed.

41 Berwick Rd. ℂ **207/361-1100.** www.arrowsrestaurant.com. Reservations strongly recommended. Main courses $41–$43; tasting menus $95–$135. MC, V. July to Labor Day Tues–Sun 6–9:30pm; rest of the year, call ahead for open hours or check website. Closed Jan–Mar. From town center, turn uphill onto Berwick Rd. at Key Bank and drive 2 miles to restaurant on your right.

Five-O Shore Road ★★ SEAFOOD/NEW AMERICAN   A fine choice if you're looking for a more casual alternative to the more formal restaurants listed, Five-O is one of those spots where just reading the menu is a decent evening's entertainment. Chef Zachary Crosby has transformed a formerly Caribbean-inspired menu into one that roams around the map. You might eat a chargrilled filet or rope-caught local mussels, but also duck nachos, escargot with shallots, local mussels roasted with almonds, wild salmon poached in a lobster-saffron bullion, mole-spiced pork, or fresh haddock stuffed with seafood. Of course, you can get a Maine lobster in season, too, perhaps served over a bed of mussels steamed with blue cheese, sweet cream, and cracked pepper. There's also a cool cocktail lounge and club, and a strong wine list. Is this Maine or Manhattan? Either way, it's a winner.

50 Shore Rd. ℂ **207/646-5001.** www.five-oshoreroad.com. Reservations strongly recommended in summer. Small plates $8–$13, main courses $14–$32. AE, DISC, MC, V. May to early Sept Mon–Fri 5–9pm, Sat–Sun 11am–2pm and 5–9pm; call for hours outside peak season.

MC Perkins Cove ★★ SEAFOOD/NEW AMERICAN   The loss of the original Hurricane in Ogunquit could have been a serious blow to Ogunquit diners, but chef-partners Mark Gaier and Clark Frasier (the "M" and "C" in "MC") of Arrows (see above) opened this bistro in its place, which manages to be fun rather than stuffy. Okay, no bathing suits are allowed in the dining room, but still: Expect big food, even on the "small" plates. Lobster rolls, chopped salads, calamari, oysters on half shell, and crab cakes give way to more sophisticated starters such as mussels in curry sauce, rustic pizzas of ham and apple, or house-cured smoked salmon with dill. Entrees might include steamed lobster, sesame-encrusted trout, Kobe burgers, grilled tuna, hanger steak, or a piece of plank-roasted fish, plus one of the so-labeled "evil carbos" (french fries, onion rings, and so forth). Desserts are wonderful: brown-butter brownies with vanilla ice cream, burnt orange caramel, and candied orange peel; mini whoopee pies; a bittersweet chocolate cake with chocolate sauce and pistachio crème anglaise; or peppermint stick ice cream with cookies.

111 Perkins Cove Rd. ℂ **207/646-6263.** www.mcperkinscove.com. Reservations recommended. Lunch entrees $8–$19; dinner entrees $19–$31. DC, DISC, MC, V. Late May to mid Oct daily 11:30am–2pm and 5:30–11pm; rest of the year closed Tues. Closed Jan.

98 Provence ★★ FRENCH The good food in this town just keeps coming. Chef Pierre Gignac incorporates local ingredients such as lobster in his French bistro–style menu; he has gained a solid local following as a result. Begin with lobster cooked in puff pastry with a sherried honey-ginger cream; a Provencal fish stew; escargots with a Parmesan crisp and some black trumpet mushrooms; a rabbit fricassee; or the daily soup or mussel dish. That's right: a daily mussel dish. Move on to veal with wild mushrooms, a grilled boar chop with a chestnut croquette and pomegranate sauce; braised beef short ribs; a cassoulet of duck confit, lamb shoulder, and pork sausage; rack of lamb roasted with cumin and garlic; or the catch of the day. There's now also a daily bistro fixed-price menu with lighter items (and prices). Look for things like vichyssoise, stewed chicken, and lemon tart, for instance, or soft-shell crab with halibut confit and Provence-style nougat, served frozen. The summery, classy interior decor is as close as you'll get in New England to Provence. An outstanding place to dine.

262 Shore Rd. ✆ **207/646-9898.** www.98provence.com. Reservations recommended. Main courses $23–$28; fixed-price menus $29–$39. AE, MC, V. Summer Wed–Mon 5:30–9:30pm; off season Thurs–Mon 5:30–9pm.

THE KENNEBUNKS ★★

10 miles NE of Ogunquit

"The Kennebunks" consist of the side-by-side villages of **Kennebunk** and **Kennebunkport,** both situated along the shores of small rivers and both claiming a portion of rocky coast. The region was first settled in the mid-1600s and flourished after the American Revolution, when ship captains, boat builders, and prosperous merchants constructed imposing, solid homes. The Kennebunks are famed for their striking historical architecture and expansive beaches; make time to explore both.

A quick primer: Kennebunk proper begins just south of the Kennebunk River bridge, stretching south and inland to the junction of Rte. 9 and Rte. 1. This is where you'll find the White Barn Inn, Tom's of Maine, and a few fast-food joints. The town also includes, a few miles to the east, the beachside community of Kennebunk Beach.

Kennebunkport's compact, trim downtown begins across the Kennebunk River, on the north side, and extends eastward to take in both million-dollar oceanfront homes (including the Bush family estate at Walker's Point) and the fishing village of Cape Porpoise.

While summer is the busy season along the coast, winter has its charms: The grand architecture is better seen through leafless trees. When the snow flies, guests find solace in front of a fire at one of the inviting inns.

Essentials
GETTING THERE

Kennebunk is just off exit 25 of the Maine Turnpike; follow signs east into town. You can also get here by taking Rte. 1 from York and Ogunquit. To reach Kennebunkport, exit for Kennebunk and continue through town on Port Road (Rte. 35) 3½ miles. At the traffic light, turn left and cross the small bridge.

VISITOR INFORMATION

The **Kennebunk-Kennebunkport Chamber of Commerce,** 17 Western Ave. (P.O. Box 740), Kennebunk, ME 04043 (✆ **800/982-4421** or 207/967-0857; www.visit thekennebunks.com), can answer questions year-round by phone or at its offices in Lower Village beside the H.B. Provisions grocery store. The **Kennebunkport**

Information Center (© 207/967-8600), operated by an association of local businesses, is off Dock Square (next to Ben & Jerry's) and is open daily in summer and fall.

Several higher-end inns in the Kennebunks offer free shuttles downtown. Otherwise, a local 'trolley' (actually a bus) makes several convenient stops in and around the two towns and also serves the best of the local beaches; it picks up passengers about once per hour from 10am until 4pm (until 3pm in spring and fall). It's expensive, though: the fare comes in the form of a day pass costing $15 per adult or $5 per child. At least the pass includes unlimited opportunities to jump on and off the trolley during the day you are using it. Call © 207/967-3686 for more details, or check the trolley's schedule online at **www.intowntrolley.com**.

Exploring Kennebunk

Kennebunk's downtown is inland, just off the turnpike, and is a dignified, compact commercial center of white clapboard and brick. If you're a history buff, the **Brick Store Museum ★**, 117 Main St. (© 207/985-4802; www.brickstoremuseum.org) should be your first stop in town. The museum hosts showings of historical art and artifacts throughout the summer, switching to contemporary art in the off season. It also holds considerable local archives. The museum is housed in a former brick store plus three adjacent buildings, all renovated and re-polished. Admission is free (though a $5 per person donation is suggested), and half-hour **walking tours ★** cost $5 per person additional. (They're a must, if you have time and interest.) The museum is open Tuesday to Friday 10am to 4:30pm, Saturdays from 10am to 1pm.

When en route to or from the coast, be sure to note the extraordinary homes that line Port Road (Rte. 35). This includes the famously elaborate **Wedding Cake House ★**, which you should be able to identify all on your own. Local lore claims that the house was built by a guilt-ridden ship captain who left for sea before his bride could enjoy a proper wedding cake.

Exploring Kennebunkport

Kennebunkport is the summer home of former President George Bush (the elder), whose family has summered here for decades, and it has the tweedy, upper-crust feel that one might expect of the place. This historic village, whose streets were laid out during days of travel by boat and horse, is subject to traffic jams. If the municipal lot off the square is full, go north on North Street a few minutes to the free long-term lot and catch the trolley back into town. Or walk back—it's a pleasant walk of 10 or 15 minutes from the satellite lot back to Dock Square.

Dock Square has a bustling, mercantile feel to it, with low buildings of mixed vintages and styles. The boutiques in the area are attractive, and many feature creative artworks and crafts. But sometimes it gets a little overcrowded or tacky here. Kennebunkport's *real* attraction is found in the surrounding blocks and side streets, where the side streets are lined with one of the nation's richest assortments of Early American homes. These neighborhoods are especially ripe with examples of Federal-style homes; many have been converted to fine B&Bs (see "Where to Stay," below).

Aimless wandering is a good tactic for exploring Kennebunkport, but at the least make an effort to stop by the **Richard A. Nott House ★★**, 8 Maine St. (© 207/967-2751), during your travels. Situated on Maine Street at the head of Spring Street, this imposing Greek Revival house was built in 1853 with sturdy Doric columns and remains a Victorian-era dream. It remained untouched by the Nott family through the years and was donated to the local historical society with the stipulation that it remain forever unchanged. The period furniture, wallpapers, and rugs will amaze you if you're into that era. The in-house tours run about 40 minutes; it's open from July through early October, 10am to 4pm and 7 to 9pm Thursday to Friday, 10am to 1pm on Saturdays. Admission is $7 for adults, free for children. The local historical **walking tours** ★ departing from here in summer are even better, some of the best on the Maine coast.

Ocean Drive from Dock Square to **Walkers Point** ★ and beyond is lined with opulent summer homes overlooking surf and rocky shore. You'll likely recognize the Bush family compound right out on Walkers Point when you arrive. If it's not familiar from the time it has spent in the national spotlight, look for crowds with telephoto lenses. If they're not out, look for a shingle-style secret service booth at the head of a driveway. That's the place. There's nothing to do here, though, but park for a minute, snap a picture, and then push on.

St. Anthony's Franciscan Monastery ★ This monastery is a peaceful spot for walks through quiet grounds, chapels, and sculptures. The estate and property were purchased by Lithuanian Franciscans in 1947, who then added the grotto, statuary, and worship spaces. There's a section of sculpture from the Vatican Pavilion at the 1964/1965 World's Fair, a chapel, an outdoor shrine, English gardens, statues, and a walking trail with some of the best river views in town. Park in the visitor's lot and be respectful of the grounds. The White Barn Inn (p. 98) is across the road.

North side of Beach Ave., less than ½ mile from Lower Village and the intersection of Rte. 9 and Rte. 35, Kennebunk. Daily dawn–dusk. Free admission.

The Seashore Trolley Museum ☺ A short drive north of Kennebunkport is a little local marvel: a scrap yard masquerading as a museum. (The "world's oldest and largest museum of its type." Um, okay.) Quirky and engaging, the museum was founded in 1939 to preserve a disappearing way of life, and today the collection boasts more than 200 trolleys, including specimens from Glasgow, Moscow, San Francisco, and Rome. Naturally, there's also a streetcar named *Desire* from New Orleans. About 40 of the cars still operate, and the admission charge includes rides on a 2-mile track. Other cars, some of which still contain early-20th-century advertising, are on display outdoors and in vast storage sheds.

195 Log Cabin Rd., Kennebunkport. ℂ **207/967-2800.** www.trolleymuseum.org. Admission $8 adults, $5.50 children 6–16, $6 seniors. Mid-May to mid Oct daily 10am–5pm; early to mid-May and mid- to late Oct Sat–Sun 10am–5pm. Closed Nov–Apr. Head north from Kennebunkport on North St. for 1¾ miles; look for signs.

South Congregational Church ★★ To me, one of Kennebunkport's lasting images is the enormous clock face of this whitewashed, meetinghouse-style church (built 1824), down a lane off Dock Square and close to the tidal river. The huge clock faces are the originals, and are made of wood (which is very unusual); they no longer keep the correct time, but this is still as lovely a church as you'll find in southern Maine. Inside, the simple spare theme continues but for some stained glass work and an outsized, impressively columnar pipe organ—though it's only from 2004.

2 North St. at Temple St., just off Spring St. ℂ **207/967-2793.** Office hours Mon–Fri 9am–2pm, Sun services 10:30am.

Beaches

The coastal area around Kennebunkport is home to several of the state's best beaches. Southward across the river (technically, this is Kennebunk, though it's much

THE beach AT PARSON'S WAY

It's certainly one of the most attractive *approaches* to a beach in Maine, and Parson's Beach itself is lovely and much less crowded than others in the area. Find the beach by heading south on Rte. 9 from Dock Square in Kennebunkport, through the traffic light; just after you cross a marsh and the Mousam River, hang a left onto Parson's Beach Road.

You'll drive down a country lane lined with maples. At the end, there's limited parking, though you can also park on the north side of the highway if it's full. This is not the best beach on the southern Maine coast for swimming—it's rocky at the mouth of the river—but it's great for lounging and reading. Be on your best behavior here. (Don't trample the dunes, don't take stuff from the tide pool, and so on.) You have to cross private land to reach the beach, and signs ominously proclaim that access can be denied at any time if the landowner so chooses.

closer to Kennebunkport) are **Gooch's Beach ★★** and **Kennebunk Beach ★★**. Head eastward on Beach Street (from the intersection of routes 9 and 35) past the White Barn Inn (below), and in a few minutes you'll wind into a handsome colony of eclectic shingled summer homes. The narrow road continues twisting past sandy beaches and rocky headlands, and this section is well worth exploring for its summer mansions and golf course, too. Hard to believe, but it sometimes gets congested along this beach in summer; avoid the gridlock by exploring on foot or by bike. Very important, you *cannot park here* if you are not a resident—unless you've moseyed down to the police station on Rte. 1 and bought a temporary parking permit, which few summer visitors know to do. (Some local inns and hotels will give you a temporary day pass.) Again, if you can avoid bringing a car to the beach, do.

Goose Rocks Beach ★, north of Kennebunkport off Rte. 9 (watch for signs), is a good choice for those who like their crowds light and prefer beaches to beach scenes. You'll find an enclave of beach homes set amid rustling oaks just off a fine sand beach. Just offshore is a narrow barrier reef that has historically attracted flocks of geese, hence the name.

Where to Stay
VERY EXPENSIVE

White Barn Inn ★★★   As it has long done, the venerable White Barn goes the extra mile and sets a standard to which other resorts can only hope to aspire. This is arguably the state's best inn-style lodging, with its best inn dining (see "Where to Dine," below). Upon checking in, guests are shown to a parlor and served a drink, while valets gather luggage and park cars. The atmosphere here is distinctly European, with an emphasis on service. Rooms are individually decorated in an upscale country style that's been recently recast to reflect the color schemes of the nearby sea. Many units have wood-burning fireplaces and Jacuzzis; suites (in an outbuilding beside the main inn) border on spectacular, each with a distinct color theme and flatscreen television, whirlpool, or similar perks. There are plenty of other amenities such as fresh flowers daily, turndown service, an attractive new spa, a lovely outdoor swimming pool, and complimentary afternoon scone service. A handful of cottages,

Kennebunk & Kennebunkport

DINING ◆
Bradbury Brothers Market **18**
Cape Porpoise Kitchen **18**
Cape Porpoise Lobster Co. **18**
Federal Jack's Restaurant
    & Brew Pub **6**
Grissini **3**
Hurricane **8**
Nunan's Lobster Hut **18**
Pier 77 Restaurant **18**
White Barn Inn **4**

ATTRACTIONS ●
Brick Store Museum **2**
Dock Square **7**
Richard A. Nott House **9**
The Seashore Trolley
    Museum **2**

ACCOMMODATIONS ■
Beach House Inn **1**
Captain Jefferds Inn **12**
The Captain Lord
    Mansion **11**
The Colony Hotel **15**
Franciscan Guest
    House **5**
Lodge at Turbat's
    Creek **14**
Maine Stay Inn &
    Cottages **10**
Old Fort Inn **16**
The Tides Inn **17**
White Barn Inn **4**
The Yachtsman Lodge &
    Marina **13**

ATLANTIC OCEAN

on the Kennebunk River across the road, are cozy and nicely equipped with modern kitchens and bathrooms; chef Cartwright's cuisine is sublime.

Ocean Ave. (¼ mile east of junction of routes 9 and 35; P.O. Box 560-C), Kennebunk, ME 04043. © **207/967-2321.** Fax 207/967-1100. www.whitebarninn.com. 25 units, 4 cottages. $280–$540 double; $565–$785 suite; $630–$1,260 cottage. Rates include continental breakfast and afternoon tea. 2-night minimum weekends; 3 nights holiday weekends. AE, MC, V. Valet parking. **Amenities:** Free bikes; concierge; conference rooms; outdoor heated pool; room service. *In room:* A/C, TV, fireplace (some units), Jacuzzi (some units).

EXPENSIVE

Beach House Inn ★★   This is a good choice if you'd like to be close to the people-watching, dog-walking action on and above Kennebunk Beach. The inn was built in 1891 but has been extensively modernized and expanded; in 1999 it was purchased by the folks who own the White Barn Inn (see above) and gussied up with down comforters, pillows, and other upgrades. The rooms here aren't necessarily historic, but they are carpeted and most have Victorian furnishings and accenting, plus nice framed photographs of beach landscapes. Suites have panoramic views of the ocean. But the main draw here might be the lovely porch, where you can stare out at the

Finding a parking spot is often difficult, and all beaches require a parking permit, which you can get at the town offices or from your hotel. You can avoid the hassle by renting a bike and leaving your car at your inn or hotel. A good spot for rentals is **Kennebunk Bike Shop** (34 Arundel Rd.; ℂ 207/967-8713), which rents a variety of bikes by the half-day, day, or week. There are also mountain bikes, along with kid trailers and baby seats. (Helmets and locks are free with rentals.) The bike shop is just north of downtown Kennebunkport: turn north on North Rd., rather than following Rte. 9 north. A few hotels and inns in town also rent bikes to guests; others provide free bikes for guests, with no strings attached (except that you have to return the bike, obviously). Ask when you book your room. The local trolley also offers beach access (see above).

pebble beach across the road and idly watch the bikers and in-line skaters. The inn has bikes and canoes for guests to use and provides beach chairs and towels.

211 Beach Ave., Kennebunk, ME 04043. ℂ **207/967-3850.** Fax 207/967-4719. www.beachhseinn.com. 35 units. $310–$620 double; $540–$925 cottage and suite. Rates include continental breakfast and afternoon tea. Packages available. 2-night minimum on weekends. AE, MC, V. Closed Jan–May. **Amenities:** Bikes; canoes. *In room:* TV.

Captain Jefferds Inn ★★   This 1804 Federal home was fully redone in 1997, and the innkeepers have done a superb job. Fine antiques abound, and guests will need persuading to emerge from their rooms once they've settled in. Among the best are the Assisi, with a restful sitting area and some rather unique interior decorating. Three of the units now have televisions, while the Winterthur and Baxter both have whirlpool tubs. The price range reflects the varying room sizes, but even the smallest rooms—like the Katahdin, with views of the town—are comfortable and exceed the usual Maine B&B experience. Bright common rooms on the first floor offer nice lounging spaces, and an elaborate breakfast is served before a fire on cool days or outside on the terrace if good summer weather permits.

5 Pearl St. (P.O. Box 691), Kennebunkport, ME 04046. ℂ **800/839-6844** or 207/967-2311. Fax 207/967-0721. www.captainjefferdsinn.com. 15 units. Memorial Day to Oct $160–$365 double; rest of the year $125–$330 double. Rates include full breakfast. 2-night minimum weekends. AE, MC, V. Dogs in carriage house only, $30 per pet, by advance reservation. *In room:* A/C, TV (some units), hair dryer, Jacuzzi (some units).

The Captain Lord Mansion ★★★   The Captain Lord is one of the most architecturally distinguished inns in Maine, housed in a pale-yellow Federal-style home on a shady lawn above the river. This is the genuine article, with grandfather clocks, Chippendale highboys, and a broad brick fireplace. There's also a conference room with a sofa and TV. Up the elliptical staircase are the rooms, furnished in splendid antiques and gas fireplaces. Among the best: the Excelsior, a large corner room with a massive four-poster bed, love seat, and a two-person Jacuzzi; the Hesper, with a big stained-glass window in the bathroom; and the Merchant, a spacious first-floor suite that pampers you with a large Jacuzzi, NordicRider bike, and foot massager. Four rooms are in the Garden House annex, a gray clapboard home behind the main inn, where guests are served breakfast at a long table in the colonial-style kitchen; this building is less opulent but still well appointed.

Pleasant and Green sts. (P.O. Box 800), Kennebunkport, ME 04046. © **800/522-3141** or 207/967-3141. Fax 207/967-3172. www.captainlord.com. 20 units. $149–$379 double; $249–$499 suite. Rates include full breakfast. 2-night minimum weekends and holidays year-round (some holidays 3-night minimum). DISC, MC, V. No children 11 and under. **Amenities:** Lounge; conference room. *In room:* A/C, fireplace, fridge, hair dryer.

Maine Stay Inn and Cottages ★   Innkeepers Janice and George Yankowski have maintained a strong sense of history in their 1860 home and its associated cottages; the decor here is traditional, without going overboard. The common room is comfortably furnished—be sure to note the exceptional staircase in the main hall—and the cottages, arrayed along the property's perimeter, are just as appealing. Constructed during the 1950s, they've since been updated with small kitchens, and many now have gas or wood fireplaces and other amenities as well. The inn is happy to accommodate kids in these cottages (there's a minimum age of 6 in the main building). Towels, umbrellas, chairs, and town parking passes make for easy beach going. The full breakfast is very good—it includes spinach frittata and fresh fruit—and can be delivered to your room or your cottage if you like. Stressed? Some rooms even have Jacuzzis.

34 Maine St. (P.O. Box 500-A), Kennebunkport, ME 04046. © **800/950-2117** or 207/967-2117. Fax 207/967-8757. www.mainestayinn.com. 17 units. $109–$319 double and cottage. Rates include full breakfast. 2-night minimum stay on weekends; 3 nights on major holiday weekends. AE, MC, V. *In room:* A/C, TV/VCR, kitchenette (some units), fireplace (some units), hair dryer, Jacuzzi (some units), kitchenette (some units).

Old Fort Inn ★★   The sophisticated Old Fort Inn surprises with its elegance. It sits on 15 acres in a quiet, picturesque neighborhood of late-19th-century summer homes 2 blocks from the ocean. Guests check in at a tidy antiques shop and park around back at the large carriage house, an interesting amalgam of stone, brick, shingle, and stucco. Rooms and suites here all have creature comforts, yet retain the charm of yesteryear: They are solidly wrought and delightfully decorated with antiques and reproductions. About half of the rooms have in-floor heated tiles in the bathrooms; all have welcome amenities such as robes, refrigerators, Aveda bath products, discreet self-serve snack bars, microwaves, and sinks. There are two large suites in the main house; light-filled no. 216 faces east and looks out over the pool. A good

PACKING A picnic IN THE KENNEBUNKS

Kennebunk Beach is a fine spot for a picnic, with long sands and good waves. Watch your parking meter here, however. This is away from the downtown, and there are no shops on the beach. So, to pick up supplies, you'll need to backtrack (or plan ahead). Try **H.B. Provisions** (© **207/967-5762**), in a grand old country store building near the Western Ave. bridge linking the two Kennebunks: it's very well stocked with local microbrews and baked goods, and groceries. Plus there's a deli fixing sandwiches and lobster rolls (those go fast).

Farther up the coast, the unlikely city of Biddeford has a few good spots, including **Rotary Park,** with river views, and **Fortunes Rock Beach.**

full buffet breakfast is also served in the main building; spa and massage services are now offered; and there's a free hour of tennis on carefully kept courts with your stay.

Old Fort Rd. (P.O. Box M), Kennebunkport, ME 04046. © **800/828-3678** or 207/967-5353. Fax 207/967-4547. www.oldfortinn.com. 16 units. High season $180–$395 double and suite; low season $125–$295 double and suite. Rates include full breakfast and 1 hr. free tennis. 2-night minimum stay weekends; 3-night minimum stay holiday weekends. AE, DC, DISC, MC, V. **Amenities:** Massage; heated outdoor pool; tennis court. *In room:* A/C, TV, fridge, hair dryer, minibar.

MODERATE

Franciscan Guest House ★ 👪 This former dormitory on the 200-acre grounds of St. Anthony's Monastery is a unique lodging choice. The 60 or so rooms are basic and clean, with private bathrooms; guests can stroll the lovely riverside grounds or walk to Dock Square, about 10 minutes away. There's also a decent pool. It's not nearly as inexpensive as it used to be, though—the brothers have wised up to modern capitalism, and rates have escalated as a result. (They even have suites now.) Nevertheless, the place is still a fairly good bargain, especially given the fine walking trails and its position close to local beaches and restaurants.

28 Beach Ave. (P.O. Box 980), Kennebunk, ME 04046. © **207/967-4865.** www.franciscanguesthouse. com. 60 units. $74–$154 double; $89–$209 suite. MC, V. Closed mid-Oct to mid-May. **Amenities:** Outdoor pool. *In room:* A/C, TV, no phone.

Lodge at Turbat's Creek 🦞 This classy and unusually clean motel isn't exactly a "lodge," but it does sit in a quiet residential neighborhood an easy 5-minute drive from Dock Square. It's a good value in a town that usually gives you sticker shock. The grounds are attractive and endowed with Adirondack chairs; the inn also supplies free mountain bikes for guests who want to cruise to town, and there's a big, seasonally open heated pool as well. Rooms, on two floors, are standard motel size. They're decorated in rustic pine furniture and painted cheerfully. The continental breakfast can be taken outside, on the lawn, in good weather.

7 Turbat's Creek Rd. (P.O. Box 2722), Kennebunkport, ME 04046. © **877/594-5634** or 207/967-8700. www.lodgeatturbatscreek.com. 26 units. $89–$179 double; holidays $129–$189 double. Rates include continental breakfast. AE, MC, V. Closed Dec–Mar. From Dock Sq., drive to top of hill, turn right on Maine St., turn left at 1st fork, and turn right at 2nd fork. Pets allowed; inquire before arriving. **Amenities:** Free use of mountain bikes; heated outdoor pool. *In room:* A/C, TV, fridge, hair dryer.

The Yachtsman Lodge & Marina ★★ The White Barn Inn took over this riverfront motel in 1997 and made it an appealing base for exploring the Kennebunk side of the river. Within walking distance of Dock Square, nice touches abound, such as down comforters, granite-topped vanities, high ceilings, CD players, and French doors that open onto patios just above the river. While rooms are all standard motel size and on one level, their simple, classical styling is far superior to anything you'll find at a chain motel. And the service is seriously kicked up a notch.

Ocean Ave. (P.O. Box 2609), Kennebunkport, ME 04046. © **207/967-2511.** Fax 207/967-5056. www. yachtsmanlodge.com. 30 units. $189–$369 double. Rates include continental breakfast. 2-night minimum stay on weekends and holidays. AE, MC, V. **Amenities:** Free bikes and canoes. *In room:* A/C, TV/VCR, fridge, hair dryer.

Where to Dine

Those looking for a quick lobster have a couple of options in the Kennebunkport area, although the prices tend to be a bit more expensive than at other casual lobster spots

Cape Porpoise ★★ is a lovely little village, nearly forgotten by time, between Kennebunk and Biddeford. (And you've got to love the name.) It makes for a superb day trip or bike ride. While in the village, think about packing a picnic and taking it to the rocks where the lobster boats are tied up; watch the fishermen, or train your binoculars on Goat Island and its lighthouse. Drop by

Bradbury Brothers Market (𝒞 207/967-3939) for basic staples, or the Cape Porpoise Kitchen (𝒞 800/488-1150 or 207/967-1150; www.capeporpoise kitchen.com) for gourmet-style prepared meals, cheeses, and baked goods. The village also has two good lobster shacks (see "Where to Dine," below), a handful of shops, and even a postage-stamp-size library.

farther north along the coast. **Nunan's Lobster Hut** (𝒞 207/967-4362), Rte. 9 north of Kennebunkport at Cape Porpoise, is a classic lobster shack, often crowded with diners and full of atmosphere, which helps make up for disappointments such as potato chips (rather than a baked potato) served with the lobster dinner. No reservations are taken, nor are credit cards accepted; it's open daily for dinner, starting at 5pm.

There's also **Cape Porpoise Lobster Co.,** 15 Pier Rd. (𝒞 800/967-4268 or 207/967-4268), a compact spot overlooking the sparkling water. There's limited outdoor dining, but most everything is served on Styrofoam plates, so beware of rogue winds that strive to dump your meal on your lap. No reservations are taken, but credit cards are accepted. It's usually open daily from 9am to 7pm for breakfast, lunch, and dinner in season; it's closed from late fall to around Memorial Day.

Federal Jack's Restaurant and Brew Pub BREWPUB This light, airy, and modern restaurant, named after a schooner built at Cape Porpoise a century ago, is in a retail complex tucked back from the bridge amid boatyards along the south bank of the Kennebunk River. From the second-floor perch (look for a seat on the spacious three-season deck in warmer weather), you can gaze across the river toward the shops of Dock Square. The place is best known for the ales, lagers, and porters that have been brewed beneath the pub since 1992. But there's also a semi-upscale pub menu of wings, burgers, calamari, and pizza plus a few nods to local cuisine (glazed salmon, lobster). Keep an eye on the specials board, which could include something as upscale as a grilled crab and Havarti sandwich, a lamb burger, or tuna sashimi—or something as lowbrow as a bowl of Texas chili.

8 Western Ave., Lower Village (south bank of Kennebunk River), Kennebunk. 𝒞 207/967-4322. www. federaljacks.com. Main courses (lunch or dinner) $3–$16; lobster dinners priced to market. AE, DISC, MC, V. Daily 11:30am–9pm (bar to 1am); Sun brunch served 10:30am–2pm.

Grissini ★★ TUSCAN Grissini is a handsome trattoria gone upscale. Oversize Italian advertising posters line the walls of a soaring, barnlike space, and burning logs in the handsome stone fireplace take the chill out of a cool evening. In fact, everything seems larger than life, including the plates, flatware, and water goblets. Meals are likewise luxuriously sized and nicely presented and include a wide range of pastas and pizza served with considerable flair. Expect delicious upscale treatments of gnocchi, lasagna, and pastas revved up with the likes of goat cheese, plus main courses such as risotto with smoked bacon and Gorgonzola; wood-grilled salmon, chicken, and steak; spicy lamb shank with chorizo; and lobster with cream cheese, scallops, and wild mushrooms. For those without completely empty stomachs, a changing "grotta" menu offers lighter fare of pizzas, ciabatta sandwiches, crepes, and glasses of wine. Desserts include panna cotta and tiramisu.

27 Western Ave., Kennebunk. © **207/967-2211.** www.restaurantgrissini.com. Reservations encouraged. Entrees $14–$28; grotto (light) menu $8–$14. AE, MC, V. Sun–Fri 5:30–9pm; Sat 5–9:30pm. Closed Wed Jan–Mar.

Hurricane ★★ AMERICAN/ECLECTIC Originally an offshoot of Brooks and Luanne MacDonald's award-winning Ogunquit restaurant, this is now the only Hurricane still blowing. The late open hours are a boon in early closing Maine. Lunch might start with a cup of lobster chowder, the "Ice Cube" (a block of iceberg lettuce with blue cheese dressing, toasted pecans, roasted pears, and croutons), a lobster Cobb salad, a bento box of Maine seafood; the main course could be a Cubano sandwich, a grilled tuna burger, or a three-cheese tortellini. Dinner entrees run to such items as a Mediterranean-inflected, lobster-based cioppino, pan-roasted chicken with pecorino mac-and-cheese, grilled beef tenderloin, a brined pork chop with sweet potatoes, a baked lobster stuffed with scallops, crab, and shrimp, or a slow-cooked rack of lamb. Finish with desserts such as vanilla bean crème brûlée, Key lime tart with coconut rum sauce, panna cotta, toffee-flavored bread pudding, or a course of cheeses.

29 Dock Sq., Kennebunkport. © **207/967-1111.** www.hurricanerestaurant.com. Reservations recommended. Main courses $15–$45; small plates $8–$22. AE, DC, DISC, MC, V. Daily 11:30am–10:30pm (winter to 9:30pm).

Pier 77 Restaurant ★★ REGIONAL Long a tony restaurant with a wonderful ocean view, Pier 77 was recently renovated and renamed by husband-and-wife team Peter and Kate Morency. The food, drawing on Peter's training at the Culinary Institute of America and 20 years in top kitchens in Boston and San Francisco, is more contemporary and skillful than almost anything else in Maine. Lunches run to slightly upscaled comfort food such as barbecue, spaghetti and meatballs, cheddar burger, and fried clams. At dinner it's again about traditional favorites (pasta, steak, lobster), but there are also some slightly more adventurous dishes: a trio of duck courses or a tomato-y seafood stew, for instance. The restaurant has earned *Wine Spectator's* awards of excellence since 1993. Worth noting: a casual section of the restaurant known as the Ramp Bar & Grill stays open all day long, even between lunch and dinner service, offering lighter meals.

77 Pier Rd., Cape Porpoise (Kennebunkport). © **207/967-8500.** www.pier77restaurant.com. Reservations recommended. Main courses lunch $9–$18, dinner $18–$30. AE, MC, V. Daily 11:30am–2:30pm and 5–9pm (Ramp Bar & Grill 11:30am–9pm); Oct–Dec closed Tues.

White Barn Inn ★★★ REGIONAL/NEW AMERICAN The White Barn Inn's (see earlier in this chapter) classy dining room—carved out of, yes, a barn—attracts gourmands from far and wide. The space is half the fun, with its soaring interior and an eclectic collection of country antiques displayed in a hayloft; window displays are changed with the seasons. Chef Jonathan Cartwright changes up the menu frequently, but always incorporates local ingredients: his signature lobster spring roll uses daikon, carrots, snow peas, and Thai sauce to accent the lobster meat. Or enjoy locally caught, pan-seared diver scallops; an intermezzo course of fruit soup or sorbet; and a main course such as pan-seared filet of salmon, grilled chicken breast over creamed spinach, or simply steamed lobster over fettuccine with cognac coral butter sauce. Cartwright's tasting menus run to seasonal items such as variations of oyster; sautéed smoked haddock rarebit; Quebec foie gras roulade; or peekytoe crab. Service is astonishingly attentive and knowledgeable, capping the experience. One of Maine's best meals.

Beach Ave., Kennebunkport. © **207/967-2321.** Reservations recommended. Fixed-price dinner $91; tasting menu $125 per person. AE, MC, V. Mon–Thurs 6:30–9:30pm; Fri 5:30–9:30pm. Closed 2 weeks in Jan.

6 PORTLAND

Maine's largest city, Portland sits on a hammerhead-shaped peninsula extending into scenic Casco Bay. It's easy to drive right past the place on I-295, admiring the skyline at 60 miles an hour, on your way to the villages and headlands farther up the coast. After all, one doesn't usually think 'urban life' when envisioning a vacation in Maine.

But Portland is worth at least an afternoon's detour, and even a weekend (or a week) isn't too much time to spend here. This historic city has plenty of charm—not only in the Old Port, with its brick sidewalks and cobblestone streets, but in several lovely residential neighborhoods of striking views and architecture. You can catch a quick ferry to an offshore island, browse boutique shops, snap photos of historic homes; crack lobsters, walk empty beaches, and pose beside lighthouses; and top off your day with top-shelf dining. (Portland is now a sort of culinary mecca, blessed with an uncommonly high number of excellent restaurants for a city its size.)

Actually, it feels more like a large town than a small city. Strike up a conversation with a resident, and you're likely to get an earful about how easy it is to live here. You can buy gourmet coffee, see art-house movies, and get good Vietnamese or Thai food to go. There's even some terrific residential architecture. Yet Portland is still compact enough that you can walk from one end to the other. Despite its outward appearance of being an actual metropolis, the city has a population of just 65,000. Traffic isn't bad at all. And there's a salty tang to local culture that you'll occasionally still glimpse in the waterfront bars and chowder houses.

Like most New England cities, Portland has been forced to reinvent itself every couple of generations as economic and cultural trends overturn old paradigms. The city was a center for maritime trade in the 19th century, when a forest of ship masts obscured the view of the harbor. It's been a manufacturing hub, with locomotive factories, steel foundries, and fish-packing plants. It's been a mercantile center, with impressive downtown department stores and a slew of wholesale dealers.

Today, as a sprawling, could-be-anywhere mall in South Portland siphons off much of the commercial business, this city is bent on reshaping its downtown core as a tourist destination, regional center for the arts, and incubator for high-tech startups.

The verdict is still out on whether Portland's current reincarnation as a mini-Boston (down to the fish market, train station, and beloved local baseball nine) will succeed.

But unlike so many other deteriorating downtowns, Portland's has few vacant storefronts. Office space is in short supply, and there's a brisk urban vitality that often eludes much bigger cities. A recent wave of immigration from Africa and Asia has given the place a shot in the cultural arm; Portland's art museum would be outstanding in a community 5 or 10 times its size; new coffee shops seem to open daily; and a downtown arts college brings a youthful spirit to the streets. Best of all, there's always an offshore island to escape to when cruise ships on the waterfront unload a few too many fellow tourists for your taste.

ORIENTATION

106 miles N of Boston and 317 miles NE of New York City

Getting There

BY CAR   Coming from the south by car, downtown Portland is most easily reached by taking exit 44 off the Maine Turnpike (I-95, which is a toll road) into the city, then following I-295 (which is free) a few miles into town. Exit I-295 onto Franklin Arterial (exit 7), then continue straight uphill and downhill to the city's ferry terminal in the Old Port. Turn right onto Commercial Street and park. There's a visitor center nearby, and plenty to do within 10 minutes' walk. Get oriented here.

BY TRAIN   Amtrak (© 800/872-7245; www.amtrak.com) runs the daily Downeaster service from Boston's North Station to Portland (passengers from other cities must change stations from South Station to North Station in Boston by taxi or subway). The train makes five round-trips daily (time: 2½ hr.), for $24 each way. Downtown is a short bus or cab ride or a drab 45-minute walk from the station, which is out on Thompson's Point.

BY BUS   Two big carriers, **Concord Coach** (© 800/639-3317 or 207/828-1151; www.concordcoachlines.com) and **Greyhound** (© 800/231-2222; www.greyound.com), provide bus service to Portland. The Greyhound bus terminal is at 950 Congress St., about a mile south of the downtown core. Greyhound runs buses from both Portland and New York City: from Boston, there are several buses daily (2 hr., $21 one-way), while from New York there's one bus daily (7 hr., $47 one-way). Concord Coach connects Portland with Boston only, but it runs more than a dozen buses daily from that city and from Logan Airport (2 hr., $21–$26 one-way; discounts for round-trips). Concord Coach's bus terminal is next to Portland's inconvenient Amtrak station (see "by Train," above) on Thompson Point Rd. City buses and taxis ferry you downtown from here.

BY PLANE   Portland International Jetport (© 207/874-8877; www.portlandjetport.org), airport code PWM, is the largest airport in Maine. It's served by flights from **AirTran** (© 800/247-8726; www.airtrain.com), **Continental** (© 800/523-3273; www.continental.com), **Delta** (© 800/221-1212; www.delta.com), **JetBlue** (© 800/538-2583; www.jetblue.com), **Northwest** (© 800/225-2525; www.nwa.com), **United Express** (© 800/864-8331; www.ual.com), and **US Airways** (© 800/428-4322; www.usair.com). The airport has grown in fits and starts in recent years, but it's small and pretty easily navigated. A taxi ride to the city is about $20 with tip; some hotels near the airport and downtown will shuttle you to your digs for free. Ask when booking.

Visitor Information

The **Convention and Visitor's Bureau of Greater Portland** (www.visitportland.com) runs *four* tourist information centers around town. The main info center is on the new Ocean Gateway Pier, just north of the Casco Bay Lines ferry terminal at the feet of Commercial St. and Franklin Arterial. Most of the year, it's open from Monday through Saturday—but in July and August it's open 7 days a week, and it closes in February. There are also tourist information kiosks at the **Portland International Jetport** (© 207/775-5809), near baggage claim, open daily year-round; in **Deering Oaks Park** at the Forest Ave. exit of I-295, open 6 to 7 days a week year-round (it's closed Sun in Sept and June); and one ad hoc kiosk that opens up outside the **cruise ship terminal** on Commercial Street for 4 hours after any cruise ship arrives.

Portland also has a free weekly newspaper, the *Portland Phoenix,* offering good listings of local events, films, nightclub performances, and the like. Copies are widely available at restaurants, bars, and convenience stores, and in newspaper boxes on curbs in the Old Port and around downtown.

City Layout

The city of Portland is divided into two areas: on-peninsula and off-peninsula. (There are also the islands, but more on that below.) Most travelers are destined for the compact peninsula, which is home to the downtown and where most of the city's cultural life and retail activity takes place.

Viewed from the water, Portland's peninsula is shaped a bit like a swaybacked horse or the hammerhead on a shark, with the **Old Port ★★★** lying in the belly near the waterfront and the peninsula's two main residential neighborhoods (Munjoy Hill and the West End) topping gentle rises overlooking downtown. Congress Street, Portland's main artery of commerce, connects these two neighborhoods. The western stretch of Congress Street (roughly btw. Monument Sq. and State St.) is home to Portland's emerging **Arts District ★**, where you can find the handsome art museum, several theaters, the campus of the Maine College of Art (located in an old department store), the original L.L.Bean outlet, and a growing number of restaurants and boutiques.

Parking

Parking is notoriously tight in the Old Port, and the city's parking enforcement is notoriously efficient. Several parking garages are convenient to the Old Port, with parking fees less than $1 per hour; you can also park in some residential neighborhoods, often for a maximum of 2 hours. Read signs carefully for news of nighttime street-sweeping hours; you *will* be towed (don't ask how I know; I just do) if you run afoul of them.

Special Events

New Year's Portland rings in January with a smorgasbord of events and entertainment throughout downtown Portland. Events for families are scheduled in the afternoon; entertainment more oriented for adults—including loads of live music—kicks off later in the evening at numerous locales, including auditoriums, shops, and churches. The emphasis is on enjoying New Year's without alcohol. One admission button buys entrance to all events.

The **Old Port Festival** (© 207/772-6828) takes place in early June, when tens of thousands of revelers descend upon the historic Old Port section to herald the arrival of summer. Several blocks of the Old Port are blocked to traffic, and the throngs order food and buy goods from street vendors. Several stages provide entertainment, ranging from kids' singalongs to raucous blues. Admission is free.

WHERE TO STAY

In addition to the lodgings listed below, there are tons of chain hotels and motels in and around the city. Check around the Maine Mall (in South Portland) for the largest agglomeration; you'll find all the usual names there, in various price ranges; see below for a few suggestions.

If you're looking for something more central (and you should), Hilton runs a hotel across the street from the main ferry dock in the Old Port neighborhood. The **Hilton Garden Inn** (65 Commercial St.; ✆ 207/780-0780; www.hilton.com) is convenient to restaurants, bakeries, and pubs—not to mention the islands of Casco Bay. You'll pay for the privilege of being in the heart of the waterfront, though: Double rooms mostly run from about $189 up to $369 per night.

The **Holiday Inn by the Bay,** 88 Spring St. (✆ 800/345-5050 or 207/775-2311; www.innbythebay.com), offers great views of the harbor from about half the rooms, along with the usual chain-hotel creature comforts. Peak-season rates are approximately $180 for a double.

Budget travelers seeking chain hotels typically head for the area surrounding the Maine Mall in South Portland, about 8 miles south of the attractions of downtown. The lowest-cost options include the **Days Inn** (✆ 207/772-3450) and the **Coastline Inn** (✆ 207/772-3838). An **Extended Stay America** (2 Ashley Dr., Scarborough; ✆ 207/883-0554) is a few minutes' drive south of the mall, and features in-room kitchenettes; doubles start around $60 nightly in the off season, $90 in summer.

Very Expensive

Black Point Inn Resort ★★ Just 10 miles south of Portland (about 15 min. driving time from downtown), the Black Point Inn is a Maine classic. The property reopened in 2007 under brand new ownership, having dispensed with one of its pools and all of the cottages (slashing the inn's room count by more than two-thirds); but the rooms that do remain open have been updated and upscaled. Situated on 9 acres with views along the coast both north and south, the inn was built as a summer resort in 1873 on the same attractive rocky point memorialized by landscape painter Winslow Homer. What remains is as elegant as ever, perhaps more so, and the expansive porch (with its constant sea breezes) thankfully remains. Rates are charged per person, and they're certainly high, but they include breakfast, dinner, and a trimmed-down afternoon tea service daily.

510 Black Point Rd., Prouts Neck, ME 04074. ✆ **207/883-2500.** Fax 207/883-9976. www.blackpoint inn.com. 25 units. $380–$520 double; $480–$580 suite. Rates include full breakfast, afternoon tea service, and dinner. Packages available. AE, DC, DISC, MC, V. Free valet parking. Closed Nov–Apr. From U.S. Rte. 1 in Scarborough, turn onto Rte. 207 east. **Amenities:** Babysitting; children's program (summers); fitness room; Jacuzzi; massage; heated outdoor pool; room service; sauna. *In room:* A/C, TV/DVD, hair dryer.

Inn by the Sea ★★★ Not so much an inn as a luxury retreat, Cape Elizabeth's best hotel has made the successful transition from relaxed seaside getaway to destination resort. Yet they've done it while retaining a wonderful sense of place: suites and dining areas emphasize Maine-themed art and foods, while summery gardens and ocean views tantalize through the windows. An expansive, lovely spa was added in 2008, as were a walk-in *cave,* fireplace rooms, and bi-level spa suites with double Jacuzzis. A further set of cottages (town-house-like suites) in an outbuilding add full kitchens and extra bedroom or bathroom space. Especially welcome is this inn's move toward green practices: It's the first hotel in Maine to burn biofuels, operate carbon neutrally, and employ printed-paper key cards. Recycled materials and low-flow toiletry also predominate. Need still more green? A walkway leads to one of Maine's best beaches.

40 Bowery Beach Rd., Cape Elizabeth, ME 04107. © **800/888-4287** outside Maine, or 207/799-3134. Fax 207/799-4779. www.innbythesea.com. 57 units. July–Aug $399–$789 suite; May–June and Sept-Oct $289–$609 suite; Nov–Apr $189–$369 suite. Packages available. AE, DC, DISC, MC, V. Pets welcome in some units. **Amenities:** Restaurant; lounge; fitness room; Jacuzzi; heated outdoor pool; room service; sauna; spa. *In room:* A/C, TV/DVD, fridge, hair dryer, kitchenette.

Expensive

The Danforth ★★   Once fading, the Danforth has recovered its former glory and is again approaching the status of "grand boutique inn" thanks to newly installed throw pillows, fireplaces, four-poster beds, televisions, and wingback chairs. The Victoria Mansion (p. 123) is just 2 blocks down the street, and the Old Port's only a 10-minute stroll.

163 Danforth St. © **800/991-6557** or 207/879-8755. www.danforthmaine.com. 10 units. $120–$275 double. MC, V. **Amenities:** Billiard room; conservatory; garden; sitting room. *In room:* A/C, TV, fireplace (most units), hair dryer, no phone.

Pomegranate Inn ★★   Located inside a 19th-century Italianate home in Portland's lovely West End, this is arguably the city's top B&B. Eight rooms feature individually distinct design touches, painted floors, faux-marble woodwork, and gas fireplaces. The carriage house room includes a private terrace whose sliding doors open onto a small garden, and breakfasts are a highlight. Also don't miss the flowery second-floor balcony and third-floor conservatory.

49 Neal St. © **800/356-0408** or 207/772-1006. Fax 207/773-4426. www.pomegranateinn.com. 8 units. $140–$295 double. Rates include full breakfast. Packages available. AE, DISC, MC, V. Children 16 and older only. **Amenities:** Afternoon refreshments. *In room:* TV, fireplace (some units).

Portland Harbor Hotel ★★   Situated adjacent to Portland's busy bar scene on the corner of Fore and Union streets, this semicircular town-house-like structure—designed to fit in with the brick facades prevailing in the Old Port—appeals to the boutique crowd with its modern amenities. The interior courtyard throws off European ambience; large rooms are furnished with queen- and king-size beds and spacious work desks. Even the standard rooms are outfitted with deep bathtubs in granite-faced bathrooms; armoires; duvets and down coverlets; two-line phones; and big TVs. Deluxe rooms and suites add Jacuzzis and sitting areas, and some units look out onto a central garden area. The house **restaurant,** Eve's at the Garden ★, is very good.

468 Fore St., Portland, ME 04101. © **888/798-9090** or 207/775-9090. Fax 207/775-9990. www.portlandharborhotel.com. 100 units. Mid-May to mid-Oct $229–$249 double, $329 suite; off season $159–$179 double, $259 suite. Packages available. AE, DC, DISC, MC, V. Valet parking in garage $10 per day. **Amenities:** Dining room; bar; babysitting; bike rental; concierge; fitness center; room service. *In room:* A/C, TV, hair dryer, Jacuzzis (some units).

Portland Regency Hotel ★★★   Centrally located on a cobblestone courtyard in the middle of the Old Port, the Regency boasts one of the city's premier hotel locations. But it's got more than location—this is also one of the most architecturally striking and better-managed hotels in southern Maine. Housed in an 1895 brick armory, the hotel is thoroughly modern and offers attractive rooms, appointed and

furnished with all the expected amenities. There are several types of rooms and suites, each fitted to the place's unique architecture; for a splurge, ask for a luxurious corner room with a handsome (nonworking) fireplace, sitting area, city views out big windows, and a Jacuzzi. The small health club is one of the best in town (it includes a sauna and hot tub), and the downstairs level conceals a restaurant and a **lounge** ★ that's possibly the nicest place in town to sip a drink in a dim room.

20 Milk St., Portland, ME 04101. ✆ **800/727-3436** or 207/774-4200. Fax 207/775-2150. www.the regency.com. 95 units. Early July to late Oct $249–$269 double, $289–$389 suite; off season $159–$219 double, $209–$329 suite. AE, DISC, MC, V. Valet parking $8 per day. **Amenities:** Restaurant; bar; free airport transfers; babysitting (with prior notice); conference rooms; fitness club w/aerobics classes; Jacuzzi; room service; sauna; spa. In room: A/C, TV, minibar.

Residence Inn Portland Downtown/Waterfront ★ Portland's newest big hotel is part of a chain, but its location—right off the Old Port—and amenities (all its units are big suites with full kitchens, including dishwashers and stovetops) have already made it a hit. Some units even have bay views; there's an indoor pool, Jacuzzi, and health club, as well.

145 Fore St. ✆ **207/761-1660.** Fax 207/761-1661. www.marriott.com. 179 units. $150–$410 suite. Rates include continental breakfast. AE, DISC, MC, V. Pets allowed ($100 fee). **Amenities:** Conference rooms; fitness club; Jacuzzi; indoor pool. In room: A/C, TV, fridge, hair dryer, kitchen.

Moderate

Embassy Suites Hotel Portland ★ Practically inside Portland's airport, this all-suite hotel gets very good reviews from business travelers. It's one of the best choices if you have a very late arrival or early departure, even if it won't win awards for innovative architecture. Business bonus: You can print remotely, for free, from all rooms.

1050 Westbrook St., Portland. ✆ **207/775-2200.** Fax 207/775-4052. www.hilton.com. 119 units. $135–$340 double. Rates include full breakfast. AE, DISC, MC, V. **Amenities:** Restaurant; bar; conference rooms; fitness club; indoor pool; room service; sauna. In room: A/C, TV, fridge (some units), hair dryer, kitchen (some units).

Fairfield Inn Portland Maine Mall ★ ☺ The Fairfield, on the southern edge of the Maine Mall's sprawl, is a good option for budget-minded families. The clean but basic rooms all have irons and ironing boards, there's a simple free breakfast in the lobby each morning, and parking's free and ample. You can practically walk to the mall (but don't). Note that there's no restaurant in the hotel.

2 Cummings Rd., Scarborough. ✆ **207/883-0300.** Fax 207/883-0572. www.marriott.com. 118 units. $69–$150 double. Rates include continental breakfast. AE, DISC, MC, V. **Amenities:** Fitness club; Jacuzzi; indoor pool. In room: A/C, TV, hair dryer.

Hampton Inn Portland–Airport ★ ☺ Of all the hotels clustered around Portland's airport and mall, this is my top "family" pick. There's a pool, a free shuttle van to and from the airport, chocolate-chip cookies, an Internet terminal in the lobby, a pretty good included breakfast, friendly staff, and a quiet-ish location. Plus they'll bring cribs and highchairs as fast as you need 'em. Downtown is a 10-minute drive away, the Maine Mall a 30-second walk.

171 Philbrook Ave., South Portland. ✆ **800/426-7866** or 207/773-4400. Fax: 207/773-6786. www. hamptoninn.hilton.com/maine. 117 units. $99–$229 double. Rates include continental breakfast. Packages available. AE, DISC, MC, V. **Amenities:** Fitness club; indoor pool. In room: A/C, TV, fridge, hair dryer.

Inn at Park Spring ★   This small, tasteful B&B is located on a busy downtown street in a historic brick home that dates back to 1835. It's well located for exploring the city on foot, and the friendly owners keep the place in good shape. Guests can linger or watch TV in a front parlor, or chat at the communal dining table in the adjacent room (communal breakfasts are a highlight—unless you're shy). The rooms are all corner rooms, and most are bright and sunny. Especially nice is the Spring Room, with its sleigh bed, hardwood flooring, and wonderful views of the historic row houses along Park Street, and crimson-hued Gables, on the third (top) floor, which gets abundant afternoon light and is furnished with a king bed, big sitting room, and nice bathroom. The Portland Museum of Art and the city's children's museum (see below) are only 2 blocks away, the Old Port a 10-minute walk.

135 Spring St., Portland, ME 04101. ℂ **800/437-8511** or 207/774-1059. www.innatparkspring.com. 6 units. Mid-Apr to Oct and holidays $129–$205 double; Nov to mid-Apr $99–$165 double. 2-night minimum weekends. Rates include full breakfast and off-street parking. AE, MC, V. No children 9 and under. *In room:* A/C, hair dryer.

La Quinta Inn & Suites Portland   Across the street from a milk plant and railroad overpass, this suite hotel won't win any prizes for location or decor—don't stay here if you're coming on a honeymoon. You get just what you'd expect: barebones accommodations, simplistic amenities. But it's the closest sleep to both Hadlock Field, home to the city's minor-league baseball team (p. 124), and the city's clean little Amtrak station.

340 Park Ave. ℂ **800/753-3757** or 207/871-0611. Fax 207/871-8243. www.lq.com. 105 units. $75–$225 double. Pets allowed (no extra charge). AE, DISC, MC, V. **Amenities:** Airport shuttle; fitness club; outdoor pool. In room: A/C, TV, hair dryer.

Wyndham Portland Airport Hotel ★★   This round, two-towered hotel looks like a pair of spaceships about to be launched, but Wyndham's transforming a formerly tired, blah chain property into a (somewhat) hip destination. The rooms are smallish and shaped like wedges of pie (the hotel is round, after all), but there's a cool bar area, a decent pool and Jacuzzi area, and updated linens, colors, bathroom amenities, and decor.

363 Maine Mall Rd., South Portland. ℂ **877/999-3223** or 207/775-6161. www.wyndham.com. 219 units. $140–$290 double. AE, DISC, MC, V. **Amenities:** Restaurant; bar; conference rooms; fitness club; Jacuzzi; indoor pool; room service; sauna. In room: A/C, TV, fridge, hair dryer.

WHERE TO DINE

Portland is nothing if not a city of creative cheap eats, so don't neglect local bakeries and coffee shops when trolling for quick or economical meals. My favorite bakery in New England, hands-down, is **Standard Baking Company** ★★, 75 Commercial St. (ℂ **207/773-2112**), across from the ferry terminal and behind the new Hilton Garden Inn hotel. Allison Bray and Matt James bake some of the best sticky buns (with or without nuts) and focaccia I've tasted, plus top-rate breads, brioche, cookies, and more. There's good coffee, too. The bakery is open 7am to 6pm daily except Sundays, when it closes at 5pm.

Among the many coffee shops around the city, I frequent both **Arabica,** 2 Free St. (ℂ **207/879-0792**), with house-roasted beans and a good choice of teas, plus pie, bagels, scones, and even toast with peanut butter (open daily until 6pm), and **Bard Coffee** at 185 Middle St. (ℂ **207/899-4788**; www.bardcoffee.com), open daily until 9pm except on Sundays, when it closes at 6pm.

For a pizza, head for **Flatbread Company** (see below); **Angelone's** (© 207/775-3114; 788 Washington Ave.), which makes outstandingly authentic local pies; or **Ricetta's** (© 207/775-7400; 29 Western Ave., South Portland), tucked into a small shopping mall en route to the larger Maine Mall.

Portland also claims to be the original home of the Italian sandwich—which may have been the original sub sandwich in America—and locals maintain the best example can still be found at the purported inventor of this creation, **Amato's,** 71 India St. (© 207/773-1682), in what's left of Portland's Italian neighborhood.

Expensive

Back Bay Grill ★★ NEW AMERICAN Back Bay Grill has long been one of Portland's best restaurants, with an upscale, contemporary ambience; the only trouble is getting there (it's near the city's main post office, far from the rest of the sights in this book). Chef Larry Matthews bought the place from founder Joel Freund in 2002, and his menu is revamped seasonally, emphasizing local produce and meats. Diners might start with some kicky Maine crab cakes, a saffron mussel chowder, beef tartare with truffle, foie gras with crispy polenta, house-cured gravlax salmon, or some local mussels steamed in white wine. Among the main courses, look for dishes like filet mignon paired with gnocchi, breast of duck, salmon paired with couscous, Casco Bay cod in a tomato-lemon-grass broth, various versions of lamb, or agnolotti pasta stuffed with goat's-milk ricotta and spinach. Finish with a crème brûlée, caramel ice cream with bourbon sauce, vanilla panna cotta, a walnut-and-lemon crepe with mead-and-caramel sauce, or one of the other extremely inventive desserts.

65 Portland St. © **207/772-8833.** www.backbaygrill.com. Reservations recommended. Main courses $18–$35. AE, DC, DISC, MC, V. Mon–Thurs 5:30–9:30pm; Fri–Sat 5:30–10pm.

Five Fifty-Five ★★ NEW AMERICAN Husband-and-wife Steve and Michelle Corry's restaurant features "small plates" with big flavors, and they've daringly plunked it down right in the heart of Portland's least scenic main street. You can mix and match your own combinations of soups, salads, cheese, foie gras—plus, they also offer a fuller menu of dishes such as pork chops, veal, lobster-flavored macaroni-and-cheese, hanger steak, hand-rolled pasta, and the like. Wine aficionados, take note: The wine list here is tops, one of the best in the entire city.

555 Congress St. © **207/761-0555.** www.fivefifty-five.com. Small plates $6–$15, main courses $31–$35. AE, MC, V. Sun 9:30am–2pm and 5–9:30pm; Mon–Thurs 5–9:30pm; Fri–Sat 5–10:30pm.

Fore Street ★★ CONTEMPORARY GRILL Fore Street has emerged as one of northern New England's most celebrated restaurants. Chef Sam Hayward gets profiled in magazines such as *Saveur* and *House Beautiful,* and his restaurant was often in *Gourmet*'s 100 Best, and so forth. Hayward's secret is simplicity: local and organic ingredients are used where possible, and the kitchen avoids fussy presentations. The dining space centers around a busy open kitchen where a team of chefs constantly stoke the wood-fired brick oven and grill, which feature prominently in the culinary philosophy here. The menu changes nightly, but entrees might run to spit-roasted pork loin, grilled duckling, grilled marinated hanger steak, or a piece of pan-seared bluefish; the wood-roasted mussels are also a big hit. Finish with a dessert such as chocolate soufflé, hand-dipped chocolates, or gelati—these are often accented in summer by seasonal Maine berries or fruits. Though it can be difficult to snag a reservation here on summer weekends, management always sets aside a few tables each night for walk-ins. Get there early and grab one.

288 Fore St. ⓒ **207/775-2717.** www.forestreet.biz. Reservations recommended. Main courses $13–$29. AE, MC, V. Sun-Thurs 5:30–10pm; Fri-Sat 5:30–10:30pm (May-Oct Sun to 9:30pm).

Hugo's ★★★ ECLECTIC/NEW AMERICAN   A decade ago this place was fading fast, but chef Rob Evans and partner Nancy Pugh bought the place and changed all that. Now it's arguably the most exciting place to eat in northern New England. Trained in star kitchens (French Laundry, the Inn at Little Washington), Evans brought a philosophy of using local ingredients and crafting unusual, exciting menus. (He was named "best chef in the Northeast" by the James Beard Foundation in 2009.) Evans offers a small-plate style of service of midsize, constantly changing portions of everything from sweetbreads with peanut and cilantro flavors to goat-cheese ravioli with mole sauce; raw Maine sea urchin over sticky rice; pan-fried Arctic char; local cod baked in parchment paper; a combo plate of rib-eye, short ribs, potato puree, and onions; crisped pork belly with fried pig's tail and a jalapeño marmalade; or breast of duck. A nightly "blind" tasting menu (you don't find out what you ate until the end) expands the journey to six courses, and chef's menus (by advance reservation only) runs to even more flights. Dessert could be a very upscale take on peanut butter cups, ice cream floats, or an apple turnover jacked up with dates, bacon, pralines, and homemade butter ice cream. A good tapas menu (charcuterie, cheese plates) is served at the bar, and the same partners also run a Belgian fries-and-shakes shop, Duckfat (see review below), down the block.

88 Middle St. ⓒ **207/774-8538.** www.hugos.net. Reservations strongly recommended. Plates $10–$25 each; tasting menus $75 and up. AE, MC, V. Tues-Thurs 5:30–9pm; Fri-Sat 5:30–9:30pm.

Sea Glass ★★ SEAFOOD/FUSION   At the house restaurant of the lovely Inn by the Sea (p. 109), Argentine chef Mitchell Kaldrovich combines European and Latin tastes and influences with fresh Maine fish and lobster. Expect seafood paella, chowder, pork chops, Argentine-style steak frites, and grilled local lobster.

40 Bowery Beach Rd., Cape Elizabeth. ⓒ **800/888-4287** or 207/799-3134. Entrees $19–$31. AE, DISC, MC, V. Mon-Fri 7:30am–3pm and 5:30–9pm; Sat-Sun 7:30am–3pm and 5:30–9:30pm.

Street & Co. ★★ SEAFOOD   Dana Street's intimate brick-walled bistro specializes in seafood, and it's possibly the city's best place to eat fish. You pass the open kitchen as you're seated in one of the two halves of a quirky dining room, then watch the talented chefs perform their magic in the tiny space. The fish is as fresh as can be (the docks are a block away), and they do lobster in interesting configurations (such as grilled and served over linguine in a buttery garlic sauce). Other fine choices include tuna, mussels, or the grilled catch of the day. Reservations are definitely recommended, although some tables are set aside for walk-ins; it can't hurt to check if you're strolling down Wharf Street and get hungry (try toward opening, rather than toward the middle of the service). During summer, outdoor seating's available at a few choice al fresco tables on a cobblestoned alley: plain but atmospheric.

33 Wharf St. ⓒ **207/775-0887.** www.streetandcompany.net. Reservations recommended. Main courses $14–$24. AE, MC, V. Mon-Thurs 5:30–9:30pm; Fri-Sat 5:30–10pm. Lounge opens 30 min. earlier.

Moderate

Beale Street BBQ ★★ 🍴 BARBECUE   Beale Street BBQ owner Mark Quigg once operated a takeout grill on Rte. 1 near Freeport, but author Stephen King got wind of his cooking; soon he was catering movie shoots and opening a restaurant. Of all the barbecue joints in Maine, this is probably my favorite: It's got an appealing roadhouse atmosphere, friendly staff, and great smoked meats. Check the board for daily specials, which usually include a fish entree as well as Creole and Cajun offerings. But I nearly always stick to the barbecue sampler (from the menu: "AKA All You Really Need to Know About BBQ"): You get your choice of pulled pork, chicken, or beef brisket; sweet, crunchy corn bread; a half slab of ribs; a quarter chicken; delicious spicy smoked links; and a mound of barbecued beans and coleslaw. Two people can comfortably split it, and it's just $24.

725 Broadway, South Portland. ✆ **207/767-0130.** www.mainebbq.com. Reservations not accepted. Main courses $9–$18. MC, V. Daily 11:30am–10pm. From Portland waterfront, cross Casco Bay Bridge (Rte. 77) and turn right onto Broadway; continue about ⅓ mile to restaurant.

Benkay ★ 🍴 SUSHI   Among Portland's sushi restaurants, Benkay is hippest, usually teeming with a lively local crowd lured by the affordable menus. Chef Seiji Ando trained in Osaka and Kyoto; his sushi, sashimi, and maki rolls deliver a lot for the price, and there's a wide range of choices and combinations. Standard Japanese bar-food items such as tempura (deep-fried vegetables), *gyoza* (dumplings), teriyaki, *katsu* (fried chicken or pork cutlets), and udon (thick noodles) are also served. It stays open pretty late, too—after midnight Friday and Saturday, which is handy in early closing Portland. For dessert, consider the green tea ice cream: deliciously bitter . . . and good for you. Sort of.

2 India St. (at Commercial). ✆ **207/773-5555.** www.sushiman.com. Reservations not accepted. Main courses $7.95–$17. AE, MC, V. Mon–Thurs 11:30am–2pm and 5–9:30pm; Fri 11:30am–2pm and 5pm–midnight; Sat 5pm–midnight; Sun 5–9pm.

Duckfat ★ CAFE   Owned by Hugo's (p. 115), this bistro serves Belgian-style fries with curried mayo, truffled ketchup, and other gourmet sauces, plus *poutine* (Canadian-style fries with cheese and gravy), soups, beignets, milkshakes of local ice cream, even a meatloaf-filled panini sandwich. Don't tell your doctor.

43 Middle St. ✆ **207/774-8080.** Entrees $6–$10. AE, MC, V. Sun–Wed 11am–9pm; Thurs–Sat 11am–10pm.

Flatbread Company ★★ ☺ PIZZA   This upscale pizzeria—an offshoot of the original Flatbread Company in Vermont, with a serious hippie tinge—might have the best waterfront location in town. It sits on a slip overlooking the Casco Bay Lines terminal, so you can watch fishermen and ferries while you eat. The inside brings to mind a Phish concert, with quirky décor and bearded staffers stoking wood-fired ovens, slicing nitrate-free pepperoni and organic vegetables, and the like. The laid-back, wood-smoky, family fun atmosphere makes the place fun to enter, but the pizza is excellent and will keep you coming back. Organic salads are also available.

72 Commercial St. ✆ **207/772-8777.** Reservations accepted for large parties only. Most pizzas $12–$15. AE, MC, V. Daily 11:30am–10pm.

The Grill Room & Bar ★★ AMERICAN   It replaced the popular Natasha's in the same space, but the Grill Room—with its bull for a sign—is off to a great start: good food, served unpretentiously. Chef Harding Lee Smith, a Portland native, left Back Bay Grill to open this mecca to meat. Most items are cooked on the open kitchen's wood-fired grills, but there's more than steak here: yummy seared-tuna sandwiches on ciabatta and thin-crust pizzas, for example. Of course, you can always get a steak (porterhouse, rib-eye, sirloin; the works) or a piece of grilled fish or chicken, and you're encouraged to do so: There's a card of tasty sauces running from "zippy" to "brandy cream" for your meat. The outdoor tables are ideal in summer, yet my favorite feature of the place is its bar area, with personable barkeeps, good beers on tap, and Red Sox on the flatscreen. This is fast becoming one of my favorite local bites.

84 Exchange St. ✆ **207/774-2333.** Appetizers and pizzas $7–$12; entrees $13–$27. AE, DISC, MC, V. Daily 11am–2:30pm and 5–10pm (Sun to 9pm).

Hi Bombay! INDIAN   The best Indian food in town, steps from the Old Port: fiery vindaloos, great mango *lassi* shakes, good *shami korma, masala,* and *biryani* dishes— and superb puffed-up *poori* fried breads. Get chutney and yogurt on the side.

1 Pleasant St. ✆ **207/772-8767.** www.hibombay.com. Entrees $9–$14. AE, DISC, MC, V. Daily 11am– 10pm.

Katahdin ★★ SEAFOOD/NEW AMERICAN   A longtime favorite of local Port-landers in the know, Katahdin is newly relocated to Forest Avenue—a more "artsy" and gritty location, but it has kept turning out the same great food. Chef Becky Lee Simmons' nightly specials range from the basic to the elaborate, with a strong lean towards the briny deep. From day-boat-caught sea scallops with house-smoked bacon and onions to flounder with a lemony brown butter; to shrimp in a buttery fondue or squid salad with lime, sea salt, and cracked pepper; to a raw bar of salmon tartare, local oysters, and ceviche. Yes, you can get a grilled steak or rib chop, too, thank good-ness. Ice creams, custards, and pastries are made for dessert. Reservations aren't accepted, so order a glass of wine—or one of the restaurant's locally famous marti-nis—while waiting to score a table.

27 Forest Ave. ✆ **207/774-1740.** www.katahdinrestaurant.com. Reservations not accepted. Small plates $5–$10, main courses $14–$24. DISC, MC, V. Daily 5–11pm.

Rí-Rá ★ PUB   This Old Port eatery is styled after an Irish pub, though it's some-what fancier than *real* Irish pubs. (Patriots and Red Sox are on the TV instead of soccer—sorry, "footie.") They've got the decor right, at least: the doors were imported from a pub in Kilkenny, and the back bar and counter are from other public drinking houses in County Louth. Upstairs beyond the pub is a dining room with a view of the docks; look for smoked turkey wraps, fish and chips, meatloaf, shepherd's pie, and Guinness bread pudding, plus a few more upscale dishes such as crab-filled salmon, Derrybeg pork (which is glazed with apricot, mustard, and cider), and *boxty,* a scal-lion-potato pancake topped with parsley sauce and meat.

72 Commercial St. ✆ **207/761-4446.** www.rira.com. Main courses $9–$20. AE, MC, V. Mon-Sat 11:30am–10pm; Sun 11am–10pm.

Shima ★ 🍴 FRENCH/JAPANESE   Just around the corner from the Regency hotel, Shima (Japanese for "island," and also the chef's last name) opened in the fall of 2009 in a space that had previously been a popular Thai eatery. It's every bit as good as that one was, owned by a Japanese-Hawaiian sushi chef who also trained in France. You can tell this guy comes from these diverse backgrounds: the huge, cre-ative menu features the expected sushi rolls, pork belly, and omakase (chef's choice) service that any self-respecting sushi joint or izakaya (bar) in Tokyo would. But it also veers off on interesting Hawaiian tangents (pineapples, bigeye), and employs creamy French sauces in more than a few spots. (Don't be surprised if a duck entree pops up, either.) The biggest surprise here is the price point: nothing's outright expensive, and many items feel like a steal. Yet the quality's very good for a just-opened place. Hip music plays in the background, and service is on two levels—upstairs has always been my preference, though it's sometimes harder to snag a table there than on street level. Good debut.

339 Fore St. ✆ **207/773-8389.** Entrees $8–$20. DISC, MC, V. Mon-Fri 11:30am–3pm and 5:30–10pm; Sat noon–11pm.

PACKING A picnic

Portland and its surrounding area is so stuffed with picnic spots you might need a week to sample them all.

For starters, don't miss the **Eastern Promenade** (p. 120), a hilltop park with expansive views of Casco Bay and its myriad (more than one for each day of the year) islands. Some have favorably compared this view with San Francisco's; even if that's stretching it a bit, you can't go wrong here watching the weather and light come and go.

The **Western Promenade** (p. 121), reached across town via Congress Street, has distant westerly views of the White Mountains (you can just make out the massive outline of Mount Washington on a clear day). The mall, airport, and paper mill in the foreground make for uninspiring scenery—but it's still a great spot for sunsets. There are a few benches, and in summer the free musical performances held here are of a pretty high caliber.

If you enjoy scenes of a gritty working waterfront, the **Casco Bay Lines** ferry terminal on Commercial Street (at the foot of Franklin Arterial) has plenty of benches.

If you seek a more tranquil water view, **Back Cove** loops around from Forest Avenue to Washington Avenue. Stopping places are scattered about the circular path around the cove, which in good weather is full of joggers, baby strollers, and walkers. A full loop takes about an hour.

Two Lights Lobster Shack ★ 🎁 SEAFOOD   This seasonal takeout shack, festooned in farm implements and plunked down on a piece of rock practically on top of one of Cape Elizabeth's string of lighthouses, is one of my favorite places to direct the new-to-Maine tourist. Yes, it's touristy. But it's been here forever; locals aren't shy about heading out here for a bite; and you absolutely cannot beat the views. You're looking at a panorama of the Atlantic while you wait for the kitchen to cook you precracked, steamed lobsters (order a platter, with coleslaw and blueberry cake included). You can also get clams. Eat in the homey dining room or out at the picnic tables right out there on the open rocks; troll through the gift shop next door; and don't forget to try or take home a whoopie pie for dessert.

225 Two Lights Rd., Cape Elizabeth. © **207/799-1677.** Lobsters market priced. MC, V. Late Mar to Oct daily 11am–8pm. Closed Nov to late Mar.

Inexpensive

Becky's DINER   This Portland institution resides in a squat concrete building at the not-so-quaint end of the waterfront. It's been written up in *Gourmet* magazine, but that's where the comparison to "fine dining" ends; this is a diner, Maine-style, complete with drop ceilings, fluorescent lights, and scruffy counters, booths, and tables. It opens early (4am) for the local fishermen grabbing a cup of joe and some eggs before heading out onto (or in from) the water; later in the day, it attracts high school kids, businessmen, and just about everyone else. The menu is extensive, offering what you'd expect: sandwiches, fried haddock, corn dogs, tuna melts, and milky bowls of chowder with just-caught fish. It's notable for its breakfasts, too, including more than a dozen omelets, eggs any way you want 'em, pancakes, French toast, and five types of home fries.

Just a few miles north of Portland along Rte. 1 in Falmouth, the Maine Audubon Society's **Gilsland Farm Sanctuary** is one of the best picnic spots I've found. Gaze out on grassy fields, wildflowers, and tidewater. Afterward, explore the society's intriguing displays, demonstration projects, and gift shops; this is clearly an organization that cares deeply about the state's natural resources. What the heck? Become a member while you're there.

And, of course, the beaches and parks in Cape Elizabeth (south of Portland, reached via Rte. 77) are all superlative picnic spots. **Two Lights State Park** and **Fort Williams Park** (which includes oft-photographed Portland Head Light) both offer sweeping vistas of lighthouses and craggy waves crashing onto dramatic rocks; **Crescent Beach State Park** is a very pleasing, sandy crescent, reached by a walk through beach roses. There's a concessions stand, too. A bit farther south, **Scarborough Beach Park** is another good choice. It's a long, sandy beach.

In metro Portland, make a quick fly-by of **Standard Baking Company** for great baked goods, sweets, and coffee (p. 113). **Cape Elizabeth** has a few general stores good for stocking up pre-beach; they're heavy on sodas, beer, and candy, but you can also score an Italian sandwich or an ice-cream treat at most.

---

390 Commercial St. ⓒ **207/773-7070.** www.beckysdiner.com. Breakfast items $2.25–$7.50; lunch and dinner items $2–$8. AE, DISC, MC, V. Daily 4am–9pm.

Federal Spice 🗲 WRAPS/GLOBAL   Parked beneath the lip of a parking garage, this has been one of Portland's prime go-to places for a quick, cheap bite ever since I can remember. Just off Temple Street, it's a breezy, informal little room with very limited seating; plan to take out. There are quesadillas, salads, and soft tacos, along with wraps full of interesting fillings such as jerk chicken, pumpkin rice, and Thai-curried slaw. The sweetish yam fries are an unusual side-dish choice when they're on the menu.

225 Federal St. ⓒ **207/774-6404.** Main courses $3–$7. V. Mon–Sat 11am–6pm.

Gilbert's Chowder House CHOWDER/SEAFOOD   Gilbert's is a very popular waterfront spot with tourists, and is nautical without taking the theme too far. The reasonable prices keep locals coming, too. The chowders are okay, if unspectacular; other choices include fried clams, haddock sandwiches, and various seafood you can order either broiled or fried. There's also a basic lobster dinner with corn on the cob and a cup of clam chowder. Limited microbrews are on tap, and they serve decent cheesecake for dessert, among other choices.

92 Commercial St. ⓒ **207/871-5636.** Reservations not accepted. Chowders $2.50–$9.75; sandwiches $3–$10; main courses $7–$23. AE, DISC, MC, V. Mon–Thurs 11am–10pm; Fri–Sat 11am–11pm; Sun 11am–9pm (closes earlier in winter).

Seng Thai Food 2 ★ SOUTHEAST ASIAN   For Thai food, this lowbrow corner eatery has been best in town for 20 years, and it must be good—doctors at the nearby hospital show up for cheap eats. Most everything costs less than $10, the Thai iced tea is excellent, and the head chefs (sisters, apparently) are unfailingly friendly. The cashew-nut entree with pineapple is great; you can't go wrong with a standard order of pad Thai, either. A good local bite.

921 Congress St. ℂ **207/879-2577.** Entrees $6–$16. AE, MC, V. Daily 10am–10pm.

Susan's Fish and Chips ☺ SEAFOOD   Zero pretense, zero frills, zero website—and what's arguably the best fried fish in a fish town. The stuff's fried up in a deliciously sandy, crunchy jacket that's never too heavy, but rather just right. Get fries, and put ketchup or vinegar on them. Or bring your *own* catch: they'll fry it! You've gotta love that.

1135 Forest Ave. ℂ **207/878-3240.** www.susansfishandchips.com. Entrees $6–$10. MC, V. Sat–Thurs 11am–8pm; Fri 11am–9pm.

Silly's ★ 📖🍴☺ ECLECTIC   Silly's has long been the favored cheap-eats joint of hip Portlanders. Situated on a busy, commercial street near the Eastern Promenade, the interior is informal, bright, and funky, with mismatched 1950s dinettes and a hodgepodge back patio beneath trees. There's also an unhealthy fascination with Einstein here; like Einstein, the menu is creative. The place is noted for its roll-ups ("Abdullahs"), a series of tasty fillings piled into soft tortillas—try one with shish kabob and feta, or a "Diesel" made with pulled pork and coleslaw. Newer menu additions include a slop "bucket," which has a messy, layered-burrito feel; the fries are hand-cut, the burgers big and juicy, and there's beer on tap. Don't overlook the dessert menu of cookies, pies, ice creams, cakes, and big milkshakes—Silly's whips its shakes up with peanut butter, tahini, bananas, malt, or almost anything else you could imagine, plus a few things (cranberry sauce? marshmallow crispies? Check.) you couldn't have.

40 Washington Ave. ℂ **207/772-0360.** www.sillys.com. Most items $5–$13; pizzas to $18. MC, V. Tues–Sun 11am–9pm.

EXPLORING THE CITY

Any visit to Portland should start with a stroll around the historic **Old Port ★**. Bounded by Commercial, Congress, Union, and Pearl streets, this area near the waterfront has the city's best commercial architecture, a mess of boutiques, fine restaurants, and one of the thickest concentrations of bars on the eastern seaboard. (The Old Port tends to transform as night lengthens, with crowds growing younger and rowdier.) The narrow streets and intricate brick facades reflect a mid-Victorian era; most of the area was rebuilt following a devastating fire in 1866. **Exchange Street** is the heart of the Old Port, with other attractive streets running off and around it.

Just outside the Old Port, don't miss the **First Parish Church,** 425 Congress St., a beautiful granite meetinghouse with an impressively austere interior that has changed little since 1826. A few doors down the block, Portland's **City Hall** is at the head of Exchange Street. Modeled after New York City's, it was built from granite in 1909. In a similarly regal vein is the **U.S. Custom House,** 312 Fore St. near the Old Port. The fine woodwork and marble floors here date to 1868.

The city's finest harborside stroll is along the **Eastern Prom Pathway ★**, which wraps for about a mile along the waterfront beginning at the Casco Bay Lines ferry terminal at the corner of Commercial and Franklin streets. This paved pathway is suitable for walking or biking, and offers expansive views of the islands and boat traffic on the harbor. The pathway skirts the lower edge of the **Eastern Promenade ★★**, a 68-acre hillside park with broad, grassy slopes extending down to the water. Little

It's been an interesting couple of years for Portland's public market, which once occupied a huge, 37,000-square-foot space a few blocks downhill from Portland's main drag. (Those few blocks, though, would prove crucial.) For a short while, this was one of *the* hip places in northern New England to grab a cup of coffee in the morning, a sandwich at lunch, a lobster and some vegetables to cook for dinner, and other gourmet goods. And they had free parking! But traffic began to wane, and the market suddenly closed its doors in 2007; the property was quickly sold off once the nonprofit foundation that had been running the place determined it could no longer subsidize the lower-than-market rents being charged to food vendors. City residents were disheartened, since the market had been a gift from Portland philanthropist Betty Noyce and had been expected to live a long, happy life.

Yet the market rose from its own ashes, and quickly. A consortium of vendors banded together and acquired a building right in the center of the city, rechristening it the **Public Market House** ★★ (② 207/228-2056; www.publicmarkethosue.com) at 28 Monument Sq., right beside a FedEx Office store. Today the market thrives once more, bursting with pizza, beer, coffee, fruits, vegetables, cheeses, and a generally lively vibe—even midday, people meet and mingle here. It's one of the most welcome possible additions to a downtown that had been looking a little tired.

East End Beach is also here, but the water is often off-limits for swimming (look for signs). The pathway continues on to Back Cove Pathway, a 3½-mile loop around tidal Back Cove.

Atop Munjoy Hill, above the Eastern Promenade, is the distinctive **Portland Observatory** ★ (② 207/774-5561), a quirky shingled tower dating from 1807, used to signal the arrival of ships into port. Exhibits inside provide a quick glimpse of Portland's past, but the real draw is the expansive view from the top of the city and the harbor. It's open daily (when flags are flying from the cupola) from Memorial Day through Columbus Day, 10am until 5pm; the last tour leaves at 4:30pm. Admission is $7 for adults and $4 for children age 6 to 16.

On the other end of the peninsula is the **Western Promenade** ★. (Follow Spring St. westward to Vaughan; turn right and then take your first left on Bowdoin St. to the Prom.) This narrow strip of lawn atop a forested bluff has views across the Fore River, which is lined with less-than-scenic light industry, to the White Mountains in the distance. It's a great spot to watch the sun set. Around the Western Prom are some of the grandest and most imposing houses in the city that include a wide array of architectural styles, from Italianate to shingle to stick.

The Top Attractions: From Lighthouses to Longfellow

Children's Museum of Maine ★ ☺   The centerpiece exhibit in Portland's kids' museum is its camera obscura, a room-size "camera" located on the top floor of this stout, columned downtown building next to the art museum. Children gather around a white table in a dark room, where they see magically projected images that include cars driving on city streets, boats plying the harbor, and seagulls flapping by. This never fails to enthrall, providing a memorable lesson in the workings of lenses. That's just one attraction; there are plenty more, from a simulated supermarket checkout counter to a firehouse pole to a mock space shuttle that kids pilot from a high cockpit.

142 Free St. (next to the Portland Museum of Art). ℰ **207/828-1234.** www.childrensmuseumofme.org. Admission $6. Free 5–8pm 1st Fri of each month. AE, MC, V. Mon–Sat 10am–5pm; Sun noon–5pm. Closed Mon Nov–Apr.

First Parish Church ★   Portland's oldest continuously operating house of worship (continuous since at least 1674, believe it or not) is right here in the heart of the city, although the present-day structure was "only" built in 1825 to replace the wooden building that had previously served as a church. Constructed of Maine granite quarried in the Brunswick, Maine area, it's a narrow, graceful counterpoint to the modern high-rises encircling it; the rough granite blocks and clock tower are topped by a surprisingly graceful spire.

425 Congress St. at Temple St. ℰ **207/773-5747.** Admission free. Interior tours possible, by appointment.

Maine Narrow Gauge Railroad Co. & Museum ★ ☺   In the late 19th century, Maine was home to several narrow-gauge railways, operating on rails 2 feet apart. Most of these versatile trains have disappeared, but this nonprofit organization is dedicated to preserving the examples that remain. There's a small fee for admission to the museum, which is waived if you purchase a more expensive ticket for the short ride on the little train that putters along Casco Bay at the foot of the Eastern Promenade. Views of the islands are attractive; the ride itself is slow and yawn-inducing, but your kids will undoubtedly enjoy it. Bring a video camera.

58 Fore St. ℰ **207/828-0814.** www.mngrr.org. Museum admission $2 adults, $1 seniors and children 3–12; train fare (includes free museum admission) $10 adults, $9 seniors, $6 children 3–12, free for children 2 and under. Memorial Day to Columbus Day daily 11am–4pm (trains run on the hour); rest of the year Mon–Fri 10am–4pm. From I-295, take Franklin Arterial exit to Fore St.; turn left and continue to museum on right.

Portland Head Light & Museum ★★   A short drive from downtown Portland, this 1794 lighthouse is one of the most picturesque in the nation. You'll probably recognize it from advertisements, calendars, or posters. The light marks the entrance to Portland Harbor and was occupied continuously from its construction until 1989, when it was automated and the graceful keeper's house (1891) was converted to a small town-owned museum focusing on the history of navigation. The lighthouse itself is still active, thus closed to the public; but visitors can stop by the museum or browse for lighthouse-themed gifts in a gift shop. The surrounding grounds of Fort Williams Park are great for picnics.

1000 Shore Rd. (in Fort Williams Park), Cape Elizabeth. ℰ **207/799-2661.** www.portlandheadlight. com. Free admission for grounds; museum admission $2 adults, $1 children 6–18. Park grounds daily year-round sunrise–sunset (until 8:30pm in summer); museum daily Memorial Day to Columbus Day 10am–4pm, weekends only mid-Apr to mid-May and mid-Oct to late Dec. From Portland, follow State St. across bridge to South Portland; bear left on Broadway. At 3rd light, turn right on Cottage Rd. (Rte. 77), which becomes Shore Rd.; follow several more miles to park on left.

Portland Museum of Art ★★★   Portland's thin brick art museum was designed by I. M. Pei & Partners in 1983, and it's top-rate by every standard. The museum features selections from its own fine collections along with a parade of touring exhibits.

(Summer exhibits are usually targeted at a broad audience.) The museum is particularly strong in its holdings of American artists with Maine connections, including Winslow Homer, Andrew Wyeth, and Edward Hopper, and it has fine displays of Early American furniture and crafts. The museum shares the Joan Whitney Payson Collection with Colby College, which includes wonderful European works by Renoir, Degas, and Picasso, among other titans. Special exhibitions have brought the landscape paintings of the Hudson River School, art by Native American high school students from northern Maine, and a mysterious *Mona Lisa* that may have been a preparatory study for the famous work. Guided tours are given daily at 2pm.

If you only time for one section, do not miss the **McLellan House ★★★**, an adjacent three-story Federal-style brick home built in 1801 by a Portland shipping and banking magnate. It's filled with the wonderful Sweat Galleries (named for the Portland congressman and wife who collected and donated them), which are fantastic and hold the museum's Winslow Homer landscapes, among other striking pieces.

7 Congress Sq. (corner of Congress and High sts.). ℭ **207/775-6148.** www.portlandmuseum.org. Admission $10 adults, $8 students and seniors, $4 students 6-17. Free admission Fri 5-9pm. Year-round Tues-Sun 10am-5pm, Fri to 9pm; Memorial Day to mid-Oct also Mon 10am-5pm.

Victoria Mansion ★★★   Perhaps no building in Portland is more famous than this imposing High Victoria manse, built from 1858 to 1860 of brownstone after plans by New Haven architect Henry Austin. This home, also known as the Morse-Libby House, is the nation's premier showpiece of Victorian architecture. Details fill the interior, from wonderful and plentiful mural work to a grand staircase, gas-fueled chandeliers ("gasoliers"), Persian-style rugs hand-woven in Scotland, stained glass, nearly all the original furniture, and plaster work and cabinets by famed interior decorator Gustave Herter. Yes, it's pricey and over the top, but a must-see for anyone serious about architectural history. December brings parties, tours, and special events.

109 Danforth St. ℭ **207/772-4841.** www.victoriamansion.org. Admission $15 adults, $14 seniors, $5 children 6-17, $35 family, free for children 5 and under. Christmas slightly higher. May-Oct Mon-Sat 10am-4pm, Sun 1-5pm; late Nov to Dec daily 11am-5pm. Tours twice per hour. Closed Nov and Jan-Apr. From the Old Port, head west on Fore St., and veer right on Danforth St. at light near Giobbi's restaurant; proceed 3 blocks to the mansion, at the corner of Park St.

Wadsworth-Longfellow House ★★   This 18th-century home is one of three structures housing the famous Portland writer Henry Wadsworth Longfellow's boyhood home *and* one of the state's best historical archives: a history campus, if you will. This home was built by Gen. Peleg Wadsworth, father of the poet, and is still furnished in early-19th-century style with some original furniture. Adjacent is the Maine History Gallery, a decent museum inside a former bank.

487-489 Congress St. ℭ **207/774-1822.** www.mainehistory.org. $8 adults, $7 seniors and students, $3 kids 6-18. Wadsworth-Longfellow House May-Oct and Dec Mon-Sat 10:30am-4pm, Sun noon-4pm (tours on the hour); museum Mon-Sat 10am-5pm.

On the Water

The 3½-mile **Back Cove Pathway ★** loops around Portland's Back Cove, offering attractive views of the city skyline across the water, glimpses of Casco Bay, and a bit of exercise. The pathway is the city's most popular recreational facility; after work in summer, Portlanders flock here to walk, bike, jog, and windsurf (there's enough water 2½ hr. before and after high tide). Part of the pathway shares a noisy bridge with

The Portland Sea Dogs are a minor league Double-A team affiliated with the Boston Red Sox (a perfect marriage in baseball-crazy northern New England). They play through summer at Hadlock Field (217 Park Ave.; ℓ 800/936-3647 or 207/879-9500; www.seadogs.com) a small stadium near downtown that still retains an old-time feel despite aluminum benches and other updating. Activities are geared toward families, with lots of entertainment between innings and a selection of food that's a couple of notches above basic hot dogs and hamburgers. (Try the tasty fries and sausages.) You might even catch future pro stars. The season runs from around April until around Labor Day.

I-295, and it can be unpleasant at a dead low tide; when the tides and the weather cooperate, however, it's a nice spot for a walk. The main parking lot is located across from Hannaford Plaza at the water's edge. Take exit 6 (Forest Ave. north) off I-295; turn right at the first light on Baxter Boulevard. At the next light, turn right again and park in the lot ahead on the left.

Another fine place to take in a water view is the **Eastern Prom Pathway ★**, which wraps for about a mile along the waterfront between the Casco Bay Lines ferry terminal and the **East End Beach** (the path continues onward to connect with the Back Cove Pathway). The paved pathway is suitable for walking or biking and offers wonderful views out toward the islands and the boat traffic on the harbor. The easiest place to park is near the beach and boat ramp. From downtown, head east on Congress Street until you can't go any farther; turn right, and then take your first left on the road down the hill to the water's edge.

Casco Bay Lines Six of Casco Bay's islands have year-round populations and are served by scheduled ferries from downtown Portland. Except for Long Island, the islands are part of the city of Portland. The ferries provide an inexpensive way to view the bustling harbor and get a taste of island life. Trips range from a 20-minute (one-way) excursion to **Peaks Island** (the closest thing to an island suburb, with 1,200 year-round residents) to the 5½-hour cruise to **Bailey Island** (connected by bridge to the mainland south of Brunswick) and back. All of the islands are well suited for walking; Peaks Island has a rocky back shore that's easily accessible via the island's paved perimeter road (bring a picnic lunch). There's also a bike rental outfit a few blocks from the island's ferry dock. **Long Island** has a good hidden beach. **Cliff Island** is the most remote of the six-pack, with a sedate turn-of-the-20th-century character.

Commercial and Franklin sts. ℓ **207/774-7871.** www.cascobaylines.com. Fares vary depending on the run and the season; summer rates $6–$9 round-trip. Frequent departures 6am–10pm.

Eagle Island ★ Eagle Island was the summer home of famed arctic explorer and Portland native Robert E. Peary, who claimed in 1909 to be the first person to reach the North Pole. (We're still not sure if he did; his accomplishments have been the subject of exhaustive debates among arctic scholars, some of whom insist he inflated his claims.) Regardless, in 1904 Peary built a simple, shingled home on a remote, 17-acre island at the edge of Casco Bay; in 1912, he added flourishes in the form of two low stone towers. After his death in 1920, his family kept up the home; they later donated it to the state, which has since managed it as a state park. The home is open to the public, maintained much as it was when Peary lived here. Eagle Tours takes one trip daily from Portland. The 4-hour Discovery tour excursion includes a 1½-hour stopover on the island.

Long Wharf (Commercial St.) ℂ **207/774-6498.** www.portlanddiscovery.com. $33 adults, $20 children 3–12; cost includes state park fee. July to early Sept, 1 boat daily Tues, Thurs, and Fri–Sun.

Shopping

Aficionados of antiques and secondhand furniture stores love Portland. Good browsing can be enjoyed along Congress Street; try the stretches between State and High streets in the arts district, or from India Street to Washington Avenue on Munjoy Hill. About a dozen shops of varying quality (mostly low-end) can be found in these two areas.

More serious antiques hounds may choose to visit an **auction house** or two. Two or three times per week, you'll be able to find an auction within an hour's drive of Portland. A good source of information is the *Maine Sunday Telegram.* Look in the classifieds for listings of auctions scheduled for the following week.

LUCKY 77: HITTING THE beaches

One of the supreme pleasures of visiting the Portland area is the opportunity to sample some of its many great beaches and lighthouse and ocean views. Even within Portland city limits, you can laze on the Eastern Promenade's tiny **East End Beach** (see above) for free; though I wouldn't swim there—a wastewater treatment plant looms nearby—you can take in great views. Across the bridge in South Portland, **Willard Beach ★** is a good neighborhood beach: small, with friendly locals, dogs, and tidal rocks to scramble over. There's plenty of parking here.

For the best of the out-of-town beaches and views, though, strike out for **Cape Elizabeth,** a moneyed suburb just south. (From Portland's State St., cross the Rte. 77 bridge going south, then follow signs.) You can choose from a trio of good beaches as you meander along **Rte. 77,** a lovely lane that occasionally recalls England with its sweeping views of marsh, ocean, or cultivated field. **Two Lights State Park ★★** (ℂ **207/799-5871**) is impressively scenic, and has the advantage of a decent lobster-and-seafood hut beside it: **Two**

Lights Lobster Shack ★★, open April through October. The lobsters are smallish, lobster rolls meaty, clam chowder pretty good, and the views are sublime. Farther south on 77, **Crescent Beach State Park ★★★** (ℂ **207/799-5871**) is a lovely mile-long curve of sand with ample parking, barbecue pits, picnic tables, and a snack bar. Both charge a fee from Memorial Day to Columbus Day. The town-operated **Fort Williams State Park ★**, located on Shore Road in Cape Elizabeth just off Rte. 77, is a bit harder to find but offers free access and supreme views of both the ocean and the much-photographed **Portland Head Light ★★** (see "Exploring the City," earlier in this chapter). Two to 3 miles farther south, turn left onto Rte. 207 for two more options: **Scarborough Beach Park ★**, on the left, another long strip of clean sand and dunes with changing facilities ($3.50 for access in summer) or—a bit farther along, on the right at the end of Ferry Road—quieter **Ferry Beach,** which is free and has good views of Old Orchard to the south.

LET'S GET HOPPING: THE beers OF PORTLAND

Portland is unquestionably the beer capital of New England. Not just northern New England, but *all* of New England. You think Boston has this many microbreweries and craft beers on tap? Think again.

Portland's Old Port is the heart of the hoppy action. **Shipyard Brewing** (📞 **800/789-0684** or 207/761-0807; www.shipyard.com) was first to hit it big (it opened in 1992, when microbrewing was still in its infancy). What began as a single Kennebunk brewpub in 1992 quickly blossomed into a thriving, nationwide operation; the product line and sales volume grew steadily as Shipyard bought or partnered with rivals like Casco Bay Brewing (which it absorbed), Sebago, and Gritty's. You can't actually tour the brewery—instead, visit the attached store, watch a video of the brewing process, and taste the results. The fruit-punch soda is great, too. You can buy their beer on-site daily at 86 Newbury St. (the entrance is on Hancock St.) on the fringes of the Old Port.

Gritty McDuff's at 396 Fore St. (📞 **207/772-2739**; www.grittys.com) is my favorite pub in town—I've covered it elsewhere (p. 129), but it's worth mentioning again. If I had time for just one beer in Portland before shipping out—this happens a lot—I'd end up at Gritty's, the second-ever brewpub to open in the city. Best beer in town? Maybe, maybe not. But the atmosphere is just right: a combination of geezers, ex-journalists, college kids, and tourists in an attractive space with big

windows front and back (plus a patio on a cobblestoned alley). The Black Fly Stout is an excellent example of the form, and the pub grub is fine. You can see the beer being born right below the pub: Those copper-and-bricked beer-works were designed in England. Yes, you can take a tour—ask the bartender about it.

Just downhill and around the corner from Gritty's is **Three Dollar Dewey's** (📞 **207/772-3310**; www.threedollar deweys.com), on a corner at 241 Commercial St., Portland's most acclaimed and prodigiously pinted (did I just say pinted?) pub. You can't believe the number of Maine and national microbrews they manage to draw on tap here—I lost count at about three dozen (with at least another 50 types of bottled beer in stock). Plus free popcorn. We're in. They're not too big on imports, but that's okay; this is local beer at its best, and the bar food's not bad. You'll run into tons of locals here, from antiques dealers to councilmen to college kids. Ask a bartender about the name.

The **Great Lost Bear** (📞 **207/772-0300**; www.greatlostbear.com), at 540 Forest Ave. feels more pubby than artisanal, but the beer card here tops Dewey's in quantity and, possibly, quality. With more than 60 tap lines and extensive storage space, they stock an extremely broad and well-chosen selection of brews from Montreal, Belgium, Brooklyn, Vermont, the other Portland (in Oregon), Germany, and other places. This is more of an international tasting than the Maine experience that

For new items, the Old Port, with its dozens of boutiques and storefronts, is well worth browsing. It's especially strong in contemporary, one-of-a-kind clothing that's a world apart from generic stuff you'll find at a mall. Artisan and crafts shops are also well represented.

Dewey's is. The layout is a bit dim and mazelike, but this place is often full.

Back uphill, **Sebago Brewing Co.** (© 207/775-2337; www.sebago brewing.com) is one of the best brew-pubs in town and has both indoor and outdoor tables. It's at 164 Middle St. and this Old Port charmer goes all-out with its central location, indoor and outdoor tables, free Wi-Fi, friendly waitstaff, and semigourmet menu of burgers, sandwiches, ribs, steaks, and fish. Oh yeah, the beer: The Boathouse Brown Ale, Frye's Leap IPA, and Lake Trout Stout are popular; or try the Full Throttle Double IPA for a more hopped-up experience.

You have to range inland to find two more of Portland's famous micro-breweries. Head west out Forest Ave-nue (off Congress St.) a few miles, then turn right on Riverside St. and take the next right after that into an industrial park. You'll soon come to **Allagash Brewing** at 50 Industrial Way (© 800/330-5385 or 207/878-5385; www.allagash.com), a fantastic craft brewer that's fast gaining nationwide buzz for its Belgian-style white, double, triple, and other beers. Allagash offers tours on weekdays from 11am to 3pm. There's also a beer store, again open weekdays only. Of the many locally brewed beers available in and around Portland, Allagash holds a special place in my palate. I still remember the first glass of owner Rob Tod's Belgian white I ever tasted—as crisp and clean as an orange rind. And, indeed, he uses cit-rus peels in the mix, as well as proprietary spices. Though that white is arguably his most famous, Tod brews other beers here, too: a Belgian dou-ble, a Belgian triple, and a bunch of specialty, limited-sale, cellared, and barrel-aged beers.

And in the very same industrial park—keep going around the circuit—is **Geary's** (© 207/878-2337; www.geary brewing.com) at 38 Evergreen Dr., usu-ally credited as Maine's very first microbrewery. It cranks out about a dozen varieties, most all of them very heavy on the hops. David Geary is usu-ally credited with kick-starting Maine's microbrew bonanza in the 1980s when he opened this brewery after several years of research and "testing" (drink-ing) in the British Isles. And brewery is still one of Portland's best-loved, pumping out their signature pale ale, plus about a dozen other (mostly hoppy) varieties. Tours are by appoint-ment, but you can visit the gift shop any weekday.

Finally, I'd be seriously remiss if I didn't mention the best place to find exotic beer in Portland. Hands-down, that's **RSVP Discount Beverage Center** (© 207/773-8808), which is at 887 Forest Ave. and doubles as a soda, juice, and beer can and bottle redemp-tion center. This isn't a bar, but no matter. The beers here are amazing—they were stocking rows of Belgian browns and *krieks* long before most of the rest of the free world had caught on. Look for exotic European and West Coast beers, and stock up for the rest of your trip.

Abacus Gallery   A wide range of bold, inventive crafts of all varieties—from fur-niture to jewelry—is displayed on two floors of this centrally located shop. Even if you're not in a buying frame of mind, this is a great place for browsing. 44 Exchange St. © 207/772-4880.

Allen & Walker Antiques ★   This is a great stop for New England, American, and Oriental items ranging from period oil paintings to antique furniture to sake sets . . . and much more. You just never know what you'll find here on a given day, and both Allen and Walker really know their stuff. 684 Congress St. ℰ **207/772-8787.**

Amaryllis Clothing Co.   Portland's original creative clothing store, Amaryllis sells unique clothing for women, plus accessories such as lingerie, belts, and jewelry. It's as comfortable as it is elegant: Colors are rich, patterns are unique, and some items are designed by local artisans. 41 Exchange St. ℰ **207/772-4439.**

D. Cole Jewelers   Jewelers Dean and Denise Cole produce lovely handcrafted gold and silver jewelry that's always attractive, and often surprisingly affordable. Browse through elegant traditional designs, as well as more offbeat ones, at the bright, low-pressure shop; the staff is extremely helpful. 10 Exchange St. ℰ **207/772-5119.**

Folia Jewelry   Original, handcrafted jewelry by owner Edith Armstrong (and some of Maine's top designers) is nicely displayed at this tasteful shop in the heart of the Old Port. The rings are especially arty and nice. 50 Exchange St. ℰ **207/761-4432.**

Green Design Furniture   This inventive shop sells beautiful mission-inspired furniture, crafted of cherry and other woods, that disassembles for easy storage and travel. "Green," by the way, isn't ecobabble: The owner's name is Doug Green. 267 Commercial St. ℰ **866/756-4730** or 207/775-4234.

Harbor Fish Market   Another of Portland's waterfront fish markets, it's worth visiting just to see piles of fish hard-working guys have pulled out of the bay. You can also buy smoked fish for your bagels, and lobsters packed safely for 24 hours' worth of traveling. You can also buy picnic fixings. 9 Custom House Wharf (across from Pearl St.). ℰ **207/775-0251.**

LeRoux Kitchen   What's a touristy shopping area without a crack kitchen store? Nothing. And this is Portland's. You'll find kitchen gadgets, made-in-Maine food products, and a good selection of wines at this Old Port shop. 161 Commercial St. ℰ **207/553-7665.**

L.L.Bean Outlet Store   Sporting goods retailer L.L.Bean opened its downtown Portland factory outlet in 1996. Look for last year's Bean fashions, returns, and slightly damaged goods, plus a small selection of first-run, nearly full-price items. 542 Congress St. ℰ **207/772-5100.**

Maine Potters Market   Maine's largest pottery collective has been in operation for 2 decades, and it's open daily. You can select from a variety of distinctive styles crafted by local potters; shipping is easily arranged. 376 Fore St. ℰ **207/774-1633.**

Rabelais Books   Finally, a decent bookstore in the Old Port! It's about time. With a motto of "thought for food," husband and wife Samantha and Don Lindgren run a great little enterprise combining classy, hard-to-find books with deep knowledge of food and wine. Foodie and reader heaven. 86 Middle St. ℰ **207/774-1044.**

Stonewall Kitchen   Stonewall is a frequent winner at trade shows for its delicious mustards, jams, and sauces: ginger peach tea jam, sun-dried tomato and olive relish, maple chipotle grill sauce, and so on. Browse (and sample the goods) at its Old Port store, which also features frequent cooking classes. 182 Middle St. ℰ **207/879-2409.**

Yes Books   Once owned by legendary local poet Pat Murphy (sadly deceased), this bookshop is about as well organized as an artist's bedroom, but so what? The first editions, philosophy, poetry, history, and prints here are amazing. 589 Congress St. © **207/775-3233.**

PORTLAND AFTER DARK

Bars & Music

Portland is usually lively in the evenings, especially on summer weekends when the testosterone level in the Old Port seems to rocket into the stratosphere, with young men and women prowling the dozens of bars and spilling out onto Fore Street and the surrounding alleys and streets.

Among the Old Port bars favored by locals are **Three-Dollar Dewey's,** at the corner of Commercial and Union streets (the popcorn is free); atmospheric **Gritty McDuff's Brew Pub ★**, on Fore Street at the foot of Exchange Street, where you'll find live music and a cast of regulars quaffing great beers brewed on-site; and the slightly rowdy Irish pub **Brian Ború,** on Center Street, with a rooftop patio. All three bars are casual and pubby, with guests sharing long tables with new companions.

Beyond the active Old Port bar scene, a number of clubs offer a mix of live and recorded entertainment throughout the year. As is common in other small cities where there are more venues than attendees, the clubs have come and gone, sometimes quite rapidly. Check the city's free weekly *Portland Phoenix* for current venues, performers, and showtimes.

Performing Arts

Portland has a growing creative corps of performing artists. Theater companies typically take the summer off, but it doesn't hurt to call or check the local papers for special performances.

Portland Stage Company ★   The most polished and consistent of the Portland theater companies, Portland Stage offers crisply produced shows starring local and imported equity actors in a handsome, second-story theater just off Congress Street. About a half-dozen shows are staged throughout the season, which runs from October to May. Recent productions have included *Proof, Arcadia, Fences, Noises Off,* Shakespeare's *Much Ado About Nothing,* and *Augusta* (a drama about small-town Maine). Performing Arts Center, 25A Forest Ave. © **207/774-0465.** www.portlandstage.com. Tickets $25–$35 adults, discounts for students and seniors.

Portland Symphony Orchestra ★★   The well-regarded Portland Symphony, now headed by Robert Moody, offers a variety of performances throughout the season

---

📷 100 **beers** old

The **Great Lost Bear** (540 Forest Ave.; © **207/772-0300**) has the best brew selection in all of northern New England, 50 to 60 offered at any given moment, including most of the numerous local brews crafted in Maine. Some of the choicest ales are even dispensed from one of three cask-conditioned hand pumps. As if that weren't enough, every Thursday the bartender showcases a particular brewer or style—a good way to get educated about the nuances of good beer. To find the Bear, head about 2 miles out on Forest Avenue (*away* from the Old Port), or ask a local for directions.

(typically Sept–May), ranging from pops concerts to Mozart; half the orchestra are Mainers, the rest New Englanders, and all are talented. Summer travelers should consider a Portland detour the week of July 4th, when the "Independence Pops" is held (weather permitting) at various sites around southern Maine, including the grounds of the Portland Head Lighthouse in Cape Elizabeth. There are also special Christmas shows. 477 Congress St. (©) **207/842-0800** for tickets, or 773-6128 for information. www. portlandsymphony.com. Tickets $16–$57, discounts for students and seniors.

SIDE TRIPS FROM PORTLAND
Old Orchard Beach

About 12 miles south of Portland is the unrepentantly honky-tonk beach town of Old Orchard Beach, which offers considerable stimulus for the senses (not to mention bikers, fried dough, and French Canadians aplenty). This venerable Victorian-era resort is famed for its amusement park, pier, and long, sandy beach, which attracts sun worshipers from all over. Be sure to spend time and money on the stomach-churning rides at the beachside amusement park of **Palace Playland** (© **207/934-2001;** www.palaceplayland.com), and then walk on the 7-mile-long beach past the midrise condos that sprouted in the 1980s like a scale-model Miami Beach.

The beach is broad and open at low tide; at high tide, space to plunk your towel down is at a premium. In the evenings teens and young adults dominate the town's culture, spilling out of the video arcades and cruising the main strip. For dinner, do as the locals do and buy hot dogs, pizza, and cotton candy—save your change for the arcades.

Old Orchard is just off Rte. 1 south of Portland. The quickest route is to leave the turnpike at exit 36 in Saco and then follow I-195 and the signs to the beach. Don't expect to be alone here: Parking is tight, and the traffic can be horrendous during the peak summer months.

Sebago Lake

Maine's second-largest lake is also its most popular. Ringed with summer homes, Sebago Lake attracts thousands of vacationers to its cool, deep waters.

You can take a tour of the outlying lakes and the ancient canal system between Sebago and Long lakes on the **Songo River Queen II,** a faux-steamship berthed in the town of Naples (© **207/693-6861**). Running from July through Labor Day, the 1-hour trips cost $12 for adults, $6 for children age 12 and under. Longer tours and group rates are also available for a little more money. Or just lie in the sun along the sandy beach at bustling **Sebago Lake State Park** (© **207/693-6613**), on the lake's north shore—the park is off Rte. 302 (look for signs on the south side of the road, btw. the towns of Raymond and South Casco). This park has shady picnic areas, a campground, a snack bar, and lifeguards on the beach (entrance fee charged). It can be uncomfortably crowded on sunny summer weekends; it's best on weekdays. Bring food and charcoal for barbecuing at the shady picnic areas off the beach. Admission costs $6.50 for non-Maine resident adults, $2 for nonresident seniors, $1 for children.

The park's **campground** has a separate beach (you need not camp to enjoy it, though), is a distance from the day-use area, and is less congested during good weather. It books up early in the season, but you might luck into a cancellation if you need a spot to pitch your tent.

Sabbathday Lake Shaker Community ★

Rte. 26, from Portland to Norway, is a speedy highway that runs past new housing developments and through hilly farmland. At one point the road pinches through a cluster of stately historic buildings that stand proudly beneath towering shade trees. That's the **Sabbathday Lake Shaker Community** (𝒞 **207/926-4597;** www. shaker.lib.me.us), the last active Shaker community in the nation. The half-dozen or so Shakers living here today still embrace their traditional beliefs and maintain a communal, pastoral way of life. The bulk of the community's income comes from the sale of herbs, which have been grown here since 1799.

Tours are offered a half-dozen times daily from Memorial Day through Columbus Day (in other words, mid-May through mid-October), providing a look at the grounds and several buildings, including the graceful 1794 meetinghouse. Exhibits in the buildings showcase the famed furniture handcrafted by the Shakers and include antiques made by Shakers at other U.S. communes. You'll learn plenty about the Shaker ideology, with its emphasis on simplicity, industry, and celibacy. The tours begin at 10:30am; last tour starts at 3:15pm. After your tour, browse the gift shop for Shaker herbs and teas. The tour lasts 1 hour and 15 minutes and costs $6.50 for adults, $2 for children ages 6–12; it's free for children 5 and under.

The village is about 45 minutes from Portland, on Rte. 26 near the attractive village of **New Gloucester.** From Portland, head northwest out Rte. 26 (Washington Ave., reachable from I-295, U.S. Rte. 1, and Congress St.). Or, from southern Maine, take exit 63 from the Maine Turnpike; after exiting, follow signs into the center of downtown **Gray** and follow signs for Rte. 26 north and into the village. Don't miss the farm stand, either, selling a wonderful array of dried herbs, flowers, and crafts farmed and crafted right on-site.

FREEPORT TO MONHEGAN ISLAND

Veteran Maine travelers contend that this part of the coast, long known as the "Midcoast" (one word, please), is fast losing its native charm—it's too commercial, they say, too developed, too highfalutin' . . . in short, too much like the rest of the United States. These grousers have a point, especially along U.S. Rte. 1. But get off the main roads, and you'll swiftly find pockets of another Maine, some of the most pastoral and picturesque meadows, mountains, peninsulas, and harbors in the entire state.

The coast is best reached via U.S. Rte. 1, which you catch in **Brunswick** by taking exit 28 from I-295. Going north, some highlights of the coastal route include the shipbuilding town of **Bath,** pretty little **Wiscasset,** and the Boothbay region on the southern end of the Midcoast; the lovely Pemaquid peninsula; lost-in-time **Monhegan Island;** and finally the power trio of **Camden, Rockland,** and **Rockport** at the northern end of the Midcoast (which are covered in chapter 8).

Beyond local tourist huts and chambers of commerce, the best source of information for the midcoast region in general is found at the **Maine State Information Center** (✆ **207/846-0833**) just off exit 17 of I-295 in Yarmouth, which isn't really *in* the Midcoast—but you'll almost certainly pass through to get there. This state-run center is stocked with hundreds of brochures, and is staffed with a helpful crew that can provide information about the entire state but that is particularly well informed about the middle reaches of coast. It's open daily year-round, though not 24 hours—but the attached restroom facilities are always open.

FREEPORT

123 miles NE of Boston, 333 miles NE of New York City, and 17 miles NE of Portland

If **Freeport** were a mall (which is not all that far-fetched an analogy), L.L.Bean would be the anchor store. It's the business that launched this town to prominence, elevating its status from just another Maine fishing village near the interstate to one of the state's major tourist draws for the outlet centers that sprang up here in Bean's wake. Freeport still has the look of a classic Maine village, but it's a village that's been largely taken over by the national fashion industry; most of the old historic homes and

ACCOMMODATIONS ■
Comfort Suites **7**
Harraseeket Inn **2**
Maine Idyll Motor Court **1**
Super 8 **7**

DINING ◆
Corsican Restaurant **3**
Gritty McDuff's **6**
Harraseeket Lunch &
    Lobster **8**
Jameson Tavern **4**
The Lobster Cooker **5**

Freeport

stores have been converted into upscale factory shops purveying name-brand clothing and housewares at cut-rate prices. Banana Republic occupies an exceedingly handsome brick Federal-style home; a Carnegie library became an Abercrombie & Fitch pumping club music (oh, the inhumanity); and even the McDonald's is inside a tasteful, understated Victorian farmhouse—you really have to look for the golden arches.

While some modern structures have also been built to accommodate the outlet boom, strict planning guidelines have managed to preserve most of the town's local charm, at least downtown. Huge parking lots are hidden from view off the main drag, and as a result Freeport is one of the more aesthetically pleasing places to shop in New England—though even with these large lots, parking can be scarce during the peak season. Expect crowds. Seeking the real Maine? Head at some point for **South Freeport,** which consists of a boat dock, general store, and lobster shack at the end of a finger of land reached via a numberless side road off U.S. Rte. 1.

Essentials
GETTING THERE
Freeport is on U.S. Rte. 1, though the downtown is most easily reached via I-295 from either exit 20 or exit 22.

Mapping Your Next Stop

Right across the road from the state information center in Yarmouth is the **DeLorme Map Store** (© **800/642-0970**), open daily from 9:30am to 6pm. You'll find a wide selection of maps here, including the firm's trademark state atlases and a line of CD-ROM map products. The store's fun to browse even if you're not a map buff, but what makes the place really worth a detour off the interstate is Eartha, "the world's largest rotating and revolving globe." The 42-foot-diameter globe occupies the entire atrium lobby and is constructed on a scale of 1:1,000,000, the largest satellite image of the earth ever produced. Far out.

VISITOR INFORMATION

The **Freeport Merchants Marketing Association,** P.O. Box 452, Freeport, ME 04032 (© **800/865-1994** automated, or 207/865-1212; www.freeportusa.com), publishes a map and directory of businesses, restaurants, and overnight accommodations. The free map is widely available around town, or you can contact the association to have one sent to you.

Exploring Freeport

While Freeport is nationally known for its outlet shopping, that's not all it offers. Just outside of town you'll find a lovely pastoral landscape, picturesque picnicking spots, and scenic drives that make for a handy retreat from all that spending.

By car head east on Bow Street (down the hill from L.L.Bean's main entrance), and wind around for 1 mile to the sign for **Mast Landing Sanctuary** ★ (© **207/781-2330**). Turn left and then right about ¼ mile into the sanctuary parking lot. A network of trails totaling about 3 miles crisscrosses through a landscape of long-ago eroded hills and mixed woodlands; streams trickle down to the marshland estuary. The 140-acre property is owned by the Maine Audubon Society and is open to the public until dusk.

Continue south on Wolfe's Neck Road, and you'll soon come to the 233-acre **Wolfe's Neck Woods State Park** (© **207/865-4465**). This compact, attractive park has quiet woodland trails that run through forests of white pine and hemlock, past estuaries, and along the rocky shoreline of the bay. Googins Island, just offshore and reached by following the park's Casco Bay Trail, has an osprey nest on it. This is a good destination for enjoying a picnic brought from town or for letting the kids burn off some pent-up energy—there are guided nature walks at 2pm daily during the summer. The day-use fee for the park is $4.50 per non-Maine resident adult, $1.50 for nonresident seniors, and $1 for children ages 5 to 11.

Shopping

Freeport has more than 140 retail shops spaced out between exit 20 of I-295 (at the far lower end of Main St.) and Mallet Road, which connects to exit 22. Some shops have even begun to spread south of exit 20 toward Yarmouth. The bulk of them are "factory" or "outlet" stores. If you don't want to miss a single one, get off at exit 17 and head north on U.S. Rte. 1. The bargains can vary from extraordinary to "huh?" Plan on wearing out some shoe leather and taking at *least* a half-day if you're really intent on finding the best deals. The sometimes-changing rotation of national chains here has recently included Abercrombie & Fitch, Banana Republic, Gap, Calvin Klein, Patagonia, North Face, Nike, Chaudier ("the cookware of choice aboard Air Force One"), Mikasa, Nine West, Timberland, and Maidenform, among many others.

Stores in Freeport are typically open daily 9am to 9pm during the busy summer and close much earlier (at 5 or 6pm) in other seasons; between Thanksgiving and Christmas, they remain open late once more.

Cuddledown Cuddledown started producing down comforters in 1973, and now makes a whole line of products much appreciated in northern climes and beyond. Some of the down pillows are made right in the outlet shop, which also carries a variety of European goose-down comforters in all sizes and weights. Look for linens, blankets, moccasins, and home furnishings, too. 475 U.S. Rte. 1 (btw. exits 17 and 20). ℭ **207/865-1713** or 207/865-4993. www.cuddledown.com.

Freeport Knife Co. ★ This store sports a wide selection of knives for kitchen and camp alike, including blades from Germany, Switzerland, and Japan. Look for their custom line, or just bring in your dull blade for a sharpening. They also sell replacement parts and do repairs on all brands of knives. 181 Lower Main St. ℭ **207/865-0779.** www.freeportknife.com.

L.L.Bean ★★★ ☺ Monster outdoor retailer L.L.Bean traces its roots from the day Leon Leonwood Bean decided that what the world really needed was a good weatherproof hunting shoe. He joined a watertight gum shoe to a laced leather upper; hunters liked it; the store grew; an empire was born. Today, L.L.Bean sells millions of dollars' worth of clothing and outdoor goods nationwide through its well-respected catalogs, and it continues to draw hundreds of thousands of customers through its doors to a headquarters building and several offshoots around town. The modern, multilevel main store is about the size of a regional mall, but it's very tastefully done with its own indoor trout pond and lots of natural wood. Selections include Bean's own trademark clothing, along with home furnishings, books, shoes, and plenty of outdoor gear for camping, fishing, and hunting (a particularly good section). The staff is incredibly knowledgeable—Bean's encourages staff to take the gear home and try it out so as to better serve customers. 95 Main St. (at Bow St.). ℭ **800/559-0747.** www.llbean.com.

Mangy Moose A souvenir shop with a twist: Virtually everything in this place is moose-related. Really. There are moose wineglasses, moose trivets, moose cookie cutters, and (of course) moose T-shirts. Somehow, this merchandise is a notch above what you'll find in most other souvenir shops around the state. 112 Main St. ℭ **800/606-6517** or 207/865-6414. www.themangymoose.com.

All Bean's, All the Time

One of the big reasons that L.L.Bean's flagship shop is such a tourist draw is that it's open 365 days a year, 7 days a week, 24 hours a day—note the lack of any locks or latches on the front doors. As such, it's a popular spot even in the dead of night, especially during summer or around holidays. Folks have been known to set out from New Hampshire at 1 or 2 in the morning to enjoy the best deals (and empty aisles) on their middle-of-the-night arrival.

TALE OF THE tags: FREEPORT VS. KITTERY

When visiting the Maine coast, many travelers only find time to shop once. Trouble is, there are *two* significant outlet centers on the southern coast. How to choose? Here's my quick take:

In **Kittery,** located at the southern edge of Maine, the malls are clumped along Rte. 1 just a couple of miles north of the New Hampshire border. Though the area appears at first glance to be a conglomerated, single huge mall, in fact there are five or six distinct areas with separate entrances. Choose carefully before you make your turn.

Generally speaking, Kittery is best for the name-brand shopper who wants to hit a large volume of places in a short time. It's easier to do Kittery more quickly than Freeport because of the side-by-side arrangement of the various stores and the malls. The trade-off is the blandness of the experience: Each of these side malls offer vast parking lots and boring architecture, and you cannot safely walk from one mall to another—you need wheels.

Among the best places to try among the various complexes are a **Gap** outlet, a **Samsonite** shop with knowledgeable sales help, a small but elegant **Coach** store, **Reebok** (I picked up swim trunks here for a fraction of the retail cost), **Polo Ralph Lauren, J. Crew** (good prices on sweaters), an **Orvis** sporting goods outlet, and a useful **Crate & Barrel** out-

let. The Native American–themed **Kittery Trading Post** is not all it's hyped up to be, but at least prices are low.

There are also a couple of good places here for a snack: **Bob's Clam Hut,** with a long line of hungry patrons awaiting superlative fried clams, and **Ben & Jerry's** for ice cream. For a sit-down meal, I like the **Weathervane,** a small New England fish-house chain that delivers value at moderate prices and is an excellent choice for families.

Freeport is a different animal. The outlets here are crunched together along and interspersed around Freeport's busy Main Street. That makes driving around town a headache, as pedestrians and cars cruising for parking bring things to a constant halt, but it's more convenient once you're out of the car. My advice? Strap on your walking shoes, park anywhere you can find a spot—even in a distant satellite lot—and just resign yourself to a lot of hoofing it. Bring a portable dolly or luggage rack to carry packages if you're expecting to buy a lot.

Freeport's outlets generally offer a higher grade of product than Kittery, and the stores have a great deal more architectural (and corporate) personality, too. You will actually find local, small manufacturers here, not just the big guys, and inventive big brands that go beyond the usual.

Thos. Moser Cabinetmakers ★★ Classic furniture reinterpreted in lustrous wood and leather is the focus at this shop, which—thanks to a steady parade of ads in the *New Yorker* and a Madison Avenue branch—has become nearly as representative of Maine as L.L.Bean has. Shaker, mission, and modern styles are wonderfully reinvented by Tom Moser and his designers and woodworkers, who produce heirloom-quality signed pieces. Nationwide delivery is easy to arrange. There's a good selection of knotted rugs made by an independent artisan, and a good gallery of rotating Maine-made art on-site. Finally, don't miss the 'Special Opportunity Room' and its samples, prototypes and refurbished pieces; you can save big bucks here. 149 Main St. ⓒ **800/708-9041** or 207/865-4519. www.thomasmoser.com.

You can troll **L.L.Bean**'s factory store (now tucked behind the flagship) for top-grade outdoors equipment and clothing, but even just sticking to Main Street you'll come across such finds as **Cuddledown of Maine**'s comfy pillows and comforters; the **Freeport Knife Co.**'s respected knife shop; **Abercrombie & Fitch**'s ever-young fashions (the girls will love this place), housed in a former Carnegie library; excellent bi-level **Gap** and **Banana Republic** outlets; the familiar **Polo Ralph Lauren** and **Coach** outlets; and plenty more distinctive factory shops.

If you love shopping and you love quality, it's a genuinely enjoyable experience to stroll around here for a day, taking a snack of chowder or lobster (see "Where to Dine" in the Freeport section, p. 139); pausing to assess your finds; grabbing a soda, grilled hot dog, or ice cream from a vendor; then planning dinner somewhere. Parking and traffic are negatives to consider, however—you may cruise a half-hour before finding an open spot (if you ever do). You'll also probably spend more on a trip to Freeport, as price tags are generally higher.

The winner? It's close, but I'll take **Freeport** for its walkability and relative elegance.

There's also a third option to consider, by the way. That's the big **Maine Mall,** which takes up a huge chunk of real estate near the Portland Jetport in South Portland (easily reached off the Maine Tpk. via its own exit). The options here are uniformly bland—this could be Anywheresville, America—and there are no outlet or factory stores; you'll pay full price, plus Maine state tax.

Still, if there's something reassuring about being able to bop among the likes of **Macy's, Bath & Body Works, Victoria's Secret, Pottery Barn, the Disney Store,** and **babyGAP,** then grabbing some chocolates from **Godiva** before settling down to coffee and a book or CD at **Borders** (in its own free-standing building), you might enjoy it. There's not much that's distinctive here, though the bookstore is very well stocked and the staff is helpful. Also check out the **Sports Authority** for low-priced sporting goods; watch for specials on exercise equipment, golf balls, camping gear, and the like.

Needless to say, there's a food court here, though it isn't very good. Consider dining at a nearby restaurant instead; a number of them surround the moatlike ring road that surrounds the mall and its acres of parking lots. Good choices include the **Weathervane** for seafood, or even the Canadian chain **Tim Horton's** (rarely seen in the U.S. outside Michigan and upstate New York) for doughnuts.

Where to Stay

Freeport has more than 700 guest rooms, ranging from quiet B&Bs with just three rooms to chain motels with several dozen. Reservations are strongly recommended during the peak summer season; the recent opening of several new midrange chain hotels and motels south of town on Rte. 1 has helped accommodate the summer crush, and in a pinch you might try the **Comfort Suites,** 500 Rte. 1 (© **877/424-6423** or 207/865-9300), or the adjacent **Super 8** (© **800/800-8000** or 207/865-1408). Both are relatively new and good enough for a night's rest.

Harraseeket Inn ★★ The Harraseeket is a large, modern hotel a short walk north of L.L.Bean on Freeport's main street. Despite its size, a traveler could drive right past

---

Need an Outlet?

L.L.Bean's campus just keeps expanding and supersizing and modernizing—though I'm not altogether sure Leon Leonwood himself would approve of the "1812 Cafe" and the huge new fishing and hunting store. That's right: In addition to the main store, L.L.Bean now maintains several new **satellite shops** stocking small, rapidly changing inventories of specialized goods, some of them used; this pair of shops replaced the old factory store just downhill from the flagship campus. **The Bike, Boat & Ski Store,** behind the flagship store, holds lots of canoes, kayaks, paddles, cycles, and helmets. Next to it is the

Hunting & Fishing Store (marked by a huge Bean boot, naturally) is the place for fly-fishing gear, hunting boots, and tons of other undeniably cool stuff—from freeze-dried camp food to hand-crank-powered LED flashlights (no batteries required), folding Adirondack chairs, 13-foot game-hunting perches, and a zillion lures, fly ties, buck knives, tent lines, and watercraft. Also adjacent is a huge new **Home Store** selling hand-crafted beds, sofas, and other furniture, plus home accessories (doormat, anyone?). Finally, Bean's **outlet shop** is downhill off Main Street in the new Freeport Village Station complex.

---

and not even notice it—which is a good thing. A 19th-century home is the soul of the hotel, though most rooms are in annexes added 1989 and 1997. Guests can relax in the dining room, read the paper in a common room while the baby grand player piano plays, or sip a cocktail in the homey Broad Arrow Tavern (with its wood-fired oven and grill, it serves dinner as well as lunch). Guest rooms are large and tastefully furnished, with quarter-canopy beds and a mix of contemporary and antique furnishings; some have gas or wood-burning fireplaces, more than half now have whirlpools, and some are even done up with wet bars and refrigerators. The big second-floor Thomas Moser Room is a nod to the local furniture craftsman, with a pencil post bed, writing desk, dresser, and flatscreen TV in the bedroom, plus a sitting room with a modern sofa, lounge chair, coffee table, Bose stereo, and stone fireplace. Plus a soaking tub. This inn is especially pet-friendly, with doggy beds and treats for four-footed guests.

162 Main St., Freeport, ME 04032. © **800/342-6423** or 207/865-9377. Fax 207/865-1684. www.harraseeketinn.com. 84 units. $125–$305 doubles; $245–$315 suites. Rates include full breakfast and afternoon tea. MAP rates available. Packages available. Pets welcome ($25 per pet per night). AE, DC, DISC, MC, V. Take exit 22 off I-295 and turn left; continue to Main St. Hotel is across road. **Amenities:** 2 restaurants; bar; concierge; indoor pool; room service. *In room:* A/C, TV, fireplace (some units), fridge (some units), hair dryer (some units), Jacuzzi (some units).

Maine Idyll Motor Court ⚓ Talk about a throwback to a happier time: This motel, 2 short miles north of Freeport's busy Main Street, doesn't take credit cards—but they *will* take your personal check. This 1930s "motor court" is a Maine classic, a cluster of 20 cottages scattered around a grove of oak and beech trees. It could have faded into oblivion, yet it hasn't: The place is still good enough for a simple night's sleep. Most cottages come with a tiny porch, wood-burning fireplace (birch logs are provided), television, modest kitchen facilities (no ovens), and dated furniture. The cabins aren't especially large, but they're comfortable enough and kept clean; some have showers, while others have bathtubs, and a good number of the cottages have two bedrooms (one even has three bedrooms). Ask for a cottage with air-conditioning if that's important—a few units have it. Kids like the play area, while dog-walkers head for nature trails accessible from the property and picnickers fire up grill sets. The only downer is the sometimes-drone of traffic: I-295 is just through the trees on one side, U.S. 1 is on the other side. Get past that traffic sandwich, though, and this place is a decent lowbrow value. They even have free Wi-Fi access.

1411 U.S. Rte. 1, Freeport, ME 04032. © **207/865-4201.** www.maineidyll.com. 20 units. May–Oct $63–$110 double. Rates include continental breakfast. No credit cards. Closed Nov–Apr. Pets on leashes allowed ($4 per pet per night). *In room:* A/C (some units), TV, fireplace (most units), fridge, kitchenette, no phone.

Where to Dine

Despite all the outlet glitz of Freeport, a couple of small-town restaurants have persisted. For a quick and simple meal, you might head down Mechanic Street (turn at the Mangy Moose, 112 Main St.) to the **Corsican Restaurant** ★, 9 Mechanic St. (© **207/865-9421**), for a surprisingly healthful 10-inch pizza, calzone, or king-size sandwich. The **Lobster Cooker,** 39 Main St. (© **207/865-4349**), serves daily seafood, sandwich, and chowder specials on an outdoor patio with views of the shopping hordes; go for salmon, lobster, or crab.

For yet another option, see the Harraseeket Inn, above, under "Where to Stay."

Gritty McDuff's ★ BREWPUB Spacious, informal, and air-conditioned in summer, Gritty's is an offshoot of Portland's original brewpub. It's a short drive south of Freeport's village center, and is best known for a varied selection of house-brewed beers like the unfiltered Black Fly Stout. The pub offers a wide-ranging bar menu of reliable salads, burgers, steaks, stone-oven pizzas, cheesesteak sandwiches, quesadillas, and pub classics such as shepherd's pie and fish and chips. There's a kids' menu as well.

187 U.S. Rte. 1 (Main St.), Freeport. © **207/865-4321.** Reservations not accepted. Main courses $10–$17. AE, DISC, MC, V. Daily 11:30am–11pm.

Harraseeket Lunch & Lobster ★ 🦞 LOBSTER Next to a boatyard on the Harraseeket River, about a 10-minute drive from Freeport's busy shopping district, this lobster pound's picnic tables get crowded on sunny days—although, with its little

---

Music to Shop By

One more of the fine reasons to come to Freeport in summer is for the abundant free music performances that take over the village's Discovery Park from mid-June through Labor Day. It's underwritten by L.L.Bean (of course) and officially known as **"Summer in the Park,"** and the performers in this summer concert series are eclectic—and impressively famous: in 2008, they ranged from folkies Martin Sexton, Richie Havens, and John Hiatt to bluesman Keb Mo', bluegrass pioneer Jerry Douglas, 1980s pop heartthrob Darryl Hall, and country superstars Kathy Mattea and Lonestar. (Not to mention the Crickets and the Portland Symphony Orchestra thrown in, too, just for good measure.) Things have gotten a little less musical since then—in 2010, the offerings mixed in more food festivals, kids' stuff, and fireworks and subtracted from the music, though country singer Tift Merritt did make an appearance. Get a schedule by picking up a brochure at Bean's information desk or checking the company website: Click on "Summer in the Park."

PACKING A picnic IN FREEPORT

South Freeport's **Winslow Park** offers camping but also day use. It's very scenic for this part of the coast, a great spot for picnics with a family. (There's a playground, too.) However, you've got to be sure to pick up food beforehand—perhaps a cup of chowder at nearby **Harraseeket Lunch & Lobster** (see above).

heated dining room, it's a worthy destination any time. Point and pick out a lobster, than take in river views from the dock as you wait for your number to be called. Advice? Come in late afternoon to avoid the lunch and dinner hordes—and don't wear your nicest clothes. This is roll-up-your-sleeves eating. You can also get fried fish, burgers, chowder, or an ice cream from the window.

Main St., South Freeport. ✆ **207/865-4888.** Lobsters market price (typically $8–$15). No credit cards. Mid-June to Labor Day daily 11am–8:45pm; May to mid-June and early Sept to mid-Oct daily 11am–7:45pm. Closed mid-Oct to Apr. From Freeport, take Bow St. to South St.; continue on South St. to South Freeport four-way. Turn left at stop sign and continue downhill to water.

Jameson Tavern ★ AMERICAN   In a farmhouse right in the shadow of L.L.Bean (on the north side), Jameson Tavern touts itself as the birthplace of Maine. And it really is: In 1820, papers were signed here legally separating Maine from Massachusetts. Mainers still appreciate that pen stroke today. The historic Tap Room is to the left, a compact spot of beer and pubby food. The rest of the house contains the main dining room, decorated in a more formal, country-Colonial style. Meals here are hearty: filet mignon wrapped in bacon, poached salmon, baked haddock, fresh pastas, and seafood salads. What's new in this old place? A nice porch, open about half of the year (not in winter, obviously) for dining semi al fresco.

115 Main St. ✆ **207/865-4196.** www.jamesontavern.com. Reservations recommended. Main courses $7–$18 in tap room and dining room at lunch; $15–$26 dining room at dinner. AE, DC, DISC, MC, V. Tap room daily 11am–11pm; dining room Sun–Thurs 11:30am–9pm, Fri–Sat 11:30am–10pm.

BRUNSWICK & BATH ★

10 miles NE of Freeport. Bath is 8 miles E of Brunswick

Brunswick and Bath are two handsome, historic towns that share a strong commercial past. Many travelers heading up Rte. 1 pass through both towns eager to reach areas with higher billing on the marquee. That's a shame, for both are well worth the detour to sample the sort of slower pace that's being lost elsewhere.

Brunswick was once home to several mills along the Androscoggin River. These have since been converted to offices and the like, but Brunswick's broad Maine Street still bustles with activity. (Idiosyncratic traffic patterns can lead to snarls of traffic in the late afternoon.) Brunswick is also home to **Bowdoin College ★★**, one of the nation's most respected small colleges. The school was founded in 1794, offered its first classes 8 years later, and has since amassed an illustrious roster of prominent alumni, including Nathaniel Hawthorne, Henry Wadsworth Longfellow, President Franklin Pierce, and arctic explorer Robert E. Peary. Civil War hero Joshua Chamberlain served as president of the college after the war. The campus green is full of interesting buildings and museums (see below), and is well worth a short stroll.

Eight miles to the east of Brunswick, **Bath ★** is pleasantly situated on the broad Kennebec River and is a noted center of shipbuilding. The first U.S.-built ship was constructed downstream at the Popham Bay colony in the early 17th century. In the years since, shipbuilders have constructed more than 5,000 ships hereabout. Bath shipbuilding reached its heyday in the late 19th century, but the business of shipbuilding continues to this day. Bath Iron Works is one of the nation's preeminent boatyards, constructing and repairing ships for the U.S. Navy. The scaled-down military has left Bath shipbuilders in a somewhat tenuous state, but it's still common to see the steely gray ships in the dry dock (the best view is from the bridge over the Kennebec) and the towering red-and-white crane moving supplies and parts around the yard.

Bath is gaining attention from young professional émigrés attracted by its fine old houses, but it's still at heart a blue-collar town, with massive traffic tie-ups weekdays at 3pm when the shipyard changes shifts. Architecture buffs will find a detour here worthwhile. (Look for the free brochure *Architectural Tours: Walking and Driving in the Bath Area,* available at information centers listed below.) The Victorian era in particular is well represented. **Washington Street**, lined with maples and impressive homes, is one of the best-preserved displays in New England of late-19th-century residences.

Front Street is the heart of Bath's compact downtown, on a small rise overlooking the river, and it's home to some remarkable Victorian commercial architecture—walk down the street slowly and try to count the brick buildings, but you'll lose track. There's also a clutch of shops, grocers, and eateries. Note especially the blond, stone Richardson-style **Patten Free Library** (at Summer St.)—its park features a gazebo, fountain, and perfect view of the Winter Street Church—and the bell tower on the big **City Hall/Davenport Memorial** (its correct name) at #55 Front St., built in 1929 during the Great Depression with money bequeathed by a wealthy local merchant. Its bell, from 1802, was probably cast by Paul Revere.

Note that **Christmas** is a big time in Bath: For a full month, from Thanksgiving to the holiday, downtown features fun window displays, a parade, and other events. Contact the local tourist office for more details.

Essentials

GETTING THERE

Brunswick and Bath are both on Rte. 1. Brunswick is accessible via exit 28 off I-95. If you're bypassing Brunswick and heading north up Rte. 1 to Bath or beyond, continue up I-95 and exit at the "coastal connector" exit in Topsham (exit 31), which avoids some of the slower traffic going through Brunswick.

For bus service from Portland or Boston, contact **Greyhound** (© **800/231-2222;** www.greyhound.com) or **Concord Coach** (© **800/639-3317;** www.ridecj.com).

VISITOR INFORMATION

The **Southern Midcoast Chamber of Commerce,** 2 Main St., Topsham, ME 04086 (© **877/725-8797** or 207/725-8797; www.midcoastmaine.com), offers information and lodging assistance Monday to Friday from 8:30am to 5pm from its offices in downtown Topsham.

What to See & Do

Collectibles buffs and aficionados of antiques malls should schedule an hour or so for **Cabot Mill Antiques,** 14 Maine St., Brunswick (© **207/725-2855;** www.cabotiques.com), located on the ground floor of a restored textile mill in downtown Brunswick. In the 15,000-square-foot showroom, more than 140 dealers purvey a wide variety of books, bottles, dolls, art, china, and porcelains. Quality is highly variable. The facility is open daily from 10am to 5pm.

IN BRUNSWICK

Bowdoin College Museum of Art ★★   This domed building on Bowdoin's main quad is one of the best small museums in New England—and it's free. The grand rotunda entrance announces the building's presence: it was designed by the prominent architectural firm of McKim, Mead & White. Collections are small but superb. The holdings include a number of American artists—some with close ties to Maine such as the Wyeths, Winslow Homer, and other landscape painters—but there's also a significant collection of work from classic European painters, and plenty of modern art. The older, upstairs galleries have soft, diffused lighting from skylights

PACKING A picnic

The campus of **Bowdoin College** (p. 140) in Brunswick is an attractive (though technically not public) place for a stroll and a bite on a bench. Better to eat in Brunswick's grassy public park (look for the gazebo), then walk it off around campus afterward. There's a big Hannaford's supermarket right downtown with a deli, but you may prefer the more natural fare of **Wild Oats Bakery and Café** (*C* **207/725-6287**) in the tiny Tontine Mall right on Maine Street.

high above; the basement galleries, which feature rotating exhibits, are modern and spacious thanks to a thorough redesign in 2008 by an Argentine architect that brought in light, color, and style.

Inside Walker Art Bldg., Bowdoin College. *C* **207/725-3275.** Free admission. Tues–Sat 10am–5pm (Thurs to 8:30pm); Sun 1–5pm.

Peary-MacMillan Arctic Museum ★★ 🎁 While Admiral Robert E. Peary (Bowdoin class of 1887) is better known for his accomplishments (he "discovered" the North Pole at age 53 in 1909), Donald MacMillan (class of 1898) also racked up an impressive string of Arctic achievements. You can learn about both men (and the wherefores of arctic exploration) in this tucked-away museum on the Bowdoin campus, just across the lawn from the college's fine museum of art (see above). Why here? Admiral Robert Peary and nonadmiral Donald MacMillan, graduated from Bowdoin in consecutive years late in the 19th century. When they returned from their respective polar travels, the two men donated many items they collected to their alma mater. The front room features mounted animals from the Arctic, including some impressive polar bears. A second room outlines Peary's historic 1909 expedition, complete with excerpts from his journal, and another room includes varied displays of Inuit arts and crafts, some historic and some modern. There are also thousands of black-and-white photographs on archive for the truly interested. It's a compact museum that can be visited in about 20 minutes or so.

Inside Hubbard Hall, Bowdoin College. *C* **207/725-3416.** Free admission. Tues–Sat 10am–5pm; Sun 2–5pm. Closed holidays.

IN BATH

Maine Maritime Museum & Shipyard ★ ☺ On the shores of the Kennebec River, this museum (just south of the big Bath Iron Works shipyard) features a wide array of displays and exhibits related to boat building. In fact, the museum is housed in the former Percy and Small shipyard, which built some 42 schooners in the late 19th and early 20th centuries. (The largest wooden ship built in the U.S.—the 329-foot *Wyoming*—was constructed here.) The centerpiece of the museum is the handsomely modern Maritime History Building, housing exhibits of maritime art and artifacts. There's also a gift shop with a good selection of books about ships. The remaining property houses a fleet of displays, including an intriguing exhibit on lobstering and a complete boat-building shop. Kids enjoy the play area (they can search for pirates from the crow's nest of a play boat, for instance), and there's always something interesting tied to the docks on the river.

243 Washington St. *C* **207/443-1316.** www.bathmaine.com. Admission $10 adults, $9 seniors, $7 children 6–17. Daily 9:30am–5pm.

Where to Stay

The Brunswick Inn ★   This handsome B&B in a rambling Federal-style house with a wraparound porch sits smack-dab in downtown Brunswick, facing the town green. It's run by enthusiastic and friendly owners, has been recently updated, and is positioned perfectly: within walking distance of Bowdoin College, a summer music theater, and restaurants lining Maine Street. Rooms are spacious, furnished in a country-modern style—some with wingback or wicker chairs, and all with attractive quilts; ask about the bright corner rooms, suites, and the Garden Cottage. The full breakfasts here are a highlight. Even better: A bar/lounge serves wine and microbrews before views of the park or a fireplace, with local acoustic musicians sometimes dropping by to play intimate sets.

165 Park Row, Brunswick, ME 04011. ✆ **800/299-4914** or 207/729-4914. Fax 207/967-8451. www. brunswickbnb.com. 15 units. $145–$195 doubles; $195 suites; $260 cottage. Prices include full breakfast. MC, V. Closed Jan. No children 5 and under. **Amenities:** Lounge. *In room:* A/C, TV (9 units), hair dryer.

Galen C. Moses House ★   This 1874 inn is an extravagant, three-story Italianate home done up in exuberant colors by innkeepers Jim Haught and Larry Keift. The whole of the spacious first floor is open to guests and includes a TV room, lots of ticking clocks, and appropriately decorated Victorian double parlor. The old friezes and stained glass are original to the house. Guest rooms vary in decor and size, but all are quite welcoming. The Victorian occupies a corner and gets a lot of afternoon light; the Suite is ideal for families, with two sleeping rooms and a small kitchen; and the Safari is zanily done up (in zebra-stripe patterns), though it does share a bathroom with the '40s Room (yes, nicely decorated in home furnishings from the 1940s).

1009 Washington St., Bath, ME 04530. ✆ **888/442-8771** or 207/442-8771. www.galenmoses.com. 7 units (2 with shared bathroom). Mid-May to Oct $119–$259 double; Nov to mid-May $119–$129 double. Rates include breakfast. 2-night minimum stay on summer weekends. AE, DISC, MC, V. *In room:* A/C, hair dryer, no phone.

Grey Havens ★   Located on Georgetown Island southeast of Bath, this gracefully aging 1904 shingled home with prominent turrets sits on a high, rocky bluff overlooking the sea. Inside, you can relax in front of a cobblestone fireplace before checking in. Guest rooms are as simple as you'd expect, with plain bathrooms; oceanfront rooms command a premium but are worth it for the views—if you're looking to save a few bucks, ask about an oceanfront room with its bathroom located across the hall. Guests can use the inn's canoes or bikes to explore the area. (There's a little stairway down to a tiny dock on the water, from which guests have reportedly caught whopping fish.) A drawback? This inn has been lightly modernized, so its character remains authentic—and the walls thin. The wonderfully big and (half-screened) porch is worth sitting on for a while, and the lounge features a big picture window.

Seguinland Rd. (P.O. Box 308), Georgetown Island, ME 04548. ✆ **800/431-2316** or 207/371-2616. Fax 207/371-2613. www.greyhavens.com. 14 units (2 with private hall bathrooms). $160–$280 double. Rates include full breakfast. 2-night minimum stay weekends. MC, V. Closed Nov–May. From U.S. Rte. 1, go south on Rte. 127 and then follow signs for Reid State Park for 11 miles; just after turning onto Reid State Rd. (also known as Seguinland Rd.), watch for inn on left. No children 11 and under. *In room:* No phone.

Where to Dine

Both downtown Brunswick and downtown Bath offer plenty of casual places to dine, ranging from burgers to barbecue and better. For informal fare, it's hard to go wrong at these cafes and restaurants.

In Bath, **Solo Bistro,** 128 Front St. (© **207/443-3373;** www.solobistro.com), is a great new addition to the area. Right on the city's main drag, this is a bistro/slash/jazz club (live music on Fri sometimes), with dinners of burgers, seared fish and seafood, lamb stews, and risotto among the possible offerings. Lunch runs more to upscale salads and sandwiches, and desserts are well thought out. The decor here is cooler than cool, including minimalist, brightly colored chairs; Scandinavian birch tabletops; and the space's native, rough-hewn stone walls. Interestingly, the husband-and-wife owners also own a Danish design shop right next door.

If you've just got to have lobster, head for Five Islands Lobster Co. (see below), or continue north across the Rte. 1 bridge a few miles to **Taste of Maine** (© **207/443-4554**), an overlarge pit stop, which nevertheless delivers the goods (read: lobster and fish) plus good marsh views.

Five Islands Lobster Co. 🍴 LOBSTER POUND   The drive alone makes this lobster pound a worthy destination. It's about 12 miles south of Rte. 1, down winding Rte. 127, past bogs and spruce forests with glimpses of the ocean. (Head south from Woolwich, just across the big bridge from downtown Bath.) Drive until you pass a cluster of clapboard homes, and then keep going until you can't go any farther. Wander out to the wharf (with great views) and place your order. This is a down-home affair, owned by local lobstermen and the proprietors of Grey Havens, a local inn (see above). The adjacent snack bar purveys soda and side dishes; gather all your grub and settle in at a picnic table or a grassy spot at the edge of the dirt parking lot. But don't expect to be alone: Despite its edge-of-the-world feel, this pound draws steady traffic and can actually get *crowded* on weekends.

1447 Five Islands Rd. (Rte. 127), Georgetown. © **207/371-2990.** Prices vary according to market. MC, V. Daily 11am–8pm June–Aug; shorter hours Mar–May and Sept to early Oct. Closed Nov–Feb.

Robinhood Free Meetinghouse ★★ FUSION   This place has attracted legions of dedicated local followers who appreciate the extraordinary attention paid to detail, such as foam baffles glued discreetly to the underside of the seats to dampen the echoes in the sparsely decorated, immaculately restored 1855 Greek Revival meetinghouse. Chef Michael Gagné features a raft of entrees, and they're wildly eclectic, with Asian accents (Szechuan-crusted seared tuna to salmon cooked in paper to two types of duck with honey butter and caramelized apples). Starters are equally fine, such as Thai crab soup or grilled shrimp adobo on homemade tortillas (served with banana salsa). Gagné almost always hits a high note—you can't go wrong on the careening menu. Even the sorbet served between courses is homemade. This is by no means a budget restaurant or waterside shack, but offers surprising skill given its out-of-the-way location.

210 Robinhood Rd., Georgetown. From Bath, cross the large bridge and turn south on Rte. 127, continue 6 miles, and turn left just after metal bridge, then continue 1 mile. © **207/371-2188.** www.robinhood-meetinghouse.com. Reservations encouraged. Main courses $22–$28. AE, DISC, MC, V. June to mid-Oct daily 5:30–9pm; rest of the year Thurs–Sun 5:30–9pm.

Sea Dog Brewing Co. PUB FARE   Relocated inside a historic old mill astride the Androscoggin River dividing Brunswick and Topsham, this brewpub makes a reasonable destination for grub such as nachos or hamburgers, plus a few more adventurous offerings that might run to a lobster bisque or a grilled-tuna sandwich. The eats won't necessarily set your taste buds on fire, but they do satisfy basic cravings. In any case, the beers here are consistently excellent, including the house hazelnut porter and India pale ale—and that's why you're here, right?

1 Main St., Topsham. © **207/725-0162.** Main courses $6–$18. AE, DISC, MC, V. Daily 11:30am–1am.

HARPSWELL PENINSULA ★★

Extending southwest from Brunswick and Bath is the picturesque Harpswell region. It's actually three peninsulas, like the tines of a pitchfork, if you include the islands of Orrs and Bailey, which are linked to the mainland by bridges. While close to some of Maine's larger towns (Portland is only 45 min. away), the Harpswell Peninsula has a remote, historical feel with sudden vistas across meadows to the blue waters of northern Casco Bay. No hiking trails, no garish attractions—just winding roads good for country drives. (Narrow shoulders and fast cars make for poor biking, however.) The islands are perfect for a beautiful drive back into an older Maine, and a good lobster dinner at the end of the peninsula (see "Where to Dine," below), on a good day. But if the weather's bad, skip it—you'll just find it monotonous. Note that, as in much of Maine, there is nothing at all to do on the peninsula at night besides enjoy the quiet.

The region is an amalgam—old houses with picturesque peeling paint next to manufactured homes, and summer houses next to the homes of Brunswick commuters. Toward the southern tips of the peninsulas, the character changes as clusters of colorful Victorian-era summer cottages displace the farmhouses found farther inland. Some of these cottages rent by the week, but savvy families book up many of them years in advance. (If you're interested, drop by any local real estate agency.)

There's no set itinerary for exploring the area. Just drive south from Brunswick on Rte. 24 or Rte. 123 until you can't go any farther, and then backtrack for a bit and strike south again. Among the "attractions" worth looking for are the wonderful ocean and island views from **South Harpswell** at the tip of the westernmost peninsula (park and wander around for a bit), and the clever **Cobwork Bridge** ★★ connecting Bailey and Orrs islands. The hump-backed bridge was built in 1928 of granite blocks stacked in such a way that the strong tides could come and go and not drag the bridge out with it. No cement was used in its construction.

Beaches

This part of Maine is better known for rocky cliffs and lobster pots than swimming beaches, with two notable exceptions.

Popham Beach State Park (✆ **207/389-1335** or 389-9125) is located at the tip of Rte. 209 (head south from Bath). This handsome park has a long and sandy strand, plus great views of knobby offshore islands such as Seguin Island, capped with a lonesome lighthouse. Parking and basic services, including changing rooms, are available; rare birds are often seen here. Admission is $6 for non-Maine resident adults, $2 for nonresident seniors, $1 for children 5 to 11 in season. There are discounts in the off season.

At the tip of the next peninsula to the east is **Reid State Park** (✆ **207/371-2303**), an idyllic place to picnic on a summer day and party with friends. Arrive early enough, and you can stake out a picnic table among the wind-blasted pines. The 1½-mile-long beach is great for strolling and splashing around. Services include changing rooms and a small snack bar. Admission is $6.50 for nonresident adults, $2 for nonresident seniors, $1 for children 5 to 11. To reach Reid State Park, follow Rte. 127 south from Bath and Rte. 1.

Where to Stay

Driftwood Inn & Cottages   The oceanside Driftwood Inn dates from 1910. This family-run retreat at the end of a dead-end road is just a compound of weathered, shingled buildings and a handful of cottages. The rooms of time-aged pine have a simple turn-of-the-last-century flavor that hasn't been gentrified in the least. Most rooms share bathrooms along the hallways, but some do have private sinks and toilets. (The inn also has seven rooms for solo travelers, a rarity these days.) Cottages on a small, private cove are furnished in budget style: Expect industrial carpeting and plastic shower stalls. Some beds could stand replacing, too, but where else in Maine can you sleep at water's edge this cheaply? The inn maintains an old saltwater pool and porches with wicker furniture to while away the afternoons, as well.

Washington Ave. (P.O. Box 16), Bailey Island, ME 04003. From Rte. 24 in Bailey Island, cross bridge and turn left onto Washington Ave. and proceed to end. (℃) **207/833-5461.** www.thedriftwoodinnmaine. com. 30 rooms (many share hallway bathrooms) and 4 cottages. $75–$115 double; $665–$700 weekly cottage; some units $115–$125 per day off season. No credit cards. Closed mid-Oct to mid-May; dining room closed Labor Day to late June. **Amenities:** Saltwater pool. *In room:* No phone.

Sebasco Harbor Resort ★ ☺ Sebasco is a grand old seaside resort fighting a mostly successful battle against time; some guests have been returning for 60 years, and spacious grounds remain the star attraction. Expect sweeping ocean views, a lovely seaside pool, and great walks, plus children's activities (including a kids' camp), a brand-new spa, and pancake breakfasts on the lawn. Most guest rooms are adequate, not elegant, although the resort has poured a pile of money into renovation. Small decks on many of the inn rooms are a plus. Better are the quirky rooms in the octagonal Lighthouse Building; most have TVs. There are also interior-court and lakefront cottages of various sizes (with up to 10 bedrooms), though some are very expensive—figure $1,000 and up per night (you read right) for primo lakeside digs.

Rte. 217 (P.O. Box 75), Sebasco Estates, ME 04565. South from Bath 11 miles on Rte. 209; look for Rte. 217, then signs to Sebasco. (℃) **800/225-3819** or 207/389-1161. Fax 207/389-2004. www.sebasco.com. 111 units, 22 cottages. Mid-June to Labor Day $199–$359 double, $459–$2,090 cottage; May to mid-June and Sept–Oct $139–$229 double, $319–$1,690 cottage. MAP rates also available. Rates do not include 10% resort service charge or state sales tax. 2-night minimum on weekends. AE, DISC, MC, V. Closed late Oct to early May. Pets allowed (some units). **Amenities:** Dining room; bike rentals; children's program; golf course; health club; pool; sauna; spa; tennis courts; hot tub; canoe and kayak rentals; sailing lessons; shuffleboard; bowling. *In room:* TV (some units), fireplace (some units), kitchenette (some units).

Where to Dine

If a steamed lobster is what you want (and you do), several sprawling establishments specialize in delivering the crustaceans fresh from the sea. On the Bailey Island side, there's **Cook's Lobster House** (℃ **207/833-2818;** www.cookslobster.com), which has been serving a choice of shore dinners since 1955 and is open daily from 11:30am until 9pm, year-round—no mean feat in a Maine winter. The restaurant has two decks for outdoor dining. Past Harpswell down Rte. 123 at the *very end* of the point (great views) is the popular **Estes Lobster House** (℃ **207/833-6340;** www.estes lobsterhouse.com), which serves various lobster plates in relaxed, festive surroundings.

Dolphin Chowder House ★ 🍴 TRADITIONAL NEW ENGLAND One of the premier places for chowder in the state is the down-home Dolphin Marina (now also known as the Dolphin Chowder House) at Basin Point. Wander inside the shingled building with small-paned windows adjacent to the boatyard, and you'll discover a tiny counter seating six and a handful of pine tables and booths with stunning views of Casco Bay. If it's crowded, you can get a meal to go—except the chowder. It's against Dolphin tradition to walk out with chowder; you have to sit down and enjoy

Get Your Kicks on Route 1? Umm . . . No.

While there's a certain retro charm in the *idea* of traveling Maine on historic Rte. 1, the reality is quite different. It can be congested and unattractive in this part of the state, and you're not missing anything if you take alternative routes. For memorable explorations, be sure to leave enough time for forays both inland and down the lesser roads along the coast.

it here. The chowders and lobster stew are reasonably priced ($4.95–$12) and absolutely delicious, and the blueberry muffins are often warm and capped with a crispy crown. Note that the servers can sometimes seem flummoxed at busy times, so bring your patience.

515 Basin Point Rd. (off Rte. 123), South Harpswell. ℂ **207/833-6000.** Breakfast items $1.25–$3; sandwiches $4–$8; complete dinners $14–$17. MC, V. May–Oct daily 7:30am–8pm. Closed Nov–Apr. Drive 12 miles south of Brunswick on Rte. 123, turn right at Ash Point Rd. near the West Harpswell School, and then take the next right on Basin Point Rd. and continue to the end.

WISCASSET ★★ & THE BOOTHBAYS ★

11 miles NE of Bath; The Boothbays are 11 miles S of Wiscasset

Wiscasset ★★ is a cute riverside town just inland from the Atlantic (no views), and it's not shy about letting you know: THE PRETTIEST VILLAGE IN MAINE, boasts a sign at the edge of town and on many brochures. Whether or not you agree with this self-assessment (and not all locals do), the town is attractive, even if the persistent line of traffic snaking through the center town through the summer diminishes its charm somewhat. Still, it makes a good stop for stretching one's legs and grabbing a bite to eat en route to other coastal destinations.

The **Boothbays ★**, 11 miles south of Rte. 1 on Rte. 27, are a string of several small, scenic villages down a peninsula—East Boothbay, **Boothbay Harbor,** and Boothbay—close to the ocean that, in some cases, actually provide frontal views of it. Bland, boxy motels hem in the harbor, where side-by-side boutiques hawk T-shirts emblazoned with puffins; still, there's some charm to be found here among the clutter and cheese, especially on days when foghorns bleat mournfully at the harbor's mouth.

Essentials

GETTING THERE
Wiscasset is right on U.S. Rte. 1, between Bath and Damariscotta. Boothbay Harbor is off Rte. 1, southeast down a peninsula on Rte. 27; coming from the south, turn right shortly after crossing the bridge in Wiscasset. Both **Greyhound** (ℂ **800/231-2222**; www.greyhound.com) and **Concord Coach** (ℂ **800/639-3317;** www.concordcoachlines.com) buses stop in Wiscasset.

VISITOR INFORMATION
As befits a place where tourism is a major industry, the Boothbay region has *three* visitor information centers in and around town. On U.S. Rte. 1, at the Rte. 27 turnoff, there's an info center open seasonally, a good place to stock up on initial brochures.

A mile before you reach the villages is the also-seasonal **Boothbay Information Center** (open June–Oct). If you zoom past that one or it's closed, don't fret: the year-round **Boothbay Harbor Region Chamber of Commerce,** P.O. Box 356, Boothbay Harbor, ME 04538 (✆ **207/633-2353;** www.boothbayharbor.com), is at the intersection of routes 27 and 96.

Exploring Wiscasset

Aside from enjoying the town's handsome architecture and general quaintness, there are a few quirky, low-key attractions good for a break while traveling up along the coast. You'll also find a handful of worthwhile antiques shops and eateries.

Castle Tucker ★ This fascinating museum at the edge of town, overlooking the river, was built in 1807 to resemble a Scottish manor house. It was then radically added onto and altered by a local cotton trader (yes, a cotton trader) named Richard Tucker who, in 1858, transformed the house, adding a rather showy piazza and other additions. Thanks to a reversal of fortune, the house wasn't renovated again—to the benefit of modern visitors, who can see what life was like for high society in Maine in the mid-19th century. Tucker's daughter eventually donated the home to New England's antiquities society, which maintains it today and Castle staff give tours of the manse, which features a wonderful, long staircase and trompe-l'oeil-style plaster that looks remarkably like solid wood. Find it overlooking the river (behind Sarah's Café).

Lee St. (at High St.). ✆ **207/882-7169.** Admission $5 per person. Tours depart hourly Wed–Sun 11am–4pm June to mid-Oct; closed rest of the year.

Musical Wonder House ★ 🏛 Danilo Konvalinka has been collecting music boxes for decades, and nothing seems to delight him more than playing them for awe-struck visitors; this offbeat museum, filling a 32-room sea captain's manse with some 5,000 of them (yes, *thousand*), is the happy result. The collection includes massive, ancient music boxes as resounding as orchestras (such as an 1870 Girard music box from Austria), as well as many smaller contraptions emitting tinnier, more tinkly sounds. The music boxes are displayed and played in four rooms of the 1852 home; admission is charged per room, and a tour can get quite pricey. If you're undecided about whether it's worth it, try this: Visit the free gift shop and sample some of the coin-operated 19th-century music boxes in the adjoining hallway first. Intrigued? Sign up for the next tour—there are three tiers of pricing.

18 High St. ✆ **207/882-7163.** www.musicalwonderhouse.com. 2-room tour $10, 3-room tour and quick upstairs walk-through $20, full tour $45; discounts for seniors. Late May to Oct daily 10am–5pm. Closed Nov to late May.

Exploring the Boothbay Region

Boothbay Harbor ★ was just another fishing village until it was "discovered" by wealthy city folks who built imposing seaside homes here. Once it embraced the tourist dollar, the village never really looked back, and in recent years it has emerged as a premier destination for tourists in search of classic coastal Maine; the village is often a mandatory stop on bus tours, which have in turn attracted kitsch, but some of the outlying areas remain beautiful.

Summer parking in the town requires either great persistence or forking over a few dollars. A popular local attraction is the long, narrow **footbridge** across the harbor,

Escaping the Crowds

Boothbay Harbor is overrun with summer visitors, but at nearby **Ocean Point**, you can leave most of the crowds behind by following a picturesque lane that twists along the rocky shore past a colony of vintage summer homes. Follow Rte. 96 southward from just outside Boothbay Harbor, and you'll pass through the sleepy village of East Boothbay before continuing on to the point. The narrow road runs through piney forests before arriving at the rocky finger. It's one of a handful of Maine peninsulas with a road edging its perimeter, allowing you fine ocean views. Colorful Victorian-era summer cottages bloom along the roadside like wildflowers. Ocean Point makes for a good bike loop, too; mountain-bike rentals are available from the Tidal Transit folks (see below).

built in 1901. It's more of a destination than a link—other than a few restaurants and motels, there's not much on the other side. The winding streets that weave through town are filled with souvenir shops purveying the usual trinkets.

In good weather, stop by a Boothbay-region information center (see above) and request a free guide to the holdings of the **Boothbay Region Land Trust** (© **207/633-4818**). More than a dozen of its properties dot the peninsula, most with quiet, lightly traveled trails good for a stroll or a picnic. Among the best: the **Linekin Preserve** ★, a 95-acre parcel en route to Ocean Point with 600 feet of riverfront. A hike around the loop trail (about 2 miles) occupies a pleasant hour. To find the preserve, drive south from Rte. 1 in Boothbay Harbor along Rte. 96 for about 3¾ miles, and look for the parking area on the left.

Coastal Maine Botanical Gardens ★   This expansive complex of waterside gardens is a work in progress, but it's well worth exploring. It's a natural habitat being gently coaxed into a more manicured state, with different pathways through the mossy forest featuring pocket gardens with different themes and flowers, plus an alley of more than 1,000 birch trees. Throughout, the walks are quiet and lush; one of the best trails runs along much of the tidal shoreline that's part of the property.

Barters Island Rd., Boothbay (near Hogdon Island). © **207/633-4333.** www.mainegardens.org. Apr–Nov, admission $10 adults, $8 seniors, $5 children age 3–17, $25 family; rest of the year free admission. Apr–Dec daily 9am–5pm; Jan–Mar Mon–Fri 9am–5pm. From Rte. 27 in Boothbay Center, bear right at monument, then make the first right onto Barters Island Rd.; drive 1 mile to stone gate on the left.

Maine State Aquarium ☺   Operated by the state's Department of Marine Resources, this compact aquarium offers a context for the marine life in the Atlantic. Kids can view rare albino and blue lobsters, or get their hands wet in a 20-foot touch tank—a sort of petting zoo of the slippery and slimy. The aquarium is located on a point across the water from Boothbay Harbor, and parking is tight; visitors are urged to take the free shuttle bus from downtown that runs daily until 5pm.

McKown Point Rd., West Boothbay Harbor. © **207/633-9542.** Admission $5 adults, $3 seniors and children age 5–16. Late May to Aug, daily 10am–5pm; Sept Wed–Sun 10am–5pm. Closed Oct to late May.

Boat Tours

The best way to see the Maine coast around Boothbay is on a boat tour. Nearly two dozen tour boats berth at the harbor or nearby. **Balmy Days Cruises**

(© **800/298-2284** or 207/633-2284; www.balmydayscruises.com), for instance, runs a half-dozen 90-minute trips daily around the harbor in summertime (mid June to mid September) from Pier 8 on Commercial St. for $15 per adult, $7.50 per child age 3 to 11. If you'd rather be sailing, ask about the five or so 90-minute harbor cruises daily from the same outfit aboard the Friendship sloop the *Bay Lady* ($22 for adults, $11 for children age 3–11). Schedules are reduced in spring and fall; call ahead for reservations.

The most personal way to see the harbor is via sea kayak. **Tidal Transit Kayak Co.** (© **207/633-7140;** www.kayakboothbay.com) offers morning, afternoon, and sunset tours of the harbor for $45 to $80 (sunset's the best bet). Single kayaks can also be rented for $20 an hour or $55 per day; tandem kayaks costs more. The shop is open daily in summer (except when it rains heavily), and is actually located on a dock at 18 Granary Way.

Where to Stay

One of the coast's best campgrounds, the **Chewonki Campground ★** (© **207/882-7426;** www.chewonkicampground.com) is located between Bath and Wiscasset. It occupies 50 acres overlooking a salt marsh and a confluence of lazy tidal streams. The 47 sites here are sizable and private; there's a nicely maintained pool with a sweeping view, and kayaks and canoes are available for rent. Campsites cost from $35 to $61 per night, which is at the 'really high' end of the camping price scale in Maine—yet it actually might be worth it. Drive 7 miles east of Bath on U.S. Rte. 1; turn right on Rte. 144, then take the next right past the airport and follow signs to the campground.

Five Gables Inn ★   East Boothbay was once home to a dozen summer hotels; now there's just one left. The handsome Five Gables was painstakingly restored in the late 1980s, and sits proudly amid a small colony of summer homes on a quiet road above a peaceful cove. It's nicely isolated from the confusion and hubbub of Boothbay Harbor. Rooms are pleasantly appointed, nearly all of them look out onto the water, and five have fireplaces burning manufactured logs; some also sport four-poster beds. Don't come expecting televisions or phones—it's a quiet place lacking both. Room no. 8 is a corner room with morning light and coastal views; room no. 14 is the biggest unit, with more watery views and a fireplace with a marble mantel. Some first-floor rooms open onto a common deck, which means little privacy, so take that into consideration when you're booking. The inn's included breakfast buffet is a good one.

Murray Hill Rd. (P.O. Box 335), East Boothbay, ME 04544. © **800/451-5048** or 207/633-4551. www.fivegablesinn.com. 16 units. $140–$235 double. Rates include breakfast. MC, V. Closed mid-Oct to May. Drive through East Boothbay on Rte. 96; turn right at blinking light onto Murray Hill Rd. Children 12 and older are welcome. *In room:* Fireplace (some units), no phone.

Newagen Seaside Inn ★   Newagen is a good, small, low-key resort with stunning ocean views amid a fragrant spruce forest, and there's been a new push here to renovate everything from rooms to amenities; a spa is said to be on the way. The inn is housed in a low, white-shingled building with cruise ship–like hallways sporting pine wainscoting and a cozy lobby. The 30 guest rooms have polished wood floors, Amish-style quilts, and country-themed decor—but *no* televisions. Downstairs, adults can relax in a pub or shoot some pool while kids try out the two candlepin lanes. (This may be the only inn in New England with its own bowling alley. If you're not from New England, know this: candlepins are maddening. Deal with it.) The 85-acre grounds are filled with decks, gazebos, a handsome in-ground pool, and walkways with magnificent water views. Five cottages with names like "Starfish" and "Spruce" offer additional privacy, eat-in kitchens, and one to three bedrooms each.

Rte. 27 (P.O. Box 29), Newagen, ME 04576. ✆ **800/654-5242** or 207/633-5242. www.newage nseasideinn.com. 35 units. $135–$235 double; $210–$285 suite; $1,500–$1,620 cottage weekly. Rates include breakfast (inn rooms only). Packages available. AE, MC, V. Closed mid-Oct to mid-May. Take Rte. 27 south from Boothbay Harbor across Southport Island bridge, continuing to the south tip of the island. **Amenities:** Dining room; pub; bikes; boat tours; bowling alley; Jacuzzi; heated outdoor pool; saltwater pool; free rowboats; tennis courts. *In room:* no TV, fridge (some units), kitchenette (some units).

Spruce Point Inn Resort ★ On a rocky point facing west across the harbor, this inn was built as a hunting and fishing lodge in the 1890s and evolved into a summer resort soon thereafter; some find it a mixed-bag experience, but it has benefited greatly from a spiffing-up that's been ongoing since the late '80s, including the addition of 55 deluxe suites with modern amenities such as Jacuzzis, marble bathrooms, private decks, woodstoves, carpeting, and new furniture. Guests typically idle in Adirondack chairs admiring the 15 acres of grounds, or partake of croquet, shuffleboard, and tennis on clay courts. Although more of a couples' place, children's programs accommodate a growing number of kids here. The spa is a welcome addition, and the formal dining room (with average food) enjoys good sunset views across the mouth of the harbor.

88 Grandview Ave. (P.O. Box 237), Boothbay Harbor, ME 04538. ✆ **800/553-0289** or 207/633-4152. www.sprucepointinn.com. 93 units. Late June to Aug $169–$359 double; spring and fall $139–$265 double; year-round $255–$560 cottage and condo. 10%–15% resort tax additional. 3-night minimum stay in summer and some holidays. AE, DC, DISC, MC, V. Closed mid-Oct to Memorial Day. From Boothbay Harbor, turn seaward on Union St.; continue 2 miles to inn. **Amenities:** 2 restaurants; pub; babysitting; concierge; conference rooms; fitness center; Jacuzzi; 2 outdoor pools; 2 tennis courts; spa. *In room:* A/C, TV, fireplace (some units), fridge, Jacuzzi (some units), kitchenette (some units).

Topside This old gray house on the hilltop looming above dated motel buildings looks a bit spooky at first glance. Fear not: Topside has spectacular ocean views at a reasonable price from its quiet perch over downtown Boothbay Harbor. The inn—a former boardinghouse for shipyard workers—has simple, clean, comfortable rooms mostly done in whites and pastels, furnished with a mixture of antiques and contemporary furniture. At the edge of the lawn there are two outbuildings stocked with basic motel-style units; these are on the smallish side, with dated paneling and furniture, though two end units (room nos. 9 and 14) might have the best views on the whole property. Most units allow some glimpse of the water, in fact, and many have decks or patios. Topside updated about one-third of its rooms and unveiled the new decor in spring of 2008; it has gotten very good reviews for both the B and the other B ever since.

60 McKown St., Boothbay Harbor, ME 04538. ✆ **888/633-5404** or 207/633-5404. Fax 207/633-2206. www.topsideinn.com. 21 units. $145–$245 double. Rates include full breakfast. 2-night minimum weekends, 3-night minimum holiday weekends. Children 6 and older welcome. DISC, MC, V. Closed Nov–Apr. *In room:* TV, fridge (some units).

Where to Dine
IN WISCASSET
Red's Eats ★ 🍴 LOBSTER/TAKEOUT Red's is a tiny red shack next to Rte. 1 smack in downtown Wiscasset—right where the traffic maddeningly backs up at the bridge—that's received more than its fair share of national ink and TV attention for

its famous lobster rolls. And they *are* good, consisting of big, moist, meaty chunks of chilled lobster in a toasted hot-dog roll with a little mayo on the side. Be aware that they're pricey—you can find less expensive, less filling versions anywhere else—and that the lines are long. Plan to spend at least 30 to 45 minutes waiting to place your order—and that's on a good day. But in my opinion, these are the best-tasting lobster rolls in Maine (those who don't agree head across the street and down the hill to Sprague's, where the lines aren't nearly as long). The few tables behind the stand fill up quickly in summer; you can also walk downhill to the public riverfront dock a minute away. Beyond the lobster rolls, very cheap fare (hot dogs, sandwiches) dominates the rest of the menu. You can also get very good ice-cream cones here.

U.S. 1 at Water St. (just before bridge). © **207/882-6128.** Most sandwiches and entrees $2–$6; lobster rolls typically $13–$16. No credit cards. Mon–Thurs 11am–11pm; Fri-Sat 11am–2am; Sun noon–6pm. Closed Oct–Apr.

Sarah's ★ 🍴 AMERICAN   Sarah's is a friendly Wiscasset family favorite that opened in 1987, then moved down the block to a place with a view of Sheepscot River a decade later. Expect personable service and filling, well-prepared food: lobster, pizzas, a changing menu of soups, stews, and more. It's usually crowded for lunch and early dinner, with items such as pita pockets, croissant sandwiches, and a cheesy local favorite called a whaleboat; the lobster rolls are uniformly excellent, and so are the dessert pies. Just want some takeout? They'll do a "bucket" of ravioli to go. This is a great choice for an informal lunch break when you're motoring up Rte. 1 and don't feel like standing in the long lines at Red's. The adjacent Twin Schooner Pub, also owned by Sarah's, is good for a beer.

Water St. and U.S. Rte. 1 (across street from Red's). © **207/882-7504.** Sandwiches and meals mostly $5–$10; pizzas $5–$18. AE, DISC, MC, V. Daily 11am–8pm (until 9pm Fri–Sat).

IN THE BOOTHBAYS

More creative dining can be found in the dining room of the Spruce Point Inn (see "Where to Stay," above).

Boothbay Lobster Wharf SEAFOOD   Across the harbor from downtown Boothbay, this place offers no-frills lobster and seafood; it's the best pick from a cluster of lobster-in-the-rough places lining the waterfront nearby. Lobsters are priced to market, and there are the usual fried-food baskets and sandwiches for those who don't dig crustaceans. This is a fine place for a classic Maine outdoor meal on a sunny day, but it's probably uninteresting in rain or fog. There's now a new fish market here, open year-round, where you can pick up cooked or live lobsters and the day's fresh catch even after the restaurant closes down for the season.

97 Atlantic Ave., Boothbay Harbor. © **207/633-4900.** Reservations not accepted. Fried and grilled foods $2–$10; dinner $7–$15. DISC, MC, V. Mid-May to mid-Oct daily 11:30am–9pm. By foot, cross footbridge and turn right; follow road for ⅓ mile to co-op.

Lobsterman's Wharf ★ SEAFOOD   On the water in East Boothbay, the Lobsterman's Wharf has the comfortable, pubby feel of a popular neighborhood bar, complete with pool table. That makes it popular with locals, but the kitchen also serves better-than-standard meals and knows how to make out-of-towners feel at home. Specials have included a mixed-seafood grill, a barbecue shrimp-and-ribs platter, grilled swordfish with béarnaise sauce, seafood fettuccine, tuna sashimi, and lobsters served at least four different ways. Blueberry pie and chocolate cake make good finishers. At lunch, there are burgers, baked haddock, lobster rolls, and steamed lobsters.

224 Ocean Pt. Rd. (Rte. 96), East Boothbay. ☎ **866/733-2057.** Reservations only accepted for parties of 6 or more. Lunch $5–$14; dinner $14–$25 (mostly $14–$16). AE, MC, V. Apr–Oct daily 11:30am–10pm. Closed Nov–Mar.

PEMAQUID PENINSULA ★★★

The **Pemaquid Peninsula ★★★** is an irregular, rocky wedge driven deep into the Gulf of Maine. Far less commercial than Boothbay Peninsula across the Damariscotta River, it's much more suited to relaxed exploration and nature appreciation than its cousin. Rugged and rocky Pemaquid Point, at the extreme southern tip of the peninsula, is one of the most dramatic destinations in Maine when the ocean surf pounds the shore.

Essentials

GETTING THERE

The Pemaquid Peninsula is accessible from the south and west by taking U.S. Rte. 1 to Damariscotta, then turning south down Rte. 129/130. Coming from the north or northeast, take U.S. 1 through Waldoboro, then turn south down Rte. 32 just south of town.

VISITOR INFORMATION

The **Damariscotta Region Chamber of Commerce,** P.O. Box 13, Damariscotta, ME 04543 (☎ 207/563-8340), is a good source of local information and maintains a seasonal information booth just off U.S. Rte. 1 during the summer months. To get there, follow Rte. 27 south, leaving Rte. 1 just east (across the bridge) after Wiscasset.

Exploring the Pemaquid Peninsula

The Pemaquid Peninsula invites slow driving and frequent stops. South on Rte. 129 toward Walpole is Damariscotta, a sleepy head-of-the-harbor village. On the left is the austerely handsome Walpole Meeting House, dating from 1772. Usually not open to the public, services are held here during the summer and the public is welcome.

Continue on Rte. 129 to picturesque **Christmas Cove,** so named because Capt. John Smith (of Pocahontas fame) anchored here on Christmas Day in 1614. While wandering about, look for the rustic **Coveside Bar and Restaurant** (☎ 207/644-8282), a popular marina with a pennant-bedecked lounge and basic dining room. The food is okay, but the views are outstanding; you might even catch a glimpse of the celebrity yachtsmen who tend to stop off here. Reservations are a good idea on summer weekends.

Continue south on Rte. 130 to the village of New Harbor, then look for signs to **Colonial Pemaquid** (☎ 207/677-2423). Open daily from Memorial Day to Labor Day, this state historic site has exhibits on the original 1625 settlement here; archaeological digs take place in the summertime. The $2 admission charge (free for children 11 and under) includes a visit to stout **Fort William Henry,** a 1907 replica of a supposedly impregnable fortress. Nearby **Pemaquid Beach** is good for a (chilly) ocean dip or a picnic with the family.

But **Pemaquid Point ★★**, owned by the town of **Bristol,** should be your final destination; it's the place to while away an afternoon (☎ 207/677-2494). Bring a

Travelers may be in for a rude surprise when they get the bill for a meal at a casual wharf-side lobster restaurant. Prices posted for lobsters are per *pound,* not per *lobster.* This can be inadvertently misleading, as a range of prices is often posted—for example, $6.99 FOR 1¼-LB. LOBSTERS, $7.99 FOR 1½-LB. LOBSTERS, and so on. That's the price per pound, not the total price, so you'll need to do a little math to figure out the final price of your lobster.

picnic and a book, and find a spot on the dark, fractured rocks to settle in. The ocean views are superb, and the only distractions are the tenacious seagulls that might take a profound interest in your lunch. While you're here, **Pemaquid Beach Park** is also worth a visit; there's a small admissions charge.

From New Harbor, you can also get a great view of the coast from the sea by taking a boat trip. **Hardy Boat Cruises ★** (℃ **800/278-3346;** www.hardyboat.com) operates summertime tours aboard the 60-foot *Hardy III,* and excursions include a 1-hour sunset-and/or-lighthouse cruise ($14 for adults, $10 for children age 3–11) and a highly acclaimed 90-minute puffin tour out to Eastern Egg Rock ($24 for adults, $15 for children age 3–11). Yes, you will see puffins. Extra clothing for warmth is strongly recommended, because it gets chilly out on the sea. The company operates from mid- or late May through Labor Day.

Rte. 32 strikes northwest out of New Harbor, and it's the most scenic way to leave the peninsula if you plan on continuing eastward on Rte. 1 to places such as Camden and Rockland. Along the way, look for the sign pointing to the **Rachel Carson Salt Pond Preserve ★★**, a Nature Conservancy property. The noted naturalist Rachel Carson studied these roadside tide pools extensively while researching her 1956 bestseller *The Edge of the Sea,* and it's still a good spot for budding naturalists and experts alike. At low tide, you can see starfish, green crabs, periwinkles, and other creatures in the tidal pools and among the rocks.

Where to Stay

Bradley Inn ★   The Bradley Inn is within easy hiking or biking distance to the point, but there are plenty of reasons to lag behind at the inn, too. Wander the nicely landscaped grounds or settle in for a game of cards at the pub. The rooms are tastefully appointed with four-poster cherry beds (though no televisions). The third-floor rooms are the best despite the hike up to them, thanks to distant glimpses of John's Bay, and a high-ceilinged second-floor suite occupying the entire floor is equipped with a full kitchen and dining room. The inn is popular for summer weekend weddings, so ask in advance if you're seeking solitude and quiet. A seaside spa, opened in 2007, offers a menu of wellness services.

Rte. 130, 3063 Bristol Rd., New Harbor, ME 04554. ℃ **800/942-5560** or 207/677-2105. Fax 207/677-3367. www.bradleyinn.com. 17 units. $160–$235 double; $225–$325 suite and cottage. Rates include full breakfast and afternoon tea. Packages available. AE, MC, V. Closed Nov–Mar. **Amenities:** Dining room; pub; free bikes; room service; spa. *In room:* Fireplace (some units), kitchen (1 unit).

Hotel Pemaquid ⚓   This 1889 coastal classic isn't directly on the water—it's about a 1- or 2-minute walk from Pemaquid Point—but the main inn has the flavor of an old-time boardinghouse. Outbuildings are a bit more modern. Though most rooms now have a private bathroom, the inn is still old-fashioned at its core, with a no-credit-cards policy, narrow hallways, and antiques, including a great collection of old radios and phonographs. It could be better, but it is what it is, and some guests love that. The two- and three-bedroom suites—one with a sun porch and one with a kitchen—are good for families, and there are cottages and a carriage house rented by the week.

3098 Bristol Rd. (Rte. 130), Pemaquid Point (mailing address: 3098 Bristol Rd., New Harbor, ME 04554). ✆ **207/677-2312.** www.hotelpemaquid.com. 23 units (4 with shared bathroom). $80–$100 double with private bathroom, $65–$75 double with shared bathroom; $125–$240 suite; $775–$825 cottage weekly. 2-night minimum stay on weekends. No credit cards. Closed mid-Oct to mid-Apr. *In room:* TV (some units), no phone.

Where to Dine

Shaw's Fish and Lobster Wharf ★ 🍴 LOBSTER   Shaw's attracts hordes of tourists, but it's no trick to figure out why: It's one of the best-situated lobster pounds, with postcard-perfect views of the working harbor. You can stake out a seat on either the open deck or the indoor dining room (go for the deck), or order some appetizers from the raw bar. This is one of the few lobster joints in Maine with a full liquor license, and the lobster rolls are considered by experts (okay, eaters like me) to be some of Maine's best.

Rte. 32, New Harbor. ✆ **207/677-2200.** Lobster priced to market (typically $7 per pound), entrees $10–$25. MC, V. Mid-May to mid-Oct daily 11am–9pm. Closed mid-Oct to mid-May.

MONHEGAN ISLAND ★★★

Monhegan Island ★★★ is Maine's premier island destination. Visited by Europeans as early as 1497, the wild, remote island was settled by fishermen attracted to the sea's bounty in offshore waters. In the 1870s, artists discovered the island and stayed for a spell, including Rockwell Kent (the artist most closely associated with the island), George Bellows, Edward Hopper, and Robert Henri.

It's not hard to figure out why artists have been attracted to this place, with its almost-mystical sense of tranquillity. It's also a superb destination for hikers, since most of the island is undeveloped and laced with footpaths.

Just be aware that this is not Martha's Vineyard. There's one ATM on Monhegan, and few pay phones—heck, even electricity is scarce. That's what most visitors seem to like about it, and an overnight at one of the island's very simple inns is strongly recommended if you've got time; the island's true character doesn't emerge until the last day boat sails back to the mainland. If you just can't stomach the complete quiet and the lack of phones, TVs, and late-night takeout, day trips are also easy to arrange.

Essentials
GETTING THERE

Access to Monhegan Island is via boat from New Harbor, Boothbay Harbor, or Port Clyde. The picturesque trip from Port Clyde is the favorite route of longtime visitors; the boat passes the Marshall Point Lighthouse and a series of spruce-clad islands before reaching the open sea and plying its way island-ward.

Several boats make the run to Monhegan from little Port Clyde. The *Laura B* is a doughty workboat (building supplies and boxes of food are loaded on first; passengers fill in the available niches on the deck and in the small cabin), and makes the run in about 1¼ hours. A newer boat—the slightly faster, passenger-oriented *Elizabeth Ann*—also makes the run, offering a large heated cabin and more seating, in about 50 minutes. You'll need to leave your car behind, so pack light and wear sturdy shoes. The fare is $32 round-trip for adults, $18 for children ages 2 to 12, and $5 for pets. They do take credit cards, but reservations are advised. Contact **Monhegan Boat Line,** P.O. Box 238, Port Clyde, ME 04855 (© **207/372-8848;** www.monhegan boat.com). Parking is available just off the Port Clyde dock for $5 per day.

You can also get out here by boarding a **Hardy Boat** (© **800/278-3346;** www. hardyboat.com) to Monhegan. There are one to two departures daily from late May through mid-October, and the journey costs $32 round-trip for adults, $18 round-trip for children age 3 to 11. See "Exploring the Pemaquid Peninsula," above, for more details on this outfit.

Finally, if you're in the Boothbays, **Balmy Days** (© **800/298-2284** or 207/633-2284; www.balmydayscruises.com) *also* does a Monhegan run in summer, from mid-June through late September. The boat leaves once daily at 9:30am, drops you off, and touches the island again at 4:15pm: perfect for day-trippers. (Or day-and-a-half-trippers.) The round-trip costs $32 for adults, $18 for children age 3 to 11.

VISITOR INFORMATION

Monhegan Island has no formal visitor center, but it's small and friendly enough that you can make inquiries of just about anyone you meet on the island pathways. Clerks at the ferry dock in Port Clyde may also be helpful. Be sure to pick up the inexpensive map of the island's hiking trails at the ticket office or various shops around the island. Also, a great website maintained by island residents dispenses very complete info to first-time visitors. Find it on the web at **www.monheganwelcome.com**.

Exploring Port Clyde

Port Clyde is located at the tip of a long finger of land about 15 miles south of Rte. 1. Its charm derives from the fact that it's still just a fishing village. While some small-scale tourist enterprises have made their mark here, it caters primarily to working fishermen and the ferrymen who keep Monhegan supplied.

Head to the **Port Clyde General Store** ★ on the waterfront and soak up the cracker-barrel ambience (there's actually a decent selection of wine here, attesting to encroaching upscalism). Order a sandwich to go, and then drive to the **Marshall Point Lighthouse Museum** (© **207/372-6450;** www.marshallpoint.org)—to find it, follow the road along the harbor east and bear right to reach the point. The museum opens weekends only during May, then daily from Memorial Day until Columbus Day. Does it look somehow familiar? It is: This small lighthouse received a few moments of fame when Forrest Gump turned around here and headed back west during his cross-country walks in the movie, but it also happens to be one of the most peaceful and scenic lighthouses in the state.

Exploring Monhegan

Walking is the chief activity on the island; it's genuinely surprising how much distance you can cover on these 700 acres (about 1½ miles long and ½ mile wide). The village clusters tightly around the harbor; the rest of the island is mostly wild land, laced with 17 miles of trails. Much of the island is ringed with high, open bluffs atop fissured cliffs; pack a picnic lunch and hike the **perimeter trail** ★★★, spending much of the day sitting, reading, and enjoying the surf rolling in against the cliffs.

The inland trails are appealing in a far different way. Deep, dark **Cathedral Woods** ★★ is mossy and fragrant; sunlight only dimly filters through the evergreens to the forest floor. **Birding** is also a popular spring and fall activity. The island is right on the Atlantic flyway, and a wide variety of birds stop here during annual migrations.

The sole attraction on the island is the good **Monhegan Museum** ★ (www.monheganmuseum.org), at 1 Lighthouse Hill next to the 1824 lighthouse on a high point above the village. The museum, open for only a short season (11:30am–3:30pm daily July–Aug, 1:30–3:30pm daily Sept), holds a quirky collection of historical artifacts and provides context for this rugged island's history. Nearby is a small and select art museum that opened in 1998 and features changing exhibits showcasing the works of illustrious island artists, including Rockwell Kent. There's no charge.

The spectacular **view** ★★ from the grassy slope in front of the lighthouse is the real prize, though. The vista sweeps across a marsh, past one of the island's most historic hotels, past Manana Island, and across the sea beyond. Get here early if you want a good seat for the sunset; folks often congregate here after dinner for the view.

Artists are still attracted to this island in great numbers, and many open their **studios** to visitors during posted hours in summer. Some of the artwork runs along the lines of predictable seascapes and sunsets, but much of it rises above the banal. Look for the bulletin board along the main pathway in the village for a listing of the days and hours the studios are open.

Where to Stay & Dine on Monhegan

Things have changed—a little—since the day when you had zero options for sleeping or dining overnight on Monhegan, and had to retreat to the mainland. There are a handful of cottages, simple inns, and plain restaurants on the island. In a pinch, hit **The Monhegan Store** (✆ 207/594-5546) for picnic supplies.

Monhegan House ★   The handsome Monhegan House has been accommodating guests since 1870, and it has the comfortable, worn patina of a venerable lodging house. The accommodations at this four-story walk-up are austere but comfortable, more so after recent renovations; it's pretty pricey, though, for what you get. There are no closets, and everyone uses clean dormitory-style bathrooms except those who stay in a newish two-bedroom suite with queen-size bed and double sofa. The downstairs lobby with fireplace is a welcome spot to sit and take the fog-induced chill out of your bones, since it can get cool on the island even in August. A dining room serves dinner nightly during the short summer season, and Monhegan's first public Wi-Fi hotspot (never thought I'd be writing *that* sentence) and ATM are in the casual eatery, the Novelty, behind the inn, which proudly touts its whoopee pies. Yes, if you're not a New Englander, those are a real food. Damned yummy, too.

Monhegan Island, ME 04852. ✆ **207/594-7983.** www.monheganhouse.com. 31 units (most with shared bathroom). $117–$154 double; $189–$220 suite. Rates include breakfast. MC, V. Closed Oct to late May. Located across road from island's church. **Amenities:** 2 restaurants. *In room:* No phone.

Trailing Yew   At the end of long summer afternoons, guests congregate near the flagpole in front of the main building of this simple, rustic hillside compound. They're waiting for the ringing of the bell that signals the start of the included-with-the-price dinner, just like at summer camp. Inside, guests sit around long tables, introduce themselves to their neighbors, and wait for the family style repast. This is a friendly, informal place popular with hikers and birders. Guest rooms are simply furnished in a pleasantly dated, summer-home style. Only one of the four guest buildings has electricity, however—guests in rooms without electricity are provided kerosene lamps and instructions for their use. Also, all rooms are unheated. Rates here are charged per person: $110 for a single adult, less for groups of two or more and for children (prorated according to age).

Lobster Cove Rd., Monhegan Island, ME 04852. © **207/596-0440.** www.trailingyew.com. 37 units (36 with shared bathroom). $190 (2 adults) double; children's rates differ according to age. Rates include breakfast, dinner, taxes, and tips. No credit cards. Closed mid-Oct to mid-May. **Amenities:** Dining room. *In room:* No phone.

MIDCOAST MAINE

et's say you're traveling east on the Maine coast along Rte. 1, and you're the sort of person who travels with one eye on the compass or GPS heading. Somewhere around Rockland, you suddenly notice something strange: you're pointed almost due north. Huh? Yet it's true. The culprit behind this geographic quirk is Penobscot Bay, a sizable bite out of the coast that forces drivers to take a lengthy northerly detour in order to cross the head of the bay, where the Penobscot River flows into it at Bucksport.

Fear not; you'll find some of Maine's most distinctive coastal scenery in this little region, which is dotted with offshore islands and hills rising above the shore. Although the mouth of Penobscot Bay is occupied by two large islands, its waters still churn when the winds and tides are right.

Thanks to both its natural beauty and architectural cuteness, the bay's western shore sees a steady stream of tourist traffic in summer, especially along the stretch of U.S. Rte. 1 passing through Rockland and **Camden.** You'll need a small miracle to find a weekend bed without a reservation in summer or early fall. Nevertheless, this is a great area to get a taste of the real Maine coast. Services for travelers are everywhere.

Forming the eastern boundary of Penobscot Bay—though you must drive north and then back *south* to get there—the lovely Blue Hill Peninsula is a sort of back-roads paradise. If you came to Maine to get lost on country lanes that dead-end at the sea or loop back on themselves, this is the place. In contrast to the western shores of Penobscot Bay, this peninsula attracts far fewer tourists and has much more of a lost-in-time, Maine-as-it-was character. The roads here are hilly, winding, and narrow, passing through forests, past old-time saltwater farms, and ticking the edge of a blue inlet here or there. The local radio station's a hoot, too.

By and large, the peninsula is overlooked by the majority of Maine's tourists, especially those who like their itineraries well structured and their destinations clear. In my book, that makes it doubly worth considering for a day or two's visit.

ENJOYING THE GREAT OUTDOORS

BEACHES Swan Lake State Park (© 207/525-4404), 6 miles north of Belfast, is a worthy beach, albeit a small one, open June through

Columbus Day. Admission is $6 per non-Maine resident adult, $2 per nonresident senior, and $1 for children.

BICYCLING **Vinalhaven** and **North Haven** in Penobscot Bay and **Swan's Island** in Blue Hill Bay are popular with bikers.

GOLFING The golf course at the **Samoset Resort** in Rockport (© **800/341-1650** or 207/594-1431; www.samoset.com) is easily the state's most dramatically scenic and challenging. It's also among the priciest, with greens fees running as high as $130 during peak season—if you can get a reservation. Six of the 18 holes literally hug the lapping edge of Penobscot Bay (don't shank one here!), and the place has got history: It dates from 1902. The course is hard enough as it is, but things become even more challenging once you hit the shifting sea breezes (worst in afternoon, believe me). There's a golf school here, with lessons available. Remember that this is a championship-caliber course and it gets busy in peak season; serious golfers will want to play it at least once, so reserve ahead, but beginners may feel intimidated.

HIKING A good destination for hilly coastal hiking is **Camden Hills State Park,** on the west shore of Penobscot Bay. *Fifty Hikes in Southern and Coastal Maine,*

Summer Camp for Families

If you're looking for an active summer destination with the family in these parts, the summer camp/retreat known as **Medomak** (© 207/845-6001; www.medomakcamp.com) offers an interesting lakeside set of options (as it has been doing since 1904), from archery and tennis to yoga and beer or cheese tastings. You sleep in pine cabins, and the emphasis is on the idea of living lightly on the earth—the director has a background in environmental education, and there are regular programs and workshops. Only catch? This is a half-hour inland from the prime coastal towns such as Camden, Rockland, and Rockport. Also bear in mind that the camp season only runs from late June through mid-August.

by John Gibson (The Countryman Press, 2003), is a reliable directory to trails in the Camden Hills area.

For a coastal walking vacation with all the details taken care of, contact **New England Hiking Holidays,** P.O. Box 1648, North Conway, NH 03860 (© 800/869-0949 or 603/356-9696; www.nehikingholidays.com), which offers guided excursions to Mount Desert Island each summer. The typically 4-night trips involve moderate days of hiking, coupled with nights at comfortable local inns; a lobster feast is included 1 night, as well, to provide calories to burn.

SAILING An ideal way to combine time in the outdoors with relative luxury and an easy-to-digest education in maritime history is aboard a windjammer cruise on the coast. Maine boasts a sizable fleet of sailing ships both vintage and modern that offer private cabins, meals, entertainment, and adventure. The ships range in size from 50 to 130 feet, and most are berthed in the region between Boothbay Harbor and Belfast. You choose your adventure: An array of excursions is available, from simple overnights to weeklong expeditions gunkholing among Maine's thousands of scenic islands and coves.

Several windjammer festivals and races are held along the Maine coast throughout the summer; these are perfect events to shop for a ship on which to spend a few days. Among the more notable events are **Windjammer Days** in Boothbay Harbor (late June) and the **Camden Windjammer Weekend** in early September. For information on windjammer vacations, contact **Maine Windjammer Association** at © 800/807- 9463 or online at www.sailmainecoast.com.

SKIING The only downhill peak of any significance along the coast would be the **Camden Snow Bowl** (p. 171), and even it's not terribly lofty. If you'd like to detour inland a bit and ski while visiting the coast, get a pamphlet with basic information about Maine skiing from the **Ski Maine Association,** P.O. Box 7566, Portland, ME 04112 (© 207/773-7669; www.skimaine.com). The association's website also offers up-to-date reports on ski conditions during the winter.

ROCKLAND & ENVIRONS ★

185 miles NE of Boston and 78 miles NE of Portland

Located on the southwestern edge of Penobscot Bay, Rockland has long been proud of its blue-collar waterfront roots. Built around the fishing industry, the city long historically dabbled in tourism but never really waded. With the recent decline of local fisheries and the rise of Maine's tourist economy, though, that balance has shifted. Rockland is swiftly being colonized by restaurateurs, innkeepers, artisans, and other folks who are transforming the place from fish-processing center to arts-and-crafts mecca.

The waterfront has a small park from which windjammers come and go, but even more appealing is Rockland's downtown—basically, one long street lined with historic brick architecture. If you're seeking picturesque harbor towns, head instead for Camden, Rockport, Port Clyde, or Stonington. Rockland is best as a local base for exploring a beautiful coastal region, especially if you like your towns to be a bit rough and salty around the edges.

Essentials

GETTING THERE

By car, U.S. Rte. 1 passes directly through the center of Rockland. **Concord Coach** (© **800/639-3317;** www.concordcoachlines.com) runs two to three daily buses from Portland and Boston.

Surprisingly, Rockland's tiny local **airport** (Knox County Regional Airport, airport code RKD) is served by daily direct flights from Boston on **Cape Air** (© **866/227-3247** or 508/771-6944; www.capeair.com) that are often surprisingly affordable. There's a local taxi on call, and a single rental car kiosk at the terminal. The airport itself is actually in Owls Head, off Rte. 73.

From spring through fall (and again in Dec), the **Maine Eastern Railroad** (© **866/637-2457;** www.maineeasternrailroad.com) runs excursion trains between Brunswick (p. 142) and Rockland (with stops in Bath and Wiscasset). Round-trip fares are $42 per adult, $37 for seniors, and $21 for children ages 4 to 15.

VISITOR INFORMATION

The **Penobscot Bay Regional Chamber of Commerce,** P.O. Box 508, Rockland, ME 04841 (© **800/562-2529** or 207/596-0376; www.therealmaine.com), staffs an information desk at Harbor Park. It's open daily from Memorial Day to Labor Day, on weekdays the rest of the year.

Events

The **Maine Lobster Festival** (© **800/562-2529** or 207/596-0376) takes place at Harbor Park the first weekend in August (plus the preceding Thurs–Fri). Entertainers and vendors of all sorts of Maine products—especially, of course, the famous Maine crustaceans—fill the waterfront parking lot for thousands of festivalgoers who enjoy the pleasantly buttery atmosphere. The event includes the Maine Sea Goddess Coronation Pageant. Admission is $8 per day for adults, $2 for children; food, of course, costs extra. Four-day passes are also available.

Rockland celebrates the changing of colors during the last 2 weeks of October—though with a unique twist: a scarecrow-making contest. It's part of the city's Festival of Scarecrows and **Harvest Day** celebrations.

Later, in late November, Rockland's **Festival of Lights** kicks off with Santa arriving not by reindeer but by Coast Guard boat—make of that what you will—then moves on to a program of caroling, horse-drawn carriage rides, a parade, and interesting tours of some of the area's most historic inns. Call © **207/596-0376** for more information.

Museums

Farnsworth Museum ★★★ Rockland, for all its rough edges, has long and historic ties to the arts. Noted sculptor Louise Nevelson grew up in Rockland, and in 1935 philanthropist Lucy Farnsworth bequeathed a fortune to establish the Farnsworth Museum, which has since become one of the most respected little art museums in New England. Located right downtown, the Farnsworth has a superb collection of paintings and sculptures by renowned American artists with connections to Maine—not only Nevelson, but also three generations of Wyeths (N. C., Andrew, and Jamie), plus Rockwell Kent, Childe Hassam, and Maurice Prendergast. The exhibit halls are modern, spacious, and well designed, and shows are professionally prepared. Equally interesting is the museum-owned **Olson House** ★, a 25-minute drive away, in the village of Cushing; it's perhaps Maine's most well-known home, immortalized in Andrew Wyeth's famous painting *Christina's World*.

356 Main St., Rockland. © **207/596-6457.** www.farnsworthmuseum.org. Museum $10 adults, $8 seniors and students 18 and older, free for children 17 and under (includes admission to Olson House and Farnsworth Victorian Homestead); Olson House only $4 per person. MC, V. Memorial Day to Columbus Day daily 10am–5pm; rest of the year Tues–Sun 10am–5pm.

Owls Head Transportation Museum ★ 👔 You don't need to be a car or plane buff to enjoy this museum, though it helps. Founded in 1974 and located 3 miles south of Rockland on Rte. 73, the museum has an extraordinary collection of cars, motorcycles, bicycles, and planes, nicely displayed in a tidy, hangarlike building at the edge of the Knox County Airport. Look for an early Harley Davidson motorcycle and a sleek Rolls-Royce Phantom dating from the roaring '20s.

Rte. 73, Owls Head. © **207/594-4418.** www.ohtm.org. $8 adults, $7 seniors, $5 children 5–17, $20 families. Apr–Oct daily 10am–5pm; Nov–Mar daily 10am–4pm.

Windjammer Tours ★★★

During the transition from sail to steam, captains of fancy new steamships belittled old-fashioned sailing ships as "windjammers." The term stuck; through a curious metamorphosis, the name evolved into one of adventure and romance.

Today, windjammer vacations combine adventure with limited creature comforts—such as lodging at a backcountry cabin floating on the water. Guests typically bunk in small two-person cabins with cold running water, a porthole to let in fresh air, and not much else. (You know it's not like a fancy inn when one ship's brochure boasts that all cabins are at least 6 ft. by 8 ft.)

Maine is the windjammer cruising capital of the U.S., and the two most active Maine harbors are **Rockland** and **Camden** on Penobscot Bay. Cruises last from 3 days to a week, during which these handsome, creaky vessels poke around tidal inlets and small coves that ring the beautiful bay. It's a superb way to explore the coast the way it's historically always been explored—from out on the water, looking in. Rates run between about $110 and $150 per day per person (which is $300–$1,000 per person for an entire trip); the best rates are offered early and late in the season.

Cruise schedules and amenities vary widely from ship to ship, even from week to week, depending on the inclinations of captains and the vagaries of Maine weather. A "standard" cruise often features a stop at one or more of the myriad spruce-studded Maine islands (perhaps with a lobster bake on shore), breakfasts served at tables below decks (or perched cross-legged on the deck), and a palpable sense of maritime history as the ships scud through frothy waters. More than a dozen windjammers cruise the Penobscot Bay region during summer (some migrate south to the Caribbean for the winter); the ships vary widely in size and vintage, and accommodations range from cramped and rustic to reasonably spacious and well appointed.

Ideally, you'll have a chance to look at a couple of ships to find one that suits you before signing up. If you can't do that, contact the **Maine Windjammer Association** (© **800/807-9463;** www.sailmainecoast.com) for a packet of brochures or simply check its good website of member ships and comparison-shop. If you're trying to book a *last-minute* windjammer cruise on a whim, stop by the chamber of commerce office on the Rockland waterfront (see above) and inquire about open berths.

Where to Stay

Captain Lindsey House Inn ★ The three-story, brick Captain Lindsey House is a couple of minutes' walk from the Farnsworth Museum: a nice advantage over farther-out digs. It was built in 1835 by a sea captain, then went through several subsequent incarnations (including one as headquarters of the Rockland Water Co.). Guests enter through a doorway a few steps off Main Street into an opulent first-floor common area done up in rich tones, dark-wood paneling, and a mix of antique and contemporary furniture. Upstairs rooms are decorated in simple country style with old-style, heavywooden beds, coffee tables, rocking chairs, and desks; rooms on the third floor have attractive exposed pine floors and Oriental carpets. All the beds are covered with feather duvets, though only a few rooms have tubs. This isn't the most luxurious inn in town (which is no knock on the place; it's plenty comfy enough), but it does have plenty of throwback-Maine character and some of the friendliest inn owners on the entire Midcoast.

5 Lindsey St., Rockland, ME 04841. © **800/523-2145** or 207/596-7950. Fax 207/596-2758. www.lindseyhouse.com. 9 units. $136–$211 double. Rates include breakfast. Packages available. AE, DISC, MC, V. *In room:* A/C, TV, hair dryer.

East Wind Inn ★ Here's how *you* become the "tenants" in Tenants Harbor: Head for the East Wind, acclaimed in places including *Architectural Digest.* It's a former sail loft converted to lodgings, perfectly situated beside the harbor with water views from all rooms and a long wraparound porch. This is your classic seaside hostelry of simple beds with white bedspreads, busy wallpaper, simple colonial reproduction furniture, and tidy rooms; some units have twin beds, though room no. 1 is a good corner suite with a queen-size bed and a sofa. (There are more rooms across the way at a former sea captain's house.) The atmosphere is relaxed almost to the point of ennui, and the service is good. Traditional New England fare is served in an Edwardian-era dining room from spring through fall.

21 Mechanic St., Tenants Harbor, ME 04860. © **800/241-8439** or 207/372-6366. Fax 207/372-6320. www.eastwindinn.com. 22 units (6 with shared bathroom). $99–$118 double with shared bathroom; $154–$176 double with private bathroom; $184–$206 suite. Rates include full breakfast. 2-night minimum stay weekends. AE, DISC, MC, V. Drive south on Rte. 131 from Thomaston to Tenants Harbor; turn left at post office. Pets allowed with advance notice ($15 per pet per night), but not in public rooms of inn. **Amenities:** Dining room.

LimeRock Inn ★★ This turreted, Queen Anne–style inn sits sleepily on a quiet side street just 2 blocks off Rockland's main drag, yet it's one of the best lodging options in town. Attention has been paid to detail throughout, from the kingly choices of country Victorian furniture to the Egyptian cotton bed sheets. All eight guest rooms are welcoming; among the best are the Island Cottage Room, a bright and airy south-of-France–like chamber wonderfully converted from an old shed (it has a private deck and a Jacuzzi); the Turret Room, with a canopy bed, cherry daybed, and French doors leading into a bathroom with a claw-foot tub and shower; and the elegant Grand Manan Room, with a big four-poster mahogany king bed, fireplace, and double Jacuzzi that puts one in mind of a southern plantation home.

96 Limerock St., Rockland, ME 04841. (C) **800/546-3762.** www.limerockinn.com. 8 units. $119–$239 double. Rates include full breakfast. DISC, MC, V. *In room:* Fireplace (some units), hair dryer, Jacuzzi (some units).

Samoset Resort ★★ Established in 1889 on a scenic hill outside Rockland, the Samoset was meant as a grown-up summer camp for the wealthy. (Even the cathedral-ceilinged lobby, constructed of massive timbers salvaged from an old grain silo in Portland, is worth photographing.) This is not the original building—the original was shuttered, auctioned off, and destroyed by fire decades ago. But the place has bounced back, big-time, as a noted golf resort and luxury property thanks to a number of exciting recent upgrades. Most recently, in 2009, a new heated pool and hot tub were added on the hill's highest point with sweeping views of the bay, plus a tiki bar serving frozen drinks and light meals; it's a huge hit already. Rooms vary in position and view, but many have balconies or porches with grand Penobscot Bay views; all have rich wood-leather headboards, flatscreen TVs, and marble vanities. Bathrooms are extra-big, some with whirlpool tubs. The golf course remains one of the most scenic in New England, while the quiet local roads are perfect for strolling, and there's even a mini-lighthouse adjacent to the property. Check out the good health club before heading to dinner—your options include seasonal **Marcel's** (see "Where to Dine," below), serving excellent resort fare, and the Breakwater Grill, serving lighter fare year-round. All in all, a great luxury comeback.

220 Warrenton St., Rockport, ME 04856. (C) **800/341-1650** or 207/594-2511. www.samoset.com. 178 units. Early July to late Aug $259–$289 double, $369 suite; May to early July and late Aug to Nov $179–$289 double, $259–$289 suite; $539–$769 cottage year-round. MAP rates available. AE, DC, DISC, MC, V. **Amenities:** 3 restaurants; babysitting; children's programs; concierge; fitness center; golf course; golf school; health club; Jacuzzi; indoor pool; heated outdoor pool; room service; sauna; 4 tennis courts. *In room:* A/C, TV, hair dryer, Jacuzzi (some units).

Where to Dine

Another good choice for the family in downtown Rockland is the Italian eatery **Rustica Cucina** ((C) **207/594-0015**), serving standard Italian favorites. It's open for lunch and dinner Monday through Saturday in high season; call for off-season hours.

Cafe Miranda ★★ 🍴 ECLECTIC Even a 2007 fire couldn't stop this place, which offers one of the best values and craziest menus in New England. Hidden on a side street, it's a tiny, contemporary restaurant with a huge ever-morphing menu of big flavors and hip attitude. "We do not serve the food of cowards," owner-chef Kerry Altiero is quoted right on top of the menu, and he's right. I could write a whole book on the regularly changing menu here, and probably should, but suffice to say you never know what you'll get 'til you get there. Small plates and entrees could include things like grilled lamb patties with parsley and garlic; "50 MPH tomatoes" deep-fried and served with spicy ranch dressing; a "squash-o'-rama" (roasted squash with cheese); fire-roasted feta with sweet peppers, tomatoes, "really good" olives, and herbs; a Portuguese seafood combo of mussels, shrimp, clams, fish, and sausage steamed in wine and pummeled with parsley; "Aunt Fluffy's Pasta" (penne with veggies, caramelized onions, and Romano); the "Polish hippie" (grilled sausage with horseradish, arugula, and beets!); "Old Bleu" (handmade pasta tossed in blue cheese

BOAT & breakfast

A growing trend in Maine is the "boat-and-breakfast" (BO-&-B), a working fishing or tour boat that takes overnight lodgers and often serves a meal or does a cruise. You wake up in the morning and disembark. Many (though not all) of Maine's BO-&-B's are berthed in Penobscot. Try one if you're looking for a different way to experience the coast (and pack Dramamine if you tend to become nauseous at sea). A few of the best current options include:

The *Rachel B. Jackson* (☎ 207/288-2216; www.downeastsail.com), 848 Eagle Lake Rd., Bar Harbor, ME 04609. A 67-foot topsail schooner based in Bar Harbor, the *Rachel B. Jackson* is a handsome reproduction ship of oak, pine, and brass. (It was built in Maine.) The overnight cruise begins at 5pm, discharges day travelers, then continues to anchorage somewhere in Acadia; cost, including breakfast but not dinner, is $500 per couple or $750 for a party of four.

The *Symbion* (☎ 207/725-0979), 252 Pinkham Point Rd., Harpswell, ME 04079. A 38-foot sloop captained by Ken Brigham, the *Symbion* ties up at Card Cove in Harpswell and circumnavigates Casco Bay, allowing guests to take the wheel from time to time (with a bit of instruction). There's a private restroom for overnight guests, and the itinerary may take in local sights such as Eagle Island, Christmas Cove, a series of lighthouses, or Monhegan Island. There's usually a 2-night minimum; a single night costs $500 per couple. (If they can fit you in for a single night, it's $600 per night.) Longer cruises of up to 5 days are also possible; rates vary by length of trip.

and basil cream); chicken paprikash; steaks; or, of course, the immortal "Pitch a Tent": sausage, gravy, onions, garlic, and mushrooms beneath a "tent" of pasta. Share everything with your fellow diners, because you'll never eat at a place this original again. Altiero again: "It's comfort food for whatever planet you're from." Amen.

15 Oak St., Rockland. ☎ **207/594-2034.** www.cafemiranda.com. Reservations strongly recommended. Small plates $9–$14, main courses $19–$27. DISC, MC, V. Daily 5–9:30pm.

Cod End Cookhouse ★ 🍴 ☺ SEAFOOD   Half the allure of Cod End is its hidden, scenic location—it's as though you'd stumbled upon a secret place. Situated between the Town Landing and the East Wind Inn in little Tenants Harbor, this is a classic lobster pound with fine views of a working harbor from its deck. To get to the cookhouse you walk through a fish market first (where you can buy fish or lobster to go, and various lobster-related souvenirs), then place your order at an outdoor shack. Steamed lobsters are the main draw, obviously, but there's actually a lot more to eat here, too—everything from chowders, stews, and lobster bisque to seafood pastas, char-broiled salmon, clam and haddock rolls, and a simple kids' menu of burgers, dogs, and sandwiches (including a classic PB&J). Yes, you probably do want to sample the sweetish blueberry cake for dessert.

Commercial St. (next to the town dock), Tenants Harbor. ☎ **207/372-6782.** www.codend.com. Main courses $5–$10 at lunch; $8–$15 at dinner. DISC, MC, V. Memorial Day to Sept daily 11am–8:30pm; closed Oct to mid-May.

Marcel's ★★ AMERICAN   This upper-crust, but never too stuffy, seasonal eatery on the ground level of the Samoset resort (see "Where to Stay," above) is a great place for a fancy bite in the Midcoast. In a room festooned with big windows on the water,

French chairs, and portraiture, chef Tim Pierce employs astounding creativity within the confines of his classic American-resort (steak Diane, lobster thermidor, filet mignon, bisque) fare. The menu changes annually, but you can always start with a Caesar salad prepared tableside (as it has been for decades), a lobster stew rich with cream and sherry, or inventive, summery salads such as one of grilled watermelon, spinach, and shallot "onion" rings. Pan-seared scallops in a knockout citrus cream are ever-popular, as are the annual permutation of lobster and steak. Pierce has even begun sneaking in some Asian influences to the menu, such as tuna tataki and yuzu sauce. Desserts run to sundaes, cakes, and ice creams—no molecular experiments here, just summery classics. Great spot; be sure to dress up (gentlemen should wear a jacket).

220 Warrenton St., Rockport, ME 04856. © **800/341-1650** or 207/594-2511. www.samoset.com. Reservations required. Entrees $24–$36. AE, MC, V. June to mid-Sept Thurs–Tues 5:30–9pm.

Primo ★★★ MEDITERRANEAN/NEW AMERICAN Primo opened in 2000 and quickly developed a buzz as one of northern New England's top eats; it still is. The restaurant occupies two nicely decorated floors of a century-old home, a short drive south of Rockland's downtown. Owner/chef Melissa Kelly graduated first in her class at the Culinary Institute of America and won a James Beard Foundation award for "best chef in the Northeast" in the 1990s. Her Italian-inflected menu reflects the seasons and draws from local products wherever available: Start with an appetizer such as wood-fired pizza with artisanal mushrooms, planked octopus with chickpea salad, seared foie gras over poached strawberries, antipasti, or fried and roasted local oysters paired with rémoulade sauce and house-cured Tasso ham. Entrees might run to seared diver scallops with fettuccine, local halibut over a white bean puree, monkfish medallions with peekytoe crab-risotto cakes, grilled steak or duck, tuna au poivre, or chicken with lavender-and-honey roasted figs and a sweet ricotta gnocchi. Finish with one of co-owner/pastry chef Price Kushner's inventive desserts: warm Belgian chocolate cake, an espresso float, a rhubarb-strawberry tartlet with vanilla gelato and strawberry sauce, homemade cannoli, a bowl of hot zeppole (small Italian doughnuts) tossed in cinnamon and sugar, or an apple *crostata* sided with pine-nut-and-caramel ice cream. The wine list is outstanding. It's hard to get a last-minute table here during summer; failing that, order off the menu from the cozy upstairs bar.

2 S. Main St. (Rte. 173), Rockland. © **207/596-0770.** www.primorestaurant.com. Reservations highly recommended. Appetizers $9–$18, main courses $25–$42. AE, DC, DISC, MC, V. Summer daily 5:30–9pm; call for dates and hours in off season.

CAMDEN ★★

8 miles N of Rockland

A quintessential coastal Maine town at the foot of wooded Camden Hills, the affluent village of Camden sits on a picturesque harbor that no Hollywood movie set could improve on. It has been attracting the gentry of the eastern seaboard for more than a century. The mansions of the moneyed set still dominate the town's shady side streets (many have been converted into bed-and-breakfasts), and Camden is possessed of a grace and sophistication that eludes many other coastal towns.

The best way to enjoy Camden is to park your car—which may require driving a block or two off U.S. Rte. 1, which unfortunately runs right up through the center of town. The village is of a perfect scale to explore on foot, with plenty of boutiques and

ACCOMMODATIONS
The Belmont Inn **4**
Blue Harbor House Inn **3**
Camden Harbour Inn **6**
Camden Maine Stay
    Inn **15**
Camden Riverhouse
    Hotel & Inns **13**
Camden Windward
    House **14**
Cedar Crest Motel **1**
The Hartstone Inn **8**
Norumbega **17**
Towne Motel **3**
Whitehall Inn **16**

DINING
Atlantica **7**
Boynton-McKay **10**
Cappy's Chowder House **11**
Francine Bistro **9**
French & Brawn **5**
Marriner's Restaurant **12**

galleries. Don't miss the hidden **town park** ★ (look behind the library), either: It was designed by none other than the firm of Frederick Law Olmsted, the famed landscape architect who designed New York City's Central Park.

On the downside, some longtime visitors say that all this attention (and Camden's growing appeal to bus tours) is having a deleterious impact on the atmosphere; yes, there are T-shirt shops here. And there are occasional cries raised about the increasing snootiness of the place. As long as you don't expect a pristine, undiscovered fishing village, you'll be in good shape to enjoy the place.

Essentials

GETTING THERE

By car, Camden is right on U.S. Rte. 1. Coming from the south, you can shave a few minutes off the trip here by turning left onto state Rte. 90 about 6 miles past Waldoboro, bypassing the downtown streets of the city of Rockland. **Concord Coach** (© 800/639-3317; www.concordcoachlines.com) runs bus service (two to three trips daily) to Rte. 1 in Rockport, a little more than a mile's walk from both downtown Camden and Rockport harbor, from Boston and Portland; the stop is at the Maritime Farms grocery store.

Rocking It in Rockport

Rockport ★ is absolutely worth a few hours during any trip to Camden. Try this route, either by bike or by car: Take Bayview Street from the center of Camden out along the bay, passing by opulent seaside estates. The road soon narrows and becomes quiet and pastoral, overarched by leafy trees. At the stop sign just past the cemetery, turn left and continue into Rockport. (Along the way, you might pass happily grazing cows.) In Rockport, stroll downstairs to the water and snoop around

the historic **harbor ★★★**, with its walking trail and outstanding photo opportunities. Then re-mount the hill and drop by the **Center for Maine Contemporary Art,** 162 Russell Ave. (✆ **207/236-2875;** www.artsmaine. org), a small gallery with decent rotating exhibits of local painters, sculptors, and craftspeople. Admission is by donation (drop in $5 if you enjoy the place); the gallery is open Tuesday to Saturday from 10am until 5pm, and Sundays from 1 to 5pm.

VISITOR INFORMATION

The **Camden-Rockport-Lincolnville Chamber of Commerce,** P.O. Box 919, Camden, ME 04843 (✆ **800/223-5459** or 207/236-4404; www.camdenme.org), dispenses helpful information from its center at the **Public Landing** (waterfront) in Camden, where there's also free parking—though spaces are pretty scarce in summer. The chamber is open year-round, daily in summer and daily except Sundays the rest of the year.

Exploring Camden

Camden Hills State Park ★★ (✆ **207/236-3109**) is about a mile north of the village center on Rte. 1. This 6,500-acre park has an oceanside picnic area, camping at 107 sites, a winding toll road up 800-foot Mount Battie with spectacular views from the summit, and a variety of well-marked hiking trails. The day-use fee is $4.50 for non-Maine resident adults, $1.50 for nonresident seniors, and $1 for children ages 5 to 11. It's open from mid-May to mid-October.

If hikes and mild heights don't bother you, I definitely recommend an ascent to the ledges of **Mount Megunticook ★★**, preferably early in the morning before the crowds have amassed (and while mists still linger in the valleys). Leave from near the state park's campground—the trail head is clearly marked—and follow the well-maintained path to open ledges. The hike takes only 30 to 45 minutes; spectacular views of the harbor await, plus glimpses of smaller hills and valleys. Depending on your stamina level, you can keep walking on the park's trail network to Mount Battie, or into lesser-traveled woodlands on the east side of the Camden Hills.

The Camden area is also great for exploring by bike. A nice loop several miles long takes you from Camden into the cute little village of **Rockport ★★**, which has an equally scenic harbor and fewer tourists. There's a boat landing, small park, cafe, one of the state's best art galleries, and a very highly regarded school of photography in Rockport, as well (see the "Rocking It in Rockport" box below).

The Camden-Rockport Historical Society has prepared a 9-mile bike (or car) tour with brief descriptions of some of the historic properties along the way. The brochure describing the tour is free; check for it at the chamber of commerce at the town's Public Landing (see above). The brochure also includes a 2-mile walking tour of downtown Camden. Bike rentals, maps, and riding advice are available in town at **Maine Sport Outfitters** on Rte. 1 in Rockport (℃ **888/236-8797** or 207/236-7120; www.mainesport.com). They're open year-round and also do a brisk business in local kayak rentals and tours.

Come winter, there's skiing at the **Camden Snow Bowl ★** (℃ **207/236-3438;** www.camdensnowbowl.com), just outside of town on Hosmer's Pond Road. This small, family-oriented ski area has a handful of trails and a modest vertical drop of 950 feet (full-day lift tickets cost $20–$33), but it also has good views of the open ocean and—maybe best of all—an exhilarating **toboggan run ★★**, open weekends only. Toboggans are available for rent, or you can bring your own; either way, it's $5 per person per hour to zip down the slopes.

On the Water

Several sailing ships make Camden their home base, and it's a rare treat to come and go from this harbor, which is considered by many to be the most beautiful in the state.

The 57-foot windjammer ***Surprise*** (www.camdenmainesailing.com) was launched in 1918 and has been based in Camden Harbor for a quarter-century now. Captain Jack Moore and his wife Barbara take a maximum of 18 passengers on 2-hour, non-smoking sailing trips from the town's Public Landing (Jack's son Joshua sometimes fills in as captain). Fruit juices and cookies are served on board; children 12 and older are permitted. Four excursions ($35 adults, discount for seniors) are offered daily from July to mid-September, and three are run daily in late May, June, and from mid-September through late October. Reservations are helpful, though you must e-mail (surprise@camdenmainesailing.com) to make them; if you can't book ahead, show up at the ticket table on the waterfront and hope for a seat.

The ***Schooner Lazy Jack II*** (℃ **207/230-0602;** www.schoonerlazyjack.com) has been plying the waters since 1947 and is modeled after the Gloucester fishing schooners of the late 19th century. They run four cruises per day on weekends from June through August, then three per day on weekdays only during May, June, September, and October. The 2-hour tours cost $35 per adult, $20 per child under age 12; snacks are available on board.

For a more intimate view of the harbor, once again **Maine Sport Outfitters** (℃ **800/722-0826** or 207/236-8797; www.mainesport.com) carries the load. The

---

PACKING A picnic

Harbor Park, on the upper part of Camden's main street, is all you could want in a park: grassy, ideal for people-watching, and possessed of outstanding bay views.

Just north of town, **Camden Hills State Park** (p. 170) is ideal for a picnic, too, whether you're on the bottom section (sea views) or drive to the top of the toll road (great bay views). I'd pick up my picnic at **Boynton-McKay,** a superlative sandwich shop just across Main Street from Harbor Park, or **French**

& Brawn, an upscale provisions shop on a corner just down the block; see "Where to Dine," later in this chapter, for more details.

A little hard to find, tiny **Rockport** (p. 170) has its own scenic public park by the boat landing—small, with only a tiny sitting area, but there's a great view of the boats in the harbor. Snag it if you can. Failing that, **Walker Park** and **Mary Lea Park,** just uphill, offer grassy expanses and nice views.

CRAFTING A vacation

The Maine coast has been a haven for visual artists, jewelers, sculptors, photographers, potters, and other creative types for as long as I can remember. Studios, galleries, arts centers, and museums of surprising quality crop up nearly everywhere, even in the tiniest coastal villages.

While cruising the coast, you'd do well to drop in to some of these crafts studios—and the best way to find them quickly is to contact the **Maine Crafts Association** (© 207/564-0041; www. mainecrafts.org), which publishes a comprehensive annual guidebook to its member artists, the *Maine Guide to Craft*

Artists and Culture (the list is also available online). It contains everything from the big Portland Museum of Art to tiny places such as Handworks Gallery (in Blue Hill) or Isleford Pottery. The guide also includes small black-and-white photographs of member work, so you can get a handle on a particular style before you barrel 30 miles down a peninsula to find it.

Speaking of that, you may wish to call ahead to get studio hours before making the trek to an out-of-the-way crafts studio or gallery. They *are* artists, after all—hours are likely to be a little whimsical.

outfit offers three to four sea-kayaking tours of Camden's scenic harbor a day, from June through August (but no tours Mon in June); the tour lasts 2 hours, costs $35 for adults ($30 for children 10–15), and takes paddlers out to Curtis Island at the outer edge of the harbor. It's an easy, delightful way to get a taste of the area's maritime culture. Longer trips and instruction are also available. The shop, located on Rte. 1 in Rockport (a few minutes' drive south of Camden), has a great selection of outdoor gear and is worth a stop if you're gearing up for some local adventures or heading up to Acadia next. Sign up for the tours either at the store or at the Camden boathouse, which is located at the head of the harbor near the town park (next to the takeout restaurant window).

Events

Fall travelers will enjoy Camden's annual **Fall Harbor Arts Show** (© 800/223-5459 or 207/236-4404), a weekend of local artworks displayed against the stunningly scenic backdrop of the Camden Hills' changing colors. Rockport has its own October crafts show, too, the annual **Work of the Hand** art show, featuring an opening bash and 9 days of contemporary crafts for sale. It's held at the Center for Maine Contemporary Art (see "Rocking It in Rockport," in box on p. 170), and there's a small admission charge. Call © **207/236-2875** for details.

Where to Stay

Camden vies with Kennebunkport, Maine, and Manchester, Vermont, for the title of "bed-and-breakfast capital of New England." They're everywhere. The stretch of Rte. 1 just north of the village center—called High Street here—is a virtual bed-and-breakfast alley, with many handsome homes converted to lodgings. Others are tucked away on side streets.

Despite the preponderance of B&Bs, though, the total number of guest rooms in town is still too small to accommodate the crush of peak-season visitors, and during summer or fall, the lodging is tight. It's best to reserve well in advance. You might also try **Camden Accommodations and Reservations** (📞 800/344-4830 or 207/236-6090; www.camdenac.com), which provides assistance with everything from booking rooms at local B&Bs to finding cottages for seasonal rentals.

If the inns and B&Bs listed below are unavailable or out of your budget, a handful of area motels and hotels might be able to accommodate you. South of the village center on Rte. 1 are the **Cedar Crest Inn,** 115 Elm St. (📞 800/422-4964 or 207/236-4839; www.cedarcrestmotel.com), a handsome seasonal motel with a coffee shop (peak-season rates $129–$144, spring and fall cheaper), and the longtime mainstay **Towne Motel,** 68 Elm St. (📞 800/656-4999 or 207/236-3377; www.camden motel.com), within walking distance of the village (open year-round; peak season rates $109–$132 double, cheaper off-season)—it's open year-round. Also right in town, just across the footbridge, is the modern, if generic, **Camden Riverhouse Hotel and Inns,** 11 Tannery Lane (📞 800/755-7483 or 207/236-0500; www. camdenmaine.com), with an indoor pool, fitness center, and new Wi-Fi and high-speed Internet access. It's open year-round; peak season rates from $189 to $239 for a double room or suite, while the off-season is far cheaper.

Also, there's camping at seasonally open **Camden Hills State Park** (see "Exploring Camden," above). Sites cost $25 to $37 per night for non-Maine residents in summer ($10 discount for nonresidents), depending on whether you snag one of the new water-and-electrical hookup sites or not. There's a discount from mid-September until the park closes.

The Belmont Inn ★ The Belmont is in a handsome, shingle-style 1890s home with a wraparound porch set in a quiet residential neighborhood of unpretentious homes away from Rte. 1. The inn has an understated, Victorian sort of theme throughout, featuring numerous floral prints by Maine artist Jo Spiller for instance (there's also a guest room with great morning light named after Spiller). All units have polished wood floors and are furnished simply with eclectic antiques and country touches such as cast-iron stoves, sleigh beds, writing desks, and wingback chairs. Downstairs, there's an elegant common room with a fireplace alcove and built-in benches. One room, the Allen Room, magically becomes a suite (and costs more) when the owners open a little door connecting it to a sitting room.

6 Belmont Ave., Camden, ME 04843. 📞 **800/238-8053** or 207/236-8053. Fax 207/236-9872. www.thebelmontinn.com. 6 units. $139–$209 double; $259–$309 suite. Rates include full breakfast. AE, MC, V. From south on Rte. 1: Turn right at 1st stop sign in Camden. Continue straight for 1 block; inn is on your left. From north: After passing through town on Rte. 1, turn left at blinking yellow light. Continue straight for 1 block; inn is on your left. No children 11 and under. *In room:* A/C.

Blue Harbor House Inn ★★ On busy Rte. 1 just south of town, this pale-blue 1810 farmhouse has been an inn since 1978, decorated throughout with a feminine country look. Rooms and suites vary in size; some are smallish, with slanting angles and low ceilings, but you can expect touches such as four-poster beds, claw-foot tubs, wicker furniture, Jacuzzis, triptych mirrors, writing desks, and slipper chairs in various configurations. And the exposed wood floors are absolutely lovely. The best rooms are the carriage-house suites, with their private entrances and extra amenities—two, Captains Quarters and Bali Hai, share a private outdoor patio. The early evening hours feature a nice cocktail service, with cocktails made to order and lovely hors d'oeuvre for a small extra charge. (Fun fact: One of the owners used to work as a cocktail bartender on the real "Love Boat" cruise ship; Gopher, Isaac, and Julie would be proud.)

67 Elm St., Camden, ME 04843. 📞 **800/248-3196** or 207/236-3196. Fax 207/236-6523. www.blueharborhouse.com. 11 units. $95–$155 double; $145–$185 suite. Rates include full breakfast. Packages

available. AE, DISC, MC, V. Closed mid-Oct to mid-May. Pets allowed in some units with prior notice. **Amenities:** Dining room. *In room:* A/C, TV, fireplace (some units), fridge (some units), hair dryer, Jacuzzi (some units).

Camden Harbour Inn ★★★ 👔 This 1871 mansion sits in a quiet neighborhood on a rise with a view of the sea and mountains beyond, on the way to Rockport—think of it as Camden's "quiet side." This had been just another fusty, Victorian-era hotel until 2007, when it got a complete makeover from the two Dutchmen who bought it. No longer a creaky place of floral wallpaper or simple antiques, it's now a luxury inn with a spa, gourmet restaurant, even a wine refrigerator in every room. The place is all about modern design. All rooms have private bathrooms and flatscreen TVs, of course, but most also sport water views, fireplaces, and/or terraces. The New Amsterdam Suite is one of the poshest in town, with its king-size featherbed and two private decks; other suites are designed in Taiwanese, Thai, and Mauritian themes. The inn's within walking distance of downtown, and there's an excellent French restaurant, **Natalie's ★**, as well.

83 Bayview St., Camden, ME 04843. ℭ **800/236-4266** or 207/236-4200. Fax 207/236-7063. www. camdenharbourinn.com. 22 units. $175–$375 double; $235–$700 suite. Rates include full breakfast. 2-night minimum in peak season. AE, DISC, MC, V. Closed Dec–Apr. Pets allowed on ground floor only. Children 12 and older welcome. **Amenities:** Restaurant; bar; spa. *In room:* A/C, TV, fireplace (some units), hair dryer.

Camden Maine Stay Inn ★ The Maine Stay is one of Camden's friendliest bed-and-breakfasts. In a home dating from 1802 (later expanded in Greek Revival style in 1840), it's your classic slate-roofed New England manse in a shady yard within walking distance of both downtown *and* Camden Hills State Park. Guest rooms, spaced out over three floors, have ceiling fans (only a few have televisions); each is distinctively furnished in antiques; things are mostly frilly and floral, but the wooden floors are often exposed as a sort of counterpoint. Note that top-floor rooms have foreshortened ceilings with intriguing angles. The downstairs Carriage House Room unit, away from the buzz of Rte. 1, is popular: Its French doors lead to a private stone patio, while a Vermont Castings stove keeps things toasty inside. The property has Wi-Fi access throughout. Interesting tidbit: The inn's owned by two Italian innkeepers—one from the south of Italy, one from Milan (the north).

22 High St., Camden, ME 04843. ℭ **207/236-9636.** Fax 207/236-0621. www.mainestay.com. 8 units. $110–$250 double and suite. Rates include full breakfast. Packages available. AE, MC, V. Children 12 and older welcome. **Amenities:** Dining room; 2 parlors; sun porch. *In room:* TV (some units), fireplace (some units), kitchenette (1 unit).

Camden Windward House ★★ One of the big complaints from travelers staying on Camden's High Street was the noise from passing traffic. The Windward's owners solved that problem by installing double windows on their historic 1854 home; as a result, when you close the door, the village feels miles away. Welcoming common rooms are decorated with a light Victorian hand and cranberry glass. Rooms vary in size and decor—some are quite frilly, some rather solid and plain—but all have flatscreen televisions, phones, and air-conditioning; some suites add gas fireplaces, Jacuzzis, claw-foot tubs, decks, or canopy beds. The Chart Room's white canopy bed is lovely and bridal-looking; the expansive Quarterdeck suite features exposed beamwork and skylights and a Jacuzzi tub; and even the simple, elegant Brass Room has a private deck. Guests choose from plenty of hot breakfast entrees, served in a pleasant dining room of maple tables, and you can order an in-room massage—rare at a B&B.

This place is better and friendlier than you might expect. There's Wi-Fi access in some, but not all, units; ask when booking.

6 High St., Camden, ME 04843. ✆ **877/492-9656** or 207/236-9656. www.windwardhouse.com. 8 units. June–Oct $190–$280 double; Nov–May $99–$240 double. Rates include full breakfast and afternoon tea. AE, MC, V. No children 11 and under. **Amenities:** Bar; library. *In room:* A/C, TV/DVD, hair dryer, Jacuzzi (some units).

The Hartstone Inn ★★★ 🏨   There are lots of great inns in the Camden area, but this one's just a little more special thanks to the great combo of friendly hospitality, fine food, and historic charm. Chef/innkeeper Michael Salmon has long drawn raves for his cooking, but the accommodations in the early-19th-century Victorian home owned by him and his wife, Mary Jo, are top-rate, too. The Hartstone's rooms are designed with grace, furnished in lovely antiques and some of the most beautiful decor in the Midcoast; suites here include Jacuzzis, Wi-Fi access, fridges, fireplaces, and other luxe touches, but even the smallest rooms are plenty comfortable, with iPod docks, flatscreen TVs, and sometimes Jacuzzis and canopy beds. I actually like the two annexes even better than the main inn—one is set across the street in a quiet neighborhood, and feels like a private home, while the other is tucked behind the inn and features the best architecture. The full breakfasts are wonderful, as are five-course **dinners** ★★★ marrying local Maine seafood with Caribbean chilies, spices, and cooking techniques—lobster with vanilla beurre blanc, for instance. It's a unique experience on a coastline already full of good inns, and the small spa and cooking school here cap the experience.

41 Elm St., Camden, ME 04843. ✆ **800/788-4823** or 207/236-4259. www.hartstoneinn.com. 14 units, 1 with bathroom across hall. $135–$190 double; $175–$275 suite. Rates include full breakfast. MV, V. Closed late Nov to late Apr. **Amenities:** Dining room; spa. *In room:* A/C, TV/DVD, fireplace (some units), fridge (some units), Jacuzzi (some units).

Inn at Ocean's Edge ★★★   On 22 gorgeous acres, this former one-building inn has committed to a far-reaching concept, remaking itself into one of Maine's premier oceanfront properties. The inn is in the process of adding new buildings, rooms, and spa services, and the inn's restaurant, the Edge, is sure to draw foodies. The grounds feature new gardens, an in-ground vanishing-edge pool, and an inlaid hot tub overlooking the sea. Units in the main inn and the hilltop annex are nearly identical: Jacuzzi tubs, four-poster beds, ocean views, TVs, VCRs, and tasteful wallpaper prints and art. Hilltop units add fridges, coffeemakers, and balconies (but sacrifice distance from the common room), while the new poolhouse suites are most luxe of all. The full breakfasts are a real highlight, too. This is as personable and well-kept a place as you'll find along this stretch of coast, and word is spreading.

Rte. 1, Lincolnville Beach (P.O. Box 74), Camden, ME 04843. ✆ **207/236-0945.** Fax 207/236-0609. www.innatoceansedge.com. 33 units. Mid-July–Aug $280–$425 double and suite; May–mid-July, Sept–Oct $175–$425 double and suite; closed Nov–April. Rates include full breakfast. AE, DISC, MC, V. **Amenities:** Restaurant; pub; fitness room. *In room:* A/C, TV/VCR, fridge (some).

Inn at Sunrise Point ★★   This peaceful, private sanctuary 4 miles north of Camden Harbor seems a world apart from the bustling town. Service is crisp and helpful, and the setting can't be beat: the edge of Penobscot Bay, down a long, tree-lined gravel road. The property is a cluster of contemporary, yet classic, shingled buildings; a granite bench and Adirondack chairs on the lawn allow guests to enjoy the views. Guest rooms and suites—all named for Maine writers and artists—are spacious, comfortable, and packed with amenities such as fireplaces, TVs with VCRs, individual heat controls, and stunning views from the plentiful windows. Breakfasts are served in a sunny conservatory. The inn's four cottages are even more luxe and private, featuring double Jacuzzis, fireplaces, wet bars, and private decks; the Fitz Hugh Lane cottage almost feels like it's *in* the bay.

U.S. Rte. 1 (P.O. Box 1344), Camden, ME 04843. (C) **207/236-7716.** Fax 207/236-0820. www.sunrise point.com. 10 units. $310–$600 double and suite; $340–$595 cottage. Rates include full breakfast. 5% inn service charge and 7% state sales tax. 2-night minimum stay Memorial Day through Columbus Day. AE, MC, V. Closed Jan–Apr. No children 11 and under. *In room:* TV/VCR, fridge (some units), hair dryer, minibar (some units).

Norumbega Inn ★★ You'll have no problem at all finding the Norumbega: just head north out of town and look for the castle on the right. Well, it's actually a mansion (built of stone in 1886 by telegraph system inventor Joseph Stearns), but it *looks* like a castle. Wonderfully eccentric and full of curves, turrets, angles, and rich materials, this hotel's on the National Historic Registry. There's extravagant carved-oak woodwork in the lobby, a stunning oak-and-mahogany inlaid floor, and a kingly downstairs billiards room. New management is currently updating all furnishings, but some "king" beds still consist of two twin beds pushed together. Still, all units have robes, some have fireplaces, most have air-conditioning, and three ground-level units sport private decks. The two suites here rank among the finest in northern New England: the bright and airy Library Suite, in the original two-story library (so big it has an *interior* balcony), and the sprawling Penthouse with its superlative bay views, king-size bed, and huge oval tub. Most rooms have free Wi-Fi access. And if you're the sort of traveler who goes gaga over Sherlock Holmes, Hercule Poirot, Angela Lansbury, or the board game Clue, don't miss Norumbega's "Murder Mystery" weekends—solve the mystery first, and you win a free stay. No lie.

63 High St., Camden, ME 04843. (C) **877/363-4646** or 207/236-4646. www.norumbegainn.com. 12 units. June–Oct $195–$525 double and suite; Nov–May $105–$375 double and suite. All rates include full breakfast. 2-night minimum in summer, Sat–Sun, and holidays. AE, DISC, MC, V. Children age 7 and older welcome. **Amenities:** Billiards room; concierge. *In room:* A/C (most units), TV, fireplace (some units), fridge (1 unit), hair dryer.

Whitehall Inn ★ 🔌 Set at the edge of town on busy Rte. 1, the Whitehall is a venerable Camden institution thanks partly to its association with local poet Edna St. Vincent Millay, who was "discovered" here by a guest who went on to fund Edna's college education. The room where the discovery happened still has a 1904 Steinway piano that Edna played. As for the three-story inn, it's all columns, gables, a long roofline, and atmospherically winding staircases. The antique furnishings—including a handsome Seth Thomas clock, Oriental carpets, and cane-seated rockers on the front porch—are well cared for. Guest rooms are simple yet appealing, and have recently been updated with important additions like flatscreen televisions (previously, there were *no* TVs in many rooms), though the "economy" rooms still share hallway bathrooms just as they did in olden days. The only drawback? That traffic—try to get a room in back.

52 High St., Camden, ME 04843. (C) **800/789-6565** or 207/236-3391. www.whitehall-inn.com. 45 units, some with shared bathroom. July–Oct $129–$199 double; mid-May to June $99–$159 double. Rates include full breakfast. AE, MC, V. Closed Nov to mid-May. **Amenities:** 2 restaurants; babysitting; conference rooms; tennis court; tour desk. *In room:* TV, no phone (some units).

Where to Dine

In addition to its fine-dining options, downtown Camden has a wealth of places to nosh, snack, lunch, and brunch. Some great doughnuts, for instance, are fried up at

Boynton-McKay, 30 Main St. (☎ **207/236-2465**), a former pharmacy that's now a great spot for lunch, coffee, a sandwich, or blue-plate special such as grilled meat-loaf. It's closed Mondays. Just up the street, pick up a bag of gourmet groceries at **French & Brawn** (☎ **207/236-3361**) on Main Street at the corner of Elm.

Atlantica ★★ ECLECTIC Atlantica gets high marks for its menu, always well-prepared under the management of chef Ken Paquin, a graduate of the Culinary Institute of America. On the waterfront with a small indoor seating area and an equally small deck, Paquin cooks subtly creative fare that leans toward seafood and takes in Asian and French influences: seared day boat scallops over lemon risotto with a steamed lobster; roasted breast of duck; porcini-dusted bass; French onion soup; local oysters baked with spinach and Pernod; small plates of seared peppered tuna with sriracha sauce; Maine shrimp in an Asian egg-drop soup; fish and chips; Kobe beef burgers; tournedos of beef with a shallot confit and shiitake mushrooms; grilled lamb chops. All good. Plus there's that great harbor view.

1 Bayview Landing. ☎ **888/507-8514** or 207/236-6011. www.atlanticarestaurant.com. Reservations recommended. Main courses $12–$24. AE, MC, V. Thurs-Mon 5-9pm. Closed Jan-Mar.

Cappy's Chowder House ☺ SEAFOOD/AMERICAN Travelers—especially families—drift in here to drink up the atmosphere and fill up on the (locally) famous thick clam chowder, which even gained a mention in *Gourmet* magazine. There's also seafood stew, rotating special chowders, burgers, club sandwiches, fried fish, lobster and lobster rolls in summer, and a wine list? It's all well worth a quick stop if you're looking for a reasonably priced and filling meal for the family late at night. But it's not going to break any new culinary ground. By the way, who is Cappy? An old salt who worked the local docks for years; he's not with us any longer—but his name lives on. There's also a little bakery around the side.

1 Main St. ☎ **207/236-2254.** www.cappyschowder.com. Main courses $8–$20. MC, V. Daily 11:30am-9pm.

Chez Michel ★ ☺ FRENCH/SEAFOOD This French-and-seafood restaurant, right across the road from the Islesboro ferry, has had a great local following since 1992 when chef Jean Michel Hetuin opened it. That's because it offers good value amid a sea of higher-priced area options, though inside it's not nearly as fancy you as might expect from the name. Instead, the menu blends elements of French, Maine, and American cooking. You might begin with mussels steamed in wine or locally smoked salmon, then move on to duck au poivre, steak Oscar, or haddock in meunière sauce . . . or you might get plunked down next to a local family enjoying a feed of lobsters, scallops, pasta, or fried oysters, and decide to join in the fun. Specials could be anything from salmon Béarnaise to pan-fried haddock or tenderloin brochette—or could be a simple chicken parm.

Rte. 1, Lincolnville Beach. ☎ **207/789-5600.** Entrees $13–$18. AE, DC, DISC, MC, V. Tues-Sat 4-9:30pm; Sun 11:30am-9pm.

Francine Bistro ★★ FRENCH This place feels more like a French brasserie in Manhattan's Meatpacking District than a coastal seafood joint—and that's a good thing. A meal from chef/owner Brian Hill (long-ago of the seminal Boston alternative-rock band Heretix, but I digress) might begin with fish, onion, or lentil soup; a seviche of halibut, serrano chilies, and red onions; mussels in bordeaux and shallots; or skewers of grilled lamb with white pesto, orange, and endive—nice to see in a state dominated by fried fish and lobster. Entrees might run to roast chicken with a chèvre gratin or a cauliflower-cheese hash; duck a l'orange; a crispy skate wing with Jerusalem artichokes; a roasted sea bass in caramelized garlic sauce; seared halibut with shrimp; a haddock stuffed with scallops; or some reliable steak frites. Hill cut his teeth in some truly great kitchens around the country, and it shows.

55 Chestnut St., Camden. ✆ **207/230-0083.** www.francinebistro.com. Reservations recommended. Main courses $17–$25. MC, V. Tues-Sat 5:30-10pm.

The Lobster Pound ★ LOBSTER POUND   Among the many lobster shacks up and down the Midcoast, this one holds its own by offering not only steamed lobsters and lobster stew but a variety of surf-and-turf combos and shore dinners (read: fried fish sided with fries). But, surprisingly, they also serve "regular" meals leaning toward the home-cooking end of things: grilled steaks, roast turkey dinners with the trimmings, grilled swordfish, and combinations thereof. The baked scallops are good, too. There's also a takeout shack for those who don't want to stick around for a sit-down meal.

U.S. Rte. 1, Lincolnville Beach. ✆ **207/789-5550.** Sandwiches $5.95–$7.20; lunch portions $9.95–$15; dinner entrees $12–$37. AE, DISC, MC, V. Daily 11:30am-8pm.

Marriner's Restaurant DINER   "The last local luncheonette" is how Marriner's sums itself up, and has used a sign with the legend DOWN HOME, DOWN EAST, NO FERNS, NO QUICHE to also get its message across: namely, that this is a no-frills affair, so don't expect snootiness or fancy food. The space is done up in a nautical theme of pine booths and vinyl seats, and the kitchen has been spooning up filling breakfasts and lunches for locals since 1942; it's a good place for early risers to get a quick start on the day and check out some local characters. Go for pancakes, chowders, or the lobster and crab rolls—and don't miss the homemade pies, either.

35 Main St., Camden. ✆ **207/236-4949.** Most breakfast items $4–$6; lunch items $4–$12 (most under $7). MC, V. Daily 6am-2pm.

BELFAST TO BUCKSPORT ★

Belfast is 18 miles N of Camden; Bucksport is 19 miles NE of Belfast.

The northerly stretch of Penobscot Bay is rich in history, especially maritime history. In the mid–19th century, Belfast and Searsport produced more than their share of ships, along with the captains to pilot them on trading ventures around the globe. In 1856 alone, 24 ships of more than 1,000 tons were launched from Belfast. The now-sleepy village of Searsport once had 17 active shipyards, which turned out some 200 ships over the years.

When shipbuilding died out, the Belfast area was sustained by a thriving poultry industry. Alas, that too declined as the industry moved south. In recent decades the area has attracted artisans of various stripes who sell their wares at various shops. Tourists tend to pass through the region quickly, en route from the tourist enclave of Camden to the tourist enclave of Bar Harbor. It's worth slowing down for.

Essentials

GETTING THERE

Rte. 1 connects Belfast, Searsport, and Bucksport.

VISITOR INFORMATION

The **Belfast Area Chamber of Commerce** (P.O. Box 58), Belfast, ME 04915 (✆ **207/338-5900;** www.belfastmaine.org), staffs an information booth at 15 Main St., near the waterfront park, that's open daily from June through September, 10am to 6pm.

If you enjoy kitsch and uniquely American things, on a rainy day in Belfast, you could do worse than making the 30-minute detour inland through the hills to little Thorndike and experience the **Bryant Stove Museum** (© 207/568-3665; www.bryantstove.com), a nothing-if-not-entertaining experience. Joe and Bea Bryant exhibit, refurbish, and sell gorgeous cast-iron woodstoves. But looking these over is only part of the fun: The premises also house a huge selection of vintage dolls, toys, antique cars, player pianos, calliopes, concertinas, and oodles of other musical instruments and mechanical contraptions. Entering the rooms where the goodies are stored is like opening a door into an alternate universe—one presided over by suspender-wearing Joe, who sings lustily along with the pianos while puppets (rigged to the instruments) bob along in time. Get there by taking Waldo Avenue (Rte. 137) west out of Belfast for about 15 miles, then turning right onto Rte. 200 and continuing a bit farther onto Stovepipe Alley. Really. A shop attached to the museum is open 8am to 4:30pm Monday to Saturday. Admission is free.

Exploring the Region

When approaching the area from the south, some splendid historic homes may be viewed by veering off Rte. 1 and entering downtown Belfast via High Street (look for the first DOWNTOWN BELFAST sign). The **Primrose Hill District** along High Street was the most fashionable place for prosperous merchants to settle during the early and mid–19th century, and their stately homes reflect an era when stature was equal to both the size of one's home and the care one took in designing and embellishing it. Downtown Belfast also has some superb examples of historic brick commercial architecture, including the elaborate High Victorian Gothic–style building on Main Street that formerly housed the Belfast National Bank.

If you'd like to explore the area by water, call Harvey Schiller at **Belfast Kayak Tours** (© 207/382-6204). With a great deal of charm and even more enthusiasm, Harvey will provide paddle instruction and take you out for a guided tour—the perfect way to get up close and personal with both the river and Penobscot Bay. (His handmade uniform is a kick, too.) Trips last about 2 hours. They also rent kayaks to kayakers intent on constructing their own itineraries.

At the northern tip of the bay, the Penobscot River squeezes through a dramatic gorge near Verona Island, which Rte. 1 spans on an attractive suspension bridge. The new **Penobscot Narrows Observatory** ★ (www.maine.gov/observatory) sits high on this bridge. However, there is an addition to the Midcoast: **a new observatory** on the lovely Verona Island bridge (U.S. Rte. 1, just outside Bucksport). It's said to be the world's *highest* public bridge observatory, some 437 feet above the river, with panoramic views of the mountains, lakes, and even Penobscot Bay. The elevator ride to the glassed-in viewing area takes just 1 minute, and placards help you interpret the landscape features you're looking at. It's open from mid-May through the end of October.

You must enter and pay admission to the adjacent **Fort Knox State Park** (© 207/469-7719) first to enjoy the views; this easily defended pinch in the river was perceived to be of strategic importance in the 1840s, when the solid and imposing fort was constructed. While it was never attacked, the fort was manned during the

Searsport has an outstanding little pocket park, **Mosman Park,** just off the hustle of busy Rte. 1; look for the post office in the center of the village, then walk downhill one block along Water St. to the water. It makes for a great quick picnic, and there's a pretty good playground—plus bay views—and it's free. Pick up rudimentary snacking foods and beverages at **Tozier's Market** (📞 **207/548-6220**), a convenience store on Rte. 1 just south of the Maritime Museum.

Civil War and Spanish-American War. It's an impressive edifice to explore, with graceful granite staircases and subterranean chambers that produce wonderful echoes.

Admission to the park only is $4.50 for non-Maine resident adults, $1.50 for nonresident seniors, and $1 for children 11 and under; there's a $2 to $2.50 per person surcharge if you want to ascend the observatory. The park is open daily from 9am until sunset from May through October, although the tower closes at 6pm (at 5pm May–June).

Across the river from Fort Knox in the paper-mill town of Bucksport is **Northeast Historic Film** (📞 **800/639-1636** or 207/469-0924; www.oldfilm.org), an organization founded in 1986 and dedicated to preserving and showing early films related to New England. In 1992 the group bought Bucksport's Alamo Theatre, which was built in 1916 and closed (after a showing of *Godzilla*) in 1956. Films are shown weekends in the renovated theater; call or check the group's website to see what's coming up. Visitors can also stop by the museum at the front of the theater (open Mon–Fri 9am–4pm) to browse videos and other items.

The Seafaring Life

Penobscot Marine Museum ★★★   The Penobscot Marine Museum is one of the best small museums in New England—and hardly anybody knows it. Housed in a cluster of historic buildings atop a gentle rise in tiny downtown Searsport, the museum does a great job of educating visitors about the vitality of the local shipbuilding industry, the essential role of international trade to daily life in the 19th century, and the hazards of life at sea. Exhibits (such as "The Art of Lobstering") are uncommonly well organized, and wandering from building to building induces a keen sense of wonderment at the vast enterprise that was Maine's maritime trade, and there's also the landscape art of Thomas and James Buttersworth and Robert Salmon. Among the most intriguing exhibits are a wide selection of dramatic marine paintings, black-and-white photographs of many of the 286 weathered sea captains who once called Searsport home, exceptional photographs of a 1902 voyage to Argentina, and an early home decorated in the style of a sea captain, complete with lacquered furniture and accessories hauled back from trade missions to the Orient. Throughout, the curators do a fine job of both educating and entertaining visitors. It's well worth the price if you're the least bit interested in Maine's rich culture of the sea.

5 Church St. (at corner of U.S. Rte. 1), Searsport. 📞 **207/548-2529.** www.penobscotmarinemuseum. org. $8 adults, $3 children 7–15, $18 families. Memorial Day to mid-Oct Mon–Sat 10am–5pm; Sun noon–5pm. Last tickets sold at 4pm.

Where to Stay

If you're stuck for a bed along this stretch of the coast and don't mind the chain-hotel ambience for a night, the **Comfort Inn,** 159 Searsport Ave. (U.S. Rte. 1) (② **207/338-2090**), is a very good backup option. Some rooms have kitchenettes and/or whirlpools; there's a pool; a small breakfast is served; and some rooms come with sublime views of the bay (if there's no fog, that is). However, check as soon as possible—the place sometimes fills up early. High season double rooms run from $109 to $209 per night; suites are more expensive.

The White House Inn ★★   This architecturally stunning Greek Revival home is just a 10-minute walk from downtown Belfast and offers a lot more B&B than you might expect for the rates, which are somewhat low for this part of the coast. Originally built as a sea captain's home in 1840 and topped with a striking eight-sided cupola, the home has been exquisitely refurnished (mainly in four-poster beds), painted, and wallpapered. Downstairs, guests have the run of a library, an elegant parlor area, and a dining room where the hearty breakfasts are served. All of the guest rooms (some with TVs) have private bathrooms stocked with soft Egyptian cotton towels and robes. The Belfast Bay unit (the most expensive) is an over-the-top Louis XVI–style room with a fireplace, crystal chandelier, Jacuzzi, and water views; the less fancy Copper Beech Suite, at the back of the house, is also appealing: it features a sitting room and classic pumpkin pine floors. Rates have escalated a bit in recent years, but that's to be expected; this is still the best place to put your feet up for the night when in Belfast.

1 Church St., Belfast, ME 04915. ② **888/290-1901** or 207/338-1901. Fax 207/338-5161. www.mainebb. com. 6 units (1 with private hall bathroom). $131–$250 double and suite. Rates include full breakfast. AE, DISC, MC, V. **Amenities:** Library. *In room:* TV (some units), hair dryer.

Where to Dine

Just south of Belfast on Rte. 1, **Seng Thai** ★ (② **207/338-0010**)—one of many Thai restaurants you'll be surprised to find as you cruise up and down the Maine coast—serves up well-spiced classic dishes such as pad Thai and various curries, but also a uniquely creative take on more upscale fare such as lobster and fish. Top off your meal with a potent Thai tea or coffee. It's open daily from 11am until 10pm in summer, until 8 or 8:30pm in winter.

A surprisingly hip new spot in downtown Belfast is **three tides** (② **207/338-1707;** www.3tides.com) at 3 Pinchy Lane right next to the boats on the waterfront—walk all the way to the end of Main St. It's got a more contemporary, urban feel than Belfast's workaday bars and pubs. They serve fancy sandwiches, salads, panini, local oysters and mussels, and a selection of beers. Jazz shows and dance parties have been known to break out. The outdoor deck is a good spot to relax while the sun goes down. It's open Tuesday to Saturday from 4pm onward.

Finally, if you're packing a picnic, one of Maine's oldest, biggest, and best natural-foods stores, the **Belfast Co-op** ★ (② **207/338-2532**), is at 123 High St. Not everything here is for the virtuous: The selection of imported beers and the cuts of organic beef are surprisingly good; the co-op also features a deli. It's open from 7:30am to 8pm daily.

Chase's Daily Restaurant ★★ VEGETARIAN   This place is special. A vegetarian restaurant that doesn't make any point at all of being politically correct, Chase's was formed by a local farm family (the Chases) with a simple philosophy: cook superlocal foods, as freshly as possible, based on the things being grown at the farm. It maintains a balance between simple, hearty food and more sophisticated offerings—so good that a line often stretches out the door, even on weekdays, even at lunch. Breakfast ranges from oatmeal to breakfast burritos to healthy fruit smoothies; lunch segues nicely into a menu of very popular pizzas, sandwiches, soups, and salads with an emphasis on Asian, Latin American, and European themes. There's also a daily pasta dish. Coffee drinks here are high quality, too: the restaurant serves fairtrade beans roasted at a New York coffeehouse. The whole room is very inviting and light-filled, with wooden floorboards and a pressed-tin ceiling, and Sunday brunches are highly regarded around town. Absolutely call ahead about table availability if you're serious about eating here in high season.

96 Main St., Belfast. ✆ **207/338-0555.** Main courses $3.50–$14. DISC, MC, V. Tues-Sat 7am-5pm (Fri to 9pm); Sun 8am-2pm.

Darby's AMERICAN/ECLECTIC   Located in a Civil War–era pub with stamped tin ceilings and a back bar with Corinthian columns, Darby's is a popular local hangout. You can order a Maine microbrew or a single-malt whiskey while you read the menu, which is more creative than you might expect given the surroundings. The kitchen serves not only bar favorites (burgers on bulky rolls), but also attempts more inventive dishes such as mahogany duck, pad Thai, and big salads; these are hit-or-miss, and nothing is out of this world, but the pubby atmosphere is pretty authentic. Desserts are homemade and basic: think cheesecake, pies, and an interesting "Russian cream." If you like the artwork on the wall, ask about it—it was probably painted by a local artist, and it's probably for sale.

155 High St., Belfast. ✆ **207/338-2339.** Reservations suggested after 7pm. Main courses $5.95–$9.95 lunch, $11–$20 dinner. AE, DC, DISC, MC, V. Mon-Sat 11:30am-3:30pm and 5-9pm; Sun noon-3:30pm and 5-8:30pm.

Young's Lobster Pound ★★ 🍴 LOBSTER   This is one of my favorite lobster shacks in Maine—although calling it a "shack" might even be a euphemism. Beyond the driveway you'll find a hangar-size door; fear not, for behind it sits a counter of friendly locals taking your order. Guys in slickers and boots do all the dirty work, plucking lobsters from long lobster tanks gurgling seawater. Eat upstairs, where picnic tables are arrayed in an open, barn-like area, or out on the deck with views across the river to Belfast. Remember: Don't wear your finest threads, and get *lots* of napkins. The lobsters, served on paper plates with butter and corn on the cob, are tasty and fairly inexpensive.

4 Mitchell St. (just off Rte. 1), E. Belfast. ✆ **207/338-1160.** Reservations not accepted. Lobster prices seasonal. MC, V. Daily 7:30am-7pm. Closed Dec-Mar. From Belfast, follow U.S. Rte. 1 north across bridge; just after bridge, look for signs to pound on right. Turn right and follow road to the water.

CASTINE & ENVIRONS ★★

Quiet little Castine, off the beaten track, must be one of the most gracious villages in Maine. It's not so much the handsome, meticulously maintained mid-19th-century homes that fill the side streets. Nor is it the location on a quiet peninsula, 16 miles south of tourist-clotted Rte. 1. No, what lends Castine most of its charm are the splendid, towering elm trees that still overarch many of the village's streets. Before Dutch elm disease ravaged the nation's elms, much of America once looked like this. Through perseverance and a measure of good luck, Castine has managed to keep several hundred of its elms alive, and it's worth the drive here to see them.

But Castine offers more than trees. It's enduringly quiet, which is probably what you're seeking in your Maine vacation. And it's full of history. This outpost served as a strategic town during various battles among the British, Dutch, French, and colonists in the centuries following its settlement in 1613 (yes, 7 years before Plymouth Rock). Castine was occupied by each of those groups at some point; and historical personages such as Miles Standish and Paul Revere passed through town. It was a very important place—strange, because now it seems almost thoroughly forgotten, except for the maritime academy at one end of the village, which still trains young sailors and cadets. Castine still looks and feels like it has it not changed much since the locals welcomed British soldiers with open arms during the American Revolution.

You'll have to work (which means drive significant distances) to find nightlife and dining, but if you like your towns quiet, you'll love it here.

Essentials

GETTING THERE

Castine is 16 miles south of U.S. Rte. 1. Turn south on Rte. 175 in Orland (east of Bucksport) and follow it to Rte. 166, which winds its way to Castine. Rte. 166A offers another, alternate route along Penobscot Bay.

VISITOR INFORMATION

Castine lacks a formal information center, though the clerks at the **town office** (© 207/326-4502) are often helpful with local information. (Don't abuse this privilege, though, since they have actual work to do running the town.) The town office is normally open weekdays from 11am to 3pm. The town also maintains a helpful web site (**www.castine.me.us/pages/business/business.html**) listing local shops, restaurants, and lodgings. For wider regional inquiries, the **Blue Hill Peninsula Chamber of Commerce** (see below) can also help you.

Exploring Castine

One of the town's more intriguing attractions is the **Wilson Museum** ★ (© **207/326-9247;** www.wilsonmuseum.org) on Perkins Street, an appealing and quirky anthropological museum constructed in 1921. This small museum contains the collections of John Howard Wilson, an archaeologist and collector of prehistoric artifacts from around the globe. His gleanings are neatly arranged in a staid, classical arrangement of the sort that proliferated in the late 19th and early 20th centuries. The museum is open from the end of May through the end of September, weekdays 10am to 5pm and weekends from 2 to 5pm; admission is free.

Next door is the affiliated **John Perkins House** (same phone number as the museum), Castine's oldest home. It was occupied by the British during the Revolution and the War of 1812, and a tour features demonstrations of old-fashioned cooking techniques. This house is only open in July and August, and only on Wednesdays and Sundays from 2 to 5pm. There *is* a fee for guided tours of this home. Two additional attractions in the Wilson-Perkins complex (it's almost like a little historical campus, really) include a cool **blacksmith shop** ★ and the **Hearse House** (where sleighlike wooden hearses of old were made, and are now archived). Both are free to tour and worth a quick look; just remember, both buildings have the same limited hours—2 days a week in summer, for 3 hours each—as the Perkins House does.

Castine is also home to the **Maine Maritime Academy** (© **207/326-4311**), which trains sailors for the rigors of life at sea with the merchant marine. The campus is on the western edge of the village, and the 500-foot T.S. (for Training Ship) **State of Maine** ★, a hulking black-and-white vessel, is often docked here—all but overwhelming the village. (It's off cruising to places such as Odessa, Germany, and Gibraltar when it's not here.) Free half-hour tours of the ship are offered in summer whenever the ship is in port.

On the Water

This is a lovely open harbor, with open land and forest edging the watery expanse. A couple of options exist for cruising on the water:

Castine Kayak Adventures (© **207/866-3506;** www.castinekayak.com) offers full- ($105) and half-day ($55) sea kayak tours departing from Dennett's Wharf restaurant. Both trips are appropriate for those without experience; a brief intro will get you started with this graceful and often meditative sport. You'll often spot wildlife, such as bald eagles, harbor seals, and ospreys.

A Tour of Cape Rosier ★★

Across the Bagaduce River from Castine is **Cape Rosier,** one of Maine's best-kept secrets. The bad news is, to reach the cape you need to backtrack to Rte. 175, head south toward Deer Isle, and then follow Rte. 176 to the turnoff for Cape Rosier—about 18 miles of driving to cross 1 mile of water. As a dead-end peninsula, there's no through traffic and roads suddenly turn to dirt in sections. The cape still has a wild, unkempt flavor with salty views of Penobscot Bay; it's not hard to imagine that you're back in 1940s Maine.

A loop of 15 miles or so around the cape starting on Goose Falls Road—begin by following Rte. 176 to **Brooksville,** then taking Cape Rosier Road—is suitable for travel by mountain bike or as a leisurely car trip. The views are uncommonly beautiful, with a mix of blueberry barrens, boreal forest, farmsteads, summer estate houses, and coves dotted with yachts and lobster boats. There's virtually no commercial development of any sort. It's no accident that Helen and Scott Nearing, the late back-to-the-land gurus and authors of *Living the Good Life,* chose to settle here when Vermont became too developed for their tastes. A number of Nearing acolytes continue to live on Cape Rosier.

If the weather's agreeable, stop for a walk on the state-owned **Holbrook Island Wildlife Sanctuary,** a 1,200-acre preserve laced with trails and abandoned roads. The sanctuary is located at the northern end of the cape (look for signs). Among the choices: The Backshore Trail passes along open meadows to the shoreline, and the Summit Trail is all mossy, mushroomy, and medieval, with teasing glimpses of the water from the top.

Where to Stay

Castine Inn ★ The Castine Inn is a Maine rarity: a hotel that was originally built *as* a hotel, not a private residence. The handsome, cream-colored inn, designed in an eclectic Georgian Federal Revival style and built in 1898, has a great wraparound porch and attractive gardens. The lobby is filled with wingback chairs, love seats, and a fireplace in the parlor. Guest rooms on the two upper floors are attractively (though sometimes unevenly) furnished in Early American style with graceful prints, pastel walls, pencil-poster beds, and sofas; three suites have been added, consolidating formerly smaller rooms and upping the amenities, and room rates, a bit.

41 Main St. (P.O. Box 41), Castine, ME 04421. ℂ **207/326-4365.** Fax 207/326-4570. www.castineinn. com. 18 units. June–Oct $90–$275 double and suite; rates lower Nov–May. Rates include continental breakfast. 2-night minimum July–Aug. MC, V. May, open weekends only; closed mid-Oct to Apr. Children 8 and older are welcome. **Amenities:** Dining room; sauna.

Pentagöet Inn ★★ At the Pentagöet, "activities" consist of sitting on the wrap-around front porch on cane-seated rockers watching the everyday goings-on along Main Street. This quirky, yellow-and-green (ca. 1894) inn with the prominent turret is tastefully, sturdily built. The lobby features hardwood floors, oval braided rugs, and a woodstove; it's all comfortable without being prissy, professional without being chilly. Most units sport king-size beds with heavy, ornate headboards and lacy white coverlets—some have claw-foot bathtubs and/or fireplaces, and one even includes a balcony with flowers. Rooms on the upper two floors of the main house are furnished eclectically in a mix of antiques and collectibles, while five units in the adjacent Perkins Street building (an austere, Federal-era house) are furnished more simply and show off painted wooden floors. The character-filled Passports **pub ★** and delicious fare in the **dining room ★** are both excellent.

26 Main St. (P.O. Box 4), Castine, ME 04421. ℂ **800/845-1701** or 207/326-8616. www.pentagoet.com. 16 units (2 with private hallway bathrooms). May–Oct $145–$280 double. Rates include full breakfast. MC, V. Closed Nov–Apr. Pets by reservation only. Suitable for older children only. **Amenities:** Dining room; pub; bikes. *In room:* Fireplace (some units).

Where to Dine

Dennett's Wharf Restaurant ★ SEAFOOD In a soaring waterfront sail loft with dollar bills tacked all over the high ceiling, Dennett's Wharf serves upscale bar food in a lively setting leavened by a good selection of microbrews. This is a quintes-sential Maine fishing-village experience. When the weather is decent, there's outside dining beneath a bright (really bright) yellow awning with superb harbor views. It's all about pub grub and seafood here. Look for sandwiches, salads, and fried clams at lunch; dinner includes local lobsters, baby back ribs, pad Thai, and hanger steak. An oyster bar serves oysters on the half-shell. But, say, how did all those bills get on the ceiling, anyway? Ask your server; it will cost you exactly $1 to find out.

15 Sea St. (next to the town dock). ℂ **207/326-9045.** www.dennettswharf.net. Reservations recom-mended in summer and for parties of 6 or more. Lunch items $5–$13; dinner items $9–$27. AE, DISC, MC, V. Daily 11am–midnight. Closed mid-Oct to Apr.

DEER ISLE ★★

The island known as **Deer Isle ★★** is well off the beaten path, yet worth the long detour from Rte. 1. Looping, winding roads cross through forest and farmland, and travelers are rewarded with sudden glimpses of hidden coves. An occasional settle-ment even crops up now and again. This island doesn't cater exclusively to tourists the way many coastal towns and islands do; it's still largely occupied by fifth- or sixth-generation fishermen, farmers, second-home owners, and artists who prize their seclusion here.

The main village—**Stonington,** on the island's southern tip—is still a rough-hewn sea town. Despite serious incursions over the past 10 years by galleries and enterprises partly or wholly dependent on tourism, it remains dominated in spirit by fishermen and the occasional quarry worker. This village does now have a handful of inns and galleries, but its primary focus is to serve locals and summer residents, not travelers. *Outside* magazine once named this one of America's 10 best towns to live in if you're an extreme/outdoorsy type. Um . . . sure, if you don't mind living several hours removed from the nearest significant population centers and airports in Maine (which are not all that significant anyway). I've yet to see a lobsterman kayaking on his downtime, either—they're too busy working—though I suppose it does happen.

Be that as it may, this is a great island on which to simply relax and smell the salt air and watch the changing landscapes.

Essentials

GETTING THERE

Deer Isle is accessible via several winding country roads that split off of U.S. Rte. 1. Coming from the south or west (Portland or Camden), turn onto Rte. 175 in Orland, then connect to Rte. 15 and continue to Deer Isle. From the east (that is, Bar Harbor), head south on Rte. 172 to Blue Hill, where you can also pick up Rte. 15. Deer Isle is connected to the mainland via a high, narrow, and graceful **suspension bridge** built in 1938—still a bit harrowing to cross in high winds.

VISITOR INFORMATION

The **Deer Isle–Stonington Chamber of Commerce,** P.O. Box 490, Deer Isle, ME 04627 (✆ **207/348-6124;** www.deerislemaine.com), staffs a seasonal information booth just beyond the bridge on Little Deer Isle. The booth is normally open daily from May through October, its opening hours dependent on volunteer availability.

Exploring Deer Isle

Deer Isle, with its network of narrow roads to nowhere, is ideal for rambling. It's a pleasure to explore by car and is also inviting to travel by bike, although hasty and careening fishermen in pickups can make this unnerving at times. Especially tranquil is **Deer Isle.** Especially tranquil is the narrow road between Deer Isle and **Sunshine** to the east. Plan to stop and explore coves and inlets along the way. To get here, follow Rte. 15; south of Deer Isle, turn east toward **Stinson Neck,** continuing on this **scenic byway** ★ for about 10 miles over bridges and causeways.

Stonington ★★, at the southern end of Deer Isle, consists of one commercial street that wraps along the harbor's edge. While B&Bs and boutiques have made inroads here in recent years, it's still a slightly rough-and-tumble waterfront town with some attractive white-clapboard homes mixed in. The best thing to see here is, well, Main Street and the waterfront behind it. Walk down side streets like Seabreeze Avenue and Atlantic Avenue for a closer look at the town.

The town opera house is home to a very good summer-stock theater company called **Opera House Arts** ★; log on to **www.operahousearts.org** for a schedule and other details or call them at ✆ **207/367-2788**.

Also worth noting: Stonington is one of those Mainesfishing villages that hosts big-time **lobster-boat racing.** Stonington's race occurs in late July—drop by if you're in the area. You'll either be amazed or horrified by how quickly one of these workhorses can get up to speed when the captain's going full throttle.

Where to Stay

Inn on the Harbor ★   This appealingly quirky waterfront inn has the best location in town—perched over the harbor and right on the main street. After a makeover, the guest rooms (more than half of which overlook the harbor) are now better appointed in antiques and carpets. The more inexpensive rooms are a bargain, in or out of season: This is a good spot for resting up before or after a kayak expedition, or as a base for day trips out to Isle au Haut. All units (except the two-bedroom suite across town in the innkeeper's home) have in-room phones; the newly updated American Eagle Suite, the most expensive unit, has a glass-fronted woodstove, private kitchen, and private deck.

45 Main St. (P.O. Box 69), Stonington, ME 04681. ⓒ **800/942-2420** or 207/367-2420. Fax 207/367-5165. www.innontheharbor.com. 14 units. Mid-May to mid-Oct $149–$225 double; mid-Oct to mid-May $85–$135 double. Rates include continental breakfast mid-May to mid-Oct. AE, DISC, MC, V. Children 12 and older welcome. **Amenities:** Spa services. *In room:* TV, kitchenette (1 unit), no phone (1 unit).

Oakland House Seaside Resort ★★ 🎁 ☺   It doesn't get much more Maine than this: Innkeeper Jim Littlefield is a great-grandson of the original owner, a sea captain who opened the inn in 1889 on land acquired from King George. (The original inn sign remains.) On the mainland just north of the bridge to Deer Isle, it's a classic coastal summer resort with that quiet and closeness to nature you've come so far to find. The main house, known as Shore Oaks, is no longer rented out as rooms, but the simple, wonderfully relaxing 10 cottages dotting the property are. Tucked among 50 acres of shoreline with extraordinary views of Eggemoggin Reach, they have one to two bedrooms each and are of varying vintages—most have fireplaces (wood is delivered); televisions or phones; and a variety of other amenities, from kitchenettes to claw-foot tubs. Lone Pine, the most expensive unit, is a nature writer's dream: it's set into the hillside, is wood-paneled, has a stone fireplace, and possesses an outstanding view of the reach. Crow's Nest feels like the top of the world and has a similar view. Less expensive cottages like Birches are set back in the woods, with no sea views. Take note that these cottages *must* be rented weekly (which is 6 days)—no shorter stays allowed—and there aren't any amenities. No pool, dining room (there used to be), business center, nothing: just a hiking trail and those great views.

435 Herrick Rd., Brooksville, ME 04617. ⓒ **800/359-7352** or 207/359-8521. www.oaklandhouse.com. 10 units. $700–$1,225 cottage weekly. Rates include breakfast and dinner mid-June to early Sept, but include no meals in spring and fall. Closed mid-Oct to early June. Inn MAP rates also available. 7-night minimum stay. MC, V. *In room:* TV (some units), fireplace (some units), kitchenette (all units), no phone (some units).

Pilgrim's Inn ★★   Set just off a town road and between an open bay and a mill pond, this is a historic, handsomely renovated inn. The inn was built in 1793 by Ignatius Haskell, a prosperous sawmill owner. His granddaughter opened the home to boarders, and it has housed summer guests ever since. The interior is tastefully decorated in a style that's informed by Early Americana but not beholden to it. The guest rooms are well appointed with antiques and decorated in muted colonial colors; expect lots of white, a little bit of lace, and flowery prints, but never oppressively so. Especially intriguing are rooms on the top floor, showing off some impressive diagonal beams. Other accents include private staircases, cherry beds, antique tubs, gas-burning stoves, and fireplaces; breakfasts are big and fancy, running to goat-cheese pancakes, eggs Benedict, smoked salmon, and the like. Three cottages near the main building allow pets and have kitchenettes for fixing your own meals. If you're not up for that, the inn also maintains a tavern-style dining room with several intriguing spaces, the Whale's Rib; expect steaks, fish, lobsters, and rack of lamb.

20 Main St. (P.O. Box 69), Deer Isle, ME 04627. © **888/778-7505** or 207/348-6615. Fax 207/348-7769. www.pilgrimsinn.com. 15 units. $119–$219 double; $189–$229 cottage. Packages available. Rates include full breakfast. MC, V. Closed mid-Oct to mid-May. Pets allowed in cottages only ($50 fee). Children 10 and older welcome in inn, all children welcome in cottages. **Amenities:** Restaurant; pub; bikes. *In room:* TV (some units), fireplace (some units), kitchenette (some units).

Where to Dine

Fisherman's Friend ★ 🍴 SEAFOOD   On a dock near the Isle au Haut ferry and attached to a general store, this is family dining: broiled and fried fresh fish, plus lobsters cooked 30 different ways. There's also a wine list and a choice of pastas. This is a local-eats place, lively and boisterous, usually as crowded as it is unpretentious. Try ordering a bowl of the lobster stew, brimming with chunks; travelers have been known to find reasons to linger in Stonington longer just to indulge in a second bowl. Dessert selections, which include such local specialties as berry pie and shortcake, are extensive and traditional New England–style.

5 Atlantic Ave. (on the dock), Stonington. © **207/367-2442.** Reservations recommended peak season and weekends. Lobsters market priced; dinner entrees $13–$20. DISC, MC, V. May–Oct daily 11am–10pm; Apr and Nov–Jan Thurs–Sun 11am–9pm. Closed Feb–Mar. Located up the hill from the harbor past the Opera House.

A Day Trip to Isle Au Haut ★★

Rocky and remote Isle au Haut offers one of the most unusual hiking and camping experiences in northern New England. This 6×3-mile island, located 6 miles south of Stonington, was originally named Isle Haut (or High Island) in 1604 by French explorer Samuel de Champlain. The name and its pronunciation evolved—today it's generally pronounced Aisle-a-*ho*—but the island itself has remained steadfastly unchanged over the centuries.

About half of the island is owned by the National Park Service and maintained as an outpost of Acadia National Park (see chapter 9). A 60-passenger ferry run by the Isle au Haut Boat Company (see below) makes a stop in the morning and late after-noon at Duck Harbor, allowing for a solid day of hiking while still returning to Stonington by nightfall.

Note: The ferry stops at two different landings. Most of the time, they stop at the "town landing"—convenient for groceries, but a 4-mile, 2-hour hike through the island's woods along the Duck Harbor Trail to the only campsite (see below). During summer, usually twice a day, special boats run directly to the Duck Harbor landing, an easy few minutes' walk to the sites. I cannot stress enough: *Check first* where your ferry is going if you are not ready or able to walk 4 miles twice. The small harborside village, which has a few old homes, a handsome church, and a tiny schoolhouse, post office, and store, is interesting, but campers and most day-trippers are better served ferrying straight to Duck Harbor.

At Duck Harbor, the NPS maintains its cluster of five Adirondack-style lean-tos, which are available for overnight **camping ★**; cost is $25 per site, and they can be used up to 3 nights in a row (5 nights outside high season). A maximum of six camp-ers can use each site, and there are no showers or electricity; there's a water pump about ⅓ mile away. These sites fill up fast, and advance reservations are essential (due by Apr 1 of the year you want to visit, though occasional cancellations merit checking afterward anyway). Contact **Acadia National Park,** Eagle Lake Road (P.O. Box 177), Bar Harbor, ME 04609; call ✆ **207/288-3338;** or download a reservation form at **www.nps.gov/acad/planyourvisit/upload/iahreserve.pdf**. Other than for camping, the park doesn't charge a fee to explore its island holdings.

Who lives here? The island is partly inhabited by some fishermen who can trace their island ancestry back 3 centuries, and partly by summer visitors whose forebears discovered the bucolic splendor of Isle au Haut in the 1880s. The summer population of the island is about 300, with about 50 die-hards remaining year-round. (One resident is writer Linda Greenlaw, the former fishing-boat captain profiled in the book and movie *The Perfect Storm* and author of *The Lobster Chronicles* as well as a cookbook of recipes from the island.)

You can stroll the often-unpaved main road that circles the island, but many hardy visitors choose to explore the excellent **island trails ★★** that penetrate and encircle the isle. Some of the more scenic ones include Western Head Trail (requiring perhaps 1¼ hr. one-way) and Cliff Trail (about 45 min. one-way), with expansive cliff and sea views. The NPS can furnish you with a trail map at the campground, and rangers sometimes ride the ferries. Be careful, however: Some of these trails are rough on the feet, and they can get wet from the sea, fog, or rain; rain, in fact, may render a few (such as Goat Trail) impassable at times.

The **Isle au Haut Boat Company** (✆ 207/367-5193; www.isleauhaut.com) operates the ferry run, leaving from the pier at the end of Sea Breeze Avenue in Stonington. In summer (roughly mid-June to mid-Sept), there are about 10 daily runs to the island, with four to six runs in spring and fall; call or check the website for exact schedules. The round-trip boat fare to either the town landing or Duck Harbor is $36 for adults and $19 for children 11 and under. (There's also a small extra surcharge if you pay by credit card.) Bikes cost $20 round-trip, kayaks $40. The crossing takes about 45 minutes to the village landing, or 1 hour and 15 minutes to Duck Harbor. Reservations are not accepted; it's best to arrive at least a half-hour before departure.

Sea Kayaking

Peer southward from Stonington, and you'll see dozens of spruce-studded islands between the mainland and the dark, distant ridges of Isle au Haut. These islands, ringed with salmon-pink granite, are collectively called Merchant's Row, and they're invariably ranked by experienced coastal boaters as among the most beautiful in the state. Thanks to these exceptional islands, Stonington is among Maine's most popular destinations for sea kayaking. Many of the islands are open to day visitors and overnight camping, and one of the Nature Conservancy islands even hosts a flock of sheep. Experienced kayakers should contact the **Maine Island Trail Association** (✆ 207/761-8225; www.mita.org) for more information about paddling here; several of the islands are open only to association members.

Old Quarry Charters ★ (✆ 207/367-8977; www.oldquarry.com), just outside the village of Stonington, offers guided kayak tours as well as kayaks for rent. (Old Quarry will rent only to those with prior experience, so it's best to call ahead to discuss your needs.) Tours range from a half-day tour ($60) to a full-day 7-hour tour that weaves out through the islands and includes a stop for a swim or a picnic at an abandoned quarry. Overnight camping trips are also offered. Other services: parking and a launch site for those who've brought their own boats, sailboat tours and lessons, charter tours aboard a 38-foot lobster boat, and camping ($24–$50 per tent site, more for RVs). For more information, visit the company's website.

Chickening Out: Maine's Folkiest Radio Station

When in the Blue Hill area, be sure to tune into the local community radio station, WERU, at 89.9 FM (and also at 102.9 FM). Started by partners including Noel "Paul" Stookey—the "Paul" in the folk trio Peter, Paul, and Mary—in a former chicken coop (only in Maine), the idea was to spread good local and rootsy music while also encouraging provocative, countercultural thinking. It's become a little bit slicker and more professional in recent years, but WERU still retains a pleasantly homespun quality and plays some of the best true folk, roots, Americana, Celtic, and blues music of any station in New England. There's also some from-the-left news and commentary during the dinner hour each day, rock and electronic music late at night, and reggae and spoken-word poetry during other time slots.

Outfitters based *outside* the region that offer guided overnight kayak trips around Merchant's Row include the **Maine Island Kayak Co.** (© **207/766-2373**; www. maineislandkayak.com) on Peaks Island (near Portland) and **Maine Sport Outfitters** (© **800/722-0826** or 207/236-8797; www.mainesport.com) on Rte. 1 in Rockport.

BLUE HILL ★★

Blue Hill ★★, population 2,400, is easy to find—just look for the dome of Blue Hill itself, which lords over the northern end of (of course) Blue Hill Bay. Set between the mountain and the bay is the quiet and historic town, clustering along the bay's shore and a little stream. There's never much going on here, which seems to be exactly what attracts repeat summer visitors; it might also explain why two excellent bookstores are located in this dot of a town. Many old-money families maintain lovely retreats along the water or in the hills around here, but the village center offers a couple choices for lodging even if you don't have local connections. It's a good place for a quiet break.

Essentials

GETTING THERE

Blue Hill is southeast of Ellsworth, at the juncture of routes 15 and 172. From Bar Harbor, follow Rte. 3 through Ellsworth, cross the bridge, then follow Rte. 172 about 14 miles to Blue Hill. Coming from the south (Rockland or Belfast) on Rte. 1/Rte. 3, turn south onto Rte. 15 about 5 miles east of Bucksport, and drive about 12 miles.

VISITOR INFORMATION

Blue Hill does not maintain a true staffed visitor information booth. Look for the "Blue Hill, Maine" brochure and map at state information centers, or drop by the **Blue Hill Peninsula Chamber of Commerce** (© **207/374-3242**; www.bluehillpeninsula. org), located at 107 Main St. Locals are also often able to answer questions you might have.

Special Events

The **Blue Hill Fair ★★** (© **207/374-3701**; www.bluehillfair.com) is a traditional country fair with livestock competitions, vegetable displays, and carnival rides. The fair takes place at the fairgrounds northwest of the village on Rte. 172 on Labor Day weekend. Admission costs $5 to $8 per person (it varies by day); rides are individually priced. Parking is free on the fairgrounds.

Exploring Blue Hill

A good way to start your exploration is to ascend the open summit of **Blue Hill ★★**, from which you'll gain superb views of the bay and the bald mountaintops on nearby Mount Desert Island. To reach the trail head from the center of the village, drive north on Rte. 172 about 1½ miles, then turn west (left) on Mountain Road at the Blue Hill Fairgrounds. Drive another ¾ mile and look for the well-marked trail; park on the shoulder of the road. The fairly easy ascent is about a mile, and takes about 45 minutes. Bring a picnic lunch.

Blue Hill has traditionally attracted more than its fair share of artists, especially potters. Family-run **Rackliffe Pottery** (② 888/631-3321 or 207/374-2297) on Rte. 172 (Ellsworth Rd.), uses native clay and lead-free glazes. Visitors are welcome to watch the potters at work. It's open year-round.

The best "museum" in town is the **Parson Fisher House ★★** (② 207/374-2459; www.jonathanfisherhouse.org), on routes 176 and 15, a half-mile west of the village. Fisher, Blue Hill's first permanent minister, was a small-town Renaissance man when he settled here in 1796. Educated at Harvard, Fisher not only delivered sermons in six different languages (including Aramaic), but was also a writer, painter, and inventor of boundless energy. On a tour of this home, which he built himself in 1814, you can view a clock with wooden works and a camera obscura that Fisher made, plus pictures he painted and books he wrote, published, and bound by hand. Outside, the property's owners are slowly recreating Fisher's original orchard.

The house is open from July to mid-October, Thursday through Saturday from 1 to 4pm. Admission is by donation; $5 per person is suggested.

If you're an ardent antiques hunter (or collector of bizarre experiences), it *might* be worth your while to detour to the **Big Chicken Barn** (② 207/667-7308; www.bigchickenbarn.com), on Rte. 1 between Ellsworth and Bucksport. (Look for it 9 miles west of Ellsworth or 11 miles east of Bucksport.) The sprawling antiques mall and bookstore is of nearly shopping-mall proportions—more than 21,000 square feet of stuff in an old poultry barn. It's open daily from 9am to 6pm during summer, 10am to 4pm in the off season.

Where to Stay

Blue Hill Farm Country Inn   Comfortably situated on 48 acres about 2 miles north of the Blue Hill's village center, this Inn (not to be confused with its similar-named neighbor; see next entry) has some of the most relaxing and comfortable common areas in the region. The first floor of a big barn was converted into a spacious living room, with sitting areas arrayed so that you can opt for either privacy or the company of others. Guest rooms are small and lightly furnished, though—none come with anything larger than a double bed. The more modern rooms are upstairs in the barn loft and are decorated in a country farmhouse style, though they're a bit motel-like. The seven older rooms in the farmhouse have more character—but they share a single bathroom with a small tub and hand-held shower. Unusually for coastal Maine, it is open year-round.

Rte. 15 (P.O. Box 437), Blue Hill, ME 04614. ② **207/374-5126.** www.bluehillfarminn.com. 14 units (7 with shared bathroom). $95–$115 double with private bathroom; $85–$95 double with shared bathroom.

Rates include continental breakfast. AE, MC, V. "Limited accommodations" for children under 12. *In room:* No phone.

Blue Hill Inn ★★   The Blue Hill Inn has been hosting travelers since 1840 on one of the village's main streets, within walking distance of everything. It's a Federal-style inn, decorated in a Colonial American motif; creaky wooden floors stamp it with authenticity. The innkeepers have pleasantly furnished all rooms with antiques and down comforters; a few units in the main house have wood-burning fireplaces (these rooms are open only from mid-May through the end of Oct), while a large contemporary suite in an adjacent, free-standing building has a cathedral ceiling, fireplace, full kitchen, living room, and deck (and it's open year-round). Breakfasts here are very good.

40 Union St. (P.O. Box 403), Blue Hill, ME 04614. ✆ **800/826-7415** or 207/374-2844. Fax 207/374-2829. www.bluehillinn.com. 12 units. $155–$205 double; $175–$275 suite. Rates include full breakfast and afternoon pastries. 2-night minimum in summer. Packages available. DISC, MC, V. Main inn closed Dec to mid-May, 1 cottage open year-round. Children 13 and older are welcome. **Amenities:** Dining room. *In room:* A/C, TV (1 unit), fireplace (some units), kitchenette (1 unit), no phone (most units).

Where to Dine

The **Fish Net** (✆ 207/374-5240), at the north end of Main St. (near the junction of routes 172 and 177), is the place where locals go for quick meals of takeout fried fish, lobster rolls, clam baskets, and ice-cream cones. It's open seasonal—figure Memorial Day to Columbus Day, at most. There's also a new and good bakery/pizzeria, **Blue Hill Hearth** (✆ 207/610-9696), at 58 Main St., serving (yes) sandwiches, pizzas, soups, and even breakfasts. So far they don't take credit cards, and it's closed Sundays.

Arborvine ★★ SEAFOOD/FUSION   The Arborvine gives sleepy Blue Hill a top-flight eatery—the best for miles and miles. In a beautifully renovated Cape Cod–style house, the restaurant's interior is warm and inviting: think rough-hewn timbers, polished wooden floors, and a cozy bar area. The owners are careful to use locally procured ingredients, such as Bagaduce River oysters on the half-shell as an appetizer. The intriguing nightly main courses change but might run to haddock Niçoise, broiled Stonington halibut with grilled polenta, coriander-crusted *ahi* with seaweed and Japanese flavorings, *gallettes* of Maine crab and shrimp, or seared local scallops in a garlicky saffron broth. The non-seafood choices are equally exciting: a rack of lamb in pine nuts and basil, beef medallions over a dollop of Vermont chèvre, crispy roast duckling glazed with kumquat with apple-ginger chutney, or just a simple boneless rib-eye with duxelle sauce. Yummy desserts could include a Grand Marnier–spiked chocolate mousse; chocolate cake with raspberry ganache; a lemon mousse napoleon; a gingery vanilla crème brûlée; or a Bartlett pear in puff pastry sided with macadamia nut-flavored cream, pomegranate sauce, and a bit of cinnamon ice cream. I highly recommend you make a detour to dine here if you're in the area.

Main St., Blue Hill, ME 04614. ✆ **207/374-2119.** www.arborvine.com. Main courses $27–$31. MC, V. Summer daily 5:30–8:30pm; off season Fri–Sun 5:30–8:30pm.

BANGOR, ORONO & OLD TOWN

The towns of Bangor (pronounced *Bayn*-gore, please—not *Bang*-er), Orono, and Old Town lie along the western banks of the Penobscot River—not far inland from Ellsworth and Belfast on the coast—and serve as gateways to the North Woods. They

One of Bangor's claims to tourist fame is that in 1977 an addled German tourist, Erwin Kreuz, accidentally disembarked here during a transatlantic refueling stop. He spent a few days wandering the city, believing the whole time he was in San Francisco. This would be an urban legend except for the fact that it's true. It's a wonder that a statue hasn't been erected of this man.

may be worth a day or a half-day if you're interested in sampling an inland slice of the real Maine.

Bangor is Maine's third-largest city (after Portland and Lewiston), the last major urban outpost with a full-fledged mall. It's a good destination for history buffs curious about the early North Woods economy. Bangor was once a thriving lumber port, shipping millions of board feet cut from the woods to the north and floated down the Penobscot River. While much of the town burned in 1911 and has since suffered from ill-considered urban-renewal schemes, visitors can still discern a robust history just below the surface. Orono and Old Town, two smaller towns to the north, offer an afternoon's diversion on rainy days.

This is a major transportation hub and the commercial center for much of eastern and northern Maine. But, quite frankly, it's not much of a tourist destination. The downtown has a handful of buildings of interest to those intrigued by late Victorian architecture, and a new and fun children's museum, but overall the city has little of the charm or urbanity of Portland. Travelers may not wish to budget a significant amount of time for exploring Bangor.

Essentials

GETTING THERE

Bangor is located just off the Maine Turnpike. Take I-395 east, exit at Main Street (Rte. 1A), and follow signs for downtown.

As with many smaller regional airports, **Bangor International Airport (BGR)** (© **207/992-4600;** www.flybangor.com) has had a tough time persuading airlines to keep a schedule of full-service flights; thus, many flights begin or end via commuter planes to or from Boston. Airlines periodically schedule summertime runs to Bangor from places like New York, Philadelphia, and Minneapolis, but these routes seem to come and go. Check online to see if you can fly in here cheaply and efficiently.

Concord Coach (© **800/639-3317;** www.concordcoachlines.com) and **Greyhound** (© **800/231-2222;** www.greyhound.com) offer bus service to Bangor from Portland and Boston—from Boston, it's a 4½- to 5½-hour ride costing $40 to $50 one-way.

VISITOR INFORMATION

The **Bangor Visitors Information Office** is staffed in summer near the big, scary statue of Paul Bunyan at the convention center on Main Street near I-395. Contact the **Bangor Region Chamber of Commerce,** 519 Main St., Bangor, ME 04401 (© **207/947-0307;** www.bangorregion.com), open year-round from 8am to 5pm Monday through Friday. The **Greater Bangor Convention & Visitors Bureau** (© **800/916-6673** or 207/947-5205; www.bangorcvb.org) also maintains listings of local accommodations, businesses, and dining options for travelers to the city. The office is located at 40 Harlow St., and the website is good for planning purposes.

Exploring Bangor, Orono & Old Town

IN BANGOR   The **Bangor Museum and Center for History** (© 207/942-5766; www.bangormuseum.com) offers a glimpse of life in Bangor during the golden days of the late 19th century. The Thomas Hill House in which part of the museum resides—a handsome brick home built in 1836 for a prominent businessman—is also worth touring. It features displays of furniture and historical artifacts, plus lots of Civil War stuff, at 159 Union St. (just off High St.). Admission costs $3 for adults, free for children under age 12. The museum is open April through December, Tuesday through Friday from noon to 4pm (last tour at 3pm); June through September, it's also open Saturday from noon to 4pm (last tour at 3pm). The museum also owns a property downtown on Broad St. and is hoping to renovate it and reopen it with expanded exhibits; time will tell.

Vintage-car and early transportation buffs will enjoy a detour to the **Cole Land Transportation Museum** ★ (© 207/990-3600; www.colemuseum.org), 405 Perry Rd., off exit 45B of I-95 near the intersection with I-395 (left at the first light, then left onto Perry Rd.). The museum features old automobiles lined up in a warehouse-size display space, along with quirky machinery such as snow rollers, cement mixers, power shovels, and tractors. Especially well represented are early trucks, appropriate given its connection with Cole Express, a Maine trucking company founded in 1917. The museum is open daily from May to mid-November from 9am to 5pm; admission is $6 for adults, $4 for seniors, and free for those 17 and under.

Despite the city's rich history and the distinguished architecture of the commercial district, Bangor is probably best known as home to horror novelist and one-man Maine industry **Stephen King.** King's sprawling Victorian home seems a fitting place for the Maine native author; it's got an *Addams Family*–like creepiness, which is only enhanced by the wrought-iron fence with bats on it. His home isn't open to the public, but it's worth a drive by. To find the house, take the Union Street exit off I-95, head toward town for 6 blocks, then turn right on West Broadway. You'll quickly figure out which one it is, trust me.

IN ORONO & OLD TOWN   Orono is home to the University of Maine, which was founded in 1868. The campus is spread out on a plain and features a pleasing mix of historic and contemporary buildings. (The campus was originally designed by noted landscape architect Frederick Law Olmsted, but its early look has been obscured by later additions.) On campus, the modern and spacious **Hudson Museum** ★ (© 207/581-1901; www.umaine.edu/hudsonmuseum) features exhibits on anthropology and native culture. The museum exhibits crafts and artwork from native cultures around the world and is especially strong in North American displays—there's even a wigwam on display. It's open Tuesday to Friday from 9am to 4pm and Saturday from 11am to 4pm. Admission is free.

A few minutes north on Rte. 178 is riverside Old Town, famous for the classic canoes made by hand here since the turn of the 20th century. The offices of **Old Town Canoe** (© 207/827-5514; www.oldtowncanoe.com), now owned by Johnson Outdoors of Wisconsin but still cranking out top-quality watercraft, are located at 35 Middle St. (Mon–Sat 9am–5pm). They do repairs at this facility, but don't operate a storefront or offer tours.

Where to Stay

Bangor has plenty of guest rooms, many along charmless strips near the airport and the mall. If you're not choosy or if you're arriving late at night, these are fine. Be aware that even these can fill up during the peak summer season, so reservations are advised. Try the **Comfort Inn,** 750 Hogan Rd. (© **877/424-6423** or 207/942-7899; www.comfortinn.com) or the **Fairfield Inn by Marriott,** 300 Odlin Rd. (© **888/236-2427** or 207/990-0001; www.fairfieldinn.com).

Other options: Connected to Bangor's airport is a **Four Points by Sheraton,** 308 Godfrey Blvd. (© **800/368-7764** or 207/947-6721; www.sheraton.com); near the Bangor Mall and other chain stores is the **Country Inn at the Mall,** 936 Stillwater Ave. (© **800/244-3961** or 207/941-0200; www.countryinnatthemall.net). Then, downtown by the Civic Center, there's also one slightly offbeat option: the **Hollywood Slots Hotel and Raceway,** 500 Main St. (© **877/779-7771;** www.hollywoodslots.com). Yes, they have slot machines, plus about 150 pretty nice units, covered parking, an airport shuttle, and—why?—an on-site laundry service.

MOUNT DESERT ISLAND

Mount Desert Island is home to spectacular Acadia National Park, and for many visitors, the two places are one and the same. Yet the park's holdings are only part of the appeal of this popular island, which is connected to the mainland by a short causeway. Besides the parklands, there are scenic harborside villages and remote backcountry roads aplenty, lovely B&Bs and fine restaurants, oversize 19th-century summer "cottages," and the historic tourist town of Bar Harbor.

The island is split in two by an inlet (see the "Fjord Tough" box below). Most of the park's land is on the eastern side of the island, though there are some vast holdings in the west, too. The eastern side is much more heavily developed. **Bar Harbor** is the island's center of commerce and entertainment, a once-charming resort now in danger of being swallowed up by T-shirt and trinket shops. The western side has a quieter, more settled air and teems with more wildlife than tourists; here, the villages are mostly filled with fishermen and second-homers rather than actual commerce.

The island isn't huge—it's only about 15 miles from the causeway to the southernmost tip at Bass Harbor Head—yet you can do an awful lot of adventuring in such a compact space and see many different kinds of towns and landscapes. The best plan is to take it slowly, exploring if possible by foot, bicycle, canoe, and/or kayak, giving yourself a week to do it. You'll be glad you did.

To help orient you, I've placed a color map of Mount Desert Island inside the front cover of this guidebook.

ENJOYING THE GREAT OUTDOORS

Acadia is a fine, even world-class, destination for those who like their coastal vacations seasoned with adventure. While southern Maine has classic beach towns where the smell of salt air mixes with coconut oil and taffy, much of the rest of the Maine coast is unruly and wild. In parts it seems to share more in common with Alaska—you can see bald eagles soaring above and whales breaching below. In between these two archetypes, you'll find remote coves perfect for a rowboat jaunt and isolated offshore islands accessible only by sea kayak.

Mount Desert Island/Acadia National Park

The best places for coastal adventure are often not the most obvious places—those tend to be crowded and more developed. You'll need to do a bit of homework to find the real treasures. A growing number of specialized guidebooks and outfitters can help point visitors in the right direction; some of the best are mentioned below.

Keep in mind that no other New England state offers as much outdoor recreational diversity as Maine. Bring your mountain bike, hiking boots, sea kayak, canoe, fishing rod, and/or snowmobile—there'll be plenty for you to do here.

If your outdoor skills are rusty or nonexistent, brush up at the **L.L.Bean Outdoor Discovery Schools** (℃ **888/552-3261;** www.llbean.com/outdoorsOnline/odp), which offers a series of lectures and workshops that run anywhere from 2 hours to 3 days. Classes are offered at various locations around the state, covering a whole range of subjects, including fly-fishing, outdoor photography, and first aid in the wilderness. L.L.Bean also hosts periodic (and popular) canoeing, sea-kayaking, and skiing festivals that bring together instructors, lecturers, and equipment vendors for 2 or 3 days of learning and outdoor diversion. Call for a brochure, or check the L.L.Bean website for a schedule.

There is some debate about how to correctly pronounce the island to which I'm referring throughout this chapter. The name is of French origin; technically, it should be Mount days-*airt,* but nobody says it that way anymore. Some locals say "Mount Des-*sert,*" like what you have after dinner, which is pretty close to the French way of saying things. (Notice the accent on the last syllable.) However, plenty of tourists, transplants, and locals *also* say Dez-ert (like the Sahara), and that's not wrong. After all, that's how it's *spelled.* As for me, I go with Des-*sert.*

BEACHGOING The average ocean temperature at Bar Harbor in summer is 54°F (12°C); farther east in Passamaquoddy Bay it's 51°F (11°C). Cold. But small, crescent-shaped **Sand Beach ★★** in Acadia National Park makes for a wonderfully scenic day outing—and the water's good for wading (but not exactly for swimming).

BICYCLING **Mount Desert Island** and **Acadia National Park** are the premier coastal destinations for bikers, especially mountain bikers who prefer easy-riding terrain—the cycling here may be some of the most pleasant in America. Its 57 miles of well-maintained national-park carriage roads offer superb cruising through thick forests and to ocean views atop rocky knolls. No cars are permitted on these grass and gravel lanes; bikers and walkers have them all to themselves. You can rent mountain bikes in Bar Harbor, which has several bike shops from which to choose. **Park Loop Road,** while often crowded with slow-moving cars, offers one of the more memorable road-biking experiences in the state. The rest of Mount Desert Island is also good for highway biking, especially on the quieter western half of the island, where traffic is almost never a problem.

CAMPING Car campers traveling the Maine coast have plenty of choices, from well-developed private campgrounds to more basic state parks. **Acadia National Park** tends to be the biggest draw, but there's no shortage of other options on and near the coast.

Among the coastal state parks worthy of an overnight are **Lamoine State Park** (© **207/667-4778**), which is convenient to Acadia National Park yet away from the thickest of the crowds (check here if you're stuck for a place to stay on Mount Desert Island), and remote **Cobscook Bay State Park** (© **207/726-4412**). Most campsites in this nearly 900-acre park are right on the water, offering a great view of the massive 28-foot tides that slosh in and out. See chapter 10 for more details on Cobscook Bay State Park.

CANOEING For many outdoors enthusiasts in the Northeast, Maine is very alluring to serious paddlers. In fact, you can't travel very far in Maine without stumbling upon a great canoe trip. The state's best canoeing tends to be far inland and deep in the woods, true, but day paddlers can still find good trips at several lakes along the coast or in some of the protected bays.

Mount Desert's ponds offer scenic if limited canoeing; most have public boat access. Canoe rentals are available at the north end of **Long Pond** (the largest pond on the island, at 3 miles long) in Somesville from **National Park Canoe & Kayak**

Rental (© 207/244-5854; www.nationalparkcanoerental.com). The cost is about $27 for 4 hours, or $44 per day.

Two excellent sources of detailed canoeing information are the *AMC River Guide: Maine* and *Quiet Water Canoe Guide: Maine,* both published by the Appalachian Mountain Club (**www.amcboston.org**). Their office is located at 5 Joy St. in Boston.

CARRIAGE RIDES ★★ Several types of carriage rides are offered by the park-managed **Wildwood Stables** (© 877/276-3622; www.acadiamagic.com/wildwood-stables.html), about a half-mile south of the Jordan Pond House. The tours depart daily in season and take in sweeping ocean views from a local mountaintop, ramble over the Rockefeller bridges, or drop by the Jordan Pond House for (optional) tea and popovers (extra charge). There's a special carriage designed for passengers with disabilities, and you can even charter your own carriage for a private group. Reservations are recommended; figure to pay about $20 per adult, or about $10 per child, for a tour.

GOLF There are several good golf courses on Mount Desert Island. The **Kebo Valley Golf Club** (© 207/288-3000; www.kebovalleyclub.com) at 136 Eagle Lake Rd. in Bar Harbor (a short walk or drive from downtown) is one of the oldest in America, open in some form or another since 1888; it's a beauty. (*Golf Digest* awarded it four stars.) Greens fees run from $49 to $99 per person for 18 holes (they're highest in summer), and it can get very busy on peak summer weekends—try to reserve well ahead. The **Northeast Harbor Golf Club** (© 207/276-5335; www.nehgc.com) is another attractive choice. Greens fees range from $45 to $85 per person for 18 holes; to find the course, drive all the way through the small downtown, then turn right on Manchester Drive, which takes you to the course. Alternately, a few miles north of town as you come south on Rte. 3/198, exit right onto Sargent Drive and continue about 2½ miles to the course.

SEA KAYAKING ★★ Sea kayaking has boomed around Mount Desert Island during the past decade. Experienced kayakers arrive in droves with their own boats. Novices sign up for guided tours that are offered by several outfitters. Many new paddlers have found their inaugural experiences gratifying; others have complained that the quantity of paddlers on quick tours in peak season makes the experience a little too much like a cattle drive to truly enjoy. A variety of options can be found on the island, ranging from a 2½-hour harbor tour to a 7-hour excursion; there are plenty of outfitters in Bar Harbor and the other towns offering guided excursions.

Details are available from **Coastal Kayaking Tours,** 48 Cottage St. (© 800/526-8615 or 207/288-9605; www.acadiafun.com), and **National Park Sea Kayak Tours,** 39 Cottage St. (© 800/347-0940; www.acadiakayak.com). Rates range from approximately $40 to $50 per person for a 2- to 3-hour harbor, sunset, or half-day tour, up to perhaps $75 for a full-day excursion.

Sea-kayak rentals are available from **Aquaterra Adventures,** 1 West St., Bar Harbor (© 877/386-4124 or 207/288-0007; www.aquaterra-adventures.com). With unpredictable weather and squirrelly tides, kayakers are advised to have some prior experience before attempting to set out on their own. They do tons of guided tours if you have any doubt about your abilities.

SKIING Cross-country skiers have a glorious mix of terrain to choose from, especially within **Acadia National Park,** where skiing is allowed for free on park grounds throughout the winter. For more about cross-country ski areas in Maine, visit the Nordic skiing website of the trade association **Ski Maine** (www.skimaine.com).

ACADIA NATIONAL PARK ★★★

It's not hard to understand why Acadia is one of the crown jewels of the U.S. national park system. (It draws the second-most visitors annually of any national park.) The landscape here is a rich tapestry of rugged cliffs, pounding ocean surf, fishing and leisure boats lolling in harbors, and quiet forest paths.

Acadia's terrain, like so much of the rest of northern New England, was shaped by the cutting action of the last great glaciers moving into and then out of the region about 18,000 years ago. A mile-high ice sheet rumbled slowly over the land, scouring valleys into deep U shapes, rounding many once-jagged peaks, and depositing boulders at odd places in the landscape—including the famous 10-foot-tall Bubble Rock, which appears perched precariously on the side of South Bubble Mountain.

In the 1840s, Hudson River School painter Thomas Cole brought his sketchbooks and easels to remote Mount Desert Island, which was then home to a small number of fishermen and boat builders. His stunning renditions of the coast were displayed in New York City, triggering a tourism boom as urbanites flocked to the island to "rusticate." By 1872, national magazines were touting Eden (Bar Harbor's name until 1919) as a desirable summer getaway. It attracted the attention of wealthy industrialists, and soon became the de rigueur summer home of Carnegies, Rockefellers, Astors, and Vanderbilts, who built massive "cottages" with dozens of rooms.

By the early 1900s, the island's popularity and growing development began to concern its most ardent supporters. Boston textile heir George Dorr and Harvard president Charles Eliot, aided by the largesse of John D. Rockefeller, Jr. (see box), began acquiring and protecting large tracts of the island for the public to enjoy. These parcels were eventually donated to the U.S. government, and in 1919, the land was originally designated as Lafayette National Park—the first national park east of the Mississippi—after the French general who assisted colonists in the American Revolution.

Renamed "Acadia National Park" in 1929, the park has now grown to encompass nearly half the island, its holdings scattered piecemeal. It is a fine, even world-class, destination for those who like coastal vacations salted with adventure. Southern Maine is full of classic beach towns where the smell of sea air mixes with coconut oil, taffy, and fried dough, but the eastern Maine coast is mostly unruly and wild, and never more so than here. In between, you'll find remote coves perfect for beach picnics, lovely offshore islands accessible only by sea kayak, clear ponds and lakes with nary a boat, and uncrowded mountaintops (reached by car or foot) with views of it all.

💬 Fjord Tough

Mount Desert Island is divided deeply right down the middle into two lobes (almost like a brain) by **Somes Sound,** a tidal inlet that is also the only true fjord—that is, a valley carved out by a glacier and then subsequently filled in with rising ocean water—in the entire lower 48 states of the U.S. No, it's not nearly as scenic as the ones in Norway and Alaska, but when you drive over that little bridge from one side to the other, you can truthfully report to friends back home that you crossed a fjord this morning. Pretty cool.

> **How the Carriage Roads Came to Be**

John D. Rockefeller, Jr., *alone* purchased and donated some 11,000 acres of Acadia National Park—about one-third of the entire park's area—and he was almost singularly responsible for its extraordinary **carriage roads.**

It happened this way. Around 1905, a dispute erupted over whether to allow noisy new motorcars onto the island. Islanders wanted these new conveniences, but Rockefeller (whose fortune had been made in the oil industry) strenuously objected, preferring the tranquillity of a car-free island for his summer vacations. The multimillionaire went down to defeat on the issue, though, and the island was opened to cars in 1913; in response, Rockefeller set about building an elaborate 57-mile system of private carriage roads on his holdings in the park, complete with a dozen gracefully handcrafted stone bridges.

These roads, open today to pedestrians, bicyclists, horses, and carriages, are concentrated most densely around **Jordan Pond,** but they also wind through wooded valleys and ascend some of the park's most scenic peaks.

Try to allow 3 or 4 days, at a minimum, for visiting the park. If you're passing through just briefly, try to work in at least two of the big three activities (hiking, biking, driving) I've described below.

And when you set out to explore the park, bring a picnic. (See "Packing a Picnic," later in this chapter.)

Essentials

GETTING THERE

Acadia National Park is near Ellsworth, reached via Rte. 3. Normally travelers take U.S. Rte. 1 to Ellsworth from southern Maine, but you can avoid coastal congestion by taking the Maine Turnpike to Bangor, then picking up I-395 to Rte. 1A and continuing south into Ellsworth. Though this is longer in terms of miles, it's a quicker route in summer.

From Ellsworth, bear right onto Rte. 3 (U.S. Rte. 1 doesn't go onto the island) and continue about 15 minutes to the island causeway in **Trenton.** Cross the bridge and you're on the island. Consult a map carefully to determine which route to take from here; there are three possible choices, all leading to very different destinations: routes 3 and 233 go to Bar Harbor, Rte. 198 goes to Northeast Harbor, and Rte. 102 leads to Southwest harbor.

Year-round, there are several flights daily from Boston on small planes to the **Hancock County-Bar Harbor airport** (airport code **BHB;** www.bhbairport.com) in Trenton, just across the causeway from Mount Desert Island. Contact **U.S. Airways Express** (© **800/428-4322;** www.usairways.com). From here, call a taxi, rent a car, or—best of all—ride the **free shuttle bus** (see below) to downtown Bar Harbor from late June through mid-October.

GETTING AROUND

A **free summer shuttle bus service** ★★ known as the *Island Explorer* (www.exploreacadia.com) was inaugurated in 1999 as part of an effort to reduce the number of cars on the island's roads. It's working; the propane-powered buses—equipped

Cost-Effective Acadia

No daily pass to Acadia is available, so if you'll be here more than 2 weeks, purchase a $40 annual Acadia pass for your car instead of several $20 weekly passes. Or, if you really travel a lot, consider buying an $80 "America the Beautiful" national parks pass—it gets you and your vehicle and your passengers into *all* national parks for an entire calendar year.

with racks for bikes—serve multiple routes covering nearly the entire island, and will stop anywhere you request outside the village centers, including trailheads, ferries, small villages, and campgrounds. (Bring a book, though; there are lots of stops.)

All routes begin or end at the central **Village Green** in Bar Harbor, but you can and should pick up the bus almost anywhere else to avoid parking hassles in town. Rte. no. 3 runs from Bar Harbor along much of the Park Loop, offering easy free access to some of the park's best hiking trails. The buses operate from late June through mid-October; ask for a schedule at island information centers, in shops, or at any hotel or campground.

Guided Tours

Acadia National Park Tours (✆ 207/288-0300; www.acadiatours.com) offers 2½-hour park tours from mid-May through October, departing twice daily (10am and 2pm) from downtown Bar Harbor. The bus tour includes three stops (Sieur De Monts Springs, Thunder Hole, and Cadillac Mountain) and plenty of park trivia, courtesy of the driver. This is an easy way for first-time visitors to get a quick introduction to the park before setting out on their own side trips. Tickets are available at Testa's Restaurant (at 53 Main St.) in Bar Harbor; the cost is $28 for adults, $15 for children 12 and under.

Entry Points & Fees

Entrance fees to the park are collected at several gates and points from May through October; the rest of the year, entrance is free—one of this nation's great outdoor bargains either way. A 1-week pass, which includes unlimited trips on the Park Loop Road (closed in winter), costs $20 per car from late June through early October and $10 per car in spring and fall; there's no additional charge per passenger once you've bought the pass. Hikers, cyclists, and anyone else traveling without a vehicle (that is, motorcyclists or boaters) must pay a $5-per-person fee.

You can enter the park at several points in the interwoven network of park and town roads—a glance at a park map, available free at the visitor center, will make these access points self-evident. The main point of entry to Park Loop Road, the park's most scenic byway, is near the official park visitor center at **Hulls Cove** (on Rte. 3 just north of Bar Harbor); the entry fee is collected at a tollbooth on the loop road, a half-mile north of Sand Beach.

Visitor Centers & Information

Acadia staffs two visitor centers. The **Thompson Island Information Center** (✆ 207/288-3411) on Rte. 3 is the first you'll pass as you enter Mount Desert Island. This center is maintained by the local chambers of commerce, but park personnel are

Early fall is the best time to miss the mobs yet still enjoy the weather here. If you come midsummer, try to venture out in early morning or early evening to the most popular spots, such as Thunder Hole or the summit of Cadillac Mountain. Setting off into the woods at every opportunity is also a good strategy. Probably four out of every five visitors restrict their tours to the loop road and a handful of other major attractions, leaving most of the gorgeous backcountry to the more adventurous.

The best guarantee of solitude is to head to the most remote outposts managed by Acadia, such as **Isle au Haut** and **Schoodic Peninsula,** across the bay to the east. Ask for more information about these areas at the visitor centers (see "Visitor Centers & Information" below).

---

often on hand to answer inquiries. Open daily 6am mid-May through mid-October, it's a good first stop for general lodging and restaurant information.

If you're interested primarily in information about the park itself, continue on Rte. 3 to the National Park Service's **Hulls Cove Visitor Center,** about 7½ miles beyond Thompson Island. This attractive, stone-walled center has professionally prepared park-service displays, such as a large relief map of the island, natural history exhibits, and a short introductory film. You can also request free brochures about hiking trails and the carriage roads, or purchase postcards and more detailed guidebooks. The center is open daily from mid-April through the end of October.

And information is available year-round, by phone or in person, at the **park headquarters** (📞 **207/288-3338**), on Rte. 233 between Bar Harbor and Somesville, open daily (except closed weekends in summer). You can also ask questions online at their website, **www.nps.gov/acad**.

Seasons

Spring is forgettable in Acadia, but summer is the peak season. The weather in July and August is perfect for just about any outdoor activity. Most days are warm (in the 70s or 80s/low to mid-20s Celsius), with afternoons frequently cooler than mornings owing to the sea breezes. (Fogs occasionally roll in from the southeast on a hot day, which gives a magical quality to the landscape.) While sun seems to be the norm, come prepared for rain; it's not uncommon at all. Once or twice each summer, a heat wave somehow settles onto the island, producing temperatures in the 90s (30s Celsius), dense haze, and stifling humidity, but this rarely lasts more than a few days. Enjoy summer: Soon enough (sometimes even during late Aug), a brisk north wind will blow in from the Canadian Arctic, forcing visitors into sweaters at night. You'll smell the approach of autumn, with winter not far behind.

Fall here is wonderful. Between Labor Day and the foliage season in early October, days are often warm and clear, nights have a crisp tang, and you can avoid the congestion, crowds, and pesky insects of summer. It's not that the park is empty in September; bus tours seem to proliferate at this time, which can mean periodic crowds and backups at the most popular sites (such as Thunder Hole). Not to worry: If you walk a minute or two off the road, you can find solitude and an agreeably peaceful walk or perch. Hikers and bikers will have the trails and carriage roads to themselves.

Before you set out to explore, pack a lunch and keep it handy. Once you get inside it, the park has very few places (other than the Jordan Pond House, see later in this chapter) to stop for lunch or snacks. Having drinks and snacks at hand will prevent you from having to backtrack into Bar Harbor or elsewhere to fend off starvation midday. The more food you bring, the more your options for a day expand, so hit up one of the charming general stores in any of the island's villages first and stock up on sandwiches, sweets, camera batteries, and hydration.

Acadia National Park is full of picnic opportunities at every turn. **Sand Beach** is gloriously scenic (bring a blanket, plus a sweater for sea winds). A hike up any of the smaller mountains such as **Day Mountain** or **Flying Mountain** is rewarded with ocean views and cooling winds (or, in fall, a blaze of colors). If you're too tired to hike, truck over to **Jordan Pond** or to **The Bubbles** for good views.

Winter is an increasingly popular time to travel to Acadia, especially among those who enjoy cross-country skiing the carriage roads. Be aware, though, that snow along the coast is inconsistent, and services—including most restaurants and many inns—are often closed down outright in winter. Expect to stay in either a really cheap motel or an expensive resort, and to often eat what locals do: pizza, burgers, and sandwiches.

Ranger Programs

Frequent ranger programs are offered throughout the year at Acadia. These include talks at campground amphitheaters and tours of various island locales and attractions. Examples include an Otter Point nature hike, walks across the carriage roads' stone bridges, cruises on Frenchman Bay (rangers provide commentary on many trips), and discussions of the changes in Acadia's landscape—there was even a small *earthquake* here in October 2006, causing rock slides that still keep a few trails closed. Ask for a schedule of park events and more information at any visitor center or campground.

DRIVING TOUR: DRIVING THE PARK LOOP ROAD

The 20-mile **Park Loop Road ★★** is to Acadia what Half Dome is to Yosemite—the park's premier attraction, and a magnet for the largest crowds. This remarkable roadway starts near the Hulls Cove Visitor Center and follows the high ridges above Bar Harbor before dropping down along the rocky coast. Here, spires of spruce and fir cap dark granite ledges, making a sharp contrast with the white surf and steel-blue sea. After following the picturesque coast and touching on several coves, the road loops back inland along Jordan Pond and Eagle Lake, with a detour to the summit of the island's highest peak, Cadillac Mountain.

Ideally, visitors should try to make two circuits of the loop road. The first time, go for the sheer exhilaration of it and to get the lay of the land. On the second time around, plan to stop frequently and poke around on foot, setting off on trails or scrambling along the coastline. Scenic pull-offs are staggered at frequent intervals. The two-lane road is one-way along its coastal sections; the right-hand lane is set aside for parking, so you can stop wherever you'd like, admire the vistas, and click away.

From about 10am until 4pm in July and August, anticipate big crowds along the loop road, at least on days when the sun is shining. Parking lots often fill up and close at some of the most popular destinations, including Sand Beach, Thunder Hole, and the Cadillac Mountain summit, so try to visit these spots early or late in a day. Alternatively, make the best of cloudy or drizzly days by letting the weather work to your advantage; you'll sometimes discover that you have the place nearly to yourself.

Ideally, visitors should try to make two circuits of the loop road. The first time, get the lay of the land. On the second time circuit (one pass gets you all-day access), plan to stop frequently and poke around on foot, setting off on trails or scrambling along the coastline and taking photos. (Scenic pull-offs are strategically staggered at intervals.) The two-lane road is one-way along some of its coastal sections; in these cases, the right-hand lane is set aside for parking, so you can stop wherever you'd like, admire the vistas from the shoulder, and click away.

From about 10am until 4pm each good-weather day in July and August, anticipate big crowds along the loop road. Parking lots often fill up and close their gates early at the most popular destinations, such as Sand Beach, Thunder Hole, and the Cadillac Mountain summit—so try to visit these spots early or late in the day. Alternatively, on cloudy or drizzly days you'll practically have the loop road to yourself.

From the Hulls Cove Visitor Center, the Park Loop initially runs atop:

1 Paradise Hill

Our tour starts with sweeping views eastward over Frenchman Bay. You'll see the town of Bar Harbor far below, and just beyond it the Porcupines, a cluster of islands that look like, well, porcupines. Sort of.

Following the Park Loop Road clockwise, you'll dip into a wooded valley and come to:

2 Sieur de Monts Spring

Here you'll find a rather uninteresting natural spring, unnaturally encased, along with a botanical garden with some 300 species showcased in 12 habitats. The original **Abbe Museum** (𝄢 **207/288-3519**) is here, featuring a small but select collection of Native American artifacts. It's open daily from late May to early October, 9am to 4pm; admission is $3 for adults, $1 for children ages 6 to 15. (A larger and more modern branch of the museum in Bar Harbor features more and better-curated displays; a ticket here gets you a discount there. See "Exploring Bar Harbor," later, for details.)

The Tarn is the main reason to stop here; a few hundred yards south of the springs via a footpath, it's a slightly medieval-looking and forsaken pond sandwiched between steep hills. Departing from the south end of the Tarn is the fine **Dorr Mountain Ladder Trail** (see "Hiking in the Park," below).

Continue the clockwise trip on the loop road; views eastward over the bay soon resume, almost uninterrupted, until you get to:

3 The Precipice Trail

The park's most dramatic walking track, the **Precipice Trail** ★★ ascends sheer rock faces on the eastern side of **Champlain Mountain.** Only about .5 mile to the summit, it's nevertheless a rigorous climb and involves scrambling up iron rungs and ladders in exposed places (those with a fear of heights and those under 5 ft. tall should *avoid* this trail). The trail is often closed midsummer to protect nesting peregrine falcons, and at these times rangers are often on hand at the trail-head parking lot to suggest alternative hikes.

Between the Precipice Trail and Sand Beach is a tollbooth where visitors have to pay the park **entrance fee.**

Picturesquely set between the arms of a rocky cove is:

4 Sand Beach

Sand Beach ★★ is virtually the only sand beach on the island, although swimming these cold waters (about 50°F/10°C) is best enjoyed on extremely hot days or by those with hardy constitutions. When it's sunny out, the sandy strand is crowded midday with picnickers, tanners, tide pool explorers, and book readers.

Two good hikes begin near this beach, too. **The Beehive Trail** overlooks Sand Beach (see "Hiking in the Park," below); it starts from a trail head across the loop road. From the east end of Sand Beach, look for the start of the **Great Head Trail,** a loop of about 2 miles that follows on the bluff overlooking the beach, then circles back along the shimmering bay before cutting through the woods back to Sand Beach.

About a mile south of Sand Beach is:

5 Thunder Hole

Thunder Hole ★ is a shallow ocean-side cave into which the ocean surges, compresses, and bursts out violently like a thick cannon shot of foam. (A road-side walking trail allows you to leave your car parked at the Sand Beach lot and hike to this point.)

If the sea is as quiet—as it sometimes is on midsummer days—don't bother visiting this attraction; there'll be nothing to see. But on days when the seas are rough, and big swells are rolling in all the way from the Bay of Fundy, this is a must-see, three-star attraction; you can feel the ocean's power and force. The best viewing time is **3 hours before high tide;** check tide tables, available at local hotels, restaurants, and info kiosks, to figure out when that is.

Just before the road curves around Otter Point, you'll be driving atop:

6 Otter Cliffs

This set of 100-foot-high precipices is capped with dense stands of spruce trees. From the top, look for spouting whales in summer. In early fall, thousands of eider ducks can sometimes be seen floating in big, raftlike flocks just offshore. A footpath traces the edge of the crags.

At Seal Harbor, the loop road veers north and inland back toward Bar Harbor. On the route is:

7 Jordan Pond

Jordan Pond ★★ is a small but beautiful body of water encased by gentle, forested hills. A 3-mile hiking loop follows the pond's shoreline (see "Hiking in the Park," below), and a network of splendid carriage roads converges at the pond. After a hike or mountain-bike excursion, spend some time at a table on the lawn of the Jordan Pond House restaurant (see "Where to Dine," below).

Shortly before the loop road ends, you'll pass the entrance to:

8 Cadillac Mountain

Reach this **mountain** ★ by car, ascending an early carriage road. At 1,528 feet, it's the highest peak touching the Atlantic Ocean between Canada and Brazil. During much of the year, it's also the first place on U.S. soil touched by the rays of sunrise. But because this is the only mountaintop in the park accessible by car (and also because it's the island's highest point), the parking lot at the summit often gets jammed.

Biking the Carriage Roads ★★

The 57 miles of **carriage roads** built by John D. Rockefeller, Jr., are among the park's most extraordinary hidden treasures. Though built for horse and carriage, they are ideal for cruising by mountain bike and offer some of the most scenic, relaxing biking found anywhere in the United States. Park your car near Jordan Pond, then plumb the tree-shrouded lanes that lace the area, taking time to admire the stonework on the uncommonly fine bridges. Afterward, stop for tea and popovers at the **Jordan Pond House** (see "Where to Dine," below), which has been a popular island destination for over a century, although it's unlikely as much Lycra was in evidence 100 years ago.

The carriage roads were maintained by Rockefeller until his death in 1960, after which they became shaggy and overgrown. A major restoration effort was launched in 1990, and today the roads are superbly restored and maintained. With their wide hard-packed surfaces, gentle grades, and extensive directional signs, they make for very smooth biking. Note that bikes are also allowed on the island's free shuttle buses (see "Getting Around," earlier in this chapter).

A useful map of the roads is available free at visitor centers; more detailed guides may be purchased at area bookshops but aren't necessary. Where carriage roads cross private land (generally btw. Seal Harbor and Northeast Harbor), they're closed to mountain bikes, which are also banned from hiking trails.

Mountain bikes can be rented along Cottage Street in Bar Harbor, with rates generally in the neighborhood of $25 for a full day or $15 for a half-day (which is 4 hr. in the bike-rental universe). High-performance and tandem bikes cost a bit more than that,

Regulations

The usual national park rules apply. Guns may not be used in the park; if you have a gun, it must be "cased, broken down, or otherwise packaged against use." Fires and camping are allowed only at designated areas. Pets must be on leashes at all times. Seat belts must be worn in the national park (this is a federal law). Don't remove anything from the park, either man-made or natural; this includes cobblestones from the shore.

It's only 1,500 or so feet high, but Cadillac Mountain feels much grander because its views seem to stretch forever—relatively speaking, that is. This is the best place on the island to get an overview of things: the fractured geology of mountains and islands, the almost Arctic-like vegetation, the subtle color changes of fall, the sea fogs (and cruise ships and ferries) rolling in like clockwork in summer. Yes, you can drive to the top (p. 204) and walk a .5-mile to the summit, and that's fine if you have limited time or mobility issues. But experienced hikers can also enjoy two trails snaking up its flanks. The 4.5-mile **North Ridge Trail** is shorter, easier (but not easy), more open, and more ocean-scenic; it departs from a parking lot on the Park Loop Rd. The 7-plus-mile **South Ridge Trail,** beginning near Blackwoods Campground (see "Camping in & near the Park" below), is better left to expert hikers: it's a bit hairy in spots. Beginners, those in questionable physical condition, or those who think mountains can be hiked in heels/flip-flops should *not* tackle either one of these hikes.

children's bikes a bit less. Most bike shops include locks and helmets as basic equipment, but ask what's included before you rent. Also ask about closing times, since you'll be able to get in a couple of extra hours with a late-closing shop. The **Bar Harbor Bicycle Shop,** 141 Cottage St. (© **207/288-3886;** www.barharborbike.com), gets many people's vote for the most convenient and friendliest. You could also try **Acadia Bike & Canoe,** 48 Cottage St. (© **800/526-8615;** www.acadiabike.com).

Hiking in the Park

Hiking is the quintessential Acadia experience, and it should be experienced by everyone at least once. The park has 120 miles of hiking trails in all, plus 57 miles of carriage roads, which are great for easier walking. Some traverse the sides or faces of low "mountains" (which would be called hills anywhere else), and almost all summits have superb views of the Atlantic. Many of these pathways were crafted by stonemasons or others with aesthetic intent, so the routes aren't always the most direct—but they're often incredibly scenic, taking advantage of natural fractures in the rocks, picturesque ledges, and sudden, sweeping vistas.

The Hulls Cove Visitor Center has a brief chart summarizing area hikes; combined with the park map, this is all you need to find one of the well-maintained, well-marked trails and start exploring. Cobble together different loop hikes to make your trips more varied, and be sure to coordinate your hiking with the weather; if it's damp or foggy, you'll stay drier and warmer strolling the carriage roads. If it's clear and dry, head for the highest peaks (Cadillac, The Bubbles) with the best views.

One of the best trails is the **Dorr Ladder Trail** ★, which departs from Rte. 3 near the Tarn just south of the Sieur de Monts entrance to the Loop Road. This trail begins with a series of massive stone steps ascending along the base of a vast slab of granite and then passes through crevasses (not for the wide of girth) and up ladders affixed to the granite. The views east and south are superb.

An easy lowland hike is around **Jordan Pond,** with the northward leg along the pond's east shore on a hiking trail and the return via carriage road. It's mostly level, with the total loop measuring just more than 3 miles. At the north end of Jordan Pond, consider heading up the prominent, oddly symmetrical mounds called **The Bubbles ★**. These detours shouldn't take much more than 20 minutes each; look for signs off the Jordan Pond Shore Trail.

On the western side of the island, an ascent of **Acadia Mountain** and return takes about 1½ hours, but hikers should schedule in some time for lingering while they enjoy the view of Somes Sound and the smaller islands off Mount Desert's southern shores. This 2.5-mile loop hike begins off Rte. 102 at a trail head 3 miles south of Somesville. Head eastward through rolling mixed forest, then begin an ascent over ledgey terrain. Be sure to visit both the east and west peaks (the east peak has the better views), and look for hidden clearings in the summit forest that open up to unexpected vistas.

Many of the ocean-side rock faces attract experienced rock climbers, as much for the beauty of the climbing areas as the challenge of the climbs and the high-grade quality of the rock. For novices or experienced climbers, **Acadia Mountain Guides** (✆ **888/232-9559** or 207/288-8186; www.acadiamountainguides.com) offers rock-climbing lessons and guide services, ranging from a half-day introduction to rock climbing to intensive workshops on self-rescue and instruction on how to lead climbs. The Bar Harbor branch (the other's in Bangor) is located at 228 Main St.

Camping In & Near the Park

The National Park Service maintains two campgrounds within Acadia National Park. Both are extremely popular; during July and August, expect both of them to fill up by early to midmorning.

The more popular of the two is **Blackwoods ★★** (✆ **207/288-3274**), on the island's eastern side, with about 300 sites. To get there, follow Rte. 3 about 5 miles south out of Bar Harbor; bikers and pedestrians have easy access to the loop road from the campground via a short trail, and the Island Explorer bus stops here as well. This campground has no public showers or electrical hookups, but an enterprising business just outside the campground entrance provides clean showers for a modest fee. Camping fees at Blackwoods are $20 per night from May through October, $10 per site in April and November. Advance **reservations** can be made to Blackwoods by calling ✆ **877/444-6777** between 10am and midnight (only until 10pm in winter), or by using a new reservations system online at **www.recreation.gov**. An Acadia pass (see above) is also required for campground entry.

The **Seawall ★** (✆ **207/244-3600**) campground is located over on the quieter, western half of the island, near the tiny fishing village of Bass Harbor (one of the Island Explorer shuttle bus lines also stops here). Seawall has about 215 sites, and it's a good base for cyclists or those wishing to explore several short coastal hikes within easy striking distance. However, it's quite a ways from Bar Harbor and Sand Beach on the other side of the island; for families, it might not be the best choice. The campground is open mid-May through the end of September, and but they *do not take reservations*. It's first-come, first-served all the way—and the lines form early. In general, if you get here by 9 or 10am you're pretty much assured of a campsite, especially if you want a walk-in site.

Camping fees at Seawall are $14 to $20 per night, depending on whether you want to drive directly to your site, or can pack a tent in for a distance of up to 150 yards. There are also no electrical or water hookups here, and (as it is with Blackwoods) prior acquisition of an Acadia entrance pass is required to stay at the campground.

Private campgrounds handle the overflow. The region from Ellsworth south boasts 14 private campgrounds, which offer varying amenities. The **Thompson Island Information Center** (② 207/288-3411), open 6am to 10pm daily from May through mid-October, posts up-to-the-minute information on which campgrounds still have vacancies; it's a good first stop for those arriving without camping reservations.

Two private campgrounds stand above the rest. **Bar Harbor Campground,** Rte. 3, Salisbury Cove (② 207/288-5185), on the main route between the causeway and Bar Harbor, does not take advance reservations. Still, you can often find a good selection of sites if you walk in before noon, even during peak season. Some of its 300 sites are set in piney woods; others are on an open hillside edged with blueberry barrens. The wooded sites are quite private. There's a pool for campers and uncommonly clean bathhouses, and campers always get to pick their own sites rather than be arbitrarily assigned one. Rates range from around $26 for a basic, no-services site to around $30 for those with hookups.

Then, at the head of Somes Sound is **Mount Desert Campground,** Rte. 198 (② 207/244-3710), which is my favorite private facility on the island and is one that's especially well suited for campers—only those RVs 20 feet long or shorter are allowed. This heavily wooded campground has many lovely sites, including some walk-in sites right at the water's edge. The rate ranges from $36 to $49 per night in high season, $29 to $38 per site in the off season. It's open from mid-June to about mid-September. (Do not confuse with the similar-named Mount Desert Narrows Campground, a bigger, more commercial campground that's much more RV-oriented. That one is located right at the end of the bridge after you arrive on the island.)

Another option is **Lamoine State Park** (② 207/667-4778), which faces Mount Desert from the mainland across the cold waters of northernmost Frenchman Bay. This is an exceptionally pleasant, quiet park with private sites, a shower house, and a small beach about a half-hour's drive from the action at Bar Harbor. The campground has been belatedly discovered by travelers in the last half-dozen years, but still rarely fills to capacity. It's open from mid-May to early September, and sites cost $20 per night for nonresidents of Maine.

Should all these options be full, don't despair: You can find a room, especially in Bar Harbor, which is teeming with motels and inns. The rest of the island also has a good, if scattered, selection of places to spend the night. See the "Where to Stay" sections for Bar Harbor and the rest of Mount Desert Island later in this chapter. Still desperate? Head off-island to Trenton (a clutch of motels along Rte. 3) and then Ellsworth.

Where to Dine

Jordan Pond House ★★ 🍴 AMERICAN The secret to the Jordan Pond House? Location, location, location. The restaurant traces its roots from 1847, when a farm was established on this picturesque property at the southern tip of Jordan Pond looking north toward The Bubbles, a picturesque pair of glacially sculpted mounds. In 1979, the original structure and its birch-bark dining room were destroyed by fire. A more modern, two-level dining room was built in its place—less charm, but it still has one of the island's best dining locations, on a nice lawn spread out before the pond. Afternoon tea with popovers and jam is a hallowed tradition here. The lobster stew is expensive but very good. Dinners include classic entrees like prime rib, steamed lobster, pasta, and lobster stew; the prix-fixe meal special is a deal.

Park Loop Rd. (near Seal Harbor), Acadia National Park. ☎ **207/276-3316.** www.jordanpond.com. Advance reservations not accepted; call before arrival to hold a table. Main courses $12–$17 at lunch, $15–$23 at dinner. AE, DISC, MC, V. Mid-May to late Oct daily 11:30am–8pm (until 9pm July–Aug).

A NATURE GUIDE TO ACADIA NATIONAL PARK

The human history of Acadia National Park is usually thought of as beginning in the early 20th century, when preservationists banded together with wealthy philanthropists to set aside and create the park we know today. In fact, its clock winds much farther back than that—beginning thousands of years ago, when local Native American tribes fished its shores and hunted its hills. But even *that* is just a flake off the deep, deep time that has been required to create Acadia. The rocks upon which you climb, sun yourself, and picnic are old—staggeringly old.

Before arriving, then, one would do well to acquaint oneself with the natural history of the place. Armed with a respect and appreciation for the landscape before you, you just might treat it a bit more reverently while you're here and help ensure it remains for future generations to behold for many years.

The Landscape

The beginnings of Acadia National Park as we see it today are perhaps a half *billion* years old. At that time, deep wells of liquid rock known as magma were moving upward, exploding in **underground volcanoes,** then hardening—still underground, mind you—into granitelike rocks. Later, as natural forces such as wind and water wore away the upper layers of rock above these rocks, the rocks began to be exposed. Their journey was only beginning, however; soon enough (geologically speaking, that is), what is now eastern North America and most of Europe began to shove up against each other, slowly but inexorably. This "collision" (which was more like an extremely

---

LANDSCAPE IS not JUST SCENERY

The places you'll be traveling are not just scenery. They are the home to millennia of natural history (volcanoes, icebergs, polar bears, whales, and caribou, oh my!), as well as a deep human history (Vikings, native Canadians fishing and hunting long before Europeans showed up, lobstermen). And the great part is, this story continues today: These layers overlap in fascinating ways to create the "place" that is now coastal Maine. Understand these creatures and landscapes you'll be interacting with *before* you get there, and you'll have a better trip—and become a more ecolog-

ically aware traveler with a deeper respect for what you're experiencing.

Pick up the books of Canadian author Farley Mowat; a locally written book on eastern Canadian geography, geology, natural history, or native Canadian culture (library book sales and local gifts shops are two great sources); or a novel by E. Annie Proulx. For information about the whales you'll be glimpsing (and how to respect them), visit the **Whale and Dolphin Conservation Society** (www.wdcs.org). For info on traveling lightly in general, see **Tread Lightly** (www.treadlightly.org) online.

---

slow-motion car wreck), heated, squeezed, transformed, and thrust up the rocks that now form the backbone of **Mount Desert Island.**

Now in place, the rocks were once again changed by everything around them. Ice ages came and went, but the rocks remained; the successive waves of great glaciation and retreat scratched up the rocks like old vinyl records, and the thick tongues of pressing ice cut deep notches out of the rock. Near Somesville it nearly divided the island in two, creating the only natural fjord in the United States; farther "inland," the slowly flowing ice pushed forward and scooped out several more narrow, parallel valleys that would later be filled by rainwater to form Jordan Pond and Eagle Lake. Huge boulders were swept up and deposited by the ice in odd places, such as the tops of mountains (**Bubble Rock** is one).

When the glaciers finally retreated for the last time, tens of thousands of years ago, the water melting from the huge ice sheet covering North America swelled the level of the Atlantic high enough to submerge formerly free-flowing river valleys and give Mount Desert Island the distinctive, knuckled-fist shape we know it for today.

Onto the bones of this landscape came plants and then animals. After each **ice age,** conifers such as spruce and fir trees—alongside countless grasses and weeds—began to reform, decompose, and form soils. It was tough work: Acadia is a rocky, acidic place. Yet they persevered, and soon the spruces, firs, and hemlocks formed an impenetrable thicket covering the bedrock. Land **animals** came here, too, some of them now extinct from the island—the caribou, elk, eastern timber wolf, and sea mink among those extirpated by human presence. Many others survived, however, and there's plenty of wildlife here today; while the lynx and eastern cougar may no longer roam the woods, hills, and fields of Acadia, plenty of other creatures do.

The park, though it appears to be fixed in time now, is actually in constant flux. Islanders got a lesson in nature's restorative powers in 1947, when a **huge forest fire** swept across the park and island, devastating most of it; in the ashes soon grew not more spruces and firs, but rather an entire new set of flowers, weeds, and trees better adapted to grow in bright, sunny, nutrient-poor meadows. Fireweeds, wildflowers, aspens, birch, oak, pine, and maple trees began to slowly fill in the denuded landscape and today help create the mixture of plants (and the fall foliage, and the deer, mice, and other animals that favor this mixture) in the park today. The spruces and firs may eventually take over again—but it will take generations to happen.

Acadia's unique position—it is very near the warm Gulf Stream, yet possesses very cold waters; it is not far from the high, shallow undersea plateau known as **Georges Bank**—has also brought an astonishing variety of marine life to its doorstep. Migrating whales make for a wonderful spectacle twice each year (and whale-watching tours out of Bar Harbor bring the lives of whales closer to the visitor). Seabirds make similar passages, lighting upon the rocks and lakes of the park coming and going. And the waters teem—though not as they once did—with fish large and small, lobsters, crabs, dolphins, and a great deal more (each creature with its particular habits, habitats, diets, life cycles, and seasonal migration patterns).

This is to say almost nothing of **Acadia's tide pools,** in that precarious zone where land and rock meet crashing ocean; a closer look at these pools reveals an ever-changing world of seaweed, snails, barnacles, darting water bugs, clams, shellfish, mud-burrowing worms, and other creatures. Interestingly, the type of life you'll find changes in well-marked "bands" as you get closer to water; rocks that are always submerged contain one mixture of seaweeds and marine organism, rocks that are exposed and then resubmerged each day by the tides contain another. Mostly dry surfaces of the shore rocks contain yet another mixture of living things. It's fascinating to note how each particular organism has found its niche, maintained it, and continues to live hardily and well—within its particular band. Move it up or down a foot, and it would perish.

What follows is only the barest sketch of the natural world in Acadia. For a real look at it, go and see it yourself—preferably by as many means as possible. Whether you choose to explore Acadia on foot, bicycle, horse-drawn carriage, kayak, charter boat, or some other way, you're almost certain to see something here you've never seen before. If you're attentive, you'll come away with a deeper respect for things natural—here, and everywhere.

The Flora

BALSAM FIR   The best-smelling tree in the park must be the mighty balsam fir, whose tips are harvested elsewhere to fabricate aromatic Christmas-tree wreaths. It's sometimes hard to tell a fir from a spruce or hemlock, though the balsam's flat, paddlelike needles (white underneath) are nearly unique—only a hemlock's are similar. Pull one off the twig to be sure; a fir's needle comes off clean, a hemlock's ragged. Still not sure you've got a fir tree on your hands? The long, glossy, almost purplish cones are absolutely distinctive.

Balsam Fir

RED, WHITE, AND PITCH PINE   The pines grow in Acadia's sandy soils and normally like some sunlight. **White pine** is the familiar "King's pine" prevalent throughout Maine; its trunk was prized for the masts of British ships of war, and countless huge pines were floated down Maine rivers by logger men. Sadly, very few virgin pine trees remain in Maine today. The white pine's extremely long, strong needles come five to a bunch. The **red pine,** not so common, can be distinguished by its pairs of needles and pitchy trunk. The presence of a **pitch pine** indicates poor, acidic soils, and this is one of the first trees to successfully rush in and take root in the wake of a fire. It can grow in the oddest places—along a cliff, on a lip of crumbling stone, in waste soil. The shorter, scrubby clumps of needles (arranged three to a group) don't look attractive but belie the tree's toughness.

Red Pine

White Pine

RED AND SUGAR MAPLE These two maple trees look vaguely alike when turning color in fall, but they're actually quite different—from the shapes of their leaves to the habitats they prefer. **Red maples** have skinny, gray trunks and like a swampy or wet area; often, several of the slim trunks grow together into a clump, and in fall the red maples' pointy leaves turn a brilliant scarlet color almost at once. **Sugar maples,** on the other hand, are stout-trunked trees with lovely, substantial leaves (marked with distinctive U-shaped notches), which autumn slowly changes to red and flame-orange. Sugar maples grow in or at the edges of mixed forests, often in combination with birch trees, oak trees, beech trees, hemlocks, and the like. Their sap, of course, can be collected and boiled down to make deli- cious maple syrup.

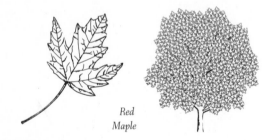

Red
Maple

LOWBUSH BLUEBERRY The lowbush blueberry, with its shrubby, tealike leaves and hardy, thick twigging, lies low to exposed rocks on sunny hillsides or some-times crops up in shady woods; most of the year, it's inconspicuous as anything, trail-ing harmlessly underfoot. Come late summer, however, and it's suddenly the island's most popular plant—among bears as well as humans. The wild blueberries ripen slowly in the sun (look behind and beneath the leaves for the best bunches), and make for fine eating, pancake baking, and jam.

The Fauna
MAMMALS
Land Mammals
BEAVER Reintroduced to Acadia in the 1920s (it had earlier nearly gone extinct from brisk world trade in beaver pelts), the beaver's lodge-building, stick-chewing, and hibernating habits are well known. You'll find it in streams, lakes, and ponds around Mount Desert Island.

BLACK BEAR   Black bears do appear in Acadia, though in small numbers (still, you may want to keep a cover on that campfire food). The bears are mostly—emphasis on mostly—plant-eaters and docile. Though they'll eat just about anything, black bears prefer easily reached foods on the woodland floor such as berries, mushrooms, and nuts. They need them for a long winter hibernation that averages 6 months.

Beaver

Black Bear

MOOSE   Nothing says Maine like a moose, and the huge, skinny-legged, vegetarian moose is occasionally seen in Acadia National Park; not very often, however. It far prefers the deep woods, lakes, ponds, and uninhabited areas of Maine's Great North Woods. You can't miss it if you see it, though—the rack of antlers (on the male), the broad, lineman shoulder, the spindly (but quick) legs, and the sheer bulk of the thing—big as a truck—ensure you won't mistake it for anything else on the planet. Hope you don't run into one late at night, on a highway: Each year cars and moose meet up in Maine. Everybody loses, but the car gets a lot more banged up than the moose.

Moose

Shellfish
AMERICAN LOBSTER   Everyone knows the lobster by sight and taste; what few know is that not so long ago it was considered ugly, tasteless, and unfit to eat. In fact, there was a time when mainly prisoners in Maine were served lobster and lobster stew—three meals a day! Today, of course, the situation is very different. Lobsters, which are related to crabs and shrimp (and more generally to spiders and insects), slowly scour the ocean bottom in shallow, dark waters, locating food by smell. They actually see very poorly. The hard shell, which they periodically shed in order to grow, is the lobster's skeleton: a greenish-black color in life, bright red only after having been cooked.

American Lobster

Whales, Dolphins, Porpoises & Seals

FINBACK WHALE   A seasonal visitor to Maine's waters twice a year when migrating between polar and equatorial waters, the finback is one of the biggest whales, and also one of the most collegial. It often travels in pairs or groups of a half-dozen or more (most whales are relatively solitary), though it does not travel close to shore or in shallow waters; you'll need a whale-watch boat to spot it. Find it by its rather triangular head and a fin that sweeps backward (like a dolphin's) rather than standing straight up like many other whales'.

Finback Whale

HUMPBACK WHALE   Though this whale's Latin name roughly translates as "large-winged New England resident," the gentle, gigantic humpback actually isn't so often seen off the coast of Acadia. (That's mostly because they were easy targets in the heyday of whaling.) But if you do see it, you'll know it: It's huge, dark black, blows tremendous amounts of water when surfacing, and does some amazingly playful acrobatics above water. The males also sing haunting songs, sometimes for as long as 2 days at a time. The world population has shrunk to perhaps 20,000 individuals.

Minke Whale

MINKE WHALE   The smallest (and most human-friendly) of the whales, the minke swims off Acadia's coast, usually moving in groups of two or three whales—but much larger groups collect in feeding areas and seasons. It has a unique habit of approaching and congregating around boats and ships, making this a whale you're quite likely to see while on a whale-watching tour. The minke is dark gray on top; the throat has grooves; and each black flipper fin is marked with a conspicuous white band.

Northern Right Whale

NORTHERN RIGHT WHALE   If you see a right whale, you've really seen something: It's the most endangered of all the living whales—there are probably fewer than a thousand left in all the oceans of the world, and the northern right is even scarcer—yet one has occasionally been seen off the coast of Acadia. Experts predict it will become extinct within a few more human generations, if not sooner. Huge and active as the humpback, the right is known for doing headstands (so to speak) underwater, poking its tail fins above. It can be spotted by its light color—often blue, brown, or even off-white—and the whitish calcium growths that often appear on its head.

Pilot Whale

PILOT WHALE   A small whale, the pilot is very rarely seen off Acadia, and very poorly understood. Its habits, world population, and diet are nearly unknown. It is known to congregate in large groups, sometimes consisting of up to several hundred, and even to swim with other species of whale at sea. Nearly unique among the whales that pass Maine, it has teeth, and the roundish fin is swept back like a dolphin's or shark's. Sightings are possible and should be cherished.

Atlantic White-Sided Dolphin

DOLPHINS   Two very similar-looking species of dolphin—the **Atlantic white-sided dolphin** and the **white-beaked dolphin**—rarely come to the coast of Maine. Cute and athletic, these dolphins sometimes also occasionally turn up on southern New England's beaches, for a more tragic reason: Large groups are occasionally stranded by the tide, then perish when they cannot get back to sea in time.

White-Beaked Dolphin

HARBOR PORPOISE   Quiet in behavior and habit, the porpoise is not the same thing as a dolphin; in fact, it's darker, much less athletic, and with a blunter, triangular fin. (The dolphin jumps out of the water, and has a pointier fin that sweeps backward.)

Harbor Porpoise

HARBOR SEAL   Related to sea lions, the whiskered harbor seal is best seen by using one of the charter boat services that leaves from Bar Harbor and other local harbors. You can also sometimes see it basking in the sun or on the rocks of an offshore island. You'll easily recognize it: The seal's flippers have five claws, almost like a human hand; its neck is stocky and strong (as are its teeth); and then there are those whiskers and that fur.

BIRDS
Waterfowl
DUCKS   Between one and two dozen species of ducks and ducklike geese, brant, and teal seasonally visit the lakes, ponds, and tidal coves of Acadia every year, including—though hardly limited to—the **red-breasted merganser, common eider,** and the **bufflehead.** Mergansers, characterized by very white sides and very red bills (males) or reddish crests (females), occur year-round in the park but are more common in winter months. So is the eider, which inhabits offshore islands and coastal waters rather than Mount Desert Island's freshwater lakes; Maine is actually the southernmost tip of its breeding range—in winter, it forms huge rafts of birds. Males are marked with a sharp black-and-white pattern. The chubby, squat bufflehead is also distinctively black and white, with a glossy green-and-purple head; it is entirely absent from the park in summer, but passes through in spring and fall, sometimes lingering for the winter. It flies much more quickly than one might imagine from its appearance.

Common Eider

Red-Breasted Merganser

GREAT BLUE HERON   Everyone recognizes a great blue at once by its prehistoric flapping wings, comb of feathers, and spindly legs. These magnificent hunters wade tidal rivers, fishing with lightning strikes beneath the surface, from May through around October. The smaller, stealthier green heron occurs less commonly, and occasional sightings of black-crowned and yellow-crowned night herons have also been recorded within the park's boundaries.

Great Blue
Heron

Red-Throated Loon

LOONS   Two species of loon visit the island's lakes and tidal inlets, fishing for dinner. The **red-throated loon,** grayish with a red neck, is mostly a spring visitor and barely present at all in the heat of summer. The **common loon** is indeed more common—it can be distinguished by a black band around the neck, as well as black-and-white stripes and dots—and can be found in Acadia year-round, though it's most easily spotted in late spring and late fall. It gives the distinctive mournful, almost laughing cry for which the birds are famous. Both have been decimated by human environmental changes such as oil spills, acid rain, and airborne mercury.

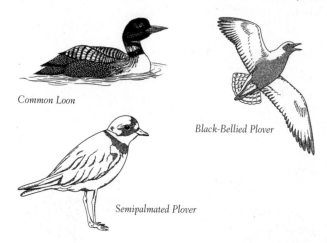

Common Loon

Black-Bellied Plover

Semipalmated Plover

PLOVERS   Plovers inhabit and breed in Acadia's muddy tidal flats, and their habitat is understandably precarious; a single human step could crush an entire generation of eggs. Only two species of plover visit the park, and they're here in significant numbers for only a relatively short time. The **black-bellied plover**—marked with a snowy black-and-white pattern—arrives in May, breeds in August and September, and is gone by Thanksgiving. The **semipalmated plover,** with its quite different brownish body and white breast, has a similar life cycle.

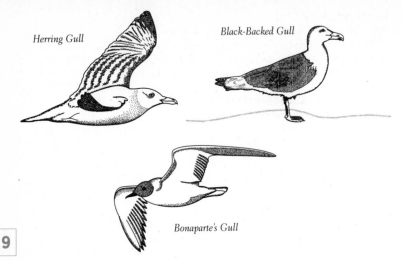

Herring Gull

Black-Backed Gull

Bonaparte's Gull

SEAGULLS   No bird is so closely associated with Maine as the seagull. But, in fact, there's more than one kind of gull here; three or four distinct gulls are commonly found here year-round, a few more visit seasonally, and a few more pop up occasionally. Most common is the grayish **herring gull,** which is also the gull least afraid of humans. It's found in prevalence every month of the year. The aggressive **great black-backed gull** is similarly common, and is nearly all white (except for that black back and wings); it will even eat the eggs of another gull, but in general avoids humans. Less common are the glaucous, **ring-billed gull,** and even the **laughing and Bonaparte's gulls** (in summer only), not to mention the related **black-legged kittiwake.** Each has a distinctive look; consult a bird guide if you're interested in telling them apart.

STORM PETRELS   The tiny storm petrel is a fascinating creature. These plucky little birds fly astonishing distances in winter, eating insects on the wing, only to return to Acadia each spring like clockwork, usually in May. They spend an amazing 4 months in the nest incubating, hatching, and tending to their single, white eggs. **Wilson's storm petrel** is here for a shorter time than the **Leach's storm petrel,** which restricts its visits and nests solely to offshore rocks and islands. Both breed in the height of summer, then pack up and head south again by fall.

Wilson's Storm Petrel

Land Birds

BALD EAGLE   Yes, they're here—year-round—and even breed in Acadia, though they're difficult to find and hardly conspicuous. (Their endangered status means you shouldn't really try to seek them out.) The bald eagle's black body, white head, and yellow bill make it almost impossible to confuse with any other bird. It was nearly wiped out by the 1970s, mainly due to environmental poisons such as DDT-based pesticides, which caused female eagles to lay eggs that were too weak to sustain growing baby chicks. However, the bird has begun to come back.

Bald Eagle

Common Raven

COMMON RAVEN   The park holds jays and crows aplenty, but the raven is a breed apart—tougher, more reclusive, more ragged, more interesting. Look (or listen) for it on cliff tops, mountains, and in deep woods.

SONGBIRDS   There are literally dozens of species of songbirds coming to roost in Acadia's open fields, forests, and dead snags—even in the rafters and bird boxes of houses. They are not so common on this rocky, shady island as in Maine's suburbia (Greater Portland, for instance) or in the farmlands of central and western Maine, but they are here. One thing is for certain: Songbirds love human company, thus look for them near the settled areas. The park hosts perhaps 15 or more distinct types of chirpy little **warblers,** each with unique and often liquid songs; a half-dozen **thrushes** occurring in significant numbers; winter **wrens, swallows, sparrows, vireos, finches, creepers,** and **thrashers;** the whimsical black-capped **chickadee;** and occasional (and lovely) sightings of **bluebirds, cardinals,** and **tanagers,** among many other species.

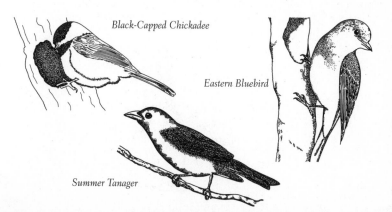

Black-Capped Chickadee

Eastern Bluebird

Summer Tanager

BAR HARBOR ★

Bar Harbor provides most of the meals and beds to travelers coming to Mount Desert Island, and it has done so since the grand resort era of the late 19th century, when wealthy vacationers first discovered this region. Sprawling hotels and boarding-houses once cluttered the shores and hillsides here, as a newly affluent middle class arrived by the steamboat and rail car from the city in droves to find out what all the fuss was about.

The tourist business continued to boom through the early 1900s, then all but collapsed when the Depression and the growing popularity of car travel doomed the era of steamship travel and extended vacations. Bar Harbor was dealt another blow in 1947, when an accidental fire spread rapidly and leveled many of the opulent cottages and a large portion of the island. Some 17,000 acres burned in all, though downtown Bar Harbor and some in-town mansions on the oceanfront were spared.

In recent years, however, Bar Harbor has bounced back with a vengeance, revived and rediscovered by visitors and entrepreneurs alike. Some see the place as a tacky place of T-shirt vendors, ice-cream cones, and souvenir shops, plus crowds spilling off the sidewalks into the street and appalling traffic. That is all true. Yet the town's history, distinguished architecture, and beautiful location on Frenchman Bay still make it a desirable base for exploring the island, and it has by far the best selection of lodging, meals, supplies, and services on the isle. (If you want to shop, fine-dine, or go out at night, you've pretty much *got* to stay here.) Otherwise, if quiet is what you're seeking, consider bunking elsewhere on the island (see below).

Essentials

GETTING THERE

Bar Harbor is on Rte. 3, about 10 miles southeast of the causeway leading onto Mount Desert Island. For plane and bus access, see "Getting There," in the Acadia National Park section earlier in this chapter.

VISITOR INFORMATION

The **Bar Harbor Chamber of Commerce** (© **800/345-4617;** www.barharborinfo.com), stockpiles a huge arsenal of information about local attractions, both at its offices on 1 West St. (at the pier) and in a welcome center on Rte. 3 in Trenton, just before the bridge onto the island. Write, call, or e-mail in advance for a directory of area lodging and attractions. The chamber's website is chock-full of information and helpful links, too.

Exploring Bar Harbor

The best water views in town are from the foot of Main Street at grassy (and free) **Agamont Park ★★**, which overlooks the town pier and Frenchman Bay. From here, stroll past The Bar Harbor Inn on the **Shore Path ★★**, a wide, winding trail that follows the shoreline for half a mile along a public right of way. The pathway also passes in front of many elegant summer homes (some converted into inns), offering a superb vantage point from which to view the area's architecture.

The **Abbe Museum ★**, 26 Mount Desert St. (© **207/288-3519;** www.abbemuseum.org), opened in 2001 as an in-town extension of the smaller, simpler museum at the Sieur de Monts spring in the national park (see above), showcasing a top-rate collection of Native American artifacts. A 17,000-square-foot gallery, this downtown

ACCOMMODATIONS ■
Acadia Hotel **25**
Balance Rock Inn **18**
Bar Harbor
 Grand Hotel **29**
Bar Harbor Hotel-
 Bluenose Inn **1**
Bar Harbor Inn **6**
Bass Cottage Inn **8**
Black Friar Inn **13**
Coach Stop Inn **1**
The Colony **1**
Highbrook Motel **1**
Ivy Manor Inn **17**
Ledgelawn Inn **22**
Maples Inn **15**
Mira Monte Inn **20**
Primrose Inn **19**
Rockhurst Motel **21**
Villager Motel **28**

DINING ◆
Alternative **27**
Ben & Bill's Chocolate
 Emporium **7**
Café This Way **26**
Eden Vegetarian Café **4**
Galyn's **5**
Havana **30**
Jordan's Restaurant **12**
Lompoc Café **9**
Mâche Bistro **14**
Maggie's Restaurant **11**
Michelle's Fine Dining **17**
Mt. Desert Ice Cream **16**
Rosalie's **10**
The Rose Garden
 Restaurant **2**

ATTRACTIONS ●
Abbe Museum **24**
Bar Harbor Historical
 Society **23**
George B. Dorr Museum
 of Natural History **3**

Frenchman Bay

9

MOUNT DESERT ISLAND | Bar Harbor

branch has an orientation center and a glass-walled lab where visitors can see archae-ologists at work preserving recently recovered artifacts, along with changing exhibits and videos that focus largely on Maine and other New England tribes. From late May through October, it opens daily from 10am to 6pm; the rest of the year, it's open Thursdays to Sundays only. Admission costs $6 for adults, $2 for children ages 6 to 15, and is free for younger children.

A short stroll around the corner from the new Abbe Museum is the **Bar Harbor Historical Society,** 33 Ledgelawn Ave. (ⓒ **207/288-0000** or 288-3807). The society moved into this handsome 1918 former convent in 1997, where it showcases artifacts of life in the old days—dishware and photos from those grand old hotels that once dotted the town, exhibits on the noted landscape architect Beatrix Farrand, and so forth. Scrapbooks document the devastating 1947 fire, too. The museum is open from June through October, Monday to Saturday from 1 to 4pm; admission is free. Even during the off season, entrance can sometimes be arranged by appointment.

Don't forget to spend an hour or two in the central **Village Green ★**, either. Bar Harbor's central park—it's at the junction of Main St. and Mount Desert St.—is a wonderful place to while away an hour or two watching the craziness unfold. You

If parking spaces are scarce downtown, head to the end of Albert Meadow (a side street across from the Village Green). At the end of the road is a small waterfront park with free parking, great views of the bay, and foot access to Shore Path. It's not well marked or publicized, so you can often find a place to park when much of the rest of town is filled up.

might see anything from protests to marriage proposals to acoustic songwriters to kids goofing off after school, plus summer tourists snapping photos and licking ice cream cones. There's sometimes music in the bandstand, and this is the pickup point for the **Island Explorer buses** that crisscross the entire island—for free. Not to be missed.

At the northern edge of town on Rte. 3 is the **College of the Atlantic** (✆ **207/288-5015**), a school founded in 1969 with a strong emphasis on environmental education. The campus, with its old and new buildings, features the **George B. Dorr Museum of Natural History** (✆ **207/288-5395;** www.coamuseum.org) at 105 Eden St. Inside the national park's original HQ (who knew?), it features exhibits that focus on interactions among island residents, from the two-legged to the four-legged, finny, and furry. From mid-June to Thanksgiving, the museum is Monday through Saturday from 10am to 5pm; the rest of the year, it's open by appointment only. Admission is by donation—drop in two or three dollars for every person in your party except young children—and check the museum's summer program: in summer, you just might stumble across a nature walk, art project, or scavenger hunt.

One of downtown's less obvious attractions is the **Criterion Theatre,** 35 Cottage St. (✆ **207/288-3441**), a movie house built in 1932 in a classic Art Deco style and that so far has avoided the degradation of multiplexification. The 900-seat theater, located on Cottage Street, shows first-run movies in summer and is worth the price of admission for the fantastic, if somewhat faded, interiors; the movie is secondary. As once was the case at most movie palaces, it still costs extra to sit in the more exclusive loges upstairs.

Whale-Watching

Bar Harbor is a base for several ocean endeavors, including whale-watching tours. Operators offer excursions in search of humpbacks, finbacks, minkes, and the infrequently seen endangered right whale. The best in the area is the Bar Harbor Whale Watch Company (✆ **888/942-5374** or 207/288-2386; www.whalesrus.com), which operates off the municipal pier at 1 West St. in downtown Bar Harbor, next to Agamont Park. Tours are on a fast, twin-hulled three-level excursion boat that can hold 200 passengers in two heated cabins. The tours run 3 hours or more; the cost is $27 to $56 per adult, $16 to $28 per child age 6 to 14. A puffin- and whale-watching tour is also offered for the same price, and there are shorter seal-watching tours for about half the price. There's free on-site parking and a money-back *guarantee* that you'll see whales—how can you go wrong? The daily tours begin each season in late May and run through late October.

Where to Stay

Bar Harbor is the bedroom community for Mount Desert Island, with hundreds of hotel, motel, and inn rooms. They're invariably filled during the busy days of summer, and even the most basic of rooms can be quite expensive in July and August. It's essential to reserve as early in advance as possible.

Bar Harbor can be an expensive town, but family owned motels have provided simple, no-frills, cheaper alternatives for decades if that's what you're seeking—some rooms still remain under $100 in peak season, which is amazing. Most are on the north end of town, along or near Rte. 3, and almost all of them open seasonally, from May through September or October. Choices in this price range include the conveniently located **Villager Motel,** 207 Main St. (𝄢 **888/383-3211** or 207/288-3211; www.barharborvillager.com); the in-town, pet-friendly **Rockhurst Motel,** 68 Mount Desert St. (𝄢 **207/288-3140**); and the **Highbrook Motel,** 94 Eden St. (𝄢 **800/338-9688** or 207/288-3591; www.highbrookmotel.com). About 4 miles west of Bar Harbor on Rte. 3 is **Hanscom's Motel and Cottages** (𝄢 **207/288-3744;** www.hanscomsmotel.com), an old-fashioned motor court with a dozen units (some of them with two bedrooms) that have been well maintained. Its rates range from $92 to $110 in summer, and go as low as $64 per night in the off season.

VERY EXPENSIVE

Balance Rock Inn ★★★   Tucked down a quiet side alley just off Bar Harbor's main drag, the Balance Rock (built in 1903 for a Scottish railroad magnate) reaches for and achieves a gracefully upscale Long Island beach house feel. The entrance alone is nearly worth the steep rack rates: You enter a sitting room, which looks out onto the sort of azure outdoor swimming pool you'd expect to find in a Tuscan villa, and just beyond looms the Atlantic. Rooms are as elegant as any on the island, with a variety of layouts, some with sea views; some have whirlpools and saunas, while the penthouse suite adds a full kitchen. The comfortable king-size beds are adjustable using controls and have been fitted with feather beds and quality linens. A poolside bar, piano room, gracious staff, and fragrant flowers lining the driveway complete the romance of the experience.

21 Albert Meadow, Bar Harbor, ME 04609. 𝄢 **800/753-0494** or 207/288-2610. www.barharborvacations. com. 17 units. July to mid-Oct $125–$525 double and suite; May–June and mid- to late Oct $115–$625 double and suite. Rates include full breakfast. AE, DISC, MC, V. Closed Nov to early May. Well-behaved

PACKING A picnic IN BAR HARBOR

Even in downtown Bar Harbor, you can have a nice picnic experience simply by settling onto a bench on the **Village Green**—that's the green, rectangular space tucked behind and between Mount Desert and Kennebec streets (beside from which island buses depart; it's a block off Cottage St.). People-watching abounds, and art shows and festivals sometimes come to the green.

Closer to the water, at the tip of the land (at the end of West and Main sts.), the pocket **Agamont Park** is superlative for its picnic spot and a view of boats and islands. There's also the quiet campus of earthy **College of the Atlantic,** back on Rte. 3; they surely won't mind if you plunk down a basket and graze—in the interest of researching the college for future enrollment, of course. You're surrounded by food in downtown Bar Harbor; but the great natural-foods store **Alternative Market,** at 16 Mount Desert St. (𝄢 **207/288-8225**), is your best bet for prepared foods, drinks, and healthy snacks. It's open daily from 10am to 6pm.

pets welcome, $30 per pet per night. **Amenities:** Poolside bar; fitness room; outdoor pool. *In room:* A/C, hair dryer.

EXPENSIVE

Bar Harbor Grand Hotel ★   Bar Harbor's newest "big" hotel (it opened in 2003) fills a gap between quaint, expensive inns and B&Bs and the island's family owned motels, hotels, and cottages. The hotel's blocky, two-tower design faithfully copies the style of the Rodick House, a now-defunct 19th-century lodging in Bar Harbor that could once boast of being Maine's largest hotel; the Grand, however, does that one better with bigger rooms and bathrooms and, of course, all-modern fixtures. Rooms and suites are decked out in the same floral bedspreads and curtains you'd expect in any upscale business hotel, and the access to downtown Bar Harbor and the nearby ocean are big pluses. It feels more like a chain business hotel than an inn. Amenities for business and tourist travelers include a guest laundry, gift shop, a heated outdoor pool, high-speed Internet access (for a fee); not surprisingly, they're booking some tour groups in here. Expect comfort, rather than local character.

269 Main St., Bar Harbor, ME 04609. ⓒ **888/766-2529** or 207/288-5226. www.barharborgrand.com. 70 units. May to mid-Oct $109–$229 double; Apr and mid-Oct to early Nov $89–$99 double. Rates include continental breakfast. Packages available. DISC, MC, V. Closed early Nov to Mar. **Amenities:** Fitness room; Jacuzzi; heated outdoor pool. *In room:* A/C, TV, fridge, Wi-Fi.

Bar Harbor Hotel—Bluenose Inn ★   This resort-style complex—situated in two buildings—offers stunning views of the surrounding terrain. Facilities here are more modern, too: Expect spacious carpeted rooms with huge bathrooms, small refrigerators, and balconies, as well as a good fitness center, indoor and outdoor pools, and one of the town's best hotel dining rooms, the **Rose Garden** ★. The two buildings are slightly different in character, but in either case upper-floor rooms with sea views are worth the extra cost, especially if the weather is good. Staff here is professional and friendly.

90 Eden St., Bar Harbor, ME 04609. ⓒ **800/445-4077** or 207/288-3348. www.barharborhotel.com. 97 units. Mid-June to mid-Oct $145–$405 double; spring and late fall $75–$299 double. Packages available. AE, DC, DISC, MC, V. Closed Nov–Apr. **Amenities:** Restaurant; fitness center; Jacuzzi; indoor pool; outdoor pool; spa. *In room:* A/C, TV, fireplace (some units), fridge, hair dryer,.

The Bar Harbor Inn ★★   The Bar Harbor Inn, just off Agamont Park, nicely mixes traditional style with contemporary touches. On shady grounds just a moment's stroll from Bar Harbor's downtown, this property offers both convenience and charm. The shingled main inn, which dates from the turn of the 19th century, has a settled, old-money feel with its semicircular dining room and a buttoned-down lobby. Guest rooms, located in the main building and two outbuildings, are much more contemporary: units in the Oceanfront Lodge and main inn both offer spectacular bay views, and many have private balconies. (The less expensive Newport Building lacks views but is still comfortable and up-to-date.) In 2006 the inn added a spa with Vichy showers, aromatherapy, heated-stone treatments, and facial treatments, while the somewhat formal **Reading Room** dining room serves resort meals with the best dining-room views in town.

Newport Dr., Bar Harbor, ME 04609. ⓒ **800/248-3351** or 207/288-3351. www.barharborinn.com. 153 units. Mid-May to mid-Oct $119–$379 double; mid-Mar to mid-May and mid-Oct to Nov $79–$215 double. Rates include continental breakfast. Packages available. AE, DISC, MC, V. Closed Dec to mid-Mar. **Amenities:** Dining room; fitness room; Jacuzzi; heated outdoor pool; room service; spa. *In room:* A/C, TV, hair dryer.

Bass Cottage Inn ★★   This tucked-away inn gets very high marks for friendliness, service, and proximity to the water. The 10 rooms here are decked out in cast-iron beds, silk canopies, love seats, armoires, writing desks, and the like. The gentle color schemes range from ivory to sky blue to taupe, reflecting the soft light of the island, and many are decorated with nautical prints; several have Jacuzzis and/or views, as well (and the entire-top-floor suite has both). This is just a 2-minute walk from downtown, yet breakfast feasts are worthy of a gourmet restaurant: They might serve cornmeal griddle cakes with blueberries, a lobster omelet, French toast with vanilla sauce, cranberry-walnut French toast, scrambled eggs with smoked salmon, or huevos rancheros. Innkeepers Teri and Jeff Anderholm are unfailingly helpful and generous with extra flourishes such as a piano, a DVD library for anytime use, and a 24-hour guest pantry stocked with snacks. Very nice place.

14 The Field (P.O. Box 242), Bar Harbor, ME 04609. ☎ **866/782-9224** or 207/288-1234. www.basscottage. com. 10 units. $185–$370 double and suite. Rates include full breakfast. 2-night stay minimum weekends, 3-day minimum stay holiday weekends. AE, MC, V. Closed Nov to mid-May. Children age 12 and over welcome. **Amenities:** Concierge. *In room:* A/C, TV, fireplace (some units), Jacuzzi (some units).

Ivy Manor Inn ★   The Ivy Manor quickly proved a welcome addition to Bar Harbor's upscale lodging pool when it opened in 1997. Located in a 1940s-era Tudor-style house, the inn has been thoroughly done over in an understated French Victorian style, mostly in rich colors such as burgundy. The rooms here are larger than average; most are carpeted and furnished with attractive, tasteful antiques from the innkeeper's collection. Some have antique claw-foot tubs; others have small outdoor sitting decks. Among the best units: no. 6, a small suite with a private sitting room and small fireplace; and no. 1, the king-size-bedded Honeymoon Room, with an imposing walnut headboard and matching armoire. The restaurant, Michelle's, is one of the town's best (see "Where to Dine," below).

194 Main St., Bar Harbor, ME 04609. ☎ **888/670-1997.** www.ivymanor.com. 8 units. Mid-June to Oct $200–$325 double; Apr to mid-June $185–$275 double. Rates include full breakfast. 2-night minimum on holiday weekends. AE, DISC, MC, V. Closed Nov–Mar. Children 11 and over welcome. **Amenities:** Restaurant; lounge. *In room:* A/C, TV, fireplace (some units).

MODERATE

Acadia Hotel ★ 🔥   The simple, seasonal Acadia Hotel is nicely situated overlooking Bar Harbor's village green, easily accessible to in-town activities and the free shuttle buses running around the island. A handsome, simple home dating from the late 19th century, the hotel features a wraparound porch; guest rooms are plain, but decorated in nice floral motifs. Units vary widely in size and amenities, however—some have simple whirlpool tubs, phones, or king beds; one has a kitchenette; and about half have small refrigerators. Others are as basic as it comes. It's a no-frills place, clean and well run—and even if prices are slowly inching up, all things considered it's still a good budget choice in a fairly pricey town.

20 Mt. Desert St., Bar Harbor, ME 04609. ☎ **888/876-2463** or 207/288-5721. www.acadiahotel.com. 11 units. July to Oct $129–$169 double; May–June $59–$109 double. Packages available. AE, MC, V. Closed late Oct to Apr. *In room:* A/C, TV, fridge (some units), no phone (some units).

Black Friar Inn ★ 🔥   The seasonal Black Friar, tucked on a Bar Harbor side street overlooking a parking lot, is a yellow-shingled home with quirky pediments and an eccentric air. A former owner "collected" interiors and installed them throughout the home, including a replica of a pub in London with elaborate carved-wood paneling (it's now a common room); stamped-tin walls (look in the breakfast room); and a doctor's office (now one of the guest rooms). Rooms are carpeted and furnished in a mix of antiques; most are smallish, though the big suite features nice paneling, a sofa, wingback chair, private porch, and gas fireplace. Other rooms sport such touches as rose-tinted stained-glass windows, brass beds, and a sort of mini spiral staircase. The least expensive units are the two garret rooms on the third floor. The inn, which is also home to a small restaurant and pub, generally asks a 2-night minimum stay.

10 Summer St., Bar Harbor, ME 04609. © **207/288-5091.** Fax 207/288-4197. www.blackfriarinn.com. 6 units. Late June to mid-Oct $125–$180 double; May-late June, mid-Oct to mid-Nov $75–$130 double. Rates include full breakfast. 2-night minimum required most times of year. MC, V. Closed mid-Nov–Apr. Children 12 and older welcome. **Amenities:** Restaurant; pub. *In room:* A/C, fireplace (1 unit).

Coach Stop Inn 🔥 Built in 1804, this claims to be Acadia's oldest inn. Surprisingly low-priced for such a well-run place, it's one of the island's best values—though it comes with the caveat of being located about as far from most of the prime attractions as you can get on Acadia. The shingled home sits on the main highway, close to the bridge to the mainland. (It's about 5 easy miles to downtown Bar Harbor, or 12 miles to Southwest Harbor.) Guests effuse about the owners' hospitality, the five simple but prettily decorated rooms; expect queen-size beds, fireplaces with mantles, claw-foot tubs, tasteful floral prints and wallpapers, sitting rooms in the suites, and (in one case) a small private porch. Three of the five rooms have televisions and DVD players. Breakfast might include pistachio-stuffed French toast, blueberry fritters, or eggs Napoleon. The grounds here include a meadow and apple trees, viewable from the patio if you're too full to walk.

715 Rte. 3, Bar Harbor, ME 04609. © **800/927-3097** or 207/288-9886. www.coachstopinn.com. 5 units. $135–$165 double. Rates include full breakfast. MC, V. From bridge, turn left onto Rte. 3 and continue 4 miles to inn on right. Not recommended for children 9 and under. *In room:* A/C, TV (some units) fridge, no phone.

Maples Inn ★ A modest home tucked away on a side street in a row of Bar Harbor B&Bs, the Maples is an easy walk downtown to a movie or dinner. It's a popular destination for those attracted to outdoor activities, and you'll often find guests swapping stories about the day's adventures on the handsome front porch, or lingering over breakfast to compare notes about hiking trails. The innkeeper, an interior designer, has a way of making guests comfortable; rooms are small to medium-size, but you're not likely to feel cramped—they have private bathrooms, wicker furniture, pencil poster beds, and handsome antique wooden writing desks. The two-room White Birch has a fireplace, a lacy canopy bed with a down comforter, and a bright blue-and-white decor; Red Oak has a private deck with plastic lounge chairs. Gourmet breakfasts are served in a sunny dining room. Curiously, peak-season rates here have shot up in the past few years (they're as much as double what they once were), while the inn's shoulder-season rates have softened a bit. Go figure.

16 Roberts Ave., Bar Harbor, ME 04609. © **207/288-3443.** www.maplesinn.com. 6 units. Mid-June to mid-Oct $160–$215 double; May to mid-June and mid-Oct to late Oct $115–$170 double. Rates include full breakfast. 2-night minimum stay, 3-night minimum on holiday weekends. DISC, MC, V. Closed Nov–Apr. Not appropriate for children. *In room:* Fireplace (1 unit), no phone.

Mira Monte Inn ★ A stay at this Italianate home (built in 1864), a few minutes' walk from Bar Harbor's restaurants and attractions and open year-round, used to feel like a trip to your grandmother's house. It's gotten a lot more contemporary since (TVs, phones, and Wi-Fi are all pretty recent additions), even if the common rooms are still furnished in a country Victorian style. The grounds are nicely landscaped, and a nice brick terrace off the street is a good place to enjoy breakfast in warm weather. Most rooms have a balcony, fireplace, or both, and some even now have Jacuzzis. Others have the feel of a spare country farmhouse. If you're a light sleeper, avoid rooms facing Mount Desert Street; those facing the gardens in the rear are much quieter. Families should ask about booking a suite in the adjacent outbuilding: these have better amenities, and some have double Jacuzzis.

69 Mount Desert St., Bar Harbor, ME 04609. © **800/553-5109.** www.miramonte.com. 12 units. $95–$209 double; $89–$259 suite. Rates include full breakfast. 2-night minimum stay in midsummer. AE, DISC, MC, V. Most units closed late Oct to mid-May. *In room:* A/C, TV, fireplace (some units), hair dryer, Jacuzzi (some units).

Primrose Inn ★★   This handsome Victorian stick–style inn, originally built in 1878, is one of the most notable properties on the "mansion row" along Mount Desert Street. Its distinctive architecture has been preserved, and was perhaps even enhanced during a 1987 addition of rooms, private bathrooms, and balconies. This inn is comfortable, furnished with "functional antiques" and modern reproductions; many of the spacious rooms have a floral theme, thick carpets, marble vanities, canopy beds, sitting or reading rooms, and handsome day beds, wingback chairs or other furniture. (Two newer "premium" rooms also have private entrances and are stocked with king beds, gas fireplaces, and such other amenities as a porch or whirlpool tub.) The owners have added flatscreen television sets and Wi-Fi access, too, while the 24/7 free soft drinks fridge remains. Breakfasts of eggs Florentine, Belgian waffles, blueberry pancakes, and the like are a hit, and the innkeepers can furnish you with a GPS unit if you'll be driving around the island and worry about getting lost. Remember that there's a 2-night minimum stay in summer and fall.

73 Mount Desert St., Bar Harbor, ME 04609. © **877/846-3424** or 207/288-4031. www.primroseinn. com. 13 units. Late June to Aug $159–$229 double; late May to late June and Sept–Oct $99–$209 double. Rates include full breakfast and afternoon tea. 2-night minimum stay summer and fall. AE, DISC, MC, V. Closed Nov to late May. *In room:* A/C, TV/DVD, fireplace (some units), hair dryer, Jacuzzi (1 unit).

INEXPENSIVE

The Colony   Owned by the same family since 1950, Colony is an aging motor court consisting of a handful of motel rooms plus a battery of cottages arrayed in an oval around a longish green. It's best appreciated by those with a taste for retro motels; others might decide to look for something fancier or better kept. But the price is low. Rooms are furnished in a simple '70s style that won't win any awards for decor (and probably won't be updated), but they're adequate. There are two classes of motel room, regular and luxury—the difference being better views and bigger beds (queens and kings instead of paired doubles). Some of the cottages have phones and kitchenettes, some don't; all of them, however, do have TVs. The complex is just across Rte. 3 from a cobblestone beach, and about a 10-minute drive into Bar Harbor. Do not expect anything fancy.

Rte. 3 (P.O. Box 56), Hulls Cove, ME 04644. © **207/288-3383.** www.acadia.net/thecolony. 55 units. $75–$135 cottage. Closed Nov–Apr. AE, DC, DISC, MC, V. *In room:* A/C (some units), TV, fridge (some units), kitchenette (some units), no phone (some units).

Where to Dine

In addition to the selections listed below, you can get good local pizza at **Rosalie's** (© **207/288-5666**) on Cottage Street; eat upstairs or down, or take out a pie to go.

There's also a superb natural foods market, **Alternative ★** (© 207/288-8225), on Mount Desert Street right across from the Village Green.

The owners of the island's best vegetarian eatery, **Eden Vegetarian Café,** shut the restaurant and have taken a hiatus, but they might reopen the place in 2011 in a new location. Ask at the tourist office—it was very good when it was open.

If you're craving something sweet, head over to **Ben & Bill's Chocolate Emporium,** 66 Main St. (© **800/806-3281** or 207/288-3281), for a big ice-cream cone. In the evenings, you may have to join the line spilling out the door. Visitors are often tempted to try the place's novelty ice cream, lobster ice cream. My suggestion: Don't do it.

Or if you enjoy experimenting with *other* ice cream flavors, **Mt. Desert Island Ice Cream ★,** 7 Firefly Lane (© **207/460-5515;** www.mdiic.com), right beside the tourist office is the place for you. It gives all the appearances of being just another ho-hum scoop shop of the vanilla-chocolate-strawberry ilk, but it's not: there's little conventional about a place featuring gourmet concoctions spiked with tarragon, chili, and wasabi, among other flavors. (President Barack Obama sampled a coconut cone during a surprise 2010 visit.) There's another branch at 325 Main St., and—flash!—one on Exchange Street in Portland. Both locations serve coffee, tea, and yerba maté, as well.

EXPENSIVE

Havana ★★ 🏨 LATINO/FUSION   Havana excited foodies all over Maine when it opened in 1999 in what was then a town of fried fish and baked haddock. The spare decor in an old storefront is as classy as anything you'll find in Boston, and the menu can hold its own in the big city, too. Chef/owner Michael Boland's menu is inspired by Latino fare, which he melds nicely with New American ideas. Expect items like appetizers of crab cakes, duck empanadas, fig-and-blue cheese tarts, or spicy beef and pork skewers dusted with cinnamon and vanilla. Entrees could include choices as adventurous as a lobster poached in butter served with a saffrony potato empanada; paella made with local lobsters and mussels; breast of duck with a blueberry glaze; broiled filet mignon with ancho gravy; pork tenderloin stuffed with cranberry and chorizo stuffing; seared black cod; or coconut-encrusted tuna steaks with a plum-red chili jam. Finish with an equally dazzling dessert such as a chocolate lava cake with cinnamon churros, apple empanadas, caramel and cream, dulce de leche cheesecake with guava sauce, a maple carrot cake, or spicy pumpkin crème brûlée kicked up with jalapeño peppers.

318 Main St. © **207/288-2822.** www.havanamaine.com. Reservations recommended. Main courses $24–$32. AE, DC, DISC, MC, V. Daily 5–10pm. Sometimes closed in late fall.

Mâche Bistro ★★ NEW AMERICAN   Little Mâche Bistro has developed a devoted local following; its soothing, plain decor conceals a sophisticated kitchen—you wouldn't expect an imported-cheese course offered in a place with plywood floors, but there is one here. Chef Kyle Yarborough's menu changes monthly; appetizers could include local crab with aioli, fish chowder, excellent house antipasti, or a wine-poached pear with Maytag blue cheese. Main courses, now more New American than French bistro, might run to herb-encrusted haddock over garlic mashed potatoes, slow-roasted pork with chorizo and vegetables, grilled hanger steak with a blue cheese butter, seared duck over white beans, or a grilled Portobello stuffed with goat cheese and caramelized onions.

135 Cottage St. © **207/288-0447.** www.machebistro.com. Reservations recommended. Main courses $16–$23. AE, MC, V. Tues–Sun 5:30–9pm (winter closed Sun).

Maggie's Restaurant ★★ SEAFOOD   The slogan for Maggie's is "Notably fresh seafood," and the place invariably delivers on that understated promise. (Only locally caught fish is used.) It's a casually elegant spot, good for a romantic evening while you enjoy the soothing music, attentive service, and excellent seafood. Appetizers could run from cheesy potatoes with lobster, grilled clams in wine sauce, a kid-size pizza, or a simple salad; main courses might include "bronzed" cod with a lime-tartar sauce, lobster crepes, Gulf shrimp with feta and olives over rice, pan-seared scallops, or salmon seared in Indian spices and served with cucumber-mint salsa. They also do nice steaks and chicken, though that's not why you come here. Desserts are home-made, and it's also worth leaving room for them: blueberry pie, lemon curd, and dark chocolate pudding cakes, and a delicious rotating menu of gourmet ice cream sundaes—the island's best.

6 Summer St. © **207/288-9007.** www.maggiesbarharbor.com. Reservations recommended July–Aug. Main courses $16–$24. MC, V. Mon–Sat 5–9:30pm.

Michelle's Fine Dining ★★ FRENCH/SEAFOOD   Michelle's, located inside the Ivy Manor Inn (see "Where to Stay," above), supplies one of the island's best dinner experiences. The three dining rooms are elegant, plus there's outside seating when the weather's good. The extensive menu elaborates on traditional French cuisine with New England twists. Nightly appetizers might include lobster bisque, French onion soup, crab cakes, or steak tartare. Main courses—divided into seafood and nonseafood entrees—are even more elaborate, with dishes such as chateaubriand for two (carved tableside); roasted rack of lamb; seared salmon with a pine-nut crisp; two versions of duck; Cornish hen; and a big bouillabaisse for two of lobster, mussels, clams, and scallops. Finish with a cheese plate, one of several soufflés, the crème brûlée, or Michelle's unique "bag of chocolate": it comes with berries and is served in an edible chocolate bag. This place is expensive but worth it.

194 Main St. © **888/670-1997** or 207/288-2138. www.michellesfinedining.com. Reservations required during peak season. Main courses $24–$54. AE, DISC, MC, V. Daily 6–9pm. Closed late Oct to early May.

MODERATE

Cafe This Way ★★ ECLECTIC   Cafe This Way is the kind of place where they know how to do wonderful Asian and Mediterranean things with simple ingredients. It has the feel of a hip coffeehouse, yet it's much more airy and creative than that. Bookshelves line one wall, and there's a small bar tucked into a nook; oddly, they serve breakfast and dinner but no lunch. Breakfasts are excellent though mildly sinful—it's more like brunch. Go for the burritos, corned beef hash with eggs, a range of omelets (build your own if you like), and the calorific Café Monte Cristo: a French toast sandwich stuffed with fried eggs, ham, and cheddar cheese served with fries and syrup. Yikes. Dinners are equally appetizing, with tasty starters that might run to Maine crab cakes in tequila-lime sauce, grilled chunks of Cyprus cheese, or lobster spring rolls. The main-course offerings of the night could include anything from lobster cooked in sherry cream or stewed in spinach and Gruyère cheese to sea scallops in vinaigrette; grilled lamb and steaks; peach-flavored pork chops; or the Korean stir-fry dish known as *bibimbap*. There's always a tasty vegetarian option, as well.

14½ Mount Desert St. ✆ **207/288-4483.** www.cafethisway.com. Reservations recommended for dinner. Breakfast items $5–$8, dinner main courses $15–$26. MC, V. Mid-Apr to Oct Mon–Sat 7–11am; Sun 8am–1pm; dinner daily 5:30–9pm.

Galyn's ★★ 🍴 SEAFOOD   Normally I avoid midpriced bistros in tourist towns like the plague, because they're generally pretty much all the same and almost never as special as their precious signs proclaim they are. But charming, unassuming Galyn's is the exception; Galyn's gets it right. From perfectly blackened and grilled Cajun shrimp, hand-cut steaks, and daily fish specials to seafood stews and penne tossed with oil, garlic, bits of feta, and all the right vegetables, everything's on point here. Finish with real Indian pudding (worth trying, and very hard to find) or the cappuccino sundae served in a cappuccino glass, which packs two helpful shots of espresso to fuel your sightseeing. There are nice dining rooms both upstairs and down, with art on the walls, but try to snag one of the tables out on the little street-side deck if you can: All face Agamont Park and stunning bay views beyond.

17 Main St. ✆ **207/288-9706.** www.galynsbarharbor.com. Reservations recommended. Main courses lunch $7–$15, dinner $14–$27. AE, MC, V. Daily 11:30am–10pm.

INEXPENSIVE

Jordan's Restaurant 🍴 DINER   This unpretentious breakfast-and-lunch joint has been dishing up filling fare since 1976, and offers a glimpse of the old Bar Harbor. It's a popular haunt of local working folks and retirees, but staff are also friendly to tourists. Diners can settle into a pine booth or at a laminated table and order off the placemat menu, choosing from basic fare such as grilled cheese sandwiches with tomato or slim burgers. The soups and chowders are all homemade, and there are some crab dishes (though no lobster). But breakfast is the star here, with a broad selection of three-egg omelets, muffins, and pancakes made with plenty of those great wild Maine blueberries (best when they're in season). With its atmosphere of "seniors at coffee klatch" and its rock-bottom prices, this is *not* a gourmet experience, but fans of big breakfasts, Americana-style cuisine, and diners will enjoy it.

80 Cottage St. ✆ **207/288-3586.** Breakfast and lunch items $3–$13. MC, V. Daily 4:30am–2pm. Closed Feb–Mar.

Lompoc Café ★ AMERICAN/ECLECTIC   The Lompoc Cafe has a well-worn, neighborhood-bar feel to it—waiters and other workers from around Bar Harbor congregate here after-hours. The cafe consists of three sections: the original bar, a tidy beer garden just outside (try your hand at bocce), and a small and open barnlike structure at the garden's edge to handle the overflow. Most of the beers are local (ask for a sample before ordering a full glass of blueberry ale). Bar menus are normally yawn-inducing, but this one has some surprises—lamb meatballs in mint, good salads, Vietnamese-style *bahn mi* sandwiches, a BLT using fried green tomatoes. There's also quite a little wine list, and some house cocktails like the lemony "Blonde with an Attitude." The outdoor tables are fun, and live music acts often play here.

36 Rodick St. ✆ **207/288-9392.** www.lompoccafe.com. Reservations not accepted. Sandwiches and salads $7–$12. MC, V. Daily 11:30am–1am.

Shopping

Bar Harbor is full of boutiques and souvenir shops along two intersecting commercial streets, Main Street and Cottage Street. Most sell the usual tourist tack, but look a little harder and you can find some original items for sale at places like these.

Bar Harbor Hemporium The Hemporium is dedicated to promoting products made from hemp such as paper, clothing, and more. Surprisingly, there's some interesting stuff here. 116 Main St. © **207/288-3014.** www.barharborhemp.com.

Cadillac Mountain Sports Sleeping bags, backpacks, outdoor clothing, and hiking boots are found at this shop, which caters to the ragged-wool and fleece set. There's a good selection of hiking and travel guides to the island, too. 26 Cottage St. © **207/288-4532.** www.cadillacmountain.com.

Island Artisans This is the place to browse for products made by local craftspeople, such as tiles, sweetgrass baskets, pottery, jewelry, and soaps. 99 Main St. © **207/288-4214.** www.islandartisans.com.

RainWise This Bar Harbor–based company manufactures weather stations for companies, agencies, and serious Weather Channel–heads; its factory store, off Cottage Street, sells these stations plus a variety of thermometers and barometers. 25 Federal St. © **800/762-5723** or 207/288-5169. www.rainwise.com.

ELSEWHERE ON MOUNT DESERT ISLAND ★★

You'll find plenty to explore outside of Acadia National Park and Bar Harbor. Quiet fishing villages, deep woodlands, and unexpected ocean views are among the jewels you can turn up once you get beyond Bar Harbor town limits.

Essentials

GETTING AROUND

The eastern half of the island is best navigated using Rte. 3, which forms a rough loop from Bar Harbor through **Seal Harbor** and past **Northeast Harbor**, then runs up along the eastern shore of Somes Sound. Rte. 102 and Rte. 102A provide access to the island's western half. Without a car, use the free **Island Explorer shuttle** (see "Getting Around" in the Acadia National Park section, earlier).

VISITOR INFORMATION

The **Thompson Island Information Center**, on the right as you are about to cross onto the island, is your single best info source. It's open daily from mid-May through mid-October. Acadia National Park information is available daily, year-round, at the **park headquarters** (© **207/288-3338**) on Rte. 233 between Bar Harbor and Somesville. Locally, the **Southwest Harbor-Tremont Chamber of Commerce,** P.O. Box 1143, Southwest Harbor, ME 04679 (© **800/423-9264** or 207/244-9264), and the **Mount Desert Chamber of Commerce, P.O.** Box 675, Northeast Harbor, ME 04662 (© **207/276-5040**), can also help you.

Exploring the Rest of the Island

Down one peninsula of the eastern lobe of the island is the staid, prosperous village of **Northeast Harbor ★★**, long a favorite retreat of well-heeled folks. You can see shingled palaces poking out from the forest and shore, but the village itself (which consists of just one short main street and a marina) is also worth investigating for its art galleries, restaurants, and general store.

One of the best, least-publicized places for enjoying views of the harbor is from the understated, wonderful **Asticou Terraces ★★** (ⓒ **207-276-3727;** www.garden preserve.org.). Finding the parking lot can be tricky: Head a half-mile east (toward Seal Harbor) on Rte. 3 from the junction with Rte. 198, and look for the small gravel lot on the water side of the road with a sign reading ASTICOU TERRACES. Park here, cross the road on foot, and set off up a magnificent path of local stone that ascends the sheer hillside, with expanding views of the harbor and the town.

Continue on the trail at the top of the hillside, and you'll soon arrive at Curtis's cabin (open to the public daily in summer), behind which lies the formal **Thuya Garden ★★**, which is as manicured as the terraces are natural. This wonderfully maintained garden, designed by noted landscape architect Charles K. Savage (he summered here) in what was once an apple orchard, attracts flower enthusiasts, students of landscape architecture, and local folks looking for a quiet place to rest. The lawns lead to a pavilion and reflecting pool; the gates were hand-carved of cedar. It's well worth the trip.

Finally, don't miss the wonderful **azalea garden ★★** 100 yards down Rte. 3 (toward Somesville). Run by the same organization as Thuya Garden and the Asticou Terraces, it's a groomed, Japanese-style wonder of water and plant life—one of my favorite places on the island to wander without getting a cardio workout.

There's no admission charge to any of these three lovely stops, but donations are requested—drop a few bucks in. There's limited free parking in a lot at both the terraces and the azalea garden.

From Northeast Harbor, visitors can depart on a seaward trip to the beguilingly remote **Cranberry Islands ★**. You have a couple of options: Either travel with a national park guide to Baker Island, the most distant of this small cluster of low islands, and explore the natural terrain; or hop one of the ferries to either Great or Little Cranberry Island and explore on your own. On Little Cranberry there's a small historical **museum ★** run by the National Park Service that's worth a few minutes. Both islands feature a sense of being well away from it all, but neither offers much in the way of shelter or tourist amenities, so travelers should head out prepared for the possibility of shifting weather.

Cranberry Cove Boating Co. (ⓒ **207/244-5882** or 207/460-1981) runs a regular ferry schedule from Southwest Harbor and Manset to the islands, and **Beal & Bunker** (ⓒ **207/244-3575**) also runs mail boats to the islands from Northeast Harbor. Figure on $20 to $25 round-trip per adult, and a half-fare for children. Be sure to check boat schedules carefully before setting off to the Cranberries to ensure that you don't miss the last ferries back to Mount Desert; there are *very* limited accommodations out here.

When leaving Northeast Harbor, think about a quick detour out to Sargent Drive. This one-way route runs through Acadia National Park along the shore of Somes Sound, affording superb views of the glacially carved inlet. On the far side of Somes

Sound, there's good hiking (see above) and the towns of **Southwest Harbor ★★** and **Bass Harbor.** These are both home to fishermen and boat-builders, and though the character of these towns is changing, they're still far more humble than Northeast and Seal harbors.

In Southwest Harbor look for the intriguing **Wendell Gilley Museum of Bird Carving** (✆ **207/244-7555;** www.wendellgilleymuseum.org), on Rte. 102 just north of town. Housed in a new building constructed specifically to display the woodcarvings, the museum contains the masterwork of Wendell Gilley, a plumber who took up carving birds as a hobby in 1930. His creations, ranging from regal bald eagles to delicate chickadees, are startlingly lifelike and beautiful. The museum offers woodcarving classes for those inspired by the displays, and a gift shop sells fine woodcarvings. It's open Tuesday to Sunday from 10am to 4pm June to October, Friday to Sunday from 10am to 4pm in May, November, and December. The museum is closed January to April, when it offers craft workshops. Admission is $5 for adults, $2 for children 5 to 12—but free Saturday mornings in July and August, and all day on Wendell Gilley's birthday (Aug 21).

Where to Stay

Asticou Inn ★   The once-grand Asticou Inn, which dates from 1883, occupies a prime location at the head of Northeast Harbor. It was once one of those "must-see" hotels on the island, but then slid slowly into a state of real neglect. Things have finally begun to turn around. Rooms are furnished in a simple summer-home style; some rooms have claw-foot tubs, and a few have fireplaces or kitchenettes, but none have phones or TVs. (Also, importantly, less than half have ocean views.) Dinner in the airy, wooden-floored main dining room focuses, as expected, on seafood. There are four quite distinct outbuildings scattered about the property, containing 17 cottagelike units, and these might be my first choice: they're more secluded, a bit more luxurious. This property is slowly getting its house in order, with some assistance from professional outside management and the coming addition of a spa. I hope the Asticou will return to its former glory soon—because this part of the island is magical.

Rte. 3 (P.O. Box 337), Northeast Harbor, ME 04662. ✆ **800/258-3373** or 207/276-3344. www.asticou. com. 44 units. Main inn July–Aug $255–$335 double; May–June and Sept–Oct $185–$265 double; "cottage" units July–Aug $255–$360, May–June and Sept–Oct $185–$265. Surcharge for every child age 3–11. Rates include continental breakfast. MAP plans available July–Aug only. DISC, MC, V. Valet parking. Closed Nov–Apr. No children 5 and under. **Amenities:** Dining room; babysitting; concierge; room service; spa; tennis court. *In room:* Fireplace (few units), kitchenette (few units), no phone.

The Claremont ★★   Early prints of the venerable Claremont show an austere, four-story wooden building overlooking Somes Sound from a grassy rise; it hasn't changed much since. The place offers classic New England grace. (It's somehow appropriate that the state's largest croquet tournament is held here each Aug.) Common areas are pleasantly appointed in country style—the library with its fireplace is popular. Most of the guest rooms are bright and airy, outfitted in antiques, old furniture, and modern bathrooms. There's also a set of 14 cottages of varied vintages and styles in the woods and on the water, all with fireplaces and kitchenettes; they sleep from two to seven people each. The dining room, **Xanthus ★**, offers fabulous views of the fjord and an upscale menu of lobster, crab cakes, fish, scallops, pork, and steaks.

P.O. Box 137, Southwest Harbor, ME 04679. ✆ **800/244-5036.** www.theclaremonthotel.com. 44 units. July–Aug $203–$308 double and cottage; late May to June and Sept to mid-Oct $152–$235 double and cottage. Rates include breakfast. Packages available. 3-night minimum in cottages. MC, V. Closed mid-Oct to late May. From center of Southwest Harbor, follow Clark Point Rd. almost to end and turn left on Claremont Rd. **Amenities:** Dining room; lounge; babysitting; free bikes; croquet; rowboats; tennis court. *In room:* Kitchenette (some units).

Inn at Southwest ★   There's a late-19th-century feel to this mansard-roofed Victorian home, which thankfully stays spare rather than frilly. All guest rooms, named for Maine lighthouses, are outfitted simply in contemporary and antique furniture, and all have ceiling fans and down comforters. Among the most pleasant rooms is Blue Hill Bay on the third floor, with its yellow-and-blue color scheme, big bathroom, sturdy oak bed and bureau, and glimpses of the harbor. The Pumpkin Island unit features a sleigh bed and rosewood sofa. The lone suite (Winter Harbor) has a pencil-poster canopy bed, French doors, and a gas-log fireplace. Breakfasts give you good incentive to rise early: the changing entrees could include Belgian waffles with raspberry sauce, poached pears, or blueberry French toast.

371 Main St. (P.O. Box 593), Southwest Harbor, ME 04679. © **207/244-3835.** www.innatsouthwest. com. 7 units. $105–$185 double. Rates include full breakfast. DISC, MC, V. Closed Nov to late Apr. *In room:* No phone.

Kingsleigh Inn ★★   In a 1904 Queen Anne–style home on Southwest Harbor's bustling Main Street, the Kingsleigh has long been a reliable place to bunk down in the area. Its living room features a wood-burning fireplace and fine art, while sitting and breakfast rooms offer further refuge. All units are outfitted with sound machines (to drown out the ambient "noise"), wine glasses, and robes; some also have air-conditioners. Prints and wallpapers are flowery in the rooms, most of which are small to moderate size, though a few have private decks. The huge third-floor penthouse suite—by far the most expensive room here—has outstanding views (plus a telescope to see them better with); the inn's only TV (with VCR and DVD players); a fireplace; and a king-size bed. Three-course, included breakfasts are filling and genuinely artistic—expect choices such as asparagus frittata, crepes, Belgian waffles, and French toast. Other nice touches include walking sticks for guests and all-day, self-service espresso.

373 Main St. (P.O. Box 1426), Southwest Harbor, ME 04679. © **207/244-5302.** Fax 207/244-7691. www. kingsleighinn.com. 8 units. $110–$195 double; $225–$305 suite. Rates include full breakfast. AE, MC, V. Closed Nov–Mar. Children 13 and older welcome. *In room:* A/C (some units), TV/DVD (1 unit), fireplace (1 unit), hair dryer, no phone.

Lindenwood Inn ★★ 🎁   Australian innkeeper Jim King gave up cabinetmaking to open a string of successful B&Bs in Southwest Harbor, and his latest is his best; it feels like renting a home with friends. In a handsome Queen Anne–style captain's home built in 1904 over harbor's edge, King has modernized the rooms in simple, bold colors and accented them with items from his collections of African and aboriginal art—a strikingly unique interior and feel you can't find anywhere else in New England. Most units have balconies and plenty of windows, some have fireplaces, French doors, and/or private porches or decks, and all possess comfy beds. The public areas remain funky and appealing, and the heated in-ground pool and Jacuzzi are wonderful in summer. There's a small honor bar for fixing a late-night cocktail upstairs, plus a lounge in the basement with a pool table, darts, and a big-screen TV. The biggest draws, however, are the outstanding hospitality, great decor, yummy breakfasts, and laid-back vibe.

CRACKING THE lobster CONUNDRUM

While you struggle to crack that lobster claw (and avoid spilling juice and butter all over your clothes), here are a few more fascinating lobster facts to chew on:

- Lobster prices in most Maine shacks vary, sometimes by a lot; it depends almost exclusively on the current year's take. (In a down year, you'll pay more.)
- There are two kinds of lobster, soft-shell and hard-shell. Many lobsters still have soft shells in the summer, because they've slipped off old ones and are still growing new ones back. People

vary in their preferences, and some say the soft-shell lobsters have less meat. Not sure about that, but I'm a hard-shell man all the way.

- In fall and early winter, hard-shell lobsters become more numerous in the sea—and their price drops. If you're in Maine after September, fill 'er up.
- The worst time to eat a lobster is probably spring, when the crustaceans are scarce, small, and overpriced. Put off that May feast; get a fish platter instead.

118 Clark Point Rd., Southwest Harbor, ME 04679. © **800/307-5335** or 207/244-5335. www.lindenwood inn.com. 8 units. $95–$215 double; $145–$295 suite. Rates include full breakfast. AE, MC, V. **Amenities:** Lounge; Jacuzzi; heated outdoor pool. *In room:* TV, fridge (2 units), kitchenette (1 unit), no phone.

Seawall Motel ★   The rooms are simple and spare at this family-run motel, but the location, just across the street from the water at the Seawall entrance to Acadia, is hard to beat. This is the closest you'll come to feeling like you've gotten away from it all without having to sleep in a tent. Ask for a room on the second floor, which offers better views of the water. And the staff here is exceptional—be sure to get their input if you're planning to explore Mount Desert Island beyond the park, as they've got fantastic suggestions for hikes and nature walks. Best of all? The motel cat, Speedbump, who keeps watch over the grounds.

566 Seawall Rd. (Rt 102A), Southwest Harbor, ME 04679. © 800/248.9250 or 207/244-3020. www. seawallmotel.com. 20 units. July–Labor Day $115; mid-May–June, mid-Sept–Oct $80; Nov–mid-May $65. Rates include continental breakfast. MC, V. *In room:* A/C, TV, free Wi-Fi, hair dryer.

Where to Dine

Ten years ago, there were virtually no serious dining options anywhere on the quiet side of Mount Desert Island. Things have definitely changed with the times. In addition to the choices listed below, you can find plenty of good restaurants in **Southwest Harbor** and several in **Northeast Harbor.** There are even decent options in tiny, one-dock fishing villages such as **Manset** and **Bernard.** Or just pack a picnic at either of the excellent local markets in Southwest Harbor and Northeast Harbor.

The current big hitters include Red Sky and Fiddlers' Green (see below for details). There's also the **Café Drydock,** 357 Main St. (© **207/244-5842**), with an extensive seafood menu, landlubber-friendly lunch and dinner options such as pasta, burgers, and salads, and a Sunday brunch.

Should you tire of eating both gourmet fare and seafood, fear not. Instead, head for one of several cafes lining the town's main street. **Quietside,** 360 Main St. (*☎* **207/244-9444**), serves inexpensive club sandwiches and ice-cream cones. The **Little Notch Pizzeria,** 340 Main St. (*☎* **207/244-3357**), an offshoot of a nearby bakery, makes decent pizzas, plus gourmet sandwiches on its own bread in the vein of grilled chicken in focaccia with onions and aioli, prosciutto with Asiago and roasted peppers on an onion roll, and grilled flank steak on a baguette. It gets crowded and convivial on summer weekend evenings. **Eat-A-Pita,** 326 Main St. (*☎* **207/244-4344**), serves pitas, salads, and egg dishes.

Find Bernard, a few miles south of Southwest Harbor, for some of Maine's outstanding lobsters at **Thurston's** (see below).

For a quick bite or a picnic lunch to go in Northeast Harbor, don't overlook the informal **Docksider Restaurant,** hidden a block off the main commercial drag at 14 Sea St. (*☎* **207/276-3965**). The crab rolls and lobster rolls are outstanding, made simply and perfectly. The small restaurant also features a host of other fare, including lobster dinners, sandwiches, chowder, fried seafood, and grilled salmon.

Finally, there's an offbeat option and a "foodie find" a few miles outside town. **XYZ ★** (*☎* **207/244-5221**) on Bennett Lane in Southwest Harbor—head south down Main Street, then bear left onto Rte. 102A toward Manset; it's off Seawall Lane—serves *very* authentic Mexican cuisine. (The acronym means Xalapa, Yucatán, and Zacatecas, three provinces in Mexico.) Expect mole sauces, spicy meals, and sweet desserts. It's open nightly from 5:30 to 9pm in summer; call ahead for opening days and hours in the off season.

Beal's Lobster Pound ★ SEAFOOD   Some says Beal's is among the best lobster shacks in Maine, and it's certainly got the right atmosphere: Creaky picnic tables sit on a plain concrete pier overlooking a working-class harbor, right next to a Coast Guard base. (Don't wear a jacket and tie.) You go inside to pick out lobster from a tank, pay by the pound, choose some side dishes (corn on the cob, slaw, steamed clams), then pop coins into a soda machine outside while you wait for your number to be called. The food will arrive on Styrofoam and paper plates, but who cares? These lobsters are good. There's also a takeout window across the deck serving fries, fried clams, and fried fish (sensing a theme?), plus ice cream.

182 Clark Point Rd., Southwest Harbor. *☎* **207/244-7178** or 244-3202. www.bealslobster.com. Lobsters market priced. AE, DISC, MC, V. Summer daily 9am–8pm; after Labor Day 9am–5pm. Closed Columbus Day to Memorial Day.

The Burning Tree ★★ 🎢 SEAFOOD   Located on a busy straightaway of Rte. 3 between Bar Harbor and Otter Creek, The Burning Tree is an easy restaurant to blow right past; that would be a mistake. This low-key place, with its bright, open, and sometimes noisy dining room, is a find: it serves some of the best and freshest seafood dinners on the island, with New American twists. Some of the produce and herbs comes from the restaurant's own gardens, while the rest of the ingredients are bought locally whenever possible. Everything's prepared with imagination and skill—expect unusual preparations like a New Orleans–style lobster, lobster fritters (great idea), and mixed seafood over noodles and cream plus old standards like salmon and halibut (served with inventive and tasty sauces). The seafood stew's good, too, but desserts are middling at best. Don't miss the bartender's house cocktails, which use local fruits and berries when possible.

Rte. 3, Otter Creek. © **207/288-9331.** Reservations recommended. Main courses $18–$23. DISC, MC, V. Mid-June to Columbus Day Wed–Mon 5–10pm. Closed Columbus Day to mid-May.

Fiddlers' Green ★★ NEW AMERICAN   Island native chef Derek Wilbur's bistro is a big hit in these seafaring parts. Begin with something from the cold seafood bar: oysters on the half shell or a trio of smoked fish and shellfish, for instance. Or start with one of Wilbur's small plates, like Thai-curried shrimp with coconut milk, fried catfish filet with a Cajun rémoulade, grilled merguez, or smoked baby back ribs. There are always steaks and pasta dishes (such as lobster strozzapreti, a type of cavatelli, with a vinho verde cream sauce) on the main menu, but seafood's the true star: tempura-fried scallops, lobster pot pie, or a good old steamed lobster. There's an extensive wine list, too, and martini drinkers should take note: Wilbur's bar serves a long list of classic and obscure versions. Desserts run to chocolate cakes, a Mayan-style fruit-and-chocolate soup, ice creams, cheese with figs, and caramel crepes filled with mascarpone cream and local blueberries.

411 Main St., Southwest Harbor. © **207/244-9416.** www.fiddlersgreenrestaurant.com. Reservations recommended. Main courses $16–$32. AE, DISC, MC, V. Tues–Sun 5:30–9pm. Closed Columbus Day to Memorial Day.

Redbird Provisions ★★ CONTINENTAL/SEAFOOD   Redbird opened in 2007 in a renovated cottage right on Northeast Harbor's cute main street, and it's been an unqualified winner so far. The kitchen cooks up local seafood and other main courses with a talented hand, using Asian, French, and Italian accents in a no-pretenses dining room. Lunches run to harvest-style soups and extremely inventive flatbreads, sandwiches, and salads (the smoked trout salad Niçoise is especially good). Dinnertime sees a broadening of the menu's scope to include appetizers like truffled cauliflower soup and ricotta-stuffed squash blossoms; pasta dishes such as risotto or a saffrony homemade orecchette with clams and lemon confit; and main courses like organic Scottish salmon with white bean ragout and roasted figs, loin of lamb, or a strip streak served with a Yukon potato gratin. The small, porch-side outdoor dining space is nice in warmer weather.

11 Sea St., Northeast Harbor. © **207/276-3006.** www.redbirdprovisions.com. Reservations recommended. Entrees lunch $9–$22, dinner $25–$34. DISC, MC, V. Tues–Sat 11:30am–2pm and 6–9pm; Sun 6–9pm. Closed late Oct to late May.

Red Sky ★★ NEW AMERICAN   Despite a change in ownership and chefs, Red Sky continues to bring big-city dining sensibilities to its little village. Meals take New England ingredients to creative heights, using French and other Continental techniques and accents. Begin with intriguing starters such as organic chicken liver pâté, baked oysters stuffed with crab and bacon, duck-pork sausage, or a crispy, layered polenta. Salads here are excellent; main courses could include a coriander-crusted piece of seared tuna, a grass-fed Maine (yes, Maine) rib-eye steak that's been grilled and topped with Maytag blue cheese, a round of grilled lamb bathed in Dijon mustard, spicy molasses-flavored scallops, a pan-roasted breast of duck with a wine sauce, a roasted half chicken, or maple-glazed baby back ribs. Finish with a *very* lemony lemon cake, bittersweet Belgian chocolate pudding, toasted gingerbread with caramel sauce and brandied whipped cream, or one of the sorbets or ice creams.

14 Clark Point Rd., Southwest Harbor. © **207/244-0476.** www.redskyrestaurant.com. Entrees $21–$30. AE, DISC, MC, V. July–Sept Wed–Sun 5:30–9pm; rest of the year closed Sun. Closed Jan.

Thurston's Lobster Pound ★ ★ 🎁 SEAFOOD   Right off the end of a dock (the same place where they load the lobsters), Thurston's possesses all three key requirements of a great Maine lobster shack: one, a great view of Bass Harbor and its fishing boats; two, great lobster and side dishes at reasonable prices; and three, an unpretentious vibe blended with a dash of friendly sass. It's like a place out of the movies. The lobsters come quickly, their claws precracked for easier access; the corn on the cob is perfectly cooked; scallop chowder, crunchy crab cakes, and bags of steamed mussels and clams all provide toothsome sides; and the "plain dinner" option ($5 extra) finishes with a wonderfully eggy cinnamon-blueberry cake. There are two decks, upstairs and down, and a convivial atmosphere pervades at both, as perfect strangers break the ice over crustaceans. This place is a true Maine classic, one of my favorite lobster shacks in the whole state.

Steamboat Wharf Rd. (at the docks), Bernard. ⓒ **207/244-7600.** Lobsters market price. MC, V. Memorial Day to Columbus Day daily 11am–8:30pm.

THE DOWNEAST COAST

The term Downeast, as in "Downeast Maine," comes from the days when ships were still powered by sail. East Coast ships heading north and east along this coastline had strong prevailing winds at their backs—making it an easy "downhill" run to the farthest eastern ports. (Returning took more skill and determination.)

Today it's a rare traveler who gets Downeast to explore the rugged coastline of Washington County. Very few tourists venture beyond the turnoff to Mount Desert Isle, discouraged by a lack of services and high-marquee attractions. Yet Downeast Maine does have appeal—so long as you're not looking for luxury. There's an authenticity here that's been lost in much of the rest of Maine. Many longtime visitors say this is how all of Maine used to look in the 1940s and 1950s, when writers and artists first arrived in earnest. Thai food, the *New York Times,* and designer coffee have yet to make serious inroads into Washington County, where a rugged, hard-scrabble way of life and tough interdependence among neighbors still predominates.

Many residents here still get by as their forebears did—scratching a living from the land and sea. Scalloping, lobstering, and fishing remain the major sources of income, as do blueberrying, logging, and other forest work. Grubbing for bloodworms in spring, picking berries in the barrens in late summer, climbing fir trees to get the fragrant tips for Christmas wreaths in the fall—that's not a vacation around here, that's what people do to make ends meet. In recent years aquaculture has also become an important part of the economy around Passamaquoddy and Cobscook bays; travelers can sometimes see vast floating pens, especially around Eastport and Lubec, where salmon are farmed for gourmet diners worldwide.

The geographical isolation of this region ensures that you'll have these back roads and tiny towns to yourself—most of your fellow travelers have long since been waylaid by the charms of Kennebunkport, Portland, Camden, or Acadia. But if you're hoping to get a peek at the *real* Maine, the one that never shows up on the tourist brochures, you'd be wise to make a trip here for a day or two. You might never see Maine the same way again.

ESSENTIALS

Getting There

Downeast Maine is usually reached via U.S. Rte. 1, coming north from Ellsworth. You can also take a more direct, less congested route via Rte. 9 from Brewer (across the river from Bangor), connecting to Rte. 1 via Rte. 193 or Rte. 192.

Visitor Information

For information on the Machias area and other parts of Downeast Maine, contact the **Machias Bay Area Chamber of Commerce,** 85 Main St. (Ste. 2), Machias, ME 04654 (© **207/255-4402;** www.machiaschamber.org), on U.S. Rte. 1. It's open from 10am to 3pm weekdays.

Events

Eastport celebrates the **Fourth of July** in extravagant fashion each year, a tradition that began in 1820 after the British gave up possession of the city (they captured it during the War of 1812). Some 15,000 New Englanders pour into this little city of 1,900 for the 4-day event, which includes vendors, games, boat races, contests, and food, culminating with a grand parade on the Fourth.

The popular **Machias Wild Blueberry Festival ★**, operated by the local Congregation Church, celebrates the local cash crop each summer. Washington County claims to produce an astonishing 85% of the world's wild blueberry harvest, so there's bound to be some for the tasting when you show up. The festivities typically begin with a children's parade and fish fry, continue with a Saturday blueberry pancake breakfast (of course) and road race, then move on to lobster feeds, the raffling of a blueberry quilt, a book sale, and a blueberry-pie-eating contest. There are also performances and the sales of blueberry-theme gift items. Stamp collectors should plan to drop by the local post office for special-issue cancellation stamps, uniquely themed to blueberries each year.

Check the festival website (www.machiasblueberry.com) or contact the local chamber of commerce (© **207/255-6665**) for the exact dates of the festival; it usually takes place in mid- to late August.

ENJOYING THE GREAT OUTDOORS

There are several good tour outfitters and boat-tour operators in these parts, offering everything from kayak day trips to whale-watches.

Bold Coast Charter Company ★ (© **207/259-4484;** www.boldcoast.com) operates cruises out of little Cutler harbor to Machias Seal Island from May through August, and to Cross Island from May through October. Captain Andrew Patterson's 40-foot *Barbara Frost* tour boat sometimes lands ashore and sometimes doesn't, but either way viewing of puffins and razorbills on Machias Seal Island (which is claimed by both Canada and the U.S. as territory; stay tuned) is almost guaranteed. You might see arctic terns, petrels, seals, eagles, or porpoises in the vicinity of Cross Island, a noted bird-and-wildlife refuge. Patterson also makes occasional trips past Libby Island and its lighthouse. The 5-hour bird-watching tours leave around 7 or 8am and

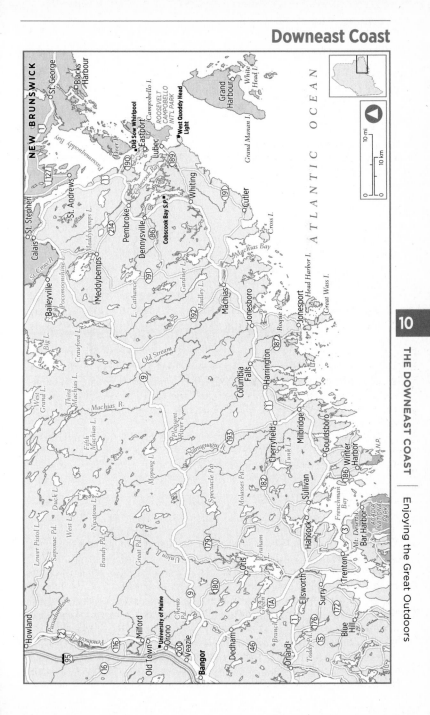

10

THE DOWNEAST COAST | Enjoying the Great Outdoors

cost $100 per person, $60 for children (there's no children's discount if the boat stops and lands on the island). Remember that many birds have already packed up and headed south by Labor Day (first week of Sept) and won't be there for the watching; come earlier than that, if you can. You board the boat at Cutler's little boat ramp on the harbor.

EXPLORING DOWNEAST MAINE

Ellsworth is 27 miles SE of Bangor

The best way to see this area—the only way, really—is to simply drive along U.S. Rte. 1 and a few associated back roads and shortcuts north from Ellsworth all the way to the Canadian border . . . and beyond, if you brought your passport.

Ellsworth to Machias

Ellsworth doesn't get much due from travelers hell-bent on making it to Mount Desert Island before dinner, but those in the know are increasingly stopping to sample a town that has significantly expanded its cultural offerings. In fact, though it seems pedestrian and overcommercialized—the town's Main Street was long ago usurped by Rte. 1, lending it a chaotic air out of step with Ellsworth's actual character—the community gives Bar Harbor a serious run for the title of Downeast arts capital.

The town was first settled by Passamaquoddy and Penobscot tribes; later, French woodsmen explored the area, and the British inevitably followed with bridges, sawmills, and ships on the Union River. By the late 19th century, Ellsworth had become both a significant port of departure for lumber cut from the big Maine woods and an important shipbuilding center. Those industries soon faded away, but Ellsworth swiftly reinvented itself as a tourist jumping-off point—playing off its proximity to Mount Desert Island—and arts center, capitalizing on the concentration of artists and musicians attracted to its services.

Traveling north from Ellsworth, it's about 13 miles from Ellsworth to **Sullivan,** nicely situated on a rise overlooking Frenchman Bay. This town was briefly home to a mini–gold rush, but today it's little more than a quiet fishing village consisting primarily of a general store and an intriguing combination smokehouse/rental cottage operation where you can buy smoked fish for picnics (see "Where to Stay & Dine," later in this chapter).

It's 8 miles farther along Rte. 1 to **Gouldsboro,** which is actually a series of five villages. The area contains a handful of accommodations. For a look at some real fishing villages, turn south off Rte. 1 down Rte. 186 and drive through Winter Harbor, Prospect Harbor, and Corea—don't expect anything fancy here. And do not miss **Schoodic Point,** at the end of this road (see later in this chapter); it's another bonus sliver of Acadia National Park, overlooked by almost all travelers, a fine spot for dramatic photographs of surf crashing over the big rocks.

Continue north 10 more miles to **Milbridge,** a former shipbuilding town, where the little **Milbridge Historical Museum** (see later in this chapter) captures some of the local history; as recently as 1983 a boat was built and launched here.

From here, it's shorter to cut north along Rte. 1A, but if you do so, you'll miss quaint Cherryfield. The **Cherryfield-Narraguargus Historical Society** (© **207/546-2076**), at 88 River Rd. in Cherryfield, maintains its own small museum of tools, photographs, and other 19th-century items. Look through preserved milk bottles, flasks, and boxes from a general store, wooden trunks, washboards, period clothing, and a hand-loom, among other items. The museum is only open in July and August, from 1 to 4pm Wednesdays through Fridays. (If you're really interested, they might let you come another time by appointment.) The museum is free, but give $5 per person as a donation.

Five miles north, the center of tiny **Columbia Falls** retains its longtime charm thanks to the good fortune of having been bypassed by Rte. 1; if you're stopping here to visit the historic **Ruggles House** (see later in this chapter), also check out April Adams's excellent **Columbia Falls Pottery** shop (© 800/235-2512; www.columbia fallspottery.com) in the restored schoolhouse next door at 150 Main St., where you can look over nature-inspired designs such as Lupine, Blueberry, Flag Iris, and Lady's-Slipper. They even take credit cards.

Just north of Columbia Falls, detour south along Rte. 187 (which makes a complete loop of its peninsula) to the end of the point. You will come to **Jonesport,** a photogenic, lost-in-time fishing village dominated by lobstermen and boat work. Beyond the pretty village and the dramatic local tides, you'll also find—should you venture offshore—some of the biggest puffin colonies in the world. July 4th is a surprisingly big deal here, featuring an impressive little parade, games, food, fireworks, and lobster boats racing in the harbor.

Jonesport is the jumping-off point for the nature preserve on **Great Wass Island** too, as well as some puffin-tour operators. **Holly Davis** runs boat tours to Machias Seal Island (and its colony of 3,000-plus puffins) out of Jonesport from June through mid-August aboard the *Chief;* call © 207/497-2560 or 497-5933 for details of the tours, which leave quite early, take about 5 hours in total (up to 2 hr. maximum on the island) and cost $100 per person. Or check her website at **www.machiassealis land.com**, which tells the interesting history of the tours—they were begun in 1939 by Captain Bana Norton. (Holly is a descendant.)

Rejoin Rte. 1 at **Jonesboro,** from where you can head east again—down empty highways—to scenic Roque Bluffs State Park (see later in this chapter), a good place to go swimming in either saltwater or freshwater pools.

Machias

The trim market town of **Machias** (pronounced Ma-*chai*-us) is the county seat of, and by far the biggest community in, Washington County—though it's not very big at all. Its year-round population of 2,400 seems positively Manhattan-esque in these parts by comparison to the rest of the towns, and a University of Maine satellite campus has attracted a welcome clutch of coffee shops, galleries, and other trappings of culture. The town's name is a native word translating approximately to "Bad Little Falls," a tribute to the rough rapids and waterfalls formed where river and coast meet here; the town was originally settled by Native Americans, who used it as a fishing camp.

Early explorers used the same river mouth as a trade port, although true colonial settlement of the town waited until the mid–18th century. This river even became the site of the Revolutionary War's first naval battle on June 12, 1775, when locals turned back the British gunboat the *Margaretta,* a story that's told and retold for visitors at the Burnham Tavern (see below).

You Light Up My Life

While in the Machias area, try to get a look at the historic **Libby Island Light,** a 42-foot-tall, solar-powered lighthouse in an extremely foggy spot 4 miles out to sea. Its granite tower was built in 1884, and the light—though visible from the local beach—is best seen by boat with a tour operator such as Bold Coast Charter Company (p. 242).

Downtown Machias still possesses a surprising number of historic structures. The **George Foster House** and Andrew Gilson House on North Street both display distinctive mansards, while Court Street is packed with historic structures: Machias's town offices are housed inside an Italianate former schoolhouse, the **Clark Perry House** has peaked lintels, and the granite **Porter Memorial Library** incorporates ballast and andirons from the *Margaretta* (talk about taking a war trophy). The **Carrie Albee House** at the corner of West and Court streets is a Victorian home dating from 1900.

Machias to Eastport

North of Machias, be sure to detour south and east along Rte. 191 to find **Cutler** (pop. 400 on a good day), an attractive small village once actively devoted to ship-building but now a sleepy place of lobster boats and enormous salmon farms. The coastal scenery north of Cutler, known here as the **Bold Coast**—and it is—makes for an impressive drive or hike. In addition to being the home of a former navy base, Cutler is also a great place to shove off on a **whale-watching cruise;** some routes also take in rare seabirds and/or basking seals on the way to the whale grounds.

Back on Rte. 1, you pass through nondescript **Whiting,** an entry point to the easternmost national wildlife refuge on the Atlantic migration corridor: **Moosehorn National Wildlife Refuge.** The refuge was created in 1934 with proceeds from President Franklin D. Roosevelt's Duck Stamp program; it's one of America's oldest such refuges, and still home to eagles, osprey, and the unusual woodcock (check out its remarkable courtship flights). Cycling, skiing, hiking, and leashed pets are allowed on the refuge roads, though not in the wildlife areas; there are more than 50 miles of trails, plus observation decks for watching some of the many birds here. Tours are often given in summer. Note that the refuge consists of two disjoined chunks of land—one here along Cobscook Bay on Rte. 1 between Dennysville and Whiting, the other to the southwest of Calais.

If you continue north along Rte. 1, north of Dennysville you cross Cobscook Bay at **Pembroke** (once the site of an ironworks) and an unusual reversing falls; the direction of the river—actually a tidal inlet—and the falls reverses twice each day, depending on the prevailing tides. From here to French-inflected **Calais** (pronounced just like *callous,* unfortunately), there are more tiny towns along Cobscook Bay and the St. Croix River. Calais is connected by bridge to St. Stephen, New Brunswick, which has a chocolate factory and museum worth checking out; go that way if you're planning to visit lovely St. Andrews or seafaring Grand Manan island, both described in chapter 11—and don't forget a passport.

If you plan to confine your explorations to American soil, split off Rte. 1 at Rte. 189 or 190, where you'll discover charming **Lubec** and **Eastport** as well as the gateways to Campobello Island (described later) and Deer Island, two lovely slices of New Brunswick. **Lubec** is the end of the line, literally: the northeasternmost community in the United States and one connected by a bridge to Canada. (Locals joke that although this isn't the end of the earth, at least you can *see* the ends of it from here.) The tidal mixing of two bays at this point has long proven to be a popular hangout for massive schools of fish, and fish canning and packing plants once filled the town. Today Lubec is notable chiefly for its vistas of the ocean and offshore lighthouses; set a course for Quoddy Head if you crave high tides, early sunrises, and a view that would stretch all the way to Europe and Africa if not for the curve of the earth.

If Lubec doesn't grab you, get back on Rte. 1 and continue north to Perry; a turn down Rte. 190 takes you to Eastport. First, however, you must pass through the **Pleasant Point Passamaquoddy Indian Reservation,** one of a handful of Maine's Native American reservations. (*Don't* speed.) The Passamaquoddy tribe here secured a landmark settlement in 1981, receiving a big land-and-cash award; in exchange, the tribe agreed to drop its series of land claims that many believe would have won in court—and probably bankrupted the state in the process. (The tribe would have received more than half of the land in the state of Maine if it had won.) There are few tourist facilities here, save a few souvenir shops and the tribal Waponahki Museum, 59 Passamaquoddy Rd. (✆ **207/853-4001;** www.wabanaki.com/museum.htm), upstairs in the Sipayik Youth Center, with its photographs, baskets, art, and cultural exhibits. It's open Monday, Wednesday, and Friday mornings in summer. Call ahead if you're intent on visiting—they just might open it for you if you can't make it then.

Eastport

Eastport, situated on a small island across a causeway at the tip of America, was once among the busiest ports on the entire East Coast; later, it became a major center for sardine canning. Today it's a sleepy fishing village rather than a shipping destination, but the historic downtown has lately begun to make itself over as an artsy place of writers, musicians, and other creative types attracted to the slow pace of life and closeness to the sea. (The fishing industry has also reinvented itself: Salmon farm pens now fill the near-shore waters.)

⦿ Radar Love

Cutler is more than a fishing village: It was once an important navy communications outpost, its proximity to Europe and northerly location making it ideal for communicating with submarines plying European waters.

Those two dozen or so big antennas poking up above the coast? They're said to make up the most powerful VLF transmitter in the world, and this quiet headland was for years considered a very high-risk target in the event of war. If you're an aficionado of things military, be sure to have a look. However, you should also know that the base's usefulness has greatly diminished in modern times, and the equipment is now operated by civilian personnel; most of the navy property, located on a scenic peninsula, is now being redeveloped.

The most interesting things here are the growing arts scene, the local historic district (see below), and an honest-to-goodness mustard mill (see below).

Eastport is also well known for its **Fourth of July** celebrations, which run several days and include pie-eating competitions, a flotilla of boats and ships in the harbor, a huge torch-lit parade (Maine's largest), parachutes, pipe bands, and the like. They go over-the-top, culminating in impressive (for the town's size) fireworks.

The **Eastport Salmon Festival ★** takes over town each year during the first weekend after Labor Day, with a very full weekend of arts, crafts, a road race, a sail-boat race, a walking tour, and plenty of seafood. Call ⓒ **207/853-4644** for more details, or check the festival website (www.eastportme.net).

Although Eastport is pretty quiet, the 90-acre peninsula of **Shackford Head State Park ★** (ⓒ **207/941-4014**) is even quieter; get there by following Rte. 190 almost into town, turn right at the gas station, and continue almost 1 mile along Deep Cove Road. There's a hiking trail here with nice views. Interestingly, you can see remains of several Civil War–era ships here at low tide. They were brought here for salvage in the early 20th century. The park is open from sunrise to sunset and is, unlike many of Maine's state parks, **free to enter.** No campfires or all-terrain vehicles are allowed.

Finally, if you're into whirlpools, you've come to the right place. Just north of East-port is the **Old Sow,** said to be the largest whirlpool in the Western Hemisphere. It's a bit finicky and is impressive only during the highest tides; the best way to see it is to take a seasonal **ferry** to Deer Island in New Brunswick, Canada (see chapter 11), and back. The ferry departs from behind the Eastport Fish and Lobster House at 167 Water St.

For more information on the Eastport area, contact the **Eastport Chamber of Commerce** (ⓒ **207/853-4644;** www.eastport.net).

WHAT TO SEE & DO

Below are some of the highlights of the region. The driving time direct from Ellsworth to Lubec via routes 1 and 189 is about 2 hours with no stops. Allow considerably more time for visiting the sites mentioned below and just plain snooping around.

Burnham Tavern   Gambrel-roofed Burnham Tavern was built on a rise overlook-ing the Machias River in 1770, and it's said to be the oldest existing building in eastern Maine. It also occupies a unique place in local history: In June 1775, a month after the Battle of Lexington, a group of locals hatched a plan here that led to the first naval battle of the Revolutionary War. The armed schooner *Margaretta* was in Machias harbor to stock up on wood for the British barracks. Locals didn't think much of that plan, and attacked the ship with smaller boats, muskets, swords, axes, pitchforks—whatever they could grab. The Mainers prevailed, killing the captain of the *Margaretta* in the process; visitors can learn all about the episode during a tour of the tavern. On display is booty taken from the British ship, along with the original tap table and other historic furniture and ephemera. The tours last around 1 hour.

Main St. (Rte. 192), Machias. ⓒ **207/255-6930.** www.burnhamtavern.com. Admission $2 adults, 25¢ children. Mid-June to early Sept Mon–Fri 9am–5pm. Closed early Sept to mid-June.

Cobscook Bay State Park ★★★   One of Maine's hidden jewels, this state park is an outstanding camping or day-trip destination for the family. Tides flow back and forth across cribworked rocks, exposing deep tidal pools, rocks, and clam–rich mud-flats; bird life is also prodigious. There are some 900 acres of trails (cross-country skiable in winter) and tidal exposure in all, and the hundred-plus campsites here include a number of waterside sites.

U.S. Rte. 1 (RR #1, Box 127, Dennysville ME 04628), 4 miles south of Dennysville. © **207/726-4412.** Open daily year-round. Mid-May to mid-Oct, $4.50 nonresident adult, $1.50 child 5–11; off season $1.50 per adult.

Cutler Coastal Trail ★   Marked by a sign in a small parking lot, this dramatic loop trail passes through diverse ecosystems, including bogs, barrens, and dark and tangled spruce forests. But the highlight of the trail, which traverses state-owned land, is a mile-long segment along rocky headlands high above the Atlantic. Some of the most dramatic coastal views in the state are located along this isolated stretch, which over-looks dark-gray-to-black rocks and the tumultuous sea. Visible on the horizon across the Bay of Fundy are the west-facing cliffs of the Canadian island of Grand Manan. Plan on at least 2 or 3 hours for the whole loop. If it's damp or foggy, rain pants are advised to fend off the moisture from the low brush along the trail.

Rte. 191, Cutler. Contact Maine Bureau of Park and Recreation © **207/827-1818.** Free admission. Open year-round. From the village of Cutler, head northeast on Rte. 191; 4½ miles north of town, look for park-ing lot and signs on right.

Eastport Historic District ★   In the late 19th century, Eastport (3 miles from Lubec by water, but 50 min. by car) was home to nearly 5,000 residents and 18 sar-dine plants. The census now counts less than 2,000, and the sardine plants are gone, but much of the handsome brick architecture remains on Water Street—a compact thoroughfare that also affords lovely views of Campobello Island and Passamaquoddy Bay. The majority of the buildings between the post office and the library are on the National Register of Historic Places. You'll mostly see the work of architect Henry Black, who designed two-thirds of these Italianate buildings during a single hectic year after an 1886 fire razed the previous downtown. Look for his hand at the East-port Savings Bank at no. 43 Water St., the Shead Building at no. 58, the M. Bradish Bakery at no. 68, the Masonic Block at no. 36, the Charles & M. A. Jackson Block at no. 74, and (we think) the Hayscale Block at no. 49.

Water St., Eastport. From Rte. 1 in Perry, take Rte. 190 south for 7 miles.

Great Wass Island Preserve ★   This exceptional 1,524-acre island, acquired by the Nature Conservancy in 1978, contains an excellent 5.5-mile loop hike covering a wide cross section of native terrain, including bogs, heath, rocky coastline, and forests of twisted jack pines. Maps and a birding checklist can be found in a stand at the parking lot. Follow one fork of the trail to the shoreline; work your way along boulders to the other fork, then back to your car. Though mostly flat, the hike is rocky and slow in places—it's no pushover. Yet it's worth doing if you're up for the challenge. If a heavy fog has settled in, it's even more beautiful; just make sure you stay on the trail. Afterward, consider making a donation to the Nature Conservancy (www.tnc.org), a great organization whose active local chapter carefully maintains this preserve as well as many other important ones in the state.

Black Duck Cove Rd. (via Wass Island Rd.), Great Wass Island, Jonesport. Contact the Nature Conservancy © **207/729-5181.** Free admission. Open daylight hours. From Jonesport, cross bridge to Beals Island (signs); continue across causeway to Great Wass Island. Bear right at next fork; pavement ends. Continue past lobster pound to a small parking lot on the left marked by Nature Conservancy logo (oak leaf).

GETTING OUT TO sea

To see the Maine Coastal Islands National Refuge, or whales, seals, or lighthouses, you'll usually need to arrange for a personalized tour from a local charter boat operator. One of the best in these parts is captain Winston Shaw's **Sea Venture** (© 207/288-3355; www.svboattours.com)—he charges $100 to $150 per hour, which covers a group of up to six travelers—if you want to view these islands. Captain Shaw ties up at the Atlantic Oakes Motel, on Rte. 3 just north of downtown Bar Harbor.

The **Bar Harbor Whale Watch Co.** (© **888/942-5374** or 207/288-2386; www.whalesrus.com) will also run you through some of these islands on its lighthouse tour; see "Whale-Watching" in chapter 9 for more details on their operations. If you set foot on those islands that are open to public for walking, please respect the rules that protect these delicate ecosystems. Tread lightly, and light no open fires or unleash any dogs.

Maine Coastal Islands National Wildlife Refuge ★★   This refuge strings together a collection of uninhabited islands and parcels of land, protecting them as habitat for nesting seabirds and birds of prey. The entire refuge now includes about 50 islands, three onshore areas, and more than 8,000 acres in all. It's home to terns, plovers, bald eagles, puffins, razorbills, storm petrels, and eiders, among other birds; hiking trails run through forests, marshes, and mudflats; there's even a loop along stony beaches (the Hollingsworth Trail, 6 miles off Rte. 1 in Steuben) and another passing through a blueberry field (Birch Point Trail). Note that some parts of the refuge are open to the public (Cross, Scotch, Halifax, and Bois Bubert islands); some are always closed (Seal Island); the rest are closed to public egress from April through August. Check ahead with administrators. To get to the refuge, you'll need your own boat—or someone else's (see the "Getting Out to Sea" box, above).

P.O. Box 279, Milbridge. © **207/546-2124.** http://petitmanan.fws.gov.

Milbridge Historical Museum   This low-key museum focuses mostly on ship-building and fishing as a local way of life, with exhibits such as *Getting Through the Long Winter, Old Ways of Fishing,* and *Rusticators* (about summer tourists seeking to escape to a more basic way of life here). The displays include vintage photos, ship-building tools, and a time capsule filled with items from Downeast Maine.

Main St. (Rte. 1), Milbridge. © **207/546-4471.** Free admission. July-Aug Tues and Sat-Sun 1-4pm; June and Sept Sat-Sun 1-4pm. Oct-Feb by appointment only. Closed Mar-May.

Raye's Mustard Mill 🎁   Foodies may feel they've gone to heaven after stumbling across Raye's artisanal mustard factory here in downtown Eastport, powered by one of the last stone mills in America. The Raye family has been cold-grinding mustard seeds and bottling various mustard concoctions here since 1903, when J. W. "Wes" Raye built the place to create mustards for a booming local sardine-canning trade. Now he supplies sardine plants as far away as Norway, too. Free hourly tours of the factory are given, where new flavors are sometimes in the offing; in the gift shop, pick up gifts for the mustard-crazed back home.

83 Washington St., Eastport, ME 04631. © **800/853-1903** or 207/853-4451. www.rayesmustard.com. Tours Mon-Fri 10am-3pm, Sat by appointment.

Roque Bluffs State Park ☺ A day-use-only park, Roque Bluffs features impressive coastal scenery plus the added attraction of both freshwater and saltwater swimming areas. Jasper Beach is particularly noteworthy for the uniformly smooth jasper stones that make it up. There are family friendly amenities here such as grills, changing areas, a playground, and a lifeguard.

145 Schoppee Point Rd. (6 miles off U.S. Rte. 1), Roque Bluffs. ℂ **207/255-3475.** $4.50 adults, $1 children ages 5–11, free for children 4 and under. Open mid-May to Sept.

Ruggles House This Federal home dates from 1818 and was built for Thomas Ruggles, a local timber merchant and civic leader. The house is grand and opulent, but in a curiously miniature sort of way. There's a flying staircase in the central hallway, pine doors hand-painted to resemble mahogany, and detailed woodcarvings in the main parlor done over the course of 3 years by an English craftsman equipped, legend has it, with just a penknife. Tours last 20 minutes to a half-hour.

146 Main St., Columbia Falls. ℂ **207/483-4637.** www.ruggleshouse.org. Tours $5 adults, $2 children ages 6–12. June to mid-Oct Mon–Sat 9:30am–4:30pm; Sun 11am–4:30pm. Closed mid-Oct to May

Schoodic Point ★★ This remote, scenic, and free unit of Acadia National Park is just 7 miles from Mount Desert Island across Frenchman Bay, but it's a 50-mile drive to get here. A pleasing one-way loop road hooks around the point (no park entry pass or fee required) and winds along the water and through forests of spruce and fir. Good views of the mountains of Acadia open up across Frenchman Bay; you can also see part of a historic naval station housed on the point. Park near the tip and explore salmon-colored rocks that plunge into the ocean, especially dramatic when the seas are agitated.

Acadia National Park, Winter Harbor. ℂ **207/288-3338.** Free admission. Drive east from Ellsworth on Rte. 1 for 17 miles to W. Gouldsboro; then turn south on Rte. 186 to Winter Harbor and look for the brown-and-white national park signs.

The Telephone Museum It's not exactly comprehensive, but the tiny telephone museum here, in a barn about 10 miles outside Ellsworth, makes for a rainy-day diversion as you explore the ins and outs of the hand-crank system that first made it possible to reach out and touch someone. Talk to a switchboard operator—the early heroines of the system (my mom was one)—and learn about telephone poles, line, linesmen, switching stations, and how they kept it all running smoothly back in a day when cellphones were just science fiction. Tours are available.

166 Winkumpaugh Rd. (P.O. Box 1377), Ellsworth. ℂ **207/667-9491.** www.thetelephonemuseum.org. Admission $5 adults, $2.50 children. July–Sept Thurs–Sun 1-4pm; May–June and Oct by appointment only. Closed Nov–Apr. From Rte. 1 in Ellsworth, go 7 miles south on Rte. 1 to Happytown Rd., turn right, and continue 6 miles to crossroads. Turn right onto Winkumpaugh Rd. Museum is on left.

West Quoddy Head Light & Quoddy Head State Park ★★ This red-and-white lighthouse, which has been likened to a barbershop pole or a candy cane, marks the easternmost point of the United States and helps guide boats into the Lubec Channel. (Interestingly, it's also the nearest geographical point in the U.S. to Africa.) The light, operated by the Coast Guard, isn't open to the public, but visitors can walk the grounds near the light and along headlands at an adjacent state park. A visitor center inside the light-keeper's house overlooks rocky shoals, pounding waves, and some of the most powerful tides on the planet. Watch for fishing boats straining against the currents and seals playing in the waves or sunning on offshore rocks. The park also includes 480 acres of coastline and bogs, with several trails winding through the forest and atop rocky cliffs; some of the most dramatic views can be found just a short walk down the path at the far end of the parking lot.

W. Quoddy Head Rd., Lubec. (*) **207/733-0911** (state park) or 207/733-2180 (lighthouse). www.west quoddy.com. Lighthouse grounds: free admission. State park admission: $3 adults, $1 seniors and children 5-11. Lighthouse late May to mid-Oct daily 10am-4pm; grounds 9am-sunset. Closed mid-Oct to mid-May.

PASSAMAQUODDY BAY

Once in Lubec or Eastport, it's only a short drive to Canada, where you'll find Campobello Island, a quiet jewel once favored by president Franklin D. Roosevelt.

From Campobello, you can catch a ferry to quiet Deer Island, then onward to New Brunswick's Passamaquoddy Bay region, which adjoins the Maine coast and is easily reached via a boat ride from Campobello. Or take a 1-minute drive across a bridge in Calais, Maine (assuming the border checks go smoothly), to St. Stephen, New Brunswick, for a look at a French town with a yummy chocolate museum.

You might also push a bit farther into New Brunswick and check out the lovely seaside town of St. Andrews. For more information about this scenic town, see chapter 11. It's a worthwhile day or overnight trip.

Campobello Island ★

Campobello is a compact island (about 10 miles long and 3 miles wide) at the mouth of Passamaquoddy Bay. Among its other distinctions, it's connected by a graceful modern bridge to Lubec, Maine, and is thus easier to get to from the United States than from Canada. Getting here from the Canadian mainland without driving through the United States requires two ferries, one of which operates only during the summer.

Campobello has been home to both humble fishermen and wealthy families over the years, and both have coexisted quite nicely. (Locals approved when summer folks built golf courses because it gave them a place to graze their sheep.) Today the island is a mix of elegant summer homes and less interesting tract homes of a more recent vintage.

The island offers excellent shoreline **walks** ★ at both Roosevelt Campobello International Park (see below for more) and **Herring Cove Provincial Park** ((*) **506/752-7010**), which is open year-round and maintains both a golf course

---

Like Bikes? You'll Love Campobello.

If you like bikes, the islands and peninsulas of Passamaquoddy Bay lend themselves nicely to cruising in the slow lane—especially pretty Campobello, which has plenty of good dirt roads perfect for mountain biking. But you'll need a guidebook to show you the way. Fortunately, Kent Thompson has written a handy one, called *Biking to Blissville.* It covers 35 lovely rides in the Maritimes, including some on the island, and costs C$15 (about US$15). Unfortunately, it was published in 1993. Try to order it through the publisher, Goose Lane Editions, 500 Beaverbrook Court, Ste. 330, Fredericton, NB E3B 5X4 ((*) **888/926-8377** or 506/450-4251; www.gooselane.com), or, failing that, through an online retailer such as **Amazon** (www.amazon.ca).

(open late Apr to Oct) and campsites (open late May to late Sept). The landscapes are extraordinarily diverse. On some trails you'll enjoy a Currier and Ives tableau of white houses and church spires across the channel in Lubec and Eastport; 10 minutes later you'll be walking along a wild, rocky coast pummeled by surging waves. Herring Cove has a mile-long beach that's perfect for a slow stroll in the fog. Camping and very scenic golf are also offered at the provincial park.

Nature lovers should note that Campobello's mixed terrain also attracts a good mix of birds, including sharp-shinned hawk, common eider, and black guillemot. Ask for a checklist and map at the visitor center.

ESSENTIALS

GETTING THERE   Campobello Island is accessible year-round from the United States. From Rte. 1 in Whiting, Maine, take Rte. 189 to Lubec, where a bridge links Lubec with Campobello. In the summer, there's another option. From the Canadian mainland, take the free ferry to Deer Island, drive the length of the island, and then board the small seasonal ferry to Campobello. The ferry is operated by **East Coast Ferries** (𝒞 **506/747-2159;** www.eastcoastferries.nb.ca) and runs from late June to September. The fare is C$13 (US$13) for car and driver, C$3 (US$2.70) for each additional passenger.

VISITOR INFORMATION   The **Campobello Welcome Center,** 44 Rte. 774, Welshpool, NB E5E 1A3 (𝒞 **506/752-7043**), is on the right side just after you cross the bridge from Lubec. It's open daily mid-May through mid-October, closed the rest of the year.

Roosevelt Campobello International Park ★★   Take a brief excursion out of the country and across the time zone. The U.S. and Canada maintain a joint national park here, celebrating the life of Franklin D. Roosevelt, who summered here with his family in the early 1900s. Like other affluent Americans, the Roosevelt family made an annual trek to the prosperous colony at Campobello Island. The island lured folks from the sultry cities with a promise of cool air and a salubrious effect on the circulatory system. ("The extensive forests of balsamic firs seem to affect the atmosphere of this region, causing a quiet of the nervous system and inviting sleep," read an 1890 real-estate brochure.) The future U.S. president came to this island every summer between 1883—the year after he was born—and 1921, when he was suddenly stricken with polio. Franklin and his siblings spent those summers exploring the coves and sailing around the bay, and he always recalled his time here fondly. (It was his "beloved island," he said, coining a phrase that gets no rest in local promotional brochures.)

You can view a brief film at the visitor center and take a self-guided tour of the elaborate mansion, which is covered in cranberry-colored shingles, to learn about Roosevelt and his early life. For a "cottage" this huge, it is surprisingly comfortable and intimate. The park is truly an international park, run by a commission with representatives from both the U.S. and Canada, making it like none other in the world. Because of Homeland Security measures currently in place, I suggest you bring with you either a passport or birth certificate, although checks are rarely enforced.

Leave some time to explore farther afield in the 2,800-acre park, which offers scenic coastline and 8.5 miles of walking trails. Maps and walk suggestions are available at the visitor center.

Remember that New Brunswick is in the *Atlantic* Standard Time (AST) zone, also known as ADT (Atlantic Daylight Time) during the summer, and that it's 1 hour *ahead* of Maine, Boston, and New York time (Eastern Standard Time). Let's just call it New Brunswick time, for now. That means if it's 9am in Eastport, Maine, when you cross the border, it's 10:01am in New Brunswick when you get across. And if you step right back across, it's 9:02am. You get the idea: reset your watch—or at least make a mental note—when crossing the border, and again when coming back. I have expressed all opening and closings times for New Brunswick attractions and restaurants in AST; in other words, in New Brunswick time.

459 Rte. 774, Welshpool NB (in Canada). ✆ **506/752-2922.** www.fdr.net. Free admission. Daily 10am–6pm (last tour at 5:45pm). Visitor center closed mid-Oct to mid-May; grounds open year-round. Reached via U.S. 1 to Whiting and then Rte. 189 to Lubec; follow signs to bridge.

St. Stephen

St. Stephen is the gateway to Canada for many travelers arriving from the United States. It's directly across the tidal St. Croix River from Calais, Maine, and the two towns share a symbiotic relationship—it's a local call across the international border from one town to the other, fire engines from one country will respond to fires in the other, and during an annual summer parade, bands and floats have sometimes marched right through Customs. Though downtown St. Stephen is hardly a destination itself, it is a handy pit stop—and the smell of chocolate (as you'll read below) does sneakily attempt to entice you into a longer stay.

ESSENTIALS

VISITOR INFORMATION The **Provincial Visitor Information Centre** (✆ **506/466-7390**) is open daily from 9am to 8pm mid-June through August and 9am to 6pm in the shoulder seasons (early June and Sept). It's in the old train station at Milltown Boulevard and King Street, about a mile from Canadian Customs; turn right after crossing the border (following signs for St. Andrews and Saint John), and watch for the information center at the light where the road turns left.

EXPLORING ST. STEPHEN

St. Stephen is a town in transition. The lumber industry and wood trade that were responsible for those handsome brick-and-stone buildings that line the main street have mostly dried up. The town now depends on its paper mill, the large Ganong chocolate factory, and pass-through tourists like yourself for its economic mainstays. (For the truly cocoa bean–obsessed, there's also a small Chocolate Festival in summer.) As a regional commercial center, it has a gritty, lived-in feel to it, though not much in the way of stylish shopping or restaurants to keep you more than a moment.

Want even more? **Ganong's Chocolatier,** an old-fashioned candy shop, is located in the storefront adjacent to the museum. Don't miss the budget bags of factory seconds. There's also a Heritage Chocolate Walk offered, which combines a factory tour with a walk through the downtown's historic areas.

Still, you can learn about the region's history with a brief stop at the **Charlotte County Museum,** 443 Milltown Blvd. (© **506/466-3295**), open June through August (and by appointment only in Sept); it's quite close to the tourist office described above. There's no charge for admission.

The Chocolate Museum ☺   Chocolate is integral to this town's history (see "The Sweet Truth About St. Stephen's Sweet Tooth," above), so of course there's a museum to the cacao bean. Here you can view an 11-minute video about the history of local chocolates. Displays and exhibits explain 19th-century chocolate boxes, and there are interactive multimedia displays about the making of candy and games for young children (such as "Guess the Centers"). One highlight is watching the expert hand-dippers make chocolates the old-fashioned way; samples, of course, are available afterward. Want more? Ganong's Chocolatier, the company's candy shop, is located in the storefront adjacent to the museum. (Don't miss the budget bags of factory seconds.) There's also a "Heritage Chocolate Walk" offered, which combines a factory tour with a walk through the downtown's historic areas. Plan to spend about an hour here altogether.

73 Milltown Blvd. © **506/466-7848.** www.chocolatemuseum.ca. Admission C$7 (US$7) adults, C$6 (US$6) students and seniors, free for children under 5, C$22 (US$22) families. Downtown tour plus museum C$13 (US$13) adults, C$10 (US$10) seniors, C$5 (US$5) children 5 and under, C$40 (US$40) families. Mid-June to Aug Mon–Sat 9:30am–6:30pm, Sun 11am–3pm; mid-Mar to mid-June and Sept to mid-Dec Mon–Fri 10am–4pm (Sept also open Sat). Closed mid-Dec to mid-Mar.

WHERE TO STAY & DINE

In Maine

Small motels, inns, and B&Bs abound along this part of the Maine coast; resorts, on the other hand, are almost nonexistent. The message: Prepare to rusticate.

The upside of this situation is that budget travelers seeking to minimize costs can do well here. Lower-end offerings on Rte. 1 in Machias include the Machias Motor Inn, with 35 air-conditioned riverside rooms (© **207/255-4861**); the Margaretta Motel (© **207/255-6500**), with a swimming pool and air-conditioning; and the

---

The Sweet Truth About St. Stephen's Sweet Tooth

St. Stephen's claim to fame is that it's purported the home of the chocolate bar—the first place where somebody thought to wrap chocolate pieces in foil and sell them individually. In 1910, they say. At least that's according to local lore. Chocolate is big around here—not as big as in Hershey, Pennsylvania, but still a big part of the local psyche and economy. The Ganong brothers began selling chocolate from their general store here in 1873, and from that an empire was built, employing some 700 people by the 1930s. Ganong was also the first place to package chocolates in heart-shaped boxes for Valentine's Day, and still holds 30% of the Canadian market for heart-box chocolates. The modern new plant on the outskirts of town isn't open to the public, but there's a museum in one of the company's early factories, a large brick structure on the main street.

Bluebird Motel (© **207/255-3332**), with 40 air-conditioned units. There are also budget options in Jonesboro, Lubec, and Eastport.

Those with RVs can camp out at Pleasant River RV Park at 11 W. Side Rd. in Addison (© **207/483-4083**). It's open May through October, though it only has a half-dozen sites from which to choose.

In addition to gleaning the listings below, you might also think about renting a cottage or farmhouse by the week or month; there are plenty to choose from along this stretch of coast in summer, though digging them up can take some doing. Among the offerings, check out the unique **Quoddy Head Station** (© **877/535-4714** or 860/535-4714; www.quoddyvacation.com), on W. Quoddy Head Road in Lubec, a former Coast Guard lifesaving station built in 1918. You can rent the five-bedroom station house, or one of five other units, all with terrific coastal views, in July and August for $80 to $275 per night or $500 to $1,800 per week—rates are lowest during the shoulder seasons.

Eats are likewise thin on the ground up here. If you're simply looking to fuel up on fast food or family style fare, Ellsworth is your main (and, actually, only) supply depot; expect the usual franchise chains along Rte. 1, especially near the point where routes 1 and 3 diverge.

On the town's main drag, you can also fuel up with standard Mexican fare at the **Mex,** 191 Main St. (© **207/667-4494;** www.themexrestaurant.com), which serves a variety of the expected Mexican dishes (taco salads, fajitas, burritos), plus some seafood surprises (crab enchiladas, seviche, haddock Veracruz) as a tip of the sombrero to Maine. Large entrees run $15 to $20 each, but you can spend much less on a small plate, burrito, or salad. More typical coastal dining is found in Ellsworth at the **Union River Lobster Pot,** 8 South St. (© **207/667-5077;** www.lobsterpot.com), featuring lobster dinners but also serving a basic menu of Maine seafood, steaks, chicken, and sandwiches. It's open daily for dinner, May through mid-October.

To stock up for a picnic at Quoddy Head, make a beeline for **Bold Coast Smokehouse** (© **888/733-0807** or 207/733-8912; www.boldcoastsmokehouse.com) on Rte. 189 in Lubec—which surely must be the nation's easternmost smokehouse. Vinny Gartmayer smokes hot salmon, gravlax, kabobs, and trout pâté, among other products. (Another Downeast smokehouse, **Sullivan Harbor Farm,** is covered in fuller detail below.)

Black Duck Inn   There isn't much to the little village of Corea, mostly just a clutch of fishing boats and some island views, but there is a bed-and-breakfast if you care to stay the night. The Black Duck consists of four no-frills rooms (two share a bathroom, while the others have private facilities), one suite, and one waterfront cottage rented out by the week. It's a simple place set among quiet scenery. Rooms here are uncluttered and dotted with antiques; three, including the studio apartment (which has a kitchenette) and the cottage, possess excellent vistas of the picturesque harbor and the lupine-strewn headland.

36 Crowley Island Rd. (P.O. Box 39), Corea ME 04624. © **207/963-2689.** Fax 207/963-7495. www.blackduck.com. 6 units (2 with shared bathroom), 1 cottage. $140–$165 double; weekly rates for cottages vary. Full breakfast included with rate. DISC, MC, V. Closed Dec to mid-May. Children 8 and older welcome. *In room:* No phone.

Captain Cates Bed & Breakfast   This trim blue house on a point of water, built by a sailor in the 1850s, is a simple yet accommodating place; five of the six units have ocean views, though all six of them do share three bathrooms. The J. W. Room, with an extralong mahogany bed from 1865 and matching commode and dresser, sports water views, while the Olevia Room is furnished with a queen-size bed and late-19th-century maple French Provincial bedroom set. Up on the third floor, the Starboard Room is done in cream and blue-green tones. There are three more units with double beds or, in the case of the Puffin Room, a single bed. The lack of TVs and phones is made up for by a communal game room with a group tube and some puzzles.

Rte. 92 at Phinney Lane (P.O. Box 314), Machiasport, ME 04655. © **207/255-8812.** Fax 207/255-6705. www.captaincates.com. 6 units (all share 3 bathrooms). $75–$95 double. AE, V. **Amenities:** 2 dining rooms; game room. *In room:* No phone.

Crocker House Country Inn   Built in 1884, this handsome shingled inn is off the beaten track on picturesque Hancock Point, across Frenchman Bay from Mount Desert Island. It's a cozy retreat, good for rest, relaxation, and quiet walks; it's only about a 4-minute walk from the water's edge. Rooms are tastefully decorated in comfortable country decor; there's nothing lavish here, but they do have phones. The common areas are more relaxed than fussy. The inn has a few bikes for guests to explore the point, the second-smallest post office in the U.S., or clay tennis courts (nearby). **Dinner** ★ here is a highlight: it's served in a fun atmosphere. Open daily from May through October and weekends in several other months, the kitchen serves mostly traditional favorites, such as oysters Rockefeller, scallops, fish, pasta, steak au poivre, and lamb.

967 Point Rd. (Box 171), Hancock Point, ME 04640. © **877/715-6017** or 207/422-6806. Fax 207/422-3105. www.crockerhouse.com. 11 units. $85–$170 double. Rates include full breakfast. AE, DISC, MC, V. Closed Jan–Feb; open weekends only in Mar. **Amenities:** Dining room; free bikes. *In room:* A/C.

Harbor House on Sawyer Cove B&B ★   Once the local telegraph office and an outpost for ship equipment, the early-19th-century Harbor House may be Jonesport's most luxurious lodging choice. There are two suites, which are set above an antiques shop, and both feature truly impressive coastal scenery from their third-floor windows. The Beachrose Room is a funkily shaped space (narrow with low ceilings) with outstanding ocean views, while the Lupine Room features a king-size feather bed and private breakfast nook; both have private entrances. Breakfast is served on a wonderful inn porch, and a backyard picnic table is yet another perfect spot from which to take in the changing light over the reach and islands. Helpfully, it's open year-round.

27 Sawyer Sq. (P.O. Box 468), Jonesport, ME 04649. © **207/497-5417.** Fax 207/497-3211. www. harborhs.com. 2 units. May–Oct $125 double; rest of the year $100 double. Rates include full breakfast. DISC, MC, V. *In room:* No phone.

Helen's Restaurant 🍴 DINER   This is the original Helen's, a cut-above-the-rest diner and one of the premier places in all of Maine to eat pie. (And, yes, there was a Helen.) You can get pork chops, fried fish, burgers, meatloaf, and other American-style square meals. But absolutely save room for the amazingly creamy and fruity pies; strawberry rhubarb or blueberry, when in season, are out of this world, but chocolate cream, banana cream, or just about anything else will satisfy the sweet tooth. Check for daily specials. There's another Helen's on the strip just north of Ellsworth.

28 E. Main St., Machias. © **207/255-8423.** Entrees $3–$16. DISC, MC, V. Daily 6am–7:30pm.

Home Port Inn ★   The 1880 Home Port was built as a family home, but converted into lodgings in 1982. On a quiet street in downtown Lubec, its rooms mostly possess tremendous views of both Cobscook Bay and the Bay of Fundy. The central living room and fireplace are the focal points; comfy guest rooms vary in size, with one occupying a former library and another a former dining room. Best bed? The Garden Overlook's king-size bed. Best view? The room known as the View, of course (though it only has a double bed). The inn restaurant is surprisingly good, serving passable seafood dinners nightly of smoked fish, lobsters, scallops, salmon, and crab, as well as landlubbing items such as chicken *cordon bleu* and steak au poivre. Note that this restaurant opens a month later (and closes a few weeks earlier) than the inn itself.

45 Main St. (P.O. Box 50), Lubec ME 04652. ⓒ **800/457-2077** or 207/733-2077. www.homeportinn. com. 7 units. $90–$105 double. Rates include continental breakfast. AE, DISC, MC, V. Closed mid-Oct to mid-May. **Amenities:** Restaurant. *In room:* No phone.

Le Domaine ★★ 💼   Located on Rte. 1 about 10 minutes east of Ellsworth, this inn somehow has the flair of a French *auberge*. While the highway in front can be a bit noisy, the garden and woodlands out back offer plenty of serenity. Rooms are comfortable and tastefully appointed without being pretentious; the innkeeper has combined several rooms to create two suites and added air-conditioning and phones to all units. Rooms are on the second floor, in the rear of the property; suites with private terraces face the woods. But the real draw is the **dining room** ★★, serving French country cooking in a handsome space of pine-wood floors and a big fireplace. Meals run to brandied pâté, filet mignon in Bordelaise sauce, grilled halibut, and quail wrapped in bacon; finish with custard-filled raspberry tarts or rich bread pudding. The wine list is great (and all French).

1513 U.S. Rte. 1 (P.O. Box 519), Hancock, ME 04640. ⓒ **800/554-8498** or 207/422-3395. Fax 207/422-3916. www.ledomaine.com. 5 units. June–Oct $200–$285 double; $285–$370 suite. Rates include full breakfast and dinner. AE, MC, V. Closed Nov–May. **Amenities:** Dining room. *In room:* A/C.

Little River Lodge   Overlooking Cutler's tiny, impressively situated harbor, this Victorian inn—once known as the Cutler Hotel—was built in the late 19th century to lodge steamship passengers bound from Boston to Canada. The inn has just five rooms, three of them facing the water; all have been decorated in nautical themes and simple, pleasing colors (forest green, eggshell blue) and stocked with old books and antiques. A warning—four of five rooms here are still furnished with twin, full, or double beds, though the Roosevelt Room (where T. R. himself is said to have slept) does contain a queen-size bed. Three of the units share a bathroom, but if you're wanting to stay in Cutler near the good coastal trails, this is really your only option.

Rte. 191 (P.O. Box 251), Cutler, ME 04626. ⓒ **207/259-4437.** www.cutlerlodge.com. 5 units (3 with shared bathroom). $110–$120 double with private bathroom; $80–$100 double with shared bathroom. Rates include breakfast. Some rooms 2-night minimum stay weekends. No credit cards. From Rte. 1 in E. Machias, turn onto Rte. 191 S. and continue 13 miles to hotel on left. **Amenities:** Dining room. *In room:* No phone.

Micmac Farm ★   Based in a 1763 home with intriguing history (the founder's family is buried in a cemetery on the premises), quiet Micmac Farm consists of just three units in a peaceful riverside setting: two rustic, wood-paneled "guesthouses" in the woods, furnished with two double beds apiece and kitchenettes, plus a more luxurious guest room located inside the main house with a big deck, king-size bed, television, and Jacuzzi tub. This third room also adjoins the home's library, which guests are welcome to use. An outdoor deck overlooks the Machias River, and it's a good spot for watching the water.

47 Micmac Lane (Rte. 92), Machiasport, ME 04655. (✆) **207/255-3008.** www.micmacfarm.com. 3 units. $125 main house double; $80–$95 daily, or $495–$595 weekly cottage double. MC, V. From Rte. 1 in center of Machias, drive south and east on Rte. 92 (Elm St.) for 2 miles; turn left on Micmac Lane. Pets and children welcome in cottages. *In room:* TV (1 unit), Jacuzzi (1 unit), kitchenette (2 units), no phone.

Milliken House B&B ★ 🍴 Guests at this friendly B&B are greeted with glasses of port or sherry in a big living room sporting two fireplaces. It's a nice welcome, and the five rooms are equally nice, done up in marble-top furnishings and outfitted with the original owner's collection of books. (Benjamin Milliken had made a small fortune building a dock and outfitting the big ships passing in and out of this once-busy port during Eastport's 19th-c. heyday.) Expect small touches such as pillow-side chocolates and fresh flowers. All rooms feature televisions and fireplaces, something of a surprise given the low, low price. The house is located only 2 blocks from Eastport's historic district, as well, making it ideal for local explorations. Breakfast might run to buttermilk pancakes served with a berry sauce, crepes, or a quiche Lorraine, sided with homemade bread.

29 Washington St., Eastport, ME 04631. (✆) **888/507-9370** or 207/853-2955. www.eastport-inn.com. 6 units. $75–$85 double. Rates include full breakfast. MC, V. Well-trained pets welcome. *In room:* TV, fireplace, no phone.

Peacock House Bed & Breakfast ★ 🍴 The Peacock House was built in out-of-the-way Lubec by an English sea captain in 1860, yet has since hosted prominent Mainers including U.S. senators Margaret Chase Smith and Edmund Muskie. The three second-floor rooms are queen-size-bedded and simple; the Margaret Chase Smith Suite has a queen-size bed, while the king-size-bedded Meadow Suite has the inn's largest bathroom and a sitting area. (It's accessible for guests with limited mobility.) The Wedgwood Suite's queen-size bed is augmented by a daybed with trundle, and is best for small families. The Peacock Suite is the most romantic choice, with a gas fireplace, four-poster queen-size bed, wet bar, refrigerator, and TV with DVD player. Tinkle the keys of the living room's baby grand piano, if you like: It's allowed and even encouraged.

27 Summer St., Lubec, ME 04652. (✆) **888/305-0036** or 207/733-2403. www.peacockhouse.com. 7 units. $90–$112 double. Rates include full breakfast. MC, V. No children 6 and under. *In room:* TV (some units), fridge (1 unit), no phone.

Redclyffe Shore Motor Inn ★ I don't recommend many motor inns or motels in this book, but this one packs a great deal more historic and scenic punch than most. The complex, consisting of a Gothic Revival main house dating from the 1860s (note the steep gables) and a cluster of motel units, perches on a cliff with awesome views of Passamaquoddy Bay and the St. Croix River. Book one of the so-called "patio rooms" with a private balcony for maximum gazing access. Whether in the main house or the motel section, all the double- and king-size-bedded rooms and suites here sport the basics: phones, televisions, and coffeemakers. The balcony rooms are a steal considering the views, and the glassed-in dining room—open every night, serving standard American meals—features yet another knockout ocean view. Remember, however, that there's no breakfast service here—you'll need to head elsewhere for that.

U.S. Rte. 1, Robbinston, ME 04671. © **207/454-3270.** Fax 207/454-8723. www.redclyffeshoremotorinn.com. 16 units. $78 double. MC, V. Closed Nov to mid-May. **Amenities:** Dining room. *In room:* A/C (some units), TV.

Riverside Inn ★   This far downeast, it isn't easy to find a frilly place, but the small three-room Riverside Inn outside of Machias offers more than the usual motel in these parts does. The second-floor Mrs. Chase Room, named for the former captain's wife, has a claw-foot tub and skylight. The two-bedroom Lower Coach Suite features a wraparound deck overlooking the river and the inn's garden, while the popular Upper Coach Suite possesses even better views—from a private balcony—plus a small true kitchen. Rooms are uniformly attractive and clean. The **dining room ★**, a rarity around here, serves surprisingly fancy dinner entrees such as lobster and scallops in champagne sauce, almond-crusted fish filets, beef Wellington, pistachio-crusted pork medallions with a cranberry-plum chutney, and the like. (The dining room is closed in winter, though the inn remains open year-round.)

U.S. Rte. 1 (P.O. Box 373), E. Machias, ME 04630. © **207/255-4134.** Fax 207/255-0577. www.riverside inn-maine.com. 4 units. $94–$129 double. Rates include breakfast. MC, V. **Amenities:** Dining room. *In room:* Fridge (1 unit), kitchenette (1 unit), no phone.

Sullivan Harbor Farm & Smokehouse 🎁   One of the last independently owned smokehouses in New England, this award-winning operation, run out of a farmhouse right on Rte. 1, specializes in delicious cuts of salmon, cured, hand-rubbed with salt and brown sugar, then cold-smoked over hickory smudge fires. They also produce gravlax, hot-roasted salmon, smoked scallops, smoked char, and pâté. If you're stumped for a place to stay near Mount Desert Island, consider renting one of three cottages on the smokehouse property; each is differently equipped—one has a full modern kitchen; another a washer/dryer, phone, and cable TV; and a third, simpler cottage comes with fewer extras. The cottages rent by the week in high summer season (shorter rentals possible in fall) from $975 to $1,700.

1545 U.S. Rte. 1 (P.O. Box 96), Sullivan, ME 04664. © **800/422-4014** or 207/422-2268. www.sullivan harborfarm.com. 3 cottages. $975–$1,700 weekly. 1-week minimum stay in summer, 3-night minimum stay (prorated rates) after Labor Day. MC, V. *In room:* TV (2 units), fireplace (2 units), kitchenette (2 units), no phone (2 units).

Todd House Bed & Breakfast   A bright yellow house out on Todd's Head overlooking Cobscook and Passamaquoddy bays, this 1775 Cape features classic New England architectural touches such as a huge center chimney and a fireplace with bake oven. It served as everything from a former Mason's Hall and temporary military barracks; today, the six inn rooms come in various configurations. Two rooms have kitchenettes. The yard features cookout equipment, too, but the ocean views are the real draw. The inn is only about a .75-mile walk from Eastport's burgeoning downtown district.

1 Capen Ave., Eastport, ME 04631. © **207/853-2328.** Fax 207/853-2328. 6 units (2 with shared bathroom). $50–$90 double. Rates include self-service breakfast. MC, V. *In room:* Fridge (2 units), kitchenette (2 units), no phone.

WaCo Diner   A touchstone in Eastport for more than 80 years, this diner has evolved somewhat from the lunch wagon that it began life as. But the WaCo still serves big breakfasts of eggs and coffee plus sandwiches at lunch and dinners of beef and fried fish, plus cocktails.

47 Water St., Eastport. © **207/853-4046.** Entrees $3–$17. MC, V. Daily 6am–closing (varies).

Weston House ★ A whitewashed, hillside 1810 Federal looking out onto the bay and Campobello, the Weston House features rooms with antiques and Asian furnishings, with classical music playing in the background. John James Audubon lodged here once upon a time, and today the three units (all sharing two bathrooms) are brightly furnished in prints and poster beds; one room has a television and a fireplace, as well. Breakfasts are better than you might expect (coddled eggs, pancakes with apricot syrup, and the like); brunches are served on the weekend along with glasses of sherry, while picnic lunches and dinners can be ordered by special arrangement. For relaxation, there's an attractive patio with wicker furniture.

26 Boynton St., Eastport, ME 04631. (✆) **207/853-2907.** www.westonhouse-maine.com. 3 units (all with shared bathroom). $80–$90 double. Rates include full breakfast. No credit cards. *In room:* TV (1 unit), no phone.

In New Brunswick

There's also camping at **Herring Cove Provincial Park** (✆ **506/752-7010**) for $19 to $22, with discounts for seniors. The campground has 76 sites in all.

Owen House, A Country Inn & Gallery This three-story clapboard captain's house dates from 1835 and sits on 10 acres filled with trees at the edge of the bay. The first-floor common rooms are nicely decorated in a busy Victorian manner with Persian and braided carpets and mahogany furniture; view the water from the nautical-feeling, airy sunroom and its big windows. The guest rooms are a mixed lot, furnished with an eclectic mélange of antique and modern furniture; some are bright and airy and filled with salty air (room no. 1 is the largest, with waterfront views on two sides); others, like room no. 5, are tucked under stairs and a bit dark, though the Owenses are renovating the house. Third-floor rooms share a single bathroom but also have excellent views. A filling hot breakfast served family style is included in the room rates, and ask to see the owner's in-house watercolor gallery if you're an art buff.

11 Welshpool St., Welshpool, Campobello, NB E5E 1G3. (✆) **506/752-2977.** www.owenhouse.ca. 9 units (2 with shared bathroom). C$96–C$189 (US$96–US$189) double. Rates include full breakfast. MC, V. Closed Nov–Apr. No children 5 and under in Aug. *In room:* No phone.

SIDE TRIPS FROM THE MAINE COAST

Once ensconced on the coast of Maine, you'd be easily forgiven if you didn't wish to do anything more strenuous than turn the pages of a book while lying in a hammock. But if you're a back-roads adventurer, an outdoors enthusiast, or a connoisseur of gourmet meals, there are some additional interesting places to be found just a little bit farther afield.

Portsmouth, New Hampshire, for instance, is well worth a quick detour across the bridge from Kittery for its coffee shops, inns, boutiques, and pleasing snugness. And coastal New Brunswick, an hour or less from Eastport, is worth seeing for its pretty seaside villages, islands, and high tides. Finally, just inland from the midcoast section of Maine, huge Baxter State Park—featuring the lofty and impressive peak of Mount Katahdin—is one of Maine's finest attractions.

I have described each of these three side trips below, going in order—as does this book—from south to north.

PORTSMOUTH, NEW HAMPSHIRE

Portsmouth ★★ is a civilized little seaside city of bridges, brick, and seagulls, and quite a little gem. Filled with elegant architecture that's more intimate than intimidating, this bonsai-size city projects a strong, proud sense of its heritage without being overly precious. Part of the city's appeal is its variety: Upscale coffee shops and art galleries stand alongside old-fashioned barbershops and tattoo parlors. Despite a steady influx of money in recent years, the town still retains an earthiness that serves as a tangy vinegar for more saccharine coastal spots. Portsmouth's humble waterfront must actually be sought out; when found, it's rather understated.

This city's history runs deep, a fact that is evident on even a quick walk through town. For the past 3 centuries, Portsmouth has been the hub of the coastal Maine/New Hampshire region's maritime trade. In the 1600s, Strawbery Banke (it wasn't called Portsmouth until 1653) was a major center for the export of wood and dried fish to Europe. Later, in the

ACCOMMODATIONS
Hilton Garden Inn **8**
Inn at Strawbery Banke **20**
Martin Hill Inn Bed &
  Breakfast **1**
Sheraton Harborside
  Portsmouth **10**
Sise Inn **2**
Wentworth by the Sea **24**

DINING ◆
Black Trumpet Bistro **12**
Blue Mermaid Island Grill **9**
Breaking New Grounds **15**
Ceres Bakery **19**
Dolphin Striker **13**
Flatbread Company **5**

Friendly Toast **7**
Jumpin' Jay's Fish Cafe **4**
Me & Ollie's **16**
Pesce Blue **6**
Portsmouth Brewery **14**
The Press Room **18**

ATTRACTIONS ●
John Paul Jones House **3**
Moffatt-Ladd House **11**
Prescott Park **22**
Strawbery Banke **21**
Warner House **17**
Wentworth-Gardner House **23**

19th century, it prospered as a center of regional trade. Just across the Piscataqua River in Maine (so important a connection that there are four bridges from Portsmouth to that state), the Portsmouth Naval Shipyard—founded way back in 1800—evolved into a prominent base for the building, outfitting, and repairing of U.S. Navy submarines. Today, Portsmouth's maritime tradition continues with a lively trade in bulk goods; look for the scrap metal and minerals stockpiled along the shores of the river on Market Street. The city's de facto symbol is the tugboat, one or two of which are almost always tied up in or near the waterfront's picturesque "tugboat alley."

Visitors to Portsmouth will discover a surprising number of experiences in such a small space, including good shopping in the boutiques that now occupy much of the historic district; good eating at many small restaurants and bakeries; and plenty of history to explore among the historic homes and museums set on almost every block of Portsmouth.

Essentials

GETTING THERE Portsmouth is served by exits 3 through 7 on I-95. The most direct access to downtown is via Market Street (exit 7), which is the last New

Hampshire exit, just before crossing the big bridge and the river to Maine. Take that exit, then bear right (coming from the south) or left (from the north). You'll come straight into town.

By train, it's trickier. **Amtrak** (© **800/872-7245;** www.amtrak.com) operates four to five trains daily from Boston's North Station to downtown Dover, New Hampshire; a one-way ticket is $19 per person, and the trip takes about 1½ hours. You can then take the no. 2 **COAST** bus (© **603/743-5777;** www.coastbus.org) from Dover station to the center of downtown Portsmouth, a 45-minute trip that costs just $1.50 (75¢ for seniors, free for kids 5 and under)—but it runs sparingly on Saturdays, and not at all on Sundays.

The bus, for once, is not a bad choice to get you to Portsmouth. **Greyhound** (© **800/231-2222;** www.greyhound.com) and **C&J Trailways** (© **800/258-7111;** www.ridecj.com) each run about five buses daily from Boston's South Station to Portsmouth, plus one to three daily trips from Boston's Logan Airport. Each service has a different pickup point: Greyhound's is the main bus stop in Market Square, while C&J's is at a modern but distant bus station about 5 miles south at the former Pease air base (call a taxi or rent a car); also C&J requests that you don't talk on cellphones while on their buses. The one-way cost for the trips is about $18 per person, with some student discounts.

A one-way Greyhound trip from New York City's Port Authority bus station to downtown Portsmouth costs from $45 to $60, depending on how far in advance you book it, and takes about 6 to 6½ hours.

VISITOR INFORMATION The **Greater Portsmouth Chamber of Commerce,** 500 Market St. (© **603/610-5510;** www.portcity.org), has an information center on outer Market Street as you approach the downtown off exit 7 (it's on the right, across the road from the piles of salt and scrap metal). From Memorial Day through Columbus Day, it's open Monday through Wednesday from 8:30am to 5pm; Thursday and Friday, from 8:30am to 7pm; and normally on weekends from 10am to 5pm. The rest of the year, however, it's usually open weekdays only, from 8:30am to 5pm. During the summer, a second staffed booth opens in **Market Square**—look for the hut right in front of the Breaking New Grounds coffee shop. Hours are irregular; the info is good.

PARKING Most of Portsmouth can be easily reconnoitered on foot, so you only need to park once. But mind the rules and signs; parking can be tight in and around the historic district in summer, and officers will ticket. The city's municipal parking garage nearly always has space and costs 75¢ per hour; it's located on Hanover Street, between Market and Fleet streets. Metered spaces cost the same. The Strawbery Banke museum (see below) also provides limited parking for visitors.

There's also now a trackless **"trolley"** (© **603/743-5777**) circulating through central Portsmouth in a one-way loop from late June through the end of August daily from 10:30am to 5:30pm, circling every half-hour. It hits all the key historical points and costs just 50¢ per person to ride. Catch it at Market Square, Prescott Park, or Strawbery Banke. There's a schedule posted online at **www.coastbus.org/routes/downtownloop.html**.

A Magical History Tour

Portsmouth's 18th-century prosperity is evident in the Georgian-style homes that dot the city. Strawbery Banke occupies the core of the historic area and is well worth visiting. If you don't have the budget, time, or inclination to spend half a day at Strawbery Banke, a walking tour takes you past many other significant homes, some of which are maintained by various historical or colonial societies and are open to the public. A helpful map and brochure, *The Portsmouth Trail: An Historic Walking Tour*, is available free at information centers.

Tired from touring? Take a break at **Prescott Park ★★**, between Strawbery Banke and the water. It's one of the best municipal parks in New England. The water views, lemonade vendors, benches, grass, lovely gardens, and full card of festivals make it worth a visit. There's a full calendar of events at the park festival website, **www.prescottpark.org**. Be amazed.

John Paul Jones House ★   Scottish Revolutionary War hero John Paul ("I have not yet begun to fight") Jones is believed to have lived in this 1758 home during the war while here to oversee construction of his sloop, the *Ranger*, which was likely the first ship to sail under the U.S. flag (a model is on display). He took a ragtag crew of locals to England and gave them no end of bother. The house is immaculately restored and maintained by the Portsmouth Historical Society; costumed guides lead tours.

43 Middle St. ✆ **603/436-8420.** Admission $6 adults, children under 14 free. Late May to Oct, daily 11am-5pm. Closed Nov to late May.

Moffatt-Ladd House ★★   Easy to miss as you ascend the hill into town, the Moffatt-Ladd's on the right as you begin to enter the commercial district but well before you penetrate it. It was built in 1763 by a successful merchant with a view right down onto his docks and operations. The gardens are as well known as wood-work and architecture. The same family kept it for nearly 2 centuries, so most of the furnishings and artwork here are absolutely original—and that's rare.

154 Market St. ✆ **603/436-8221.** House and gardens $6 adults, $2.50 children 11 and under; gardens only $2 per person. Mon-Sat 11am-5pm; Sun 1-5pm. Tours mid-June to mid-Oct; last tour at 4:30pm.

Strawbery Banke ★★★   This is one of New England's most impressive concentration of old buildings under an organized historical banner. Here you get a true feel for the late 17th century colonial period, not only because the actual buildings have been restored—but because they're actually open to the public for once, rather than privately owned. In 1958, the city of Portsmouth was finalizing plans to raze this neighborhood (which was settled in 1653) to make way for urban renewal. A group of local citizens resisted the move, and they prevailed, establishing an outdoor history museum that's become one of the largest and best in New England.

Today the attraction consists of 10 acres and more than 40 historic buildings, some restored with period furnishings, situated around a big open lawn (which was once an inlet); it all has a settled, picturesque quality. One ticket gains you entry to about half the buildings—the other half, you can only view from outside. Coopers, boat builders, and potters demonstrate colonial crafts, and the Drisco House is two exhibits of Americana within one house: 1790s Portsmouth and 1950s Portsmouth. While the Banke employs staffers to assume the character of historical residents, the emphasis is more on the buildings, architecture, and history than on the costumed reenactors—as it should be.

Visitor's center on Hancock St. at Marcy St. ✆ **603/433-1100.** www.strawberybanke.org. Summer $15 adults, $10 children 5-17, $40 family; winter rates lower. May-Oct daily 10am-5pm; Nov-Apr Sat-Sun 10am-2pm and must take 90-min. guided tour.

Heading South: Exploring Around the Wentworth-Gardner House

Most travelers tend to visit just Strawbery Banke, do a little shopping at the downtown boutiques, grab a bite, and hustle onward to Maine. To get a fuller sense of historic Portsmouth, though, take the time to stroll a bit off the beaten track. The so-called "South End" neighborhood around the Wentworth-Gardner House and Prescott Park is a great area to snoop around in, with lanes too narrow for SUVs to fit into, twisting roads, fish and lobster shacks, and wooden-frame houses of all shapes and sizes. It's a great taste of the early 19th century, and definitely off the beaten tourist track.

Warner House ★ This house, built in 1716, was the governor's mansion during the mid–18th century, when Portsmouth was the state capital. (Who knew?) After a period as a private home, it was opened to the public in the 1930s. This stately brick structure with graceful Georgian architectural elements is a favorite among architectural historians for its wall murals—said to be the oldest murals still in place in the U.S.—early wall marbleizing, and original white pine paneling.

150 Daniel St. ✆ **603/436-8420.** www.warnerhouse.org. Admission $5 adults, $4 seniors, $2.50 children 7-12, free for children 6 and under. Mid-June to mid-Oct Mon-Sat 11am–4pm; Sun noon–4pm. Closed mid-Oct to mid-June.

Wentworth-Gardner House ★★★ Arguably the most handsome mansion in the Seacoast region, this is considered one of the nation's best examples of Georgian architecture. The 1760 home features many period elements, including pronounced *quoins* (blocks on the building's corners), pedimented window caps, plank sheathing (to make the home appear as if made of masonry), an elaborate doorway with Corinthian pilasters, a broken scroll, and a paneled door topped with a pineapple, the symbol of hospitality. Perhaps most memorable is its scale—though a grand home of the Colonial era, it's modest in scope; some architectural circles today may not consider it much more than a pool house.

50 Mechanic St. ✆ **603/436-4406.** Admission $5 adults, $2 children 6-14, free for children 5 and under. Mid-June to mid-Oct Wed-Sun noon–4pm. Closed mid-Oct to mid-June. From rose gardens on Marcy St. across from Strawbery Banke, walk south 1 block, turn left toward bridge, make a right before crossing bridge; house is down the block on your right.

Boat Tours

Portsmouth is especially attractive when seen from the water. A small fleet of tour boats ties up at Portsmouth, taking scenic tours of the Piscataqua River and the historic Isle of Shoals throughout the summer and fall.

The **Isles of Shoals Steamship Co.** ★★ (✆ **603/431-5500;** www.islesofshoals.com) sails from Barker Wharf on Market Street and is the most established of the city's tour companies. The firm takes a variety of tours on the 90-foot, three-deck MV *Thomas Laighton* (a modern replica of a late-19th-c. steamship). Most popular are the excursions to the Isle of Shoals, at which passengers can disembark and wander about Star Island, a dramatic, rocky landmass that's part of an island cluster far out in the offshore swells. Reservations are strongly encouraged. Other popular trips include a sunset lighthouse cruise. Fares range from $25 to $33 per adult, depending on the length of the cruise; dinner cruises cost extra. Parking is an additional charge, as well.

Portsmouth Harbor Cruises ★ (© **800/776-0915** or 603/436-8084; www.portsmouthharbor.com) specializes in seasonal tours of the historic Piscataqua River aboard the *Heritage,* a 60-foot, 49-passenger cruise ship with plenty of open deck space. It leaves from the Ceres Street docks, beside the tugboats. Cruise past five old forts or enjoy the picturesque tidal estuary of inland Great Bay, a scenic trip upriver from Portsmouth. Trips run daily in summer, weekend only in spring and fall; reservations are suggested. Fares are $16 to $21 for adults, $11 to $19 for seniors, and $9 to $14 for children ages 2 to 12.

Where to Stay

Downtown accommodations are preferable, as everything is within walking distance, but prices tend to be high. The newish **Courtyard Portsmouth,** 1000 Market St. (© **603/436-2121**), is big and modern, with business amenities and comfortable beds right off I-95 about 2 or 3 minutes' drive from downtown. But the service is highly variable; hopefully that will improve. It books up fast on summer weekends or when conventions come to town, so specify and confirm your room type in advance. Since 2006, there's also a **Hilton Garden Inn** (© **603/431-1499**) in a very central downtown location with a nice indoor pool.

For more downscale, budget-priced accommodations, less-stylish chain and family owned hotels and motels clump up at the edges of town along I-95 and around the big traffic circle on the Rte. 1 bypass. I can't vouch for all of these; it's buyer beware.

Inn at Strawbery Banke ★ 🎐 This historic little inn is tucked away in an 1814 home on Court Street, an ideal base for exploring Portsmouth: Strawbery Banke is just a block away, and Market Square (the center of the city's cafe action) is just 2 blocks away. The friendly innkeepers have done a nice job of taking a cozy antique home and making it comfortable for guests. Rooms are tiny and simply furnished, yet brightened up by stenciling, pencil-poster beds, wooden shutters, and their beautifully preserved pine floors; one has a bathroom down the hall. Two sitting rooms are

PACKING A picnic IN PORTSMOUTH

Portsmouth's **Prescott Park** is about as pretty a spot as you could expect to find for an alfresco bite, with views of the harbor, a well-kept green, free gardens, summer-long music festivals, and vendors dispensing slushies and other fun treats in the summer. And it's free. There are a few benches, but tote a blanket just in case—the lawn makes a great spot for splaying out and catching some rays. Get provisions nearby at the simple, aptly named **Portsmouth**

Provisions (© **603/436-5104**), 2 blocks away at 148 State St. It's open from early in the morning until almost midnight, daily. There's a selection of beers, an attached sandwich counter where locals eat lunch on the fly, and plenty of snacks. Or just hit the vendors in the park for a hot dog, ice cream, or a lemonade. For those with a sweet tooth, a summertime ice-cream shop has also opened its doors across the street in the Strawbery Banke complex.

stocked with TVs, phones (there are none in the rooms), and lots and lots of books, and you take full breakfast in a dining room each morning.

314 Court St., Portsmouth, NH 03801. ℂ 800/428-3933 or 603/436-7242. www.innatstrawberybanke. com. 7 units (1 with detached bathroom). Mar–Sept $145–$150 double; Oct–Feb $100–$150 double. Rates include full breakfast. 2-night minimum stay Aug and Oct weekends. AE, DISC, MC, V. Children 10 and older welcome. *In room:* A/C, no phone.

Martin Hill Inn Bed & Breakfast ★★   This B&B in a residential neighborhood is just a short walk from downtown. The inn consists of two period buildings: a main house (built ca. 1815) and a second guesthouse built 35 years later. All rooms have queen-size beds, writing tables, and sofas or sitting areas, and are variously appointed with distinguished wallpapers, porcelains, antiques, love seats, four-poster or brass beds, and the like. The relaxing, expansive Greenhouse Room is basically a suite with its own sitting room and wicker-furnished sun porch. More good stuff: a stone path from the inn leads to a small, beautiful water garden, and the included full breakfast is a highlight. It might consist of johnnycakes (a delicious New England specialty of cornmeal pancakes), "goldenrod" eggs, quiche, nutty waffles, or cooked fruit. When checking out, remember there's an automatic $3 charge for housekeepers' tips.

404 Islington St., Portsmouth, NH 03801. ℂ 603/436-2287. 7 units. May–Oct $130–$210 double; rest of the year $115–$210 double. Holiday rates higher. Off-season discounts possible. 2-night minimum stay summer and holiday weekends. Rates include full breakfast. MC, V. No children 15 and under. *In room:* A/C.

Sheraton Harborside Portsmouth ★★   This five-story, in-town brick hotel is nicely located on the way into town—the attractions of downtown Portsmouth are virtually at your doorstep (Strawbery Banke is about a 10-min. walk, and waterfront bars are a block or two away). With plenty of parking both underground and across the street, a stay here makes for a relatively stress-free visit. The modern building was inspired by the low brick buildings of the city, and wraps around a circular courtyard; it's a well-maintained and -managed property popular with business travelers as well as leisure travelers looking for the amenities of a larger hotel, if a bit bland in its decor. Some rooms and suites have views of the working harbor.

250 Market St., Portsmouth, NH 03801. ℂ 888/627-7138 or 603/431-2300. Fax 603/431-7805. www. sheratonportsmouth.com. 200 units. $130–$310 double and suite; off-season discounts available. AE, DISC, MC, V. **Amenities:** Restaurant; fitness center; executive-level rooms; room service; spa. *In room:* A/C, TV, hair dryer, minibar.

Sise Inn ★   A modern, elegant hotel in the guise of a country inn, this solid Queen Anne–style home was built for a prominent merchant in 1881; the hotel addition was constructed in the 1980s, amid other renovations. The effect is happily harmonious, with antique stained glass and copious oak trim meshing well with the more contemporary elements. An elevator serves the three floors; modern carpeting is throughout, but many rooms have antique armoires, updated Victorian styling, and whirlpool or soaking tubs. I like room no. 302, a bi-level, two-bedroom suite with a claw-foot tub; no. 406, a suite with soaking tub and private sitting room; no. 120, with its private patio; and no. 216 (in the carriage house), with an actual working sauna, a two-person whirlpool, and lovely natural light.

40 Court St. (at Middle St.), Portsmouth, NH 03801. ℂ 877/747-3466 or 603/433-0200. Fax 603/433-1200. www.siseinn.com. 34 units. $120–$280 double and suite. Rates include continental breakfast. AE, DISC, MC, V. *In room:* A/C, TV, hair dryer, Jacuzzi (some units).

Three Chimneys Inn ★★   About 20 minutes northwest of Portsmouth at the edge of the university town of Durham, this is a wonderful retreat. The main section of the inn dates to 1649, but later additions and a full-scale renovation in 1997 have given it more of a regal Georgian feel now. All of the units are above average in size, and have been lushly decorated with four-poster or canopied beds, mahogany armoires, and Belgian carpets. Most rooms sport either gas or Duraflame log fireplaces. One of my favorite rooms is the William Randolph Hearst Room, with photos of starlets on the walls and a massive bed that's a replica of one at San Simeon. Five rooms on the ground-floor level beneath the restored barn have private entrances, Jacuzzis, and gas fireplaces; these tend to be a bit more cavelike than the other units, but luxurious and romantic. This is a popular place for weddings on summer weekends, and is always booked up long in advance of University of New Hampshire events such as graduation, football games, and homecoming weekend. Be sure to book well ahead at those times.

17 Newmarket Rd., Durham, NH 03824. © **888/399-9777** or 603/868-7800. Fax 603/868-2964. www. threechimneysinn.com. 23 units. $129–$209 double. MAP rates available. Rates include full breakfast. 2-night minimum stay on weekends Sept–Oct. AE, DISC, MC, V. Children 6 and older welcome. **Amenities:** 2 restaurants; bar. In room: A/C, TV.

Wentworth by the Sea ★★★   The reopening of this historic resort in 2003 was a major event; it's now one of the top resorts in New England. The photogenic grand hotel, which opened on New Castle Island in 1874 but later shut down, was refurbished by the owners of the Samoset (p. 166) and is operated jointly with Marriott in professional, luxurious fashion. As befits a grand old hotel, the main building's rooms vary in size, but most are spacious with good views of ocean or harbor; particularly interesting are the suites occupying the three turrets. Some of the rooms have gas-powered fireplaces or private balconies, while all have luxury bath amenities, new bathroom fixtures, and lovely detailing and furnishings. (Families might appreciate that many contain two queen-size beds.) Downhill, a set of luxury suites beside the marina are truly outstanding, with water views, modern kitchens, and marble bathrooms with Jacuzzis. A full-service spa offers a range of treatments and body wraps.

Wentworth Rd. (P.O. Box 860), New Castle NH 03854. © **866/240-6313** or 603/422-7322. Fax 603/422-7329. www.wentworth.com. 161 units. $229–$459 double and suite; off-season discounts possible. Packages available. AE, DISC, MC, V. **Amenities:** 2 restaurants; bar; golf course privileges; indoor and outdoor pools; spa. In room: A/C, TV, fireplace (some units), hair dryer, Jacuzzi (some units), kitchenette (some units).

Where to Dine

For two more dining options beyond those listed below, visit the **Wentworth by the Sea** resort (above) on Rte. 1B a few miles south of the city. There are two choices: a main dining room and a casual bar and grill. The **dining room** fare is top-rate, served beneath a remarkable (and original) frescoed dome; entrees might include grilled swordfish, lobster with filet mignon, seared yellowfin tuna, a clambake, a lobster pie, or something more Continental. There is a moderate dress code: Men are asked to wear a collared shirt. The **Latitudes** grill is simpler in menu, but offers something the main inn can't—an outdoor patio of tables with lovely views overlooking the water. It's softly lit at night.

Downtown Portsmouth now also has a branch of the terrific **Flatbread Company** (© **603/436-7888**) pizzeria at 138 Congress St. It's *the* place to eat a terrific

Portsmouth has one of the best cafe scenes in northern New England, nearly comparable to Cambridge's or Boston's. There are numerous places in the compact downtown alone where you can get a decent-to-very good cup of coffee and better-than-average baked goods; new coffeehouses open all the time. There's a Starbucks (of course), but two of my favorite spots to quaff a coffee drink or pot of tea with a book are **Breaking New Grounds**, 14 Market Sq. (✆ 603/436-9555), with outstanding espresso shakes, good tables for chatting out on the square, and late hours; and **Me and Ollie's,** 10 Pleasant St. (✆ 603/436-7777), known locally for its good bread, sandwiches, and homemade granola.

If you want a bit more of a bite to go with your coffee, Portsmouth's got that covered, too. Two places leap to mind. The tie-dyed **Friendly Toast,** 121 Congress St. (✆ 603/430-2154), serves a variety of eggs and other breakfast dishes all day long, plus heartier items such as burgers. (At press time, there was talk it might close; call ahead if you're intent on visiting.) The funky little **Ceres Bakery,** 51 Penhallow St. (✆ 603/436-6518), on a side street off the main square, has a handful of tiny interior tables; grab a sandwich, cookie, or slice of cake to go and walk to the waterfront rose gardens nearby.

organic-wheat crust pizza cooked in an open brick oven. Seriously: this is among the best pizza I've ever had in America. Augment it with a beer and a good salad. Pizzas cost $10 to $18 each; they take credit cards; and the place is open daily until 10pm.

Black Trumpet Bistro ★★ BISTRO/WINE BAR   When the former owners of this restaurant space decided to sell it in early 2007, their own executive chef Evan Mallett jumped at the chance to buy it. Now he cooks exotically spiced comfort food in an intimate, two-story space carved out of a former warehouse. The menu is subtly influenced by Spain and Latin America: you partake of starters that might include quahog chowder, tomatoey octopus with chorizo, bacalao salad, local mussels steamed in porter (a dark beer), or a Moroccan-spiced beet soup. Among the entrees, the Black Trumpet burger is fun, incorporating foraged mushrooms and Gouda cheese, as is an ostrich filet served with pine nuts in a Concord grape demiglace. The wine list is obviously strong. If they're full, just sit in the bar.

29 Ceres St. ✆ **603/431-0887.** www.blacktrumpetbistro.com. Reservations recommended. Main courses $16–$26. AE, DC, MC, V. Sun–Thurs 5:30–9:30pm; Fri–Sat 5:30–10pm.

Blue Mermaid Island Grill ★★ 🏝️ GLOBAL/ECLECTIC   The Blue Mermaid is a Portsmouth favorite for its good food, good value, and refusal to take itself too seriously. It's a short stroll from Market Square, in a historic area called the Hill, and is not pretentious—locals congregate here, Tom Waits tunes play in the background, and the service is casual but professional. The menu is adventurous in a low-key global way, leaning ever so slightly toward Mexico and the Caribbean—you might try a tortilla pizza or a salmon club sandwich for lunch, or a dinner of short ribs in guava-soy sauce, served with corn bread; Bimini-style grilled chicken with bananas and walnuts in bourbon sauce, sided with a sweet-potato hash; or beef medallions spiced up with horseradish cream and chipotle peppers. For fun, make a dinner out of small-plate offerings such as wontons, Jamaican beef patties, and the seafood-coconut wrap. They also cook seafood on a wood-fired grill, burgers, pasta, and pizzas; libations include local draft brews plus a full menu of coolers, mojitos, Goombay smashes, and margaritas.

409 The Hill (at Hanover and High sts., facing the municipal parking garage). © **603/427-2583.** www. bluemermaid.com. Reservations recommended for parties of 6 or more. Main courses $6–$12 lunch, $16–$22 dinner. AE, DISC, MC, V. Mon–Thurs 11:30am–9pm; Fri–Sat 11:30am–10pm; Sun 10am–9pm.

Dolphin Striker ★ NEW ENGLAND   Housed in a historic brick warehouse in Portsmouth's most charming area, the Dolphin Striker is a little fancier than it looks at first glance. Yes, the kitchen serves traditional New England seafood dishes, but some of them come in new clothes, such as a mushroom-crusted filet of cod or a piece of salmon "lacquered" in tomatoey balsamic vinaigrette and then grilled. But the redoubtable Maine lobster potpie hasn't changed since, well, probably 1700. Seafood loathers can find refuge in a duet of organic beef (hanger steak and wine-braised ribs), a rack of lamb when it's on the menu, or the grilled duck breast with risotto and fruity sauce. The main dining room here has a rustic, public house atmosphere with wide pine-board floors and wooden furniture; downstairs is a comfortable pub known as the Spring Hill Tavern, with quite good acoustic acts. After 9pm, the Striker shelves the heavy fare and switches over to a lighter "tavern" menu.

15 Bow St. © **603/431-5222.** www.dolphinstriker.com. Reservations recommended. Main courses $21–$27 dinner. AE, DC, DISC, MC, V. Daily 5–11pm.

Jumpin' Jay's Fish Café ★★ SEAFOOD   One of Portsmouth's best eateries, Jay's is a hopping destination, and it's especially good for those travelers who want to eat seafood that has *not* been cooked in a deep-fryer. A sleek and spare dining room is dotted with splashes of color, with an open kitchen and polished-steel bar; locals seem to have fun eating here, and the place attracts a younger, hipper clientele than most other spots in town. The catch of the day is posted on blackboards; you pick your fish, then pair it with a sauce such as spicy orange-sesame glaze, lobster velouté, citrusy mustard sauce, or simple olive oil and herbs. Pasta dishes are also an option— you can add scallops, mussels, or even chicken.

150 Congress St. © **603/766-3474.** www.jumpinjays.com. Reservations recommended. Dinner main courses $19–$25. AE, DISC, MC, V. Mon–Thurs 5:30–9:30pm (closes 9pm in winter); Fri–Sat 5–10pm; Sun 5–9pm.

Pesce Blue ★★★ SEAFOOD/ITALIAN   Another upscale seafood eatery in downtown Portsmouth? Yes, and again it's a smashing success, thanks to a youthful drive that starts with ownership and trickles on down. Chef James Walter serves seafood and other dishes with a strong Italian accent. Lunch might be a piece of grilled flatbread topped with smoked salmon; a salad of mussels, San Marzano tomatoes, marinated olives, and capers; or a cut of pan-roasted haddock with baccala-whipped potatoes and ramps. Plenty of antipasti are available, as well. Dinner entrees could include a crispy piece of sockeye salmon, lasagna with house lamb sausage, oil-poached halibut, a mixed seafood grill, a wild boar steak, a small plate of tuna tartare with pickled apples and capers (the small plates are great), or salt-baked branzino. Desserts include mascarpone-ricotta cheesecake, fennel-flavored panna cotta, molten chocolate cake, gelati, and a lovely olive oil-orange cake topped with vanilla cream.

106 Congress St. © **603/430-7766.** www.pesceblue.com. Main courses $9–$21 lunch, $14–$30 dinner. AE, DISC, MC, V. Mon–Tues 5–9pm; Wed–Sun 11:45am–2pm and 5–9pm.

Portsmouth Brewery ECLECTIC/PUB FARE   In the heart of the historic district (look for the tipping tankard suspended over the sidewalk), New Hampshire's first brewpub opened in 1991 and still draws a clientele loyal with its superb beers. The tin-ceiling, brick-wall dining room is open, airy, echoey, and redolent of hops. Brews are made in 200-gallon batches and include specialties such as Old Brown Dog ale and a delightfully creamy Black Cat Stout. A rather eclectic menu complements these robust beverages. It includes the expected pizzas, burgers, and sandwiches (including a steak bomb), but also offers a changing rotating of some pretty adventurous choices such as tamarind-grilled shrimp, crispy green tomatoes with Parmesan cheese, artichoke-stuffed ravioli, and cioppino. The food is hit-or-miss, frankly, but the beer is great.

56 Market St. (✆ **603/431-1115**. www.portsmouthbrewery.com. Reservations accepted for parties of 10 or more. Main courses $7–$22. AE, DC, DISC, MC, V. Daily 11:30am–12:30am.

The Press Room TAVERN FARE   Locals flock here more for convivial atmosphere and easy-on-the-budget prices than creative cuisine. An in-town favorite since 1976, the Press Room boasts that it was the first place in the area to serve Guinness beer, so it's appropriate that the place has a rustic, vaguely Gaelic charm. On cool days, a fire burns in the woodstove, and drinkers flex their elbows throwing darts in an atmosphere of brick walls, pine floors, and heavy wooden beams. Choose from a bar menu of inexpensive selections, such as burgers, fish and chips, and stir-fries. The jazz here is justifiably popular among locals (see "Portsmouth After Dark," below).

77 Daniel St. (✆ **603/431-5186**. Reservations not accepted. Sandwiches $4–$7; main courses $8–$13. AE, DISC, MC, V. Sun–Thurs 5–11pm; Fri–Sat 11:30am–11pm.

Shopping

Portsmouth's historic district is home to dozens of boutiques offering unique items. The fine contemporary **N.W. Barrett Gallery,** 53 Market St. (✆ **603/431-4262**), features the work of area craftspeople, with a classy selection of ceramic sculptures, glassware, lustrous woodworking, and handmade jewelry. The **Robert Lincoln Levy Gallery,** operated by the New Hampshire Art Association, 136 State St. (✆ **603/431-4230**), frequently changes exhibits and shows and is a good destination for some quality fine art produced by New Hampshire artists.

Chaise Lounge, 57 Congress St. (✆ **603/430-7872**), has a wonderfully eclectic range of home furnishings, including wonderful photo lamps. **Nahcotta,** 110 Congress St. (✆ **603/433-1705**), is a gallery purveying high-end paintings and sculptures, many of which are quietly edgy and entertaining.

Bailey Works, 909 Islington St. (✆ **603/430-9577**), is an offbeat choice but young people might like to have a look. The company makes rugged, waterproof bike messenger–style bags in several styles and colors. The attention to detail is superb; the "253" style is quite popular; and the bags are sold as far abroad as Tokyo. 'Nuff said.

Paradiza Boutique, 63 Penhallow St. (✆ **603/431-0180**), has an array of clever greeting cards, along with exotica such as soaps and bath products from Israel and Africa. **Macro Polo,** 89 Market St. (✆ **603/436-8338**), sports arguably the best name of *any* shop in New Hampshire. It specializes in adolescent gag gifts, toys, unsightly dolls that will make you laugh out loud, magnets, and gadgets. It also recently opened two annexes, including a pet-accessories store next door called **Macro, Unleashed** (✆ **603/436-8887**).

Seabrook Side Trip: Lobsters Galore!

If you're driving Rte. 1 or I-95 south of Portsmouth, heading to or from Massachusetts, make a detour to **Seabrook** for some of the best lobsters in New Hampshire—and the amazing spectacle of two (gently) competing shacks right across the road from each other.

Brown's (© **603/474-3331**) got here first, and it's a bit more like the typically unadorned shack you'd find in, say, Downeast Maine. (Its patio also frames a view of Seabrook's infamous nuclear power plant—and, yes, it's active.) **Markey's** (© **603/474-2851**) opened later and more closely resembles a small-town diner. The pounds frame both sides of state Rte. 286, easily reached from Portsmouth or Boston via the exits to Seabrook off both U.S. Rte. 1 and the New Hampshire Turnpike (I-95; drive east a few miles). From Hampton Beach, head south on coastal Rte. 1A a few miles and turn inland (west) on Rte. 286.

Finally, I'd be remiss if I didn't mention **Bull Moose Music ★★**, 82–86 Congress St. (© **603/422-9525**). There's nothing glamorous about this cavelike space, but it is *the* place in northern New England to pick up new and used CDs, vintage (gasp) vinyl records, and rock memorabilia—often at special prices—and it's open until 11pm daily. I can't count the hours I've whiled away here, but I'd never call them wasted.

Portsmouth After Dark

PERFORMING ARTS

The Music Hall ★★   This historic theater dates from 1878 and was restored to its former glory by a local arts group. A variety of shows are staged here, from film festivals and comedy revues to *The Nutcracker* and concerts by visiting symphonies and pop artists (David Crosby, Graham Nash). Call or check the website for a current calendar. 28 Chestnut St. © **603/436-2400.** www.themusichall.org.

BARS & CLUBS

The Press Room ★   A popular local bar and restaurant (see "Where to Dine," above), the Press Room also offers casual entertainment almost every night, either upstairs or down. It's best known locally for its live jazz; the club brings in quality performers from Boston and beyond. You might also hear beat poetry or blues. 77 Daniel St. © **603/431-5186.**

Spring Hill Tavern   Quality acoustic noodling, live jazz, classical guitar, and low-key rock is offered most evenings of the week here. It's the pub located right beneath the popular Dolphin Striker seafood restaurant (see "Where to Dine," above). 15 Bow St. © **603/431-5222.**

BAXTER STATE PARK & MOUNT KATAHDIN

There are two versions of the Maine Woods. There's the grand and unbroken forest threaded with tumbling rivers that unspools endlessly in the popular perception, and then there's the reality.

THE debate OVER MAINE'S NORTH WOODS

Much of Maine's outdoor recreation takes place on private lands—and that's especially true in the North Woods, 9 million acres of that are owned by fewer than two dozen **timber companies.** This sprawling, uninhabited land is increasingly at the heart of a simmering debate over land-use policies.

Hunters, fishermen, canoeists, rafters, bird-watchers, and hikers have been accustomed to having the run of much of this forest, with the tacit permission of most of the timber companies, many of which had long and historic ties to Maine's woodland communities because the companies were founded here.

But a lot has changed in recent years. One of the biggest factors has been the increasing **value of lakefront property,** which has suddenly made this land far more valuable as second-home property than as standing timber. A number of parcels have been sold off, and some formerly open land has been closed to visitors.

At the same time, **corporate turnovers** in the paper industry have led to increased debt loads and greater pressure from shareholders to produce more from the woodlands; this, in turn, has led to accelerated timber harvesting and big land sales, parcels sometimes changing hands at a dizzying speed. **Environmentalists** maintain this is a disaster in the making. They believe the forest can't provide jobs in the timber industry *or* remain a viable recreational destination if the state continues on its present course, and they believe that tree-cutting and herbicide spraying are both done far too recklessly. The timber companies deny this, insisting they're practicing responsible forestry.

A number of proposals to restore and conserve the forest have circulated in recent years, ranging from sweeping steps (such as establishing a new 2.6-million-acre **national park** here) to more modest notions such as encouraging timber companies to practice **sustainable forestry** and keep access open for recreation through tax incentives.

In the 1990s, statewide referendums calling for a clear-cutting ban and sweeping new timber-harvesting regulations were twice defeated, but the land-use issue still hasn't sorted itself out yet. The debate over the future of this forest isn't as volatile here as it is in the Pacific Northwest, where public lands are involved, but still—few residents around here lack opinions on the matter.

The perception is that this region is the last outpost of big wilderness in the East, with thousands of acres of unbroken forest, miles of free-running streams, and more azure lakes than you can shake a canoe paddle at. A look at a road map seems to confirm this, with only a few roads shown here and there amid terrain pocked with lakes; but undeveloped does not mean untouched.

The reality is that this forestland is a massive plantation, largely owned and managed by a handful of international paper and timber companies. An extensive network of small timber roads feeds off major arteries and opens the region to extensive clear-cutting. This is most visible from the air. In the early 1980s, *New Yorker* writer John McPhee noted that much of northern Maine "looks like an old and badly tanned pelt. The hair is coming out in tufts." That's even more the case today following the acceleration of timber harvesting thanks to technological advances in logging and demands for faster cutting to pay down large debts incurred during the large-scale buying and selling over the past decade and a half.

While the North Woods are not a vast, howling wilderness, the region still has fabulously remote enclaves where moose and loon predominate, and where the turf hasn't changed all that much since Thoreau paddled through in the mid–19th century and found it all "moosey and mossy." If you don't arrive expecting utter wilderness, you're less likely to be disappointed.

Baxter State Park is one of Maine's crown jewels, even more spectacular in some ways than Acadia National Park. This 200,000-plus-acre park in the remote north-central part of the state is unlike most state parks you may be accustomed to in New England—don't look for fancy bathhouses or groomed picnic areas. When you enter Baxter State Park, you enter near-wilderness.

Former Maine governor and philanthropist Percival Baxter single-handedly created the park, using his inheritance and investment profits to buy the property and donate it to the state in 1930. Baxter stipulated that it remain "forever wild." Caretakers have done a good job fulfilling his wishes: You won't find paved roads, RVs, or hookups at the campgrounds. (Size restrictions keep all RVs out.) Even cellphones are banned. You will find rugged backcountry and remote lakes. You'll also find Mount Katahdin, a granite monolith that rises above the sparkling lakes and boreal forests around it.

To the north and west of Baxter State Park lie several million acres of forestland owned by timber companies and managed for timber production. These concerns also control public recreation. If you drive on a logging road far enough, expect to run into a gate eventually; you'll be asked to pay a fee for day use or overnight camping on their lands.

Don't try to tour these woodlands by car. Industrial forestland is boring at best, downright depressing at its overcut worst. A better strategy is to select one pond or river for camping or fishing, then spend a couple of days getting to know the small area around it. Like a Hollywood set, buffer strips of trees have been left along the pond shores, streams, and rivers in this region, so it can feel like you're getting away from it all as you paddle along.

Essentials

GETTING THERE Baxter State Park is 85 miles north of Bangor. Take I-95 to Medway (exit 244), then head west 11 miles on Rte. 11/157 to the mill town of

---

Grinning & Bearing It in Baxter

There are a few dozen black bears in Baxter State Park, and while they are not out to eat you, they do get ornery when disturbed, and they do get hungry at night. The park has published these tips to help you keep a safe distance:

- Put all food and anything else with an odor (toothpaste, repellent, soap, deodorant, perfume) in a sealed bag or container and keep it in the car.
- If you're camping in the backcountry without a car, put all your food, dinner leftovers, and other "smellable" things in a bag and hang it between two trees (far from your tent) so that a bear can't reach it easily. Never keep any food in your tent.
- Take all your trash with you from the campsite when you leave.
- Do not feed bears or any other animals in the park. They may bite that hand that feeds them! And don't toss any food on the trail.

Millinocket, the last major stop for supplies. Go through town and follow signs to Baxter State Park. Another, less-used entrance is in the park's northeast corner. Follow I-95 to exit 259, then take Rte. 11 north through Patten and west on Rte. 159 to the park. Speed limit in the park is 20 mph; motorcycles and ATVs are not allowed here.

VISITOR INFORMATION   Baxter State Park provides maps and information from its **park headquarters** at 64 Balsam Dr. in Millinocket (📞 **207/723-5140;** www.baxterstateparkauthority.com). Note that no pets are allowed into the park, and all trash you generate must be brought back out. For information on canoeing and camping *outside* of Baxter State Park, contact **North Maine Woods, Inc.,** P.O. Box 425, Ashland, ME 04732 (📞 **207/435-6213;** www.northmainewoods.org). This is the consortium of paper companies, other landowners, and concerned individuals that controls and manages recreational access to private parcels of the Maine woods.

For help in finding cottages, rentals, and tour outfitters in the region, contact the **Katahdin Area Chamber of Commerce,** 1029 Central St., Millinocket, ME 04462 (📞 **207/723-4443;** www.katahdinmaine.com), open weekdays from 9am to 1pm.

FEES   Baxter State Park visitors driving cars with out-of-state license plates are charged a per-day fee of $14 per car. (It's free to Maine residents.) This fee is charged only once per stay if you're coming to camp; otherwise, you need to repay each day you enter the park. *Tip:* A season pass costs $39 per car for out-of-staters. If you'll be in the park more than 3 days during any given year, buy the pass instead.

Getting Outdoors

BACKPACKING   The park maintains about 180 miles of backcountry hiking trails and more than 25 backcountry campsites, some of them accessible only by canoe. Most hikers coming to the park are intent on ascending **Mount Katahdin** (see below), Maine's highest peak; but dozens of other peaks are well worth scaling as well, and simply walking through the deep woods here is a sublime experience in stretches; you will hear no chainsaws. Reservations are required for backcountry camping; many of the best spots fill up quickly in early January when reservations open for a calendar year (see "Camping," below).

En route to Mount Katahdin, the Appalachian Trail winds through the "100-Mile Wilderness," a remote stretch where the trail crosses few roads and passes no settlements. It's the quiet habitat of loons and moose. Trail descriptions are available from the **Appalachian Trail Conference,** 799 Washington St., Harpers Ferry, WV 25425 (📞 **304/535-6331;** www.appalachiantrail.org).

CAMPING   Baxter State Park has eight **campgrounds** accessible by car and two more backcountry camping areas that must be walked into; most are open from mid-May until mid-October. Don't count on finding a spot if you show up without reservations in mid-summer; the park starts processing requests on a first-come, first-served basis the first week in January, and dozens of die-hard campers traditionally spend a cold night outside headquarters to secure the best spots. Call well in advance (as in, during the previous year) for the forms to mail in. The cost of camping inside the park ranges from $7 to $30 per site (a night in a bunkhouse is $11 per person per night), while entire cabins can be rented for from $55 to $130. Reservations can be made by mail, in person at the headquarters in Millinocket (see "Visitor Information," above), or (sometimes) by phone, though *only* less than 14 days from arrival. Don't call them about any other dates. And remember: **they don't accept credit cards inside the park,** only when reserving by mail or online ahead of time.

North Maine Woods, Inc. (see above), also maintains a small network of **primitive campsites** on its 2-million-acre holdings. While you may have to drive through massive clear-cuts to reach them, some are positioned on secluded coves or picturesque points. A map showing logging road access and campsite locations is available for a small fee plus postage from the North Maine Woods headquarters (see "Visitor Information," above). Daily camping fees are minimal, though you must also pay an access fee to the lands.

CANOEING   The state's premier canoe trip is the **Allagash River ★★**, starting west of Baxter State Park and running northward for nearly 100 miles, finishing at the village of Allagash. The **Allagash Wilderness Waterway** (© **207/941-4014**) was the first state-designated wild and scenic river in the country, protected from development since 1970. Most travelers spend between 7 and 10 days making the trip from Chamberlain Lake to Allagash. The trip begins on a chain of lakes involving light portaging. At Churchill Dam, a stretch of Class I–II white water runs for about 9 miles, then it's back to lakes and a mix of flatwater and mild rapids. Toward the end, there's a longish portage (about 450 ft.) around picturesque Allagash Falls before finishing up above the village of Allagash.

About 80 simple campsites are scattered along the route; most have outhouses, fire rings, and picnic tables. The camping fee is $10 per night, $6 for Maine residents (no fee for kids under 15 and seniors 70 and older).

HIKING   With 180 miles of maintained backcountry trails and 46 peaks (including 18 that are higher than 3,000 ft.), Baxter State Park is a serious destination for serious hikers. The most imposing peak is 5,267-foot **Mount Katahdin ★★★**, the northern terminus of the **Appalachian Trail.** An ascent up this rugged, glacially scoured mountain is a trip you'll not soon forget. The raw drama and grandeur of the rocky, windswept summit is equal to anything you'll find in the White Mountains.

Allow at least 8 hours for the round-trip, and abandon your plans if the weather takes a turn for the worse while you're en route. The most popular route departs from **Roaring Brook Campground.** In fact, it's popular enough that it's often closed to day hikers—when the parking lot fills, hikers are shunted off to other trails. You ascend first to dramatic **Chimney Pond,** which is set like a jewel in a glacial cirque, then continue upward toward Katahdin's summit via one of two trails. (The **Saddle Trail** is the most forgiving, the **Cathedral Trail ★** the most dramatic.) From here, descent begins along the aptly named **Knife Edge,** a narrow, rocky spine between Baxter Peak and Pamola Peak. Do not take this trail if you are afraid of heights: In spots, the trail narrows to 2 or 3 feet with a drop of hundreds of feet on either side. Obviously, it's also not the spot to be if high winds move in or thunderstorms are threatening. From the Knife Edge, the trail follows a long and gentle ridge back down to Roaring Brook.

Katahdin draws the biggest crowds, but the park also maintains numerous other trails where you'll find more solitude and wildlife than on the main peak. One pleasant day hike is to the summit of **South Turner Mountain,** which offers wonderful views across to Mount Katahdin and blueberries for picking (in late summer). This trail also departs from Roaring Brook Campground, and requires about 3 to 4 hours for a round-trip. To the north, more good hikes begin at the **South Branch Pond Campground.** My advice? Talk to rangers and buy a trail map at park headquarters first.

WHITE-WATER RAFTING   One unique way to view Mount Katahdin is by rafting the west branch of the Penobscot River. Flowing along the park's southern border, this wild river has some of the most technically challenging white water in the East. At least a dozen rafting companies take trips on the Penobscot, with prices around $90 to $115 per person, including a lunch. Among the better-run outfitters in the area is **New England Outdoor Center** (© **800/766-7238;** www.neoc.com), on the river southeast of Millinocket. Its **River Drivers Restaurant** ★ is among the best in Millinocket; the owners also run nearby **Twin Pine Guest House,** a lodge and cottages on the shores of Millinocket Lake with stellar views of Mount Katahdin. For other rafting options, the trade group **Raft Maine** (© **800/723-8633;** www.raft maine.com) can connect you to one of its member outfitters.

ST. ANDREWS & GRAND MANAN ISLAND

Once you've reached the northernmost limits of coastal Maine, it's just a skip (well, boat ride) onward to the pleasures of maritime Canada. For a sampling of one pocket of briny goodness, head for the **Bay of Fundy.** Its top attractions close to Maine include Campobello, Deer Isle, Grand Manan, and St. Andrews.

Note that the bay is rich with plankton, and therefore rich with whales. Some 15 types of whales can be spotted in the bay, including finback, minke, humpback, the infrequent orca, and the endangered right whale. Whale-watching expeditions sail throughout the summer from Campobello Island, Deer Island, Grand Manan, St. Andrews, and St. George. Any visitor information center can point you in the right direction; the province's travel guide also lists many of the tours, which typically cost around C$40 to C$50 (US$32–US$40) for 2 to 4 hours of whale-watching.

St. Andrews ★★

The lovely village of St. Andrews—or St. Andrews By-the-Sea, as the chamber of commerce persists in calling it—traces its roots back to the days of the Loyalists. After the American Revolution, New Englanders who supported the British in the struggle were made to feel unwelcome. They decamped first to lovely little Castine, Maine, which they presumed was safely on British soil. But it wasn't; the St. Croix River was later determined to be the border between Canada and the United States. Forced to uproot once again, the Loyalists dismantled their new homes, loaded the pieces aboard ships, and rebuilt them on the welcoming peninsula of St. Andrews, which is not so far away by water. Some of these remarkably resilient saltbox houses still stand in town today.

This community later emerged as a fashionable summer resort in the late 19th century, when many of Canada's affluent and well-connected built homes and gathered annually here for social activities. Around this time, the Tudor-style Algonquin hotel (now known as the Fairmont Algonquin) was built on a low rise overlooking the town in 1889, and quickly became the town's social hub and defining landmark.

St. Andrews is beautifully sited at the tip of a long, wedge-shaped peninsula. Thanks to its location off the beaten track, the village hasn't been spoiled much by modern development, and walking the wide, shady streets—especially those around the Algonquin—invokes a more genteel era. Some 250 homes around the village are more than a century old. A number of appealing boutiques and shops are spread along

ACCOMMODATIONS ■
The Fairmont Algonquin 3
Kingsbrae Arms Relais &
    Châteaux 7
Picket Fence Motel 1

DINING ◆
Europa 5
The Gables 4

ATTRACTIONS ●
Kingsbrae Garden 8
Ross Memorial Museum 6
St. Andrews Blockhouse 2

Water Street, which stretches for some distance along the town's shoreline, and it's easy to grab a boat tour from the waterfront as well. I definitely recommend this town if you're seeking a tame, easy tourism dip into New Brunswick. Also don't miss the weekly farmer's market, held Thursday mornings in summer on the waterfront.

ESSENTIALS

GETTING THERE   St. Andrews is located at the apex of Rte. 127, which dips southward from Rte. 1 between St. Stephen and St. George. It's an easy drive north from St. Stephen or south from Saint John (more scenic coming from Saint John), and the turnoff is well marked from either direction. In case you don't have wheels, **Acadien Bus Lines** (⌀ 800/567-5151; www.acadianbus.com) runs one daily bus trip between St. Andrews and Saint John; the fare is C$29 (US$29) adult one-way, C$49 (US$49) round-trip. The bus line offers discounts for children, students, and seniors.

VISITOR INFORMATION   St. Andrews' seasonal **Welcome Centre** (⌀ 506/529-3556) is located at 46 Reed Ave., on your left as you enter the village. It's in a handsome 1914 home overarched by broad-crowned trees. It's open daily from 8am to 8pm in July and August, from 9am to 5pm in May, June, and from September until it closes in early October. The rest of the year, contact the **Chamber of Commerce** in the same building (© **800/563-7397** or 506/529-3555) by writing P.O. Box 89, St. Andrews, NB E0G 2X0.

EXPLORING ST. ANDREWS

The chamber of commerce produces a Town Map and Directory and the *St. Andrews By-the-Sea Historic Guide,* both of which are free and can be found at the two visitor information centers listed above. Also look for *A Guide to Historic St. Andrews,* produced by the St. Andrews Civic Trust. With these in hand you'll be able to launch an informed exploration. To make it even easier, many of the private dwellings in St. Andrews feature plaques with information on their origins. Look in particular for the saltbox-style homes, some of which are thought to be the original Loyalist structures that traveled here by barge.

The village's compact and handsome downtown flanks Water Street, a lengthy commercial street that parallels the bay. You'll find low, understated commercial architecture, much of it from the turn of the 20th century, that encompasses a gamut of styles. Allow an hour or so for browsing at boutiques and art galleries. There's also a mix of restaurants and inns.

Two blocks inland on King Street, you'll get a dose of local history at the **Ross Memorial Museum,** 188 Montague St. (© **506/529-5124**). The historic home was built in 1824; in 1945 the home was left to the town by Rev. Henry Phipps Ross and Sarah Juliette Ross, complete with their eclectic and intriguing collection of period furniture, carpets, and paintings. The museum is open June to early October, Monday through Saturday from 10am to 4:30pm. Admission is by donation (give 'em C$3 [US$3] per person).

Walk up the hill to the head of King Street, and you'll eventually come to the **Kingsbrae Garden** (see below).

On the west end of Water Street, you'll come to Joe's Point Road at the foot of Harriet Street. The stout wooden **blockhouse** that sits just off the water behind low grass-covered earthworks was built by townspeople during the War of 1812, when the British colonials anticipated a U.S. attack that never came. This structure is all that remains of the scattered fortifications created around town during that war.

Across the street from the blockhouse is the peaceful Centennial Gardens, established in 1967 to mark the centenary of Canadian confederation. The compact, tidy park has views of the bay and makes a pleasant spot for a picnic.

At the other end of Water Street, headed east from downtown, is the open space of Indian Point and the Passamaquoddy Ocean Park Campground. The views of the bay are panoramic; somehow it's even dramatic on foggy days, and swimming in these icy waters will earn you definite bragging rights.

Look for history right at your feet when exploring the park's rocky beaches: You'll sometimes turn up worn and rounded flint and coral that has washed ashore. It's not native, but rather imported—early traders sailing here from afar loaded up their holds with flint from Dover, England, and coral from the Caribbean to serve as ballast on their crossings. When they arrived, the ballast was just dumped offshore, and today it still churns up from the depths.

For a more protected swimming spot, wander down **Acadia Drive,** which runs downhill behind the Algonquin. You'll come to popular Katy's Cove, where floating docks form a sort of natural saltwater swimming pool along a lovely inlet. You'll find a snack bar, a playground, and an affable sense of gracious ease here, and it's a fine place for families to while away an afternoon. There's a small fee.

BOAT TOURS

St. Andrews is an excellent spot to launch an exploration of the bay, which is very much alive, biologically speaking. On the water you'll look for whales, porpoises, seals, and bald eagles, no matter which trip you select. Two to 3-hour tours generally run C$45 to C$50 (US$45–US$50) per adult, less for children.

Quoddy Link Marine (© 877/688-2600 or 506/529-2600; www.quoddylink marine.com) offers seasonal (late June to early Oct) whale-watching tours on a 17m (55-ft.) power catamaran, and the tour includes seafood snacks and use of binoculars; the tours take 2½ to 3 hours. Two-hour tours in search of wildlife aboard 7.2m (24-ft.) rigid-hull Zodiacs are offered by **Fundy Tide Runners** (© 506/529-4481; www. fundytiderunners.com); passengers wear flotation suits as they zip around the bay. This outfitter is open for a longer season than many others, from mid-May to mid-October.

For a more traditional experience, sign up for a trip aboard the 22m (72-ft.) square-rigged cutter the *Jolly Breeze of St. Andrews* ★ with **Tall Ship Whale Adventures** (© 506/529-8116; www.jollybreeze.com). The outfit offers 3-hour tours, three times daily, from mid-June through mid-October; tickets cost C$53 (US$53) per adult, C$38 (US$38) for children age 3 to 14. A discount for families of four or more is available. Watch for seals, dolphins, and eagles—all have been sighted from the ship's deck.

Seascape Kayak Tours (© 866/747-1884 or 506/747-1884; www.seascape kayaktours.com), in nearby Deer Island (see "Getting There," in the "Campobello Island" section in chapter 10), offers an up-close and personal view of the bay on half-day tours, with snacks provided. No kayaking experience is needed. The 2-hour sunset trip costs C$75 (US$75) for adults. The outfit also offers 2-hour, full-day, and longer trips for the serious kayaker throughout the summer; contact Seascape for more details.

GOLF

In St. Andrews, the **Fairmont Algonquin** hotel's newly expanded and redesigned golf course is a beauty—easily among Eastern Canada's top 10, right behind the bigger-name stars on Cape Breton Island and Prince Edward Island. It features 9 newer inland holes (the front 9) and 9 older seaside holes that become increasingly spectacular as you approach the point of land separating New Brunswick from Maine. All 18 of them are challenging, so bring your "A" game. Service and upkeep are impeccable here, and there are both a snack bar on premises and a roving club car with sandwiches and drinks. Greens fees are C$39 to C$99 (US$39–US$99) for 18 holes (carts cost extra; fees are lowest after 3pm). You can also rent clubs and take lessons, and there's a short-game practice area in addition to a driving range; call © 888/460-8999 or 506/529-8165 for tee times.

WHAT TO SEE & DO

Atlantic Salmon Interpretive Centre   The splashy visitor center of the Atlantic Salmon Federation, sometimes called Salar's World after the main exhibit, is dedicated to educating the public about the increasingly rare and surprisingly intriguing

Atlantic salmon. Located in a bright and airy post-and-beam facility, the center allows visitors to get oriented through exhibits, presentations, and viewing salmon through underwater windows or strolling the outdoor walkways along Chamcook Stream. Plan to spend about a half-hour here.

24 Chamcook Rd. (6.5km/4 miles from St. Andrews via Rte. 127). © **506/529-1384.** www.salarstream. ca. Admission C$5 (US$5) adults, C$4 (US$4) students, C$3 (US$2.70) children, C$13 (US$13) families. Daily 9am–5pm. Closed Sept to mid-May.

Kingsbrae Garden ☺   This 11-hectare (27-acre) public garden opened in 1998, using the former grounds of a long-gone estate. The designers incorporated the existing high hedges and trees, and have ambitiously planted open space around the mature plants. The entire project is very promising, and as the plantings take root and mature, it's certain to become a noted stop for garden lovers. The grounds include almost 2,000 varieties of trees (including old-growth forest), shrubs, and plants. Among the notable features: a day lily collection, an extensive rose garden, a small maze, a fully functional Dutch windmill that circulates water through the two duck ponds, and a children's garden with an elaborate Victorian-mansion playhouse.

With views over the lush lawns to the bay below, the on-site Garden Cafe is a pleasant place to stop for lunch. (Try the thick, creamy seafood chowder and one of the focaccia bread sandwiches.) There's also a gift shop and art gallery. Those with a horticultural bend should plan to spend at least a few hours here.

220 King St. © **866/566-8687** or 506/529-3335. Admission C$9.75 (US$9.75) adults, C$8.25 (US$8.25) seniors, C$23.50 (US$21) family, free for children 5 and under. Daily 9am–6pm. Closed early Oct to mid-May.

Ministers Island Historic Site/Covenhoven ★★   This rugged, 200-plus-hectare (500-acre) island is linked to the mainland by a sandbar at low tide, and the 2-hour tours are scheduled around the tides. (Call for upcoming times.) You'll meet your tour guide on the mainland side, then drive your car out convoy-style across the ocean floor to the magical island estate created in 1890 by Sir William Van Horne.

Van Horne was president of the Canadian Pacific Railway, and the person behind the extension of the rail line to St. Andrews. He then built a sandstone mansion (Covenhoven) with some 50 rooms (including 17 bedrooms), a circular bathhouse (where he indulged his passion for landscape painting), and one of Canada's largest and most impressive barns. The estate also features heated greenhouses, which produced grapes and mushrooms, along with peaches that weighed up to 2 pounds each. When Van Horne was home in Montreal, he had fresh dairy products and vegetables shipped daily (by rail, of course) so that he could enjoy fresh produce year-round. You'll learn all this, and more, on the tours.

199 Carriage Rd. (off Rte. 127, northeast of St. Andrews), Chamcook. © **506/529-5081.** www.ministers island.ca. Admission C$15 (US$15) adults, C$10 (US$10) seniors and students. Closed mid-Oct to mid-May.

WHERE TO STAY

Those traveling on a budget instead of seeking the luxury digs below might head for the **Picket Fence Motel,** 102 Reed Ave. (© **506/529-8985;** www.picketfencenb. com). This trim and tidy property is near the handsome Algonquin golf course (see "Golf," above) and within walking distance of St. Andrews' village center. Rooms cost C$70 to C$95 (US$70–US$95) double.

Or, for something slightly more upscale yet unlikely to break your bank, contact the **Europa** ★★ restaurant (see "Where to Dine," below); the owners rent out a series of rooms, suites, and an apartment collectively rated at 3½ stars by Canada's government hotel-rating agency for C$95 to C$165 double (US$95–US$165), breakfast included; you can also buy plans including dinner at the restaurant. The suites and apartment have kitchenettes.

The Fairmont Algonquin ★★

The Algonquin dates from 1889. The original structure was destroyed by fire in 1914, but the surviving annexes were rebuilt in Tudor style; in 1993 an addition was built across the road, linked by a gatehouse-inspired bridge. The red-tile–roofed resort commands one's attention through its sheer size and aristocratic bearing (not to mention the kilt-wearing, bagpipe-playing staff). The inn is several long blocks, affording panoramic bay views from a second-floor roof garden and many rooms. The rooms have been refreshed, and are comfortable and tasteful. In addition to the outstanding seaside golf course (see "Golf," above), there's a full spa. Note that the hotel markets itself to bus tours and conferences, and if your timing is bad you might feel a bit overwhelmed by one or more of them.

184 Adolphus St., St. Andrews, NB E5B 1T7. ⓒ **800/441-1414** or 506/529-8823. Fax 506/529-7162. www.fairmont.com. 234 units. C$99–C$459 (US$99–US$459) double; C$299–C$1,169 (US$299–US$1,169) suite. Rates include continental breakfast. AE, DC, MC, V. Valet parking. Small cats and dogs C$25 (US$25) per night. **Amenities:** 2 restaurants; 2 bars; babysitting; bike rentals; children's programs; concierge; game room; golf course; health club; Jacuzzi; outdoor heated pool; sauna; spa; 2 tennis courts. *In room:* TV, hair dryer.

Kingsbrae Arms Relais & Châteaux ★★★

Kingsbrae Arms, part of the Relais & Châteaux network, is a five-star inn informed by an upscale European feel. The inn occupies an 1897 manor house built by prosperous jade merchants in 1897, and features a heated pool amid rose gardens at the foot of a lawn, and immediately next door are the 11-hectare (27-acre) Kingsbrae Horticultural Gardens; some rooms have wonderful views of the gardens, while others offer a view sweep of the bay. Guests will feel pampered, with amenities including high-thread-count sheets, plush robes, and a guest-services suite stocked with snacks and refreshments. Some rooms have Jacuzzis; all have gas fireplaces. Guests can also enjoy a five-course meal in the dining room during peak season. (This dining room is not open to the public.) Entrees on a given visit might include Fundy salmon, PEI mussels, roasted guinea hen, goat cheese in a hazelnut glacé, New Zealand rack of lamb, or Alberta steaks.

219 King St., St. Andrews, NB E5B 1Y1. ⓒ **506/529-1897.** Fax 506/529-1197. www.kingsbrae.com. 8 units. C$395–C$995 (US$395–US$995) double. 2-night minimum; 3-night minimum July–Aug weekends. 5% room service charge additional. AE, MC, V. Closed Nov–Apr. Pets allowed with advance permission. **Amenities:** Babysitting. *In room:* A/C, TV, hair dryer, Jacuzzi (some units).

WHERE TO DINE

Europa ★★ 🍴 CONTINENTAL   In an intriguing yellow building that once housed a movie theater and dance hall, Bavarian husband-and-wife transplants Markus and Simone Ritter whip up great French-, Swiss- and German-accented Continental cuisine for a 35-seat room. Starters include smoked salmon with rösti and capers; a house specialty of seared scallops in Mornay sauce, baked with cheese; French onion soup; and escargots. Main courses run to several versions of schnitzel (grilled pork or veal steak), each with distinct fillings, toppings, and sauces; beef stroganoff; duck a l'orange; rack of lamb; haddock in lemon butter or champagne sauce; steak in béarnaise sauce; and tiger shrimp in mango-curry sauce. All are prepared with skill and restraint. Finish with chocolate mousse, homemade almond parfait, or one of about a dozen homemade ice creams or sorbets. The wine list is also surprisingly strong given that this is such a small, out-of-the-way town. All in all, consider this restaurant a gem—a should-get-there spot if you're at all in the area.

48 King St. ✆ **506/529-3818.** Reservations recommended. Main courses C$18-C$27 (US$18-US$27). MC, V. Mid-May to Sept daily 5-9pm; Oct Tues-Sat 5-9pm; Nov to mid-Feb Thurs-Sat 5-9pm. Closed mid-Feb to mid-May.

The Gables SEAFOOD/PUB FARE   This informal eatery is located in a trim home with prominent gables fronting Water Street, though you enter down a narrow alley where sky and water views suddenly break through a soaring window from a spacious outside deck. It's all about maritime decor and plastic-porch–furniture informality, and the food matches that—this is not a foodie spot. Breakfast is served during summer only, with homemade baked goods and rosemary potatoes. Lunch and dinner options include burgers, steaks, and seafood items such as breaded haddock, daily catches, and sometimes a lobster "clubhouse"—a chopped lobster salad with cheese, cucumber, lettuce, and tomato mixed in. There's a kids' menu, too, and margaritas and sangria are available by the pitcher for adults. The view definitely pulls rank on the menu, but if you like simple family restaurants, it's an option.

143 Water St. ✆ **506/529-3440.** Main courses C$4-C$7 (US$4-US$7) breakfast, C$8-C$25 (US$8-US$25) lunch and dinner. MC, V. July-Aug daily 8am-11pm; Sept-June daily 11am-9pm.

Grand Manan Island ★

Geologically rugged, profoundly peaceable, and indisputably remote, this handsome island of 2,800 year-round residents is a 90-minute ferry ride from the port of Blacks Harbour, which is just southeast of St. George. Despite being located incredibly close to Maine (and the U.S.), Grand Manan is a much-prized destination for adventurous travelers—sometimes a highlight of their vacation. Yet the island also remains a mystifying puzzle for others who fail to be smitten by its rough-edged charm. Either this is your kind of place, or it isn't; perhaps there's no in between. The only way to find out is to visit.

Grand Manan is a special favorite both among serious **birders** and serious enthusiasts of Pulitzer Prize–winning novelist Willa Cather, who found her way from Nebraska and New York to a summer cottage here. Hiking the island's famous trails, don't be surprised to come across knots of very quiet people peering intently through binoculars. These are the birders, not the Cather fans. Nearly 300 different species of birds either nest here or stop by the island during their long migrations, and it's a good place to add mightily to your "life list," if you're into such a pursuit; with birds ranging from bald eagles to puffins (though you'll need to sign up for a boat tour to catch a glimpse at the latter) here, you're sure to see something with wings you've never seen before except in books.

Cather kept a cottage here and wrote some of her books while staying on the island. Her die-hard fans are as easy to spot as the birders, say locals, and something of a wild breed; during one Cather conference some years ago, several dozen got up, wrapped themselves in sheets, and danced around a bonfire during the summer solstice.

ESSENTIALS

GETTING THERE   Grand Manan is connected to Blacks Harbour on the mainland via frequent ferry service in summer. **Coastal Transport ferries** (✆ **506/642-0520;** www.coastaltransport.ca), each capable of hauling 60 cars, depart from the mainland and the island every 2 hours between 7:30am and 5:30pm during July and August; a ferry makes three to four daily trips the rest of the year. The round-trip fare is C$11 (US$11) per passenger (C$5.40/US$5.40 ages 5–12), plus C$33 for your car if you're bringing one. To speed up the initial crossing, boarding the ferry on the mainland is free; you purchase the tickets when you *leave* the island.

A couple of tips: Reserve your return boat at least a day ahead to avoid getting stranded on the island an extra night, and get in line early to secure a spot. A good strategy for departing from Blacks Harbour is to bring a picnic lunch, arrive an hour or two early, put your car in line, and head to the grassy waterfront park adjacent to the wharf. It's an attractive spot; there's even an island to explore at low tide.

VISITOR INFORMATION   The island's **Visitor Information Centre,** on Rte. 776 in Grand Harbour (✆ **888/525-1655** or 506/662-3442), is usually open daily in summer. It's closed from mid-September through early June, though; if you're coming and it's not open, ask at island stores or inns for a free island map published by the **Grand Manan Tourism Association** (www.grandmanannb.com), which has a listing of key island phone numbers and spots.

EXPLORING THE ISLAND

Start your explorations before you arrive. As you come abreast of the island aboard the ferry, head to the starboard side. You'll soon see **Seven Day's Work** in the rocky cliffs of Whale's Cove, where seven layers of hardened lava and sill (intrusive igneous rock) have come together in a sort of geological Dagwood sandwich.

You can begin to open the puzzle box that is local geology at the **Grand Manan Museum** (✆ **506/662-3524;** www.grandmananmuseum.ca) at 1143 Rte. 776 in Grand Harbour, one of three villages on the island's eastern shore. The museum's geology exhibit, located in the basement, offers pointers about what to look for as you roam the island. Birders will enjoy the Allan Moses collection upstairs, which features 230 stuffed and mounted birds in glass cases. The museum also has an impressive lighthouse lens from the Gannet Rock Lighthouse, and a collection of stuff that's washed ashore from the frequent shipwrecks. The museum is open from June to September Monday through Friday 10am to 4pm; it's also open Saturdays from 10am to 4:30pm in July and August. The requested admission is C$4 (US$4) adults, C$2 (US$2) seniors and students, and free for children 11 and under.

This relatively flat and compact island is perfect for exploring by bike; the only stretches to avoid are some of the faster, less scenic segments of Rte. 776. All the side roads offer **superb biking.** Especially nice is the **cross-island road ★★** (paved) to **Dark Harbour,** where you'll find a few cabins, dories, and salmon pens. The route is wild and hilly at times but offers a memorable descent to the ocean on the island's west side.

Bike rentals are available at **Adventure High ★** (✆ **800/732-5492** or 506/662-3563; www.adventurehigh.com) in North Head, not far from the ferry. (Day-trippers who are fit enough should consider leaving their cars at **Blacks Harbour** and exploring the island by bike alone, then returning on the last ferry.) Kevin Sampson's

Adventure High also offers sea kayak tours of the island's shores for those who prefer a **cormorant's-eye view ★** of the impressive cliffs. Bikes rent for C$22 (US$22) per day, C$16 (US$16) for a half-day. Kayak tours run from C$45 (US$45) for a 2-hour sunset tour to C$110 (US$110) for a full-day's excursion. Sampson also rents out cabins and offers multiday tours.

While Grand Manan is very quiet, you can find more solitude and cross one more island off your life list on **White Head Island.** To get there, drive to Ingalls Head (follow Ingalls Head Rd. from Grand Harbour) and catch the half-hour ferry to this rocky island, home to about 200 locals. On the island, you can walk alongshore to the lighthouse guarding the way between Battle Beach and Sandy Cove. The ferry holds 10 cars, is free of charge, and sails up to 10 times daily in summer.

Hiking

Numerous hiking trails lace the island, and they offer a popular diversion throughout the summer. Trails can be found just about everywhere, but most are a matter of local knowledge. Don't hesitate to ask at your inn or the tourist information center, or to ask anyone you might meet on the street. *A Hiking Guide to New Brunswick* (Goose Lane Editions; © **506/450-4251**) lists 12 hikes with maps; this handy book is often sold on the ferry.

The most accessible clusters of trails are at the island's northern and southern tips. Head north up Whistle Road to Whistle Beach, and you'll find both the **Northwestern Coastal Trail ★** and the **Seven Day's Work Trail ★**, both of which track along the rocky shoreline. Near the low lighthouse and towering radio antennae at Southwest Head (follow Rte. 776 to the end), trails radiate out along cliffs topped with scrappy forest; the views are remarkable when the fog's not in.

Whale-Watching & Boat Tours

A fine way to experience island ecology is to mosey offshore. Several outfitters offer complete nature tours, providing a nice sampling of the world above and beneath the sea. On an excursion you might see minke, finback, or humpback whales, along with exotic birds including puffins and phalaropes. **Sea Watch Tours** (© **506/662-8552;** www.seawatchtours.com), run by Peter and Kenda Wilcox, operates a series of 5-hour excursions from mid-June to early August, with whale sightings guaranteed or your money back, aboard a 13m (42-ft.) vessel with canopy. The rate is C$63 (US$63) for adults and C$43 (US$43) per child age 12 and younger.

WHERE TO STAY

Anchorage Provincial Park ★ (© **506/662-7022**) has about 100 campsites scattered about forest and field, available late May to mid-September. There's a small beach and a hiking trail on the property, and it's well situated for exploring the southern part of the island. It's very popular midsummer; call before you board the ferry to ask about campsite availability. Sites run from about C$22 to C$35 (US$22–US$35), some with hookups for RVs and some that are much better suited for a simple tent.

Inn at Whale Cove Cottages ★★ The Inn at Whale Cove is a delightful, family run compound set in a grassy meadow overlooking a quiet and picturesque cove. The original building is a cozy 1816 farmhouse. It's been restored rustically with a nice selection of country antiques. The three guest rooms in here are comfortable (Sally's Attic has a small deck and a big view). Five cottages are scattered about the property, varying in size from one to four bedrooms. One of the older units was author Willa Cather's famous cottage, while the newer John's Flat and Cove View cottages are the most modern, with extra bedrooms, dining rooms, decks, televisions, and so forth. The grounds, especially the path down to the quiet beach, are wonderful. Innkeeper Laura Buckley received her culinary training in Toronto, and the **dining room** ★ demonstrates a deft touch with local ingredients. From June through mid-October, dinner is served nightly. Some of the cottages are only rented by the week; nearly all units are pet-friendly.

Whistle Rd. (P.O. Box 233), North Head, Grand Manan, NB E0G 2M0. ℭ **506/662-3181.** www.whale covecottages.ca. 8 units. Inn rooms and selected cottages C$125–C$160 (US$95–US$135) double; C$825–C$950 (US$825–US$950) weekly cottage. Rates include full breakfast. MC, V. All but 1 unit closed Nov–Apr. Pets accepted for C$5 (US$4.50) per day. **Amenities:** Dining room. *In room:* TV (2 units), Jacuzzi (1 unit), kitchenette (3 units).

Shorecrest Lodge ★ 🎣 ☺   This century-old inn is a place to put your feet up and unwind. Located just a few hundred yards from the ferry, the inn is nicely deco-rated with a mix of modern furniture and eclectic country antiques. Most of the guest rooms have private bathrooms, a rarity for Grand Manan. The best might be room no. 8 with its burgundy leather chairs and great harbor view. Kids like the TV room in back, which also stocks games and a library that's long on local natural history. Note that breakfast is not included with rates, but you can buy it in the country-style dining room with a fireplace and hardwood floors. Dinner features local fresh seafood, pizza, chicken, and beef tenderloin. Don't feel like sitting inside? The lodge also maintains an outdoor grill area.

100 Rte. 776, North Head, Grand Manan, NB E5G 1A1. ℭ **506/662-3216.** www.shorecrestlodge.com. 10 units (8 with private bathroom). C$65–C$120 (US$65–US$120) double. MC, V. Closed Nov–May. **Ameni-ties:** Restaurant; fitness room. *In room:* No phone.

WHERE TO DINE

Options for dining out aren't exactly extravagant on Grand Manan. The inns listed above offer good meals, and you'll encounter a few more family restaurants and gro-cers along the road, as well. If you're here on Saturday morning, check out the weekly **farmer's market** in North Head.

FAST FACTS & WEBSITES

FAST FACTS: COASTAL MAINE

Area Codes   Maine's area code is **207** throughout.

Business Hours   Shops in Maine are usually open weekdays from 9am to 6pm, Saturdays from 10am until 5 to 7pm, and Sundays from noon until 5 or 6pm. But in bigger cities like Portland, and in shopping-mall and outlet-shop areas, shops stay open as late as 9pm during peak shopping days and/or seasons.

Cellphones (Mobile Phones)   See "Staying Connected," p. 56.

Drinking Laws   The legal age for purchase and consumption of alcoholic beverages is 21; proof of age is required and often requested at bars, nightclubs, and restaurants, so it's always a good idea to bring ID when you go out. Do not carry open containers of alcohol in your car or any public area that isn't zoned for alcohol consumption. The police can fine you on the spot. Don't even think about driving while intoxicated.

Liquor of some sort is sold at special, state-operated stores; some supermarkets; and many convenience stores in Maine. Restaurants without liquor licenses sometimes allow patrons to bring in their own—ask first. Bars sell liquor until 1am in Maine.

Driving Rules   See "Getting Around," p. 37.

Electricity   Like Canada, the United States uses 110 to 120 volts AC (60 cycles), compared to 220 to 240 volts AC (50 cycles) in most of Europe, Australia, and New Zealand. Downward converters that change 220–240 volts to 110–120 volts are difficult to find in the United States, so bring one with you.

Embassies & Consulates   All embassies are located in the nation's capital, Washington, D.C. Some consulates are located in major U.S. cities, and most nations have a mission to the United Nations in New York City. If your country isn't listed below, call for directory information in Washington, D.C. (℃ **202/555-1212**), or check **www.embassy.org/embassies**.

For travelers from the British Isles, however, consular services *are* relatively close to Maine. The **British Consulate ℃ 617/245-4500**) is at 1 Broadway in Cambridge, Mass. on the campus of MIT. And the **Irish Consulate** (℃ **617/267-9330**) is on the 5th floor of 535 Boylston St. in Boston, near Copley Square.

The embassy of the **United Kingdom** is at 3100 Massachusetts Ave. NW, Washington, DC 20008 (📞 **202/588-7800**; www.britainusa.com), while other British consulates are located in Atlanta, Chicago, Cleveland, Houston, Los Angeles, New York, San Francisco, and Seattle. The embassy of **Ireland** is at 2234 Massachusetts Ave. NW, Washington, DC 20008 (📞 **202/462-3939**; www.irelandemb.org). Other Irish consulates are located in Chicago, New York, and San Francisco. See website for complete listing.

The embassy of **Australia** is at 1601 Massachusetts Ave. NW, Washington, DC 20036 (📞 **202/797-3000**; www.austemb.org). There are consulates in New York, Honolulu, Houston, Los Angeles, and San Francisco.

The embassy of **Canada** is at 501 Pennsylvania Ave. NW, Washington, DC 20001 (📞 **202/682-1740**; www.canadianembassy.org). Other Canadian consulates are in Buffalo (New York), Detroit, Los Angeles, New York, and Seattle.

The embassy of **New Zealand** is at 37 Observatory Circle NW, Washington, DC 20008 (📞 **202/328-4800**; www.nzemb.org). New Zealand consulates are in Los Angeles, Salt Lake City, San Francisco, and Seattle.

Emergencies For fire, police, and ambulance, find any phone and dial 📞 **911.** If this somehow fails, dial 0 (zero) and report an emergency.

Gasoline (Petrol) Gasoline in the U.S. is sold in gallons, at stations known variously as "gas stations" or "service stations." One gallon is equal to 3.8 liters or 0.85 imperial gallons. Gas in Maine is a bit more expensive than it is in some other parts of the U.S., but still much cheaper than it is in Canada, Europe, Asia, and Australia. Taxes are included in the price listed on gas station signs. You can often save money by pumping the gas yourself (this is known as "self-serve"), and the discount for doing so if often noted on gas station signs. Allowing an attendant to pump ("full serve) is becoming an increasingly rare practice in Maine, and it costs more.

Holidays Banks, government offices, post offices, and many stores, restaurants, and museums are closed on the following legal national holidays: January 1 (New Year's Day), the third Monday in January (Martin Luther King, Jr., Day), the third Monday in February (Presidents' Day), the last Monday in May (Memorial Day), July 4 (Independence Day), the first Monday in September (Labor Day), the second Monday in October (Columbus Day), November 11 (Veterans' Day/Armistice Day), the fourth Thursday in November (Thanksgiving Day), and December 25 (Christmas). The Tuesday after the first Monday in November is Election Day, a federal government holiday in presidential-election years (held every 4 years, and next in 2012).

For more information on holidays see "Calendar of Events," beginning on p. 29.

Insurance Although it's not required of travelers, health insurance is always a good idea. Many health insurance policies cover you if you get sick away from home—but check your coverage before you travel to be sure.

International visitors to the U.S. should note that the United States does *not* offer free or low-cost medical care to either citizens or visitors. Doctors and hospitals are relatively expensive, and sometimes require advance payment or proof of coverage before they even treat you.

Canadians should check with their provincial health plan offices or contact **Health Canada** (www.hc-sc.gc.ca) to learn about their coverage and what documentation and receipts they will need to get in case they are treated in Maine.

British travelers should carry their European Health Insurance Cards (www.ehic. org.uk). Note, however, that an EHIC covers "necessary medical treatment" only, not return flights, lost wages, baggage, or trip-cancellation costs

Travel Insurance: If you don't have health insurance, it's smart to buy a temporary travel insurance policy for the length of your trip. It isn't usually expensive; the premium is determined by the length of your trip, where you're going, and how much you think you'll spend on the trip. There are any number of providers, of which I can recommend **Travel Guard** (© **800/826-4919;** www.travelguard.com) because I have used it more than once and customer service was exemplary.

Trip-Cancellation Insurance: Trip-cancellation insurance is a way to get a refund when you must cancel a trip, cut it short, or your travel supplier goes bankrupt and cancels it for you. Of course, it's a gamble; chances are, you'll never use it. This insurance usually covers such events as sudden illness and natural disasters. You won't get back *all* of a prepaid trip's cost, of course—but you might recover a substantial portion. Again, there are many providers; check online and compare premiums and coverage.

Internet Access   Many of Maine's **public libraries** maintain computer terminals with free public Internet access, enabling travelers to check e-mail on the fly. An increasing number of Maine inns and hotels offer free Wi-Fi with your stay; ask when booking or checking in. Internet cafes come and go, but any reasonably hip **coffee shop** on the coast is also likely to have free Wi-Fi. For more info, see "Staying Connected," p. 56.

Legal Aid   If you are "pulled over" for a minor infraction (such as speeding), never attempt to pay the fine directly to a police officer; this could be construed as attempted bribery, a much more serious crime. Pay fines by mail, or directly into the hands of the clerk of the court. If accused of a more serious offense, say and do nothing before consulting a lawyer. Here the burden is on the state to prove a person's guilt beyond a reasonable doubt, and everyone has the right to remain silent, whether he or she is suspected of a crime or actually arrested. Once arrested, a person can make one telephone call to a party of his or her choice. The international visitor should call his or her embassy or consulate.

Lost Property   Most bus and train stations, stores, and hotels keep lost items for a few weeks. Ask for **"lost and found."** If your credit card disappears or is stolen, contact your credit card companies immediately. (If theft was involved, also call police and get a printed police report.) Be sure to tell all of your credit card companies the minute you discover your wallet has been lost or stolen, and file a report at the nearest police precinct. Your credit card company or insurer may require a police report number or record of the loss. Most credit card companies have an emergency toll-free number to call if your card is lost or stolen; they may be able to wire you a cash advance immediately or deliver an emergency credit card in a day or two.

Visa's emergency number is © **800/847-2911;** MasterCard's is © **800/307-7309;** and American Express is at © **800/221-7282**.

If you need emergency cash over the weekend when all banks and American Express offices are closed, you can have money wired to you via **Western Union** (© **800/325-6000;** www.westernunion.com).

Mail   Every town and city in Maine has a post office—in the smallest towns, it may double as a grocer or other business. At press time, domestic letters cost 44¢ (up to

1 oz.) and postcards cost 28¢. International rates are always higher. For more information on rates, go to the website **www.usps.com** and click on "Calculate Postage."

If you aren't sure what your address will be in the United States, mail can be sent to you, in your name, c/o General Delivery at the main post office of the city or region where you expect to be. (Call ☎ **800/275-8777** for information on the nearest post office.) The addressee must pick up mail in person and must produce proof of identity (driver's license, passport, etc.). Most post offices will hold mail for up to 1 month, and are open Monday to Friday from 8am to 6pm, and Saturday from 9am to 3pm.

Always include zip codes when mailing items in the U.S. If you don't know your zip code, visit www.usps.com/zip4.

Newspapers & Magazines   See "Staying Connected," p. 56.

Passports   See "Embassies & Consulates," above, for whom to contact if you lose your passport while traveling in the U.S. For other information, contact the following agencies:

For Residents of Australia   Contact the Australian Passport Information Service at ☎ 131-232, or visit www.passports.gov.au.

For Residents of Canada   Contact the central Passport Office, Department of Foreign Affairs and International Trade, Ottawa, ON K1A 0G3 (☎ 800/567-6868; www.ppt.gc.ca).

For Residents of Ireland   Contact the Passport Office, Setanta Centre, Molesworth Street, Dublin 2 (☎ 01/671-1633; www.foreignaffairs.gov.ie).

For Residents of New Zealand   Contact the Passports Office, Department of Internal Affairs, 47 Boulcott Street, Wellington, 6011 (☎ 0800/225-050 in New Zealand, or 04/474-8100; www.passports.govt.nz).

For Residents of the United Kingdom   Visit your nearest passport office, major post office, or travel agency or contact the Identity and Passport Service (IPS), 89 Eccleston Sq., London, SW1V 1PN (☎ 0300/222-0000; www.ips.gov.uk).

For Residents of the United States   To find your regional passport office, check the U.S. State Department website (travel.state.gov/passport) or call the National Passport Information Center (☎ 877/487-2778) for automated information.

Police   Dial ☎ **911.** You can also find the direct phone numbers for many of Maine's small-town police stations in the local phone book.

Smoking   Smoking is now banned in *all* workplaces and public places (restaurants, bars, offices, hotel lobbies) in Maine.

Taxes   The United States has no value-added tax (VAT) or other indirect tax at the national level. Every state, county, and city may levy its own local tax on all purchases, including hotel and restaurant checks and airline tickets. These taxes will not appear on price tags.

Telephones   See "Staying Connected," p. 56.

Time   The continental United States is divided into four time zones. The entire Maine coast lies within the **Eastern Standard Time zone (EST).** When it's noon in Bar Harbor and Portland, it's also noon in New York City, and it's 11am in Chicago (CST), 10am in Denver (MST), 9am in Los Angeles (PST), and 5pm in London (GMT).

Daylight saving time is in effect from 1am on the second Sunday in March to 1am on the first Sunday in November, except in Arizona, Hawaii, the U.S. Virgin Islands, and Puerto Rico. Daylight saving time moves the clock 1 hour ahead of standard time.

Tipping   Tips are a very important part of certain workers' income, and gratuities are the standard way of showing appreciation for services provided. However, tipping is certainly not compulsory if service is poor. In hotels, tip **bellhops** $1 or more per bag ($2–$3 if you have a lot of luggage) and tip **housekeeping staff** a few dollars per day (more if you have a large suite). Tip the **doorman** or **concierge** if some specific service was provided (for example, calling a cab or obtaining difficult-to-get theater tickets). Tip **valet-parking attendants** $1 to $5 each time you get your car.

In restaurants, bars, and nightclubs, tip **service staff** 15% to 20% of the check, tip **bartenders** 10% to 15%, tip **checkroom attendants** $1 per garment.

Tip **cabdrivers** 15% of your fare; tip **skycaps** at airports at least $1 per bag ($2–$3 if you have a lot of luggage); and tip **hairdressers** and **barbers** 15% to 20%.

Toilets   In coastal Maine, they're called **bathrooms** or restrooms. Find them in hotel lobbies, bars, coffee shops, restaurants, fast-food places, museums, department stores, train stations, and some gas stations. (Sometimes, you will need to ask the cashier for a key, or make a purchase first.)

Visas   For information about U.S. Visas go to **http://travel.state.gov** and click on "Visas." Or go to one of the following websites:

Australian citizens can obtain up-to-date visa information from the **U.S. Embassy Canberra,** Moonah Place, Yarralumla, ACT 2600 (☎ **02/6214-5600**) or by checking the U.S. Diplomatic Mission's website at **http://canberra.usembassy. gov/consular**.

British subjects can obtain up-to-date visa information by calling the **U.S. Embassy Visa Information Line** (☎ **0891/200-290**) or by visiting the "Visas to the U.S." section of the American Embassy London's website at **www.usembassy. org.uk**.

Irish citizens can obtain up-to-date visa information through the **U.S. Embassy Dublin,** 42 Elgin Rd., Ballsbridge, Dublin 4 (☎ **353/1-668-8777; http://dublin. usembassy.gov**.

Citizens of **New Zealand** can obtain up-to-date visa information by contacting the **U.S. Embassy New Zealand,** 29 Fitzherbert Terrace, Thorndon, Wellington (☎ **644/472-2068; http://newzealand.usembassy.gov**).

Visitor Information   For a comprehensive overview of what's what in the state, Maine's state office of tourism (☎ **888/624-6345** or 207/287-5711; www.visit maine.com) at #59 State House Station, Augusta, ME 04333 should be your first call or e-mail.

For more specialized local and regional information, local chambers-of-commerce often carry the load. The addresses and phone numbers of local tourist offices are provided in the previous chapters—most towns of size on the Maine coast operate such an office, but tiny fishing villages usually *don't*. Call in advance and ask for information to be mailed to you from the local or regional tourist office long before you depart.

Wi-Fi   See "Staying Connected," p. 56.

AIRLINE WEBSITES

Major airlines flying into Maine or nearby Boston

Air Canada
www.aircanada.com

Air France
www.airfrance.com

Alaska Airlines/ Horizon Air
www.alaskaair.com

Alitalia
www.alitalia.com

American Airlines
www.aa.com

British Airways
www.british-airways.com

Cape Air
www.flycapeair.com

Continental Airlines
www.continental.com

Delta Air Lines
www.delta.com

Frontier Airlines
www.frontierairlines.com

Iberia Airlines
www.iberia.com

Icelandair
www.icelandair.com

Israir Airlines
www.israirairlines.com

JetBlue Airways
www.jetblue.com

Lufthansa
www.lufthansa.com

Nantucket Airlines
www.nantucketairlines.com

Porter Airlines
www.flyporter.com

Swiss Air
www.swiss.com

TACA
www.taca.com

United Airlines
www.united.com

US Airways
www.usairways.com

Virgin America
www.virginamerica.com

Virgin Atlantic Airways
www.virgin-atlantic.com

Budget airlines flying into Maine or nearby Boston

Aer Lingus
www.aerlingus.com

AirTran Airways
www.airtran.com

Frontier Airlines
www.frontierairlines.com

JetBlue Airways
www.jetblue.com

Southwest Airlines
www.southwest.com

Spirit Airlines
www.spiritair.com

WestJet
www.westjet.com

Index

Restaurants